DATE DUE

JA 9 '97			
17			
FE '01			

DEMCO 38-296

United Nations in action

David J. Whittaker

M.E. Sharpe

Armonk, New York
London, England

s book may be reproduced in any form
)m the publisher, M. E. Sharpe, Inc.,
, Armonk, New York 10504.

.n 1995 by UCL Press

ress Limited
University College London
Gower Street
London WC1E 6BT

The name of University College London (UCL) is a registered
trade mark used by UCL Press with the consent of the owner.

Library of Congress Cataloging-in-Publication Data

Whittaker, David J., 1925–
United Nations in action / David J. Whittaker.
p.   cm.
Includes index.
ISBN 1-56324-742-9 (hardcover). —
ISBN 1-56324-743-7 (pbk.)
1. United Nations.   I. Title.
JX1977.W4663   1995
341.23′1—dc20   95-20701
CIP

(c)   10   9   8   7   6   5   4   3   2   1
(p)   10   9   8   7   6   5   4   3   2   1

Typeset in Sabon and Gill Sans.
Printed and bound by
Biddles Ltd, Guildford and King's Lynn, England.

Contents

	Preface	v
	Abbreviations	ix
	Illustrations and maps	xii
Part One	**Purpose, principles and structure**	
1	The purpose and principles of the UN	3
2	The structure of the UN	14
Part Two	**Peacekeeping and collective security**	
3	Peacekeeping in principle	27
4	The UN and Korea, 1950–3	38
5	Cyprus	50
6	The Palestinian problem	61
7	Afghanistan	77
8	The Gulf conflict, 1990–1	88
Part Three	**Nuclear questions**	
9	Nuclear proliferation	105
10	Nuclear testing	118
Part Four	**Human rights**	
11	Human rights	133
12	Women's rights	148
13	Apartheid	161

14	Former Yugoslavia (Bosnia)	175
Part Five	**New nations**	
15	West Irian, 1962–9	193
16	Namibia	204
17	Cambodia	215
Part Six	**New initiatives**	
18	The environment	231
19	The control of drugs	246
20	The control of AIDS	256
21	Africa's food crisis	266
	Appendix: where to find out more about the UN	279
	Index	281

Preface

The reader may wonder whether one more book about the United Nations (UN) is needed. This is a book, however, with a number of differences. Its main purpose is to illustrate the UN in action. A selection of case-studies is presented to show the UN dealing with threats to peace and the violation of basic human rights, aiding social and economic development in many lands and meeting the global challenges of AIDS, drug abuse and famine. Fifty years have elapsed since the foundation of the UN and this seems a particularly appropriate time for appraisal of the organization's work and achievements.

Again, this is offered as an introductory text. The case-studies are written straightforwardly and end with brief notes and suggestions for further reading. Each chapter has a *Quick reference page* as a brief guide to complex facts and legislation and the chronology of events. An Appendix, *Where to find out more about the UN*, directs the reader to sources of further information. A page of *Abbreviations* at the beginning of the book lists some of the commonly used acronyms, including UN missions.

Essentially, this is a critical book in the sense that T. S. Eliot once thought of criticism as "strong black coffee". Seeking to be as objective as possible, it is aimed at stimulating the reader to learn about the work of a great international organization, the United Nations, and then discuss findings with others, speculate, and go on to read more widely.

The book is organized in six parts. Part I introduces the institutional shape of the UN, its purpose, principles, and its structure. Part II, *Peacekeeping and collective security*, considers the major field of UN action. It has been said that peacekeeping operations are like a set of tools that the UN *may* be allowed to use by parties to a dispute. After a preliminary survey of theory and practice since 1945, set against the larger issues of collective security, selected case-studies are presented to suggest the possibilities and limitations of UN approaches. The scenarios are all dramatically different. Part III, *Nuclear questions*, deals with the efforts UN members have exercised over half a century to cope with the proliferation and testing of nuclear weaponry. Two case-studies record strenuous debate, some experiment, and the stubborn persistence of argument and delay.

Part IV, *Human rights*, centres on the UN's concern to establish and preserve individual and collective human rights. Three case-studies range over decades of steady work against sex inequality, racial intolerance and gross violation of basic rights. Part V, *New nations*, shows the UN as midwife bringing groups of people from a state of dependence into self-determination and full statehood. Three case-studies show the UN active in the New York Headquarters and in the field, engaged in risky but carefully executed programmes of community development, in Namibia, West Irian and Cambodia. Understandably, these operations have not lacked controversy. Part VI is called *New initiatives*. The world today has changed dramatically since the time of the UN's birth. In many respects the world has shrunk in size as the interrelationship of problems has expanded. No nation can ignore the vulnerable fragility of our environment, escape the pervasive influence of drug-dependence by its people, or the spread of AIDS. Nor can people in some regions of Africa be left to starve. Four case-studies here highlight the UN grappling with a major global challenge.

This selection of case-studies has been assembled to illustrate the breadth and variety of UN work. Inevitably, they record the UN sometimes succeeding, sometimes floundering, and, at times, failing. They reveal complexity and delay for, after all, the UN is an organization supported by people from 185 states. Above all, the case-studies pose questions and it is right that they should. Questions are a prelude to re-examination and reform.

Should the myth of the primacy of the great-powers now be replaced by a fairer composition of the Security Council? Are there archaic and complacent elements in the UN Charter that could be modified, even removed, by a two-thirds majority of the General Assembly? And then there is the General Assembly itself. It is sometimes suggested that the Assembly is "pure theatre" and the nations' delegates mainly "actors". The UN Charter begins with a reference to "the Peoples of the United Nations". Are there ways in which they could be represented more appropriately and with a permanence that is not granted to the accredited non-governmental organizations?

Keeping the peace, working for collective security, and promoting and protecting human rights, are three great areas for states acting together. First, in regard to peacekeeping, the case-studies show states now demanding the impossible of the UN – politically, financially and logistically. Each crisis and each response is different, yet they point to many issues still undecided. Would, for example, the establishment and deployment of some sort of standing force, say, a rapid deployment force, be able to act quickly and save lives? What is the point of anaesthetizing a conflict as has happened in Cyprus? Are UN members so bankrupt in cash and creative ideas that they cannot push the process of peace*building* more urgently and more systematically? Cambodia and Namibia will be seen as instances of experiment taking some hold.

Secondly, there is the whole notion of collective security. Is there a way for the UN to work towards "packages" of regional security, using organizations such as the Organization (formerly the Conference) on Security and Cooperation in Europe (OSCE), the Organization of African Unity (OAU), or the Organization of American States (OAS) rather than continue to strive for the hazy ideal of a global scheme? In any case, some regional security arrangements appear to be contrived by bilateral negotiation, where the UN is sidelined, as has happened in the Middle East. Is this inevitable?

Thirdly, there is the matter of human rights. The UN does not hesitate to legislate, to monitor, to condemn, even to isolate. Yet enforcement is difficult as Cambodia, Bosnia, Rwanda and Haiti show. Elsewhere, there is discrimination in various forms and constant evasion. The campaign against apartheid suggests ways in which a world community can influence an erring and stubborn government to change its ways. External influence apart, there is frequent speculation about circumstances that would justify the UN crossing "inviolable" national frontiers to check unacceptable and gross violation of human rights.

Finally, the pace of most UN work is never that of the "quick fix". Most of it is steady, perhaps imperceptible, possibly erratic. The UN in its fiftieth year seems to be moving forward on many fronts with a consensus and with publicity never seen before in the darker days of international politics. The recent words of the present UN Secretary-General, Boutros Boutros-Ghali, seem an appropriate foreword to the task of this book. He says:

> This is a critical time for the United Nations and the principle of the Charter. The need to reach out to public opinion to explain the purpose of the United Nations and to seek support for our work is greater than ever. . . . No simple blueprint for a future world system has painlessly emerged. But the outlines of a new vision are already taking shape. . . . The United Nations is a fragile human achievement. It is more than an investment of peace and cooperation among nations. It is the repository of hope for humanity.

The Secretary-General has elaborated further his thoughts about necessary UN reforms in his booklet *Agenda for peace*, published in 1992.

A book such as this inevitably owes a great deal to sharing the thoughts of others in print, correspondence and conversation. My dependence on printed sources will be clear from the Notes (which I have kept as brief as possible) and in the suggestions for Further Reading. Advice on certain points from Dr Frank Barnaby, Dr Peter van den Dungen, Lord Ennals, Lord Gladwyn, Brigadier Michael Harbottle, and Mr E. H. Hodge, has been particularly helpful. The comments of Professor G. R. Berridge after patiently reading the whole manuscript were sharp, constructive and much appreciated. Mr Malcolm Harper, Director of the United Nations Association, London, and members of staff of the United Nations Information Centre, London, and in the Universities of Bradford (the School of Peace Studies), Durham and Teesside, all kindly and readily met my need for up-to-date information. I acknowledge with gratitude the encouragement and constructive suggestion of colleagues with whom I have shared so many ideas in the University of Teesside, particularly Caroline Kitching and Dick Richardson. Above all, it was during the stimulating and affable work with students in the University of Teesside that this book was conceived. I am deeply indebted to all of them. Lastly, without the indefatigable word-processing and patience of Jane Thompson, the knowledgeable counsel and proofreading of Marianne, my wife, and the encouragement, enterprise and watchfulness of Steven Gerrard, Senior Editor at UCL Press, this work of mine would never have come into being. For any shortcomings or mistakes I alone am responsible.

Abbreviations

Acronyms denoting UN peacekeeping operations are given on pp. 36–7.

AIDS acquired immunodeficiency syndrome
ANC African National Congress
ASEAN Association of South East Asian Nations
CFC chlorofluorocarbon
CIA Central Intelligence Agency (US)
CIS Commonwealth of Independent States
CND Commission on Narcotic Drugs
CSCE Council for Security and Cooperation in Europe (now OSCE)
CTB Comprehensive Test Ban
CTBT Comprehensive Test Ban Treaty
DND Division of Narcotic Drugs
DOMREP Mission of the Representative of the Secretary-General in the Dominican Republic
EC European Community
ECOSOC Economic and Social Council
EU European Union, formerly EC (European Community)
EOKA Ethniki Organosis Kypriou Agoniston (National Organization of Cypriot Fighters)
FAO Food and Agriculture Organization
GATT General Agreement on Tariffs and Trade
GEMS Global Environment Monitoring System
GIEWS Global International Emergency Warning System
GNP gross national product
GPA Global Programme against AIDS
GRID Global Resource Information Database
HIV human immunodeficiency virus
IAEA International Atomic Energy Agency
ICAO International Civil Aviation Organization
ICJ International Court of Justice
IFAD International Fund for Agricultural Development
ILO International Labour Organization

IMO	International Maritime Organization
INCB	International Narcotics Control Board
INFOTERRA	International Referral System for Sources of Environmental Information
INSTRAW	International Research and Training Institute for the Advancement of Women
KPNLF	Kampuchean People's National Liberation Front
MINURSO	United Nations Mission for the Referendum in Western Sahara
MNC	multinational corporation
MNF	multinational force
MPLA	People's Movement for the Liberation of Angola
MTCR	Missile Technology Control Régime
NATO	North Atlantic Treaty Organization
NFZ	nuclear-free zone
NGO	non-governmental organization
NNWS	non-nuclear weapon states
NPT	Non-proliferation Treaty
NWS	nuclear weapon states
OAS	Organization of American States
OAU	Organization of African Unity
OEOA	Office of Emergency Operations Africa
ONUC	United Nations Operation in the Congo
ONUCA	United Nations Observer Group in Central America
ONUMOZ	United Nations Operation in Mozambique
ONUSAL	United Nations Observer Mission in El Salvador
OPEC	Organization of Arab Petroleum Exporting Countries
OSCE	Organization for Security and Cooperation in Europe (previously CSCE)
P5	the five Security Council Permanent Members (i.e. the US, the UK, Russia (USSR before December 1991), China and France)
PDPA	People's Democratic Party of Afghanistan
PLO	Palestine Liberation Organization
PNET	Peaceful Nuclear Explosions Treaty (1976)
PTBT	Partial Test Ban Treaty (1963)
ROC	Republic of Cyprus
SADF	South Africa's Defence Force
SALT II	Strategic Arms Limitation Treaty
SEATO	South East Asia Treaty Organization
START	Strategic Arms Reduction Treaty (1991)
STD	sexually transmitted disease
SWAPO	South West Africa People's Organization
TRNC	Turkish Republic of Northern Cyprus
TTBT	Threshold Test-Ban Treaty
UK	United Kingdom
UN	United Nations
UNAMIC	United Nations Advance Mission in Cambodia
UNAMIR	United Nations Assistance Mission for Rwanda
UNASOG	United Nations Aouzou Strip Observer Group
UNAVEM I	United Nations Angola Verification Mission I
UNAVEM II	United Nations Angola Verification Mission II

UNCHE   Conference on the Human Environment
UNCTAD   United Nations Conference on Trade and Development
UNDOF   United Nations Disengagement Observer Force
UNDP   United Nations Development Programme
UNDRC   United Nations Disaster Relief Coordinator
UNDRO   United Nations Disaster Relief Organization
UNEF I   First United Nations Emergency Force
UNEF II   Second United Nations Emergency Force
UNEP   United Nations Environment Programme
UNESCO   United Nations Educational, Scientific and Cultural Organization
UNFDAC   United Nations Fund for Drug Abuse Control
UNFICYP   United Nations Peacekeeping Force in Cyprus
UNGOMAP   United Nations Good Offices Mission in Afghanistan and Pakistan
UNHCR   United Nations High Commissioner for Refugees
UNHUC   United Nations Humanitarian Centres
UNICEF   United Nations Children's Fund
UNIFIL   United Nations Interim Force in Lebanon
UNIIMOG   United Nations Iran–Iraq Military Observer Group
UNIKOM   United Nations Iraq–Kuwait Observation Mission
UNIPOM   United Nations India–Pakistan Observation Mission
UNITA   National Union for the Total Independence of Angola
UNITAF   Unified Task Force in Somalia
UNMIH   United Nations Mission in Haiti
UNMOGIP   United Nations Military Observer Group in India and Pakistan
UNOGIL   United Nations Observation Group in Lebanon
UNOMIG   United Nations Observer Mission in Georgia
UNOMIL   United Nations Observer Mission in Liberia
UNOMSA   United Nations Observer Mission in South Africa
UNOMUR   United Nations Observer Mission Uganda–Rwanda
UNOSOM I   United Nations Operation in Somalia I
UNOSOM II   United Nations Operation in Somalia II
UNPAAERD   United Nations Programme for African Economic Recovery and Development
UNPROFOR   United Nations Protection Force
UNRWA   United Nations Relief and Works Administration
UNSCOP   United Nations Special Committee on Palestine
UNSF   United Nations Security Force in West New Guinea (West Irian)
UNTAC   United Nations Transitional Authority in Cambodia
UNTAG   United Nations Transition Assistance Group
UNTEA   United Nations Temporary Executive Authority
UNTSO   United Nations Truce Supervision Organization
UNYOM   United Nations Yemen Observation Mission
US   United States
USSR   Union of Soviet Socialist Republics
VOP   Vance–Owen Plan
WFP   World Food Programme
WHO   World Health Organization

Illustrations and maps

The UN system   16

Korea   40

Cyprus   53

The Middle East   65

Afghanistan   80

The Gulf   94

League table of equality in literacy   150

The former Yugoslavia   176

Indonesia and West Irian   194

Namibia   208

Estimated and projected annual AIDS incidences (number of new cases each year) by "macro" region, 1980–2000   262

Drought in southern Africa   267

PART ONE

Purpose, principles and structure

CHAPTER ONE

The purpose and principles
of the UN

With all the convulsions in global society, only one power is left that can impose order on incipient chaos: it is the power of principles transcending changing perceptions of expediency. (Boutros Boutros-Ghali to Security Council, January 1992)

Principles tend to outlast opportunities and convenience. This chapter begins by tracing the rebirth of an international organization: the reassertion of earlier purposes and principles and the encoding of new ones. A discussion of the main principles of the UN Charter follows. Major principles of collective security, regionalism, trusteeship and law are briefly explained, as is the UN's essential purpose of putting principles into practice. The chapter ends by reviewing a number of modern developments that direct a searchlight at the UN's original purpose and founding principles.

SOMETHING OLD, SOMETHING NEW

Affirmed in 1945 by 51 nations, the ideals of the UN are rooted in a great tradition of liberal, Utopian thought that was given particular stimulus by the pragmatic resolve after the First World War to build a better world. The result then was the League of Nations. Similar resolve gripped the victors after the Second World War, who were determined that only a team effort of nations, established world actors, could achieve a better order. The League of Nations, which was the forerunner of the UN, came into being in 1919 at a time of political and military fluidity and uncertainty when two things seemed particularly to matter: seeing the war through by ensuring the Allied victory and reconstructing a shattered Western Europe. Over two decades later, after even more extensive world hostilities, the purpose was to restore order and civilization. This time the uniting of nations would be less experimental, not so much concerned with what was wrong with the League as with restoring what seemed right and feasible.

In the wake of each World War, two lines of thought seemed to converge – one idealistic, the other realistic. In each case this was a merger between what was thought desirable and what was considered possible. Idealists discerned three elements that should be realized: first, a state of what might be termed "disarmed peace" among nations rather than armed isolation; secondly, a collective resolve to deal with conflicts and aggression and build a system of shared security; thirdly, a code binding on all members of the syndicate, called the Covenant of the League in 1919 and the Charter of the UN in 1945. Partnership and law were the criteria for success. The secret dealings of the old diplomacy would be replaced by openness and trust. The concept of "action the right of the powerful" gives way to "action the duty of members" of a responsible and responsive association. Unilateralism is inherently unstable.[1]

Realists, on the other hand, were less sure about the application of principles that worked best within the *status quo*, otherwise there were few guarantees. Sovereignty was non-negotiable. Equality has limits for there are, after all, great and small states. In the shadow of a peace settlement, peace would be maintained (not necessarily created) on "terms" settled by a concert of powers rather than built vaguely out of hopes and unrealistic expectations.

A call for a reconstituted world body issued from a meeting between UK Prime Minister Winston Churchill and US President Franklin D. Roosevelt in August 1941 when they framed a statement of eight principles, the Atlantic Charter. Roosevelt thought tentatively about Four Policemen, that is, great-powers exercising a custodial role and taking on prime responsibility for peacekeeping. Churchill, stressing the principle of moral leadership by great-powers, did not find it easy either to accommodate his idealism in regard to common unity and shared enterprise within his realistic urge to safeguard British (Imperial) interests, or to preserve a special relationship across an Atlantic bridge. His concept of universalism narrowed down to a conviction that the victors would keep the peace and that a regional sub-organization would give peacekeeping firmer substance. Many of his cabinet ministers and advisors deplored the Prime Minister's obstinacy and procrastination, perceiving an element of hard-headedness in reasserting the influence of a near-exhausted Britain. Worse, though, they suspected that Western leaders were compromising principles at the major conferences at Tehran (1943), Yalta (1945) and Potsdam (1945) in conceding Soviet demands for a sphere of influence in exchange for Moscow's agreement to the proposed UN constitution and voting procedures.

DRAFTING THE UN CONSTITUTION

In autumn 1944 a constitution was drafted filling out ideas discussed in Moscow a year earlier. Known as the Dumbarton Oaks Proposals, it envisaged that all member-states would collaborate to maintain peace and build a better world. Two tiers of membership were approved, a General Assembly and a Security Council, with the latter needing the unanimity of five great-powers, namely, the US, the USSR, the UK, China and France, the Permanent Members (or P5). The Yalta Conference in 1945 confirmed the title "United Nations", and set a seal on the membership and voting procedures, especially the disputed "veto".

Roosevelt was anxious to have a Charter drafted well before war's end to provide a touchstone for the populace. It would take time to compile the final part of the document where there was emphasis on social and economic aspects and on the constitution of an international court. Everything must be ready for inauguration in San Francisco in April 1945. In no sense must the California venue repeat the meeting of bemedalled Allies in Paris in 1919. This was to be a forum proclaiming ideals such as justice, equality, compassion and unity as the bases of a resuscitated world community. Unhappily, there were already signs of tension between the great-powers and disagreement as to priorities and ways of working the code. During 62 hectic days more than 3,000 drafters of documents met in working parties and plenary sessions to put the views of 51 states. It was Roosevelt's democratic impulse, reminiscent, perhaps, of his efforts to give pre-war America a "new deal", that the new organization should recruit from as wide a spectrum as possible.

Thus, UN principles were fashioned in impressive liaison between governments and an unprecedented array of people from professional, religious and labour groups. Roosevelt's preferred name, the United Nations, was the one adopted. New York, not "unlucky Geneva" was to be its home. The UN Charter was signed on 26 June 1945 and ratified on 24 October 1945; there was now the tremendous task for a Preparatory Commission, working in ten committees night and day in London, to go beyond the enumerated principles and devise rules and agendas for a first meeting of 51 member-states at the General Assembly in London on 10 January 1946.

THE CHARTER PRINCIPLES

The UN Charter plainly states the determined purpose of an association of subscribing nations. The four purposes of the UN set out in Article 1 of Chapter I are to maintain international peace and security; to develop friendly relations among nations; to achieve collaboration in solving global problems and the promotion of fundamental freedoms; and to act as a centre for harmonizing these efforts. Eighteen further chapters describe structure and ways and means. Agreement about purpose and management is to be the means of moving forward, although it is unlikely that the founders ever saw consensus as easily obtainable. Working with realities of interstate relations rather than in spite of them, a rebuilt international body would offer a static function as conference convenor, information provider, and initiator of enquiry as well as performing a more dynamic role in facilitating action that is constructive and preventive. The obligation of member-states to work in concord for common aims was to be structurally reinforced by the executive action of a Security Council, the debating forum of a General Assembly, and the impartial judgement of an International Court of Justice. Fundamental to the promotion of these concepts was the loyalty, integrity and competence of a Secretary-General and Secretariat. Charter Articles assert principles; they also empower those principles by outlining courses of action to deal with threats to peace, breaches of peace, acts of aggression and conflicts. The Charter, unlike the Ten Commandments, is not a mandatory set of rules. Functionally, it is a skeletal framework of principles and voluntary obligations.

THE PRINCIPLE OF COLLECTIVE SECURITY

Collective security is the crowning UN principle (as it was for the League of Nations). The Charter's very first article charges its members in the interests of maintaining international peace and security "to take effective collective measures for the prevention and removal of threats to the peace, and for the suppression of acts of aggression or other breaches of the peace".

The principle here is that states unite to maintain, develop and protect a world progressively freed from conflict, poverty and threat. An actual or potential aggressor is to be identified and dealt with by a guarantee of prompt and unified response. It is not difficult to see the obstacles. Aggression may take many forms, overt or covert. An aggressor may act alone or find appreciable support elsewhere. Preventive or enforcement action by the UN originally provided for a range of responses (outlined in Chapter VII of the Charter) with force envisaged only as a last resort and co-ordinated by a Military Staff Committee. Which responses, however, would be the most appropriate? Would they be likely to bring about a lasting enhancement of security? Unless security is a collective attainment any unilateral effort by a member who breaks ranks to protect or accentuate their own security may be viewed as reducing the security of others. Effective translation into action of this cardinal principle may well lie in preferring the term "co-operative security" to provide for states employing a range of dialogue-centred techniques that seek gradually to address diverse and complex problems imperilling everybody's security.[2]

The heady days of "peace at last" in 1945 made the P5 aim at consensus in regard to security unless one of them resorted to veto power – "blackballing" any resolution likely to be unacceptable and hazardous to harmony. Chapter 2 will look again at the issue of the veto in the Security Council, which some see as a disabling mechanism, rendering the concept of collective security unrealizable. This is repudiation, they claim, a complete inability to appreciate the implications of a principle. Nor does this appear to be the only escape clause in the UN Charter. Prohibiting UN intervention, as Article 2.7 does in matters "essentially within the domestic jurisdiction of any state", might be thought to restrict collective initiatives. Permitting resort to regional arrangements (Article 52) or recognizing "the inherent right of individual or collective self-defence" (Article 51), surely weakens the notion of universal responsibility.[3] Wasn't this, critics asked, a curious blend of collective security in idealistic terms and of balance of power in pragmatic terms? Mikhail Gorbachev has not been the only one to wonder whether collective security seen in this light could ever reassure individual states.

Another instance of the power of expediency bearing on the power of principles is that UN peacekeeping has evolved largely because the ideal of collective security has never materialized. Neutral interposition and observation, improvised often with difficulty, have aimed rather at political and preventive measures far short of the effective, forceful removal and suppression called for in the Charter. This distinction, between the principle of collective security and the approach of peacekeeping in the field, will be outlined again in Chapter 3.

There is now a wider understanding of the concept of "security".[4] Two-thirds of mankind have been born since the UN was set up. A large proportion finds existence and expectations menaced by threats that are political, social, economic and ecological. Inevitably, as the Cold War brought something of a military stalemate and more and more developing states joined the UN, the economic gulf between the haves and the have-nots cemented resentful dependence of the one on the other. It has become increasingly clear that the promotion of human rights and fundamental freedoms means very little without determined application of development and relief programmes to ensure such vital resources as shelter, food, fresh water, hygiene and health aid. This is, of course, the field of activity of the UN's Specialized Agencies and the constant concern of a large number of non-governmental organizations (NGOs) accredited to the UN.

The vital principle of helping to settle disputes and dealing effectively with threats to the peace is addressed in two chapters of the Charter. A range of techniques is outlined in Chapter VI, from investigation to mediation, conciliation and arbitration. The obligation of pacific settlement is stressed, and responsibility is clearly laid on the disputants to search for means of reconciliation. Legal wrangles could in principle be referred to the International Court of Justice. Although the wording of the articles in Chapter VI is fairly loose, Article 37 states that if a continuing dispute is likely to endanger the maintenance of international peace and security it will be referred to the Security Council, which may then recommend appropriate procedures for adjustment. While such a concept is in theory endorsed, in practice some states have made use of discretion or evasion or resorted to the protective armour of domestic jurisdiction. Thus, in such cases as the US and Central America, the USSR and Afghanistan, Iran and Iraq, Jew and Arab in the Middle East, South Africa and apartheid, the UN has found it difficult to bring decisive influence to bear despite rhetoric proclaiming justice for all as an indispensable prelude to peace. As the case-studies following this chapter will show, the "changing perceptions of expediency" have all too often emasculated the "power of principles".

THE PRINCIPLE OF REGIONALISM

In consequence of doubts about collective security and some reservations about mediation, UN members have never been sure how far the concept of universalism is affected by regional instincts and schemes. Although the founders disapproved of alliances that were exclusive, the Charter gives over the whole of Chapter VIII to recognizing how useful regional arrangements may be, provided their activities are consistent with the purposes and principles of the UN. This strikes an unconvincing note where the main criterion is united action, or, at least, preparedness for it. Quite clearly, states frequently act within regional parameters because of basic autonomous preference, and they may not consider the UN to be any sort of regulator mechanism in general terms. Moreover, where there is a dispute or a threat one party may believe that to contain, divert or oppose the power potentials of others is best done in a limited area and presumably with limited means. The principles of the UN are essentially transnational and regional politicians find little difficulty in giving them lip-service at the same time as they manoeuvre in very much tighter terms. There is no evidence that inconsistency in this respect worried the sponsors of the North Atlantic Treaty Organization (NATO) in 1947 or of the Warsaw Treaty (Pact) in 1955. Regional security in theory depended on a demonstrated harmony of the watchful and strong. Nevertheless, in the last two decades, the General Assembly has granted formal consultative status to a number of regional organizations, including the OAU, the OAS, the European Union (EU) and the 35-nation OSCE.

PRINCIPLES OF TRUSTEESHIP AND LAW

Rounding off the Charter are two great humanistic precepts: trusteeship of dependent territories and international law constituted in an International

Court of Justice. It is sometimes remarked at the UN that the Trusteeship Council, set up to administer the scheme, has worked itself out of a job while the International Court of Justice has never held one down. Three chapters of the Charter are devoted to the interests of people who have no self-government. Powers administering Trust Territories in Africa and Asia were required as soon as possible to bring their subjects out of "alien subjugation, domination and exploitation", in the words of the Declaration on the Granting of Independence to Colonial Countries and Peoples passed by the General Assembly in 1960. This can be seen as a collective effort to put urgency and vigour into the broad aims of the Charter, which, while they established a trust over 11 territories, had a much looser role in 72 others, nearly all small dependencies of large states. The basic ideals were those of encouraging the hopes of these people (many millions of them, in fact), of assisting them in the development of free political institutions, or protecting them against abuses and discrimination, and recognizing their needs as paramount. This was a difficult campaign to mount given the doubts, fears and conservative attitudes of the 1940s and 1950s. Putting the UN concepts into practice is a remarkable success story, for by 1975 all but one Trust Territory (Micronesia in the Pacific) had attained independence. As for the 72 non-Trust Territories, now less than 20 are not self-governed. Over 80 nations, comprising some 700 million people, have now been brought out of colonial rule and have joined the UN as full members. Despite UN principles and sustained public pressure, more than three million people still live under some form of colonial rule. Bitterness and violence have not been avoided but the earning of independence for Namibia has been a triumph for patient campaigning and negotiation.

PUTTING PRINCIPLES INTO PRACTICE

The essential purpose of the UN is to translate principles into practice. Three procedures to bring this about are adopted by the General Assembly, namely, the Declaration, the Covenant and the Convention. Having most carefully debated an issue and come to a conclusion, the Assembly can formally express its firm Resolution in a Declaration as a prelude to anticipated action. The case-studies in this book provide many examples of the UN following this course. The Covenant is a promise to act in a way that reaffirms an agreed principle. Most obligatory of all is a Convention, a formal instrument of international law derived from general agreement on terms. A Convention does not necessarily require all member-states to assent to a principle. For instance, the Convention against Torture, adopted by the General Assembly in 1984, had only 20 states ratifying it five years later.[5]

Regretfully, some member-states readily began to use the principles of the UN to win votes in the General Assembly or as elements in propaganda disputation – not too often in major issues like the quarrels over Berlin, Austria and Trieste, but in secondary areas where proxy supporters might be recruited. By 1950 the state of play was discernible. On the one hand, there was also an Utopian belief that law and cohesion could transform state centrism into ordered, principled progress. This held ground, albeit shakily. Otherwise, realists put it that we were back to the old dogmas where politics, however transnationally they might be staged, were still pragmatic and defensive and often coercive. Idealists, of course, spoke differently. Contention in the world and the threat of war could surely be minimized, in Henry Morgenthau's words, "through the continuous adjustment of conflicting interest by diplomatic action". According to this stern American "realist" in 1948, wishful thinking ought to be renounced, the ardour of crusading dampened, "realities" acknowledged, and a search for compromise begun.

FOUNDING PRINCIPLES 50 YEARS LATER

The world of the mid-1990s is dramatically different from that of 1945. The harsh glare of confrontation in the Cold War era has been dissipated. The "security" of the Armed Peace of those years paradoxically maintained by a four-minute threat of Armageddon is replaced by insecurity, partly because nobody seems to have quite the muscle and the resolve to ensure control. Over half a century a number of significant developments suggest that the principles of 1945 should be taken down, dusted, reviewed and perhaps reshaped.

The pattern of UN membership has become asymmetrical where founders are heavily represented on the governing boards of Specialized Agencies and pull the main financial levers in the World Bank. Particularly, developing countries complain that their interests are not sufficiently represented. The UN appears to be set to one side when nations resort to bilateral and multilateral "fixing" and the popular use of "summitry". UN principles seem to be observed unevenly when the great-powers hold on to nuclear superiority while they bow towards the ideal of multilateral arms reduction. General Assembly debates expose contradiction when states affirm belief in transnational association while they link up their strongly national identities in smaller scale alliances for defence or protectionist trade in Europe, Latin America or South East Asia. UN principles are unlikely to be observed consistently by any government that lacks stability and the trust of its people. Tensions are raised by the uncompromising methods of nationalistic and fundamentalist groups and by the acts of terrorists. Civil strife at times has rendered almost hopeless the restoration of normal life in the Middle East, Central America, Ethiopia and Bosnia. Developments such as these point to the UN's 185 members interpreting its purpose and its principles in diverse and even devious ways. Peace never comes about if communities are torn by violence, savaged by famine, thirst and disease, or denied effective trade and transport. The plight of 18 million refugees is a stern and searching challenge to any upholder of human rights. The world over, the UN's members individually and collectively also have to cope with a great range of human and natural emergencies.

Finally, in view of these and other issues, and in the light of the UN's own setbacks and shortcomings, a straight question must be asked: does the United Nations today represent active or inactive nations? This chapter has described the purpose and principles of the UN; readers may judge from the case-studies that follow and from other reading that the UN has not had an easy ride. Controversy and questions abound.

NOTES

1. A detailed account of the transition from League of Nations to the UN is in F. P. Walters, *A History of the League of Nations* (London: Oxford University Press, 1952). An article by Goodrich (1947) is still useful. My own *Fighter for Peace, Philip Noel-Baker 1889–1982* features an outline discussion.
2. Security problems and possible responses are carefully elaborated in Gareth Evans, *Cooperating for Peace* (Sydney: Allen and Unwin, 1993). It includes an excellent discussion of peacekeeping and UN reform.
3. For some critics, today's Bosnia casts doubt on the continued soundness of these principles. Does Article 2.7 entirely rule out UN humanitarian intervention to deal with "ethnic cleansing"? Does Article 51 invalidate a UN embargo on beleaguered Bosnians arming themselves?
4. See discussion in Gareth Evans (1993), Chapter 12, and in G. R. Berridge (1992), Chapter 12.
5. If delegates agree to the text of a Convention (or a treaty) their adopting *signatures* mean no more than an indication of willingness to accept it provisionally and to refer it back to their home government for *ratification* (formal government acceptance of binding obligation) or refusal to ratify (rejection).

FURTHER READING

Baehr, P. R. *The United Nations: reality and ideal*. New York: Praeger, 1984.

Buzan, B. New patterns of international security in the twenty-first century. *International Affairs* 67(3), pp. 431–51, 1991.

Franck, T. M. *Nation against nation: what happened to the UN dream and what the US can do about it?* New York: Oxford University Press, 1985.

Goodrich, L. M. From League of Nations to United Nations. *International Organization* 1, pp. 3–21, 1947.

Jensen, E. & T. Fisher. *The United Kingdom – the United Nations*. London: Macmillan, 1990.

Kirkpatrick, J. J. The United Nations as a political system. *World Affairs* 146(4), pp. 358–68, 1984.

Morgenthau, H. J. *Politics among nations*, revised 5th edn. New York: Knopf, 1978.

Moynihan, P. *A dangerous place*. New York: Berkeley Books, 1980.

Parsons, A. The UN in the post-Cold War era. *International Relations* (December 1992) 11(3), pp. 189–200.

Pines, B. Y. *A world without a UN: what would happen if the UN shut down?* Washington DC: Heritage Foundation, 1984.

Saksena, K. P. Forty years of the United Nations: a perspective. *International Studies* 22(4), pp. 289–317, 1985.

Whittaker, D. J. *Fighter for peace, Philip Noel-Baker 1889–1982*. York: Sessions, 1989.

Chapter One

THE PURPOSE AND PRINCIPLES OF THE UN

August 1941	Atlantic Charter	⎫ Preliminary shaping
Autumn 1944	Dumbarton Oaks Proposals	⎬ of the organization
February 1945	Yalta Conference	⎭
26 June 1945	UN Charter signed in San Francisco by 51 states	
24 October 1945	UN Charter ratified by 51	
January 1946	General Assembly meets for the first time (London, later years, New York)	
October 1952	UN enters new permanent home in New York	

Charter (in brief)

The purposes are to:
  (a) maintain international peace, security by appropriate collective measures;
  (b) develop friendly international relations based on equality, self-determination;
  (c) work collectively on problem solution; and
  (d) be centre for harmonizing collective action.

The principles are:
  (a) members to respect states' sovereign equality, domestic jurisdiction;
  (b) members have right to self-defence, regional association; and
  (c) members pledge to refrain from threat, use of force, assist UN settle disputes peacefully, deal firmly with threats, breaches of peace, promote human rights observance, economic, social betterment (via ECOSOC), assume trusteeship of non-self-governing territories, comply with decisions of ICJ.

The structure of the UN

The structure of the UN is fairly straightforward. The Charter established seven principal elements: the General Assembly, the Security Council, the Secretary-General, the Secretariat, the International Court of Justice, the Economic and Social Council, and the Specialized Agencies. Expectations in 1945 were high among the 51 founders that organizing the enterprise in this way would meet the expressed purposes of the UN. A representative Assembly was to investigate, debate and recommend. A Security Council would be an extra powerhouse for preventive diplomacy using the maximum of persuasion and the minimum of force. The separate functions of the two bodies would be administered by a Secretariat. Economic and social development work would be the sphere of activity of Specialized Agencies co-ordinated by an Economic and Social Council (ECOSOC). Lastly, a judicial organ would be established to advise and adjudicate.

THE GENERAL ASSEMBLY

Essentially, the General Assembly has four principal functions: to provide a forum for open debate; to promote and disseminate the principles and purpose of the UN; to carry out a quasi-legislative role; and to co-ordinate, monitor and approve work done by Agencies, committees and commissions. Each of the 185 (since December 1994) member-states in the General Assembly has up to five delegates (with advisors) but only one vote, regardless of its size or power.[1] Convened annually from late September for three months, the General Assembly has the right to discuss and make recommendations on any question within the scope of the Charter. The General Assembly is not conceived as a "parliament" in the sense that democracies use the term for constitutional assemblies that frame mandatory legislation. It is a place of rhetoric and persuasion where proposals are aired, rejected or adopted in Resolutions generally long on hope and short on guarantee. (If the Security Council already has the matter in hand the Assembly must stand aside and await its decision.) No single member has power to force action but pronouncements carry the weight of informed Assembly opinion. Perfunctory, perhaps heated, plenary sessions are complemented by steady work done in seven main committees that consider security and disarmament, political, economic, social-humanitarian-cultural, decolonization, administrative and budgetary, and legal matters.

The Assembly serves both as a safety-valve and as a central exchange in a communications system. Assembly members adopt Resolutions, affirm Declarations, frame Conventions, and draft agreements as a prelude to signature and ratification by governments. Co-ordination of UN activities is facilitated by special reports from studies, enquiry commissions and committees and from the Specialized Agencies. Facts obtained this way enable the Assembly to decide about the agenda and international programmes. The UN budget is scrutinized every two years. The General Assembly appoints a Secretary-General, admits new members, and elects officers and committee members. Particular issues to do with water, youth, women, disabled people, literacy and so on, may be highlighted through an International Year or even a Decade. Special Sessions have been convened to focus on such urgent topics as Palestine (1947, 1968), Lebanon (1978), Disarmament (1978, 1982, 1988).

Funding the UN is a permanent headache for New York. Member-states' contributions are assessed according to a formula that takes account of a state's economic health and population and the scale of these levies ranges from 0.01% to 25% with the US contributing 25%, France 6.25%, and the UK 5%. Most states, in fact, pay less than 1%. Unfortunately, many governments are in arrears and there is a constant battle to urge them to underwrite the principles they have endorsed.[2] The budget allocated for the two years 1994 and 1995 is $2,749 million. This is to cover the expense of substantial programmes in economic, social and humanitarian activities, 17 peacekeeping operations, special disaster relief initiatives, and administrative costs such as staff, management, library and a host of conferences. A great spread of UN activities results from General Assembly deliberations.[3] Four critical areas seen as needing priority are disarmament, human rights, development programmes and disaster relief. Although many arms reduction measures have been secured through bilateral negotiation, highlighted by presidential signing ceremonies, the General Assembly has steered notable treaties through to international endorsement as we shall see in a later chapter. Human rights issues and development work, on occasion provoking vigorous Assembly debate, have been handed over to commissions and committees and then to workers and observers in the field.

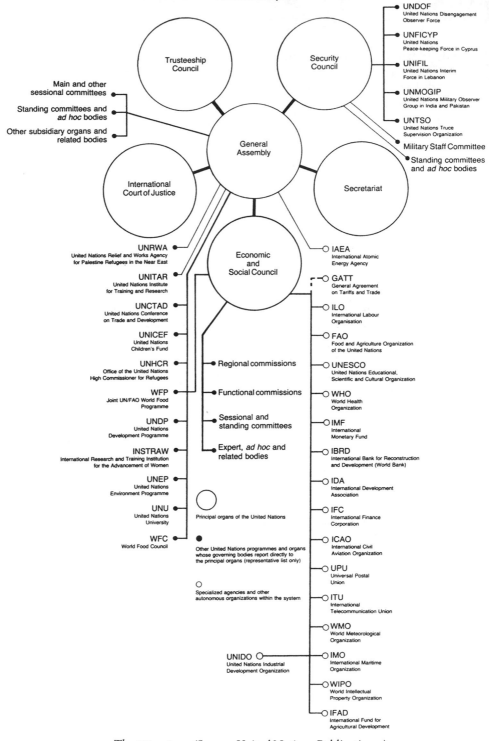

United Nations system

Trusteeship Council

Security Council

- UNDOF
  United Nations Disengagement
  Observer Force
- UNFICYP
  United Nations
  Peace-keeping Force in Cyprus
- UNIFIL
  United Nations Interim
  Force in Lebanon
- UNMOGIP
  United Nations Military Observer
  Group in India and Pakistan
- UNTSO
  United Nations Truce
  Supervision Organization

Military Staff Committee

- Standing committees
  and ad hoc bodies

Main and other
sessional committees

Standing committees and
ad hoc bodies

Other subsidiary organs and
related bodies

General
Assembly

International
Court of Justice

Secretariat

Economic
and
Social Council

UNRWA
United Nations Relief and Works Agency
for Palestine Refugees in the Near East

UNITAR
United Nations Institute
for Training and Research

UNCTAD
United Nations Conference
on Trade and Development

UNICEF
United Nations
Children's Fund

UNHCR
Office of the United Nations
High Commissioner for Refugees

WFP
Joint UN/FAO World Food
Programme

UNDP
United Nations
Development Programme

INSTRAW
International Research and Training Institution
for the Advancement of Women

UNEP
United Nations
Environment Programme

UNU
United Nations
University

WFC
World Food Council

Regional commissions

Functional commissions

Sessional and
standing committees

Expert, ad hoc and
related bodies

○ Principal organs of the United Nations

● Other United Nations programmes and organs
whose governing bodies report directly to
the principal organs (representative list only)

○ Specialized agencies and other
autonomous organizations within the system

IAEA
International Atomic
Energy Agency

GATT
General Agreement
on Tariffs and Trade

ILO
International Labour
Organisation

FAO
Food and Agriculture Organization
of the United Nations

UNESCO
United Nations Educational,
Scientific and Cultural Organization

WHO
World Health
Organization

IMF
International
Monetary Fund

IBRD
International Bank for Reconstruction
and Development (World Bank)

IDA
International Development
Association

IFC
International Finance
Corporation

ICAO
International Civil
Aviation Organization

UPU
Universal Postal
Union

ITU
International
Telecommunication Union

WMO
World Meteorological
Organization

IMO
International Maritime
Organization

WIPO
World Intellectual
Property Organization

IFAD
International Fund for
Agricultural Development

UNIDO
United Nations Industrial
Development Organization

The UN system. (Source: United Nations Publications.)

THE SECURITY COUNCIL

The Security Council alone is empowered to take executive decisions and to "call upon" member-states under the Charter to carry them out. This is an attempt to put authority, agreement and force into its duty to safeguard a peaceful world. There are now 15 member-states, the original Permanent Five (P5) and 10 others who are elected by the General Assembly for two-year terms. Each member of the Council has one vote. They meet in continuous session, almost always in New York, with a representative of each member always on call. If an urgent threat to world peace is perceived, disputing parties will be advised to seek a solution through a range of measures such as enquiry, conciliation, arbitration, judicial settlement, or using mediation and observers, or inviting the Secretary-General's "good offices". Should fighting break out, the Security Council can issue cease-fire directives or despatch a peacekeeping force. If all else fails, the Council may decide on enforcement measures such as economic sanctions or even move reluctantly towards using military force. Events in Korea, the Congo, the Persian Gulf, Cambodia and Bosnia demonstrate the range of activities, even if the effectiveness of some has been questioned.

Voting procedures in the Security Council have attracted much attention from those anxious about stalemate and manipulation. Inis Claude has described the dilemma of the founder peace-seekers in 1945, convinced that unanimity among the P5 was "certainly necessary" but fearing that it was not "necessarily certain". After much argument, several points were eventually agreed, among them that the P5 could rule off the agenda (i.e. veto) any substantive matter likely to lead to rupture, and, further, that any P5 member not supporting a decision and not wishing to block discussion by veto could abstain. In any case, a party to a dispute was to abstain from voting. Procedural matters would be decided by an affirmative vote of nine members including the concurring votes of the P5. In the first few years after 1945 the veto was frequently employed by P5 members influenced by ideological considerations. If the veto is a system-preserver in the Security Council, rather like a fuse, on the other hand it also has had a stimulating (if a divisive) effect on the General Assembly.

The privileged position of the P5 is today a controversial aspect of UN structure. That five out of 185 UN members are able to freeze UN action on a substantive matter by exercising a veto, and the unrepresentativeness of this elite group, have led to calls for enlargement of the Security Council (perhaps to 20 or 25 members), which could usefully be part of a general structural reappraisal. Why, one asks, should the victors of the Second World War, 50 years later, still hog the top table? In Henry Kissinger's words, "the realities of power rather than the canons of legitimacy" should determine the privileged status of the P5 – it is no longer an equitable or a sensible reflection of the very different economic and political make-up of today's state system. Should Germany and Japan, defeated in 1945, still be excluded from executive responsibility?[4] Surely other states, such as Brazil, Egypt, Nigeria, India and possibly Indonesia and Mexico, could use their influence beneficially as permanent members?

The P5, confronted by calls for enlargement, at first protested that it would entail revision of the Charter. They were uneasy that their conferred right to use a veto might be abused by others. The compromise of five permanent members with veto power and five without it did not appeal to them. It would never be easy to resolve the rival claims of intending states knocking on the exclusive door.[5] At the UN's fiftieth anniversary, and with reform in the air, some of these timid and unconvincing responses will lose ground quickly. The Charter can surely be modified by assent. Voting procedures can be reviewed and changed if necessary after five decades. An organization that claims to be democratic, and is now happily free from the old East/West divisions, must find ways of securing representative and vital membership if it is not to die on its feet. Enlargement will need the approval of a General Assembly two-thirds majority. Extending veto power would do nothing to ensure the prime objectives in reform, namely, fairer representation and more efficient decision-making.

THE SECRETARY-GENERAL

More than one Secretary-General has seen his office on the 38th floor of the UN headquarters building in New York as the loneliest place in the world. This is the focal point of political and administrative leadership. Here, one man, serving a five-year term, has to balance the power of quiet diplomacy with assertiveness. The six Secretary-Generals since 1946 have worked hard both to resolve international conflicts and to avoid them. The most perceptive holder of the post was Dag Hammarskjöld (1953–61), whose death on active service appalled the world. Eminent in consistency, integrity and intellect, he saw himself as needing to exercise not the sleight of hand of the juggler but the harder, patient work of the builder and the unflurried commitment of honest broker. Two things, above all, were essential for success in his office. First, to see the UN not as static conference machinery but as a dynamic instrument enabling governments to develop forms of anticipatory action before a crisis boiled over – "preventive diplomacy". Secondly, to realize that the only hope of finding a lasting solution to conflict was to learn to see the solution objectively and to experience contestants' difficulties subjectively. This was to lead to this Secretary-General's initiatives in peacekeeping intervention (bringing a degree of reconciliation in 16 out of 24 disputes).

THE UN SECRETARIAT

The UN Secretariat in New York and in the main world offices numbers 13,000. Overall, the entire UN system, that is, including all the Specialized Agencies, employs 51,000 staff (less than 10% of that employed by the British Civil Service). On appointment these officials solemnly swear that they will uphold the interests of the UN in loyalty, discretion and conscience and not seek or accept instructions from any external authority. To divest yourself of national preconceptions might be thought a superhuman problem. The UN has gone about the task of securing the highest standards in efficiency, competence and integrity by recruiting from a wide geographical area.

On the whole, the UN has been remarkably fortunate in recruiting people of real calibre. In its early days the organization found it difficult to persuade governments to release some of their brightest officials especially where a government was trying to get on its feet again after war. Many of these officials, trained in elitist circles at home, did not find it easy to be "universalist" and "impartial" in a novel, polyglot community. Two out of three of them came from the US, Britain or France. The balance has been somewhat redressed, but 42% still hail from Western Europe or the Americas, despite an attempt to spread recruitment by appointing one in three on short fixed-term contracts. Secretariat personnel are charged with enormous responsibilities. They must prepare the ground meticulously for General Assembly meetings, they must service committees and organize conferences. Liaison with 185 governments must be maintained. Representatives, individuals and groups from NGOs are continually visiting the UN building in New York, observing meetings, and conferring with staff. This management of the UN system supports a wealth of detailed and wide-ranging activity involving delicate diplomacy and a mass of paperwork. Every day HQ staff have to deal with delegates who may be uncertain or confused or stubborn. Their approach has to take account of entrenched state autonomies and prejudice, and even of the difficulties of cultural bias. Like most bureaucrats they can be the whipping-boys of those who suspect mistakes or who may just be under a misunderstanding.

THE INTERNATIONAL COURT OF JUSTICE

The International Court of Justice (ICJ) was established in 1947. The outline of its competence (which is spelled out in the UN Charter), not only its codification but its continued development, is based on international law. The sources are treaties and Conventions, international custom, the general principles of law recognized by civilized nations, and the teachings of eminent lawyers in various nations. One might think there is enough breadth there to confuse everybody and to encourage time-wasting legalism. Nevertheless, it does represent an attempt to bring into the mainstream of UN practice, procedure and established convention, elements that reflect many different legal traditions and cultures. Much ICJ work is to do with interpretation of treaties and settlement of disputes over territorial rights on land and at sea. From time to time the UN asks for an advisory opinion on a legal question (for instance, the South African presence in Namibia before its independence, or the shooting down of an aircraft).

Two factors limit the Court's usefulness. First, only states, not individuals or organizations, may be parties to any dispute heard by the ICJ. Secondly, the parties are required to accept the Court's findings. There are states prepared to acknowledge the jurisdiction of the ICJ provided that it does not compromise their own domestic jurisdiction. They may be discouraged from using the Court if they fear a dispute may be settled on terms resulting in embarrassment at home or injurious to important national interests. The ICJ is an adjudicating body without extra powers of enforcement and arrest. Perhaps it should be seen as an international experiment aimed at gradually building up a set of judgments and rules demonstrating that notions of overriding sovereignty and selfish unilateral action are outdated. While the ICJ and its 15 judges are primarily concerned with adjustment and settlement of international disputes by peaceful and legal means, the actual development and codification of international law is the task of a separate International Law Commission, established in 1947. Its 34 members serve in their individual capacity, not as governmental representatives. Their job is to prepare drafts on topics of international law, often referred to them by the General Assembly or ECOSOC, and after careful examination of all the implications, to take them back to the General Assembly as a basis for Conventions, say, on the law of the sea, statelessness, or human rights, which all Assembly members are invited to sign.

THE ECONOMIC AND SOCIAL COUNCIL

ECOSOC was set up by the Charter to co-ordinate the work of the Specialized Agencies. Fifty-four members serve for three years. This body is a forum for discussion and for the formulation of policy recommendations. Research and reports are commissioned, conferences are convened. As with the Secretariat, liaison is maintained with government representatives and with a host of advisors who can be approached or brought to headquarters.

Systematic inventories and careful programming steer the long-term efforts at community resuscitation of Agencies like the World Health Organization (WHO), Food and Agriculture Organization (FAO), the United Nations Children's fund (UNICEF), and the International Labour Organization (ILO). Each Agency has its independent Council responsible for administration and budget, and there is a network of supervising management units in all the continents, serviced by native and foreign personnel. The FAO is in Rome, WHO in Geneva, the United Nations Educational, Scientific and Cultural Organization (UNESCO) in Paris, and the International Atomic Energy Agency (IAEA) in Vienna. Research institutes and survey teams monitor progress and forecast trends. Radiating back to New York and ECOSOC are action reports and comparative data that have enabled ECOSOC to devise for the General Assembly universal Covenants and codes to protect human rights, standard procedures for the control and eventual eradication of disease, and guidelines for international transport and postal services. Twenty million refugees have been aided by the High Commissioner for Refugees (UNHCR), some resettled, others offered temporary relief. Other Agencies fight illiteracy on a global scale, promote the use of basic and alternative technologies, or seek to curb exploitation of outerspace and the ocean floor while encouraging its exploration, or demonstrate the peaceful uses of atomic energy. They study the effects of pollution and uncontrolled use of natural resources. Something like eight out of ten dollars spent by the UN goes to economic and social development in a struggle to achieve better living standards globally.

Nowhere is all this Agency work more necessary (and more uneven and difficult) than in the developing countries where two-thirds of the world's people live, menaced by poverty, hunger, disease and ignorance. Three UN Development Decades since 1960 have focused on strategic programmes. In May 1974 members of the UN signalled their determination to work together on such programmes, "to correct inequality and redress existing injustices . . . to eliminate the widening gap between developed and developing countries and ensure steadily accelerating economic and social development".

The work of the Specialized Agencies reflects the different spheres of UN activity over five decades. Initially, after the Second World War, the UN was involved in large-scale rehabilitation of industry, agriculture and transport in Europe and Asia – economic reconstruction. There followed political spearheading in the 1950s and 1960s to transform the hitherto dependent colonies into states responsible for their own fortunes – political revitalization. More recently, the Agencies have come together to lend a hand, certainly, but also to encourage self-help and studiously targeted development programmes managed in partnership by the agents of change in receiving countries – political regeneration. Workers in the Specialized Agencies have to contend with world recession, with the enormous pressures of population growth, and with violence resulting from nationalist rivalries and ethnic tensions. Much that is done is threatened by the indebtedness and lack of security of developing nations. Security, in the fullest sense of the term, was only partly understood in 1945 and then mainly in political terms. Fifty years later, in country after country, we see demonstrated the dramatic fact that "security" entails "wellbeing" for individuals and for groups. Security, like peace, is rarely conferred and almost always has to be earned. The case-studies that follow show something of the endless mission of the UN in action.

NOTES

1. Only sovereign states are granted UN membership. Does this principle in practice deny large minority groups (e.g. in the former USSR) a voice or place in the New York forum? Recently, the former Yugoslavia split off into two smaller units, and both were subsequently admitted to the UN as sovereign states. The tally of 185 members may well increase as a result of a similar "fission" elsewhere.
2. The major reason for the UN's continuing financial straits is the failure of the US to honour more than half of its assured dues during the last ten or so years. Presidents Bush and Clinton have had to wrestle with US Congress delay and obstruction. Most of the US arrears should have been paid by the end of 1995.
3. Perceptive scrutiny of the General Assembly at work can be found in two books by Inis L. Claude Jnr: *Swords into plowshares*, 4th edition (1971) and *The changing United Nations* (1967), both published by Random House in New York.
4. Germany and Japan, both likely to become permanent members in 1995, are campaigning vigorously for enlargement. Their constitutions after joining the Security Council would need amendment to permit their defence forces to contribute to UN peacekeeping operations.
5. There is a very full record of British reservations about enlargement in *House of Commons Foreign Affairs Committee 3rd Report Session 1992–93: The Expanding Role of the United Nations and its Implications for United Kingdom Policy, Vol II. Minutes of evidence* (London: HMSO). It makes illuminating and controversial reading.

FURTHER READING

Baehr, P. R. & L. Gordenker. *The United Nations: reality and ideal.* New York: Praeger Publishers, 1984.

Bailey, S. D. *The United Nations: a short political guide.* London: Macmillan, 1989.

Falk, R. A., S. S. Kim, S. H. Mendlovitz. *The United Nations and a just world order.* Oxford: Westview Press, 1991.

Kostakos, G., A. J. R. Groom, S. Morphet, P. Taylor. Britain and the new UN agenda: towards global riot control? *Review of International Studies* 17, pp. 95–105, 1991.

Lister, F. Exploiting the recent revival of the United Nations. *International Relations* 9(5), pp. 419–38, 1989.

Luard, E. *The United Nations. How it works and what it does,* 2nd edn. London: Macmillan, 1994.

Peterson, M. J. *The General Assembly in world politics.* Boston: Allen & Unwin, 1986.

Riggs, R. E. & J. C. Plano. *The United Nations, international organization and world politics.* Chicago: Dorsey Press, 1988.

Roberts, A. & B. Kingsbury. *United Nations, divided world,* 2nd edn. Oxford: Clarendon Press, 1993.

Ruggie, J. G. The United States and the United Nations: toward a new realism. *International Organization* 39(2), pp. 343–56, 1985.

Williams, Douglas. *The specialized agencies: the system in crisis.* London: Hurst, 1987.

Williamson, R. S. The United Nations: some parts work. *Orbis* 32(2), pp. 187–97, 1988.

Chapter Two

THE STRUCTURE OF THE UN

The Charter

General Assembly	Forum for open debate; promotes principles and purposes of UN; quasi-legislative role; co-ordinates, monitors and approves work of the agencies, committees and commissions. 185 member-states with one vote each.
Security Council	Executive body; preventive diplomacy. 15 member-states.
Secretary-General	Appointed by General Assembly • Trygve Lie (1945–53) (Norway) • Dag Hammarskjöld (1953–61) (Sweden) • U. Thant (1961–71) (Burma) • Kurt Waldheim (1972–81) (Austria) • Perez de Cuellar (1982–92) (Peru) • Boutros Boutros-Ghali (1992–) (Egypt)
Secretariat	Administers General Assembly & Security Council.
International Court of Justice (ICJ)	Judicial body, advises and adjudicates.
Economic and Social Council (ECOSOC)	Co-ordinates activity of specialized agencies.
Specialized Agencies	Economic and social development work.

PART TWO

Peacekeeping and collective security

Peacekeeping in principle

The term "peacekeeping" is not to be found in the Charter of the UN, yet every newspaper and the daily TV screen are filled with the pictures and the dramatic accounts of the UN's peacekeepers, the Blue Berets, at work. Currently there are 17 peacekeeping operations and 71,000 peacekeepers. Peacekeeping missions have been resorted to increasingly in recent years, with a total of 36 operations since 1948 at a cost of more than $10,400 million; 650,000 men and women from 70 countries have donned the blue beret and launched into a score of arduous and imaginative enterprises – over 1,000 have paid with their lives. There is a wealth of controversy, sometimes ill-informed, as to the effectiveness and validity of some of these operations. At times the UN has been seen not so much active as inactive. This chapter will consider, first, some of the UN's early approaches to the task of peacekeeping; the Cold War era apparently rendered many of these impotent and questionable. Efforts to modify peacekeeping principles by successive Secretary-Generals are next described, followed by the most recent proposals for UN peacekeeping. Finally, this chapter briefly explores the transition from peacekeeping to peacebuilding, emphasising particularly the controversial issue of UN intervention within a state's frontiers.

APPROACHES TO PEACEKEEPING

Part II of this book shows the UN in action to address the problem of collective security in general terms and to deal with specific breaches of the peace. Collective security and peacekeeping are fundamentally different both as concepts and in practice. Since a collective response to aggression has never materialized in the shape envisaged by the UN founders, first, in New York, the organization has had to resort to enquiry, calls for restraint, even condemnation and sanctions; and secondly, in the field, neutral forms of interposition and observation have been mounted, relying on volunteer forces and slender funds. Two operations alone have depended on enforcement: Korea in 1950–3 and the 1991 Gulf conflict. The other operations in peacekeeping, as far as possible, have followed a non-violent course to explore ways of preventing conflict, maintaining cease-fire, and working through negotiation towards peacemaking and rehabilitation.

At the foundation of the UN in 1945, there were two main approaches to the maintenance of peace. There was what might be called a realistic style, which relied on a balance-of-power rather than a moral position. Five Great Defenders (the US, the USSR, the UK, China and France) proclaimed responsibility as protector-guarantors, encouraging others to share the watch. The plan overall was to forestall aggression by strengthening weak states and weakening strong states (it was never entirely clear which of the two might cause most trouble). This rather simplistic scheme depended on a hierarchy of large, medium and small states maintaining vigilance. The other approach was more idealistic, reminiscent of the old League of Nation hopes that a collective will could identify likely sources of belligerence, would then be prepared to deal with the situation, and would muster and employ non-violent means of resolution. Collective action would separate disputants and offer them various options for reconciliation, and threaten transgressors.

This suggests a dual-track of custodial function (force up one's sleeve) and pacification function (not enforced). The principles above, for instance, are hedged about with difficulties. How are disputants to be held at arm's length and for how long? Exactly who is disputing most – the administration of the state, officials in the provinces, or ordinary people? The case of Cyprus showed the impossibility of neat isolation and insulation. What happens if suggested measures are not acceptable? Stalemate, rancour, violence may result. Suppose, as in the case of Saddam Hussein's Iraq, penalties and threats are not taken seriously? Law and order, the objectives of a peace mission, may only be partly established, remain temporary, or even be ignored, as happened in the Congo. Elsewhere, the buffer force may be bogged down with little prospect of effecting any firm or lasting settlement, as happened in Lebanon.

THE IMPACT OF THE COLD WAR

However creative and however optimistic the views of early UN supporters, the onset of the Cold War both impeded progress and subjected principle to scrutiny. Within 18 months or so of the UN's 1945 inauguration in San Francisco, it was being rent by dissension as 30 states scrambled to throw off imperial shackles and turn towards new allegiances and alignments. The nuclear monopoly of the war victors seemed with every successive year a threat inhibiting moves towards a more peaceful and secure world community. Very clearly this tremendous impasse was fragmenting resolve and initiative. Paralysis in the Security Council led to the General Assembly searching for peacekeeping alternatives. Even when *détente* eased tension the slight hopes of peace were often those that marginalized the UN. The real work of maintaining peace became more realistically peace-through-understanding-of-strength on two levels: (a) the macro approach of facing a potential rival with postures of armed might and determined alliance; and (b) the micro approach of mopping up proxy conflicts without pushing the grand East/West rivals beyond the *nth* degree. Peace during those years of challenge and insecurity seemed to depend on the double maxim that "one man's security is another man's threat". This reassures your allies and deters your enemies, but it does not provide a basis for a lasting and dependable coexistence. Inevitably it encourages complacent justification along the lines of, "we can't solve most political problems, therefore it is not the job of *peacekeepers* to solve political problems". In the Cold War world, viewed at large, and in areas of super-power dominance such as Europe and the Americas, peacekeeping by the UN was not welcome. The P5 were to supply the pivot. In areas where the superpowers were not dominant or were exercising some influence through "friendly" states, UN peacekeeping forces might be allowed in as a stabilizing instrument provided they stayed neutral – such as UN missions in the Congo (1960–4), in Lebanon (1978 to date), in India and Pakistan (1949 to date), and in Yemen (1963–4).

In areas where UN peacekeeping was not permitted, observers, since they were less obtrusive, might be authorized; for example, in the Dominican Republic (1965–6), in Central America (1989 to date) and in Afghanistan (1988–90). In areas of major power tension UN peacekeeping was believed to freeze the situation usefully, discouraging potential change that might turn out to be destructive; for example, operations in Cyprus (1964 to date), and two in the Middle East (the Disengagement Observer Force (UNDOF), 1974 to date), and the Truce Supervision Organization (UNTSO), 1948 to date). It is not difficult now to add to the criticism of UN peacekeeping in those early years. It was certainly inflexible and conservative. Measures recommended by the General Assembly were thought of as "the right thing to do"; essentially restorative, they were not enforceable and lacked preventive capacity. Moreover, Africa, South East Asia and Latin America, where so many conflicts erupted or were just dormant, were inadequately represented on the UN's executive body, the Security Council.

UN PEACEKEEPING OPERATIONS: MODIFIED PRINCIPLES

Two Secretary-Generals made stalwart efforts to move peacekeeping from negative (restoring the *status quo*) to positive (regenerative) approaches. Trygve Lie in 1948 took bold steps over UNTSO and in 1950 over Korea. He proposed what today we would call a "rapid deployment force" to which states would contribute earmarked units. The idea never got off the ground. In those early days UN peacekeeping was thought of as operating largely in three stages: first, deterring aggression and facilitating armistice and withdrawals; then, patrolling and policing a bridged divide; and finally, aiding resettlement. Lie valiantly tried to get a number of questions discussed. If there were to be national contingents how would personnel be recruited and trained? What could be the possible arrangements for political direction, command and legal status? How would such a force be financed? By general levy? By *pro rata* payment from contributing states?

During Lie's term of office (1945–53) the altercation over North Korea's invasion of the south flared into a situation where the UN had to resort to force. The operation was authorized under Chapter VII of the Charter as an enforcement action and so had nothing to do with peacekeeping proper. Among other things, as we shall see in the next chapter, the initiative was not impartial and goals were not clearly defined. The case-study of Korea demonstrates that a presence lacking a policy provides neither viable barrier nor bridge. Unpreparedness to understand a developing situation and eagerness to restore a discredited *status quo* almost collapsed the UN in disrepute. The whole Korean saga still raises more questions than it has ever answered.

Dag Hammarskjöld (1953–61) more carefully set about improving techniques of conflict management. He realized that by carefully and slowly addressing the sensitive issues of national sovereignty, interstate politics, national and international law, and military strategy, it should be possible to use a variety of mediation measures in comprehensive and co-ordinated fashion. This he termed "preventive diplomacy", working, as he put it, "at the edge of developing human society".[1] For the peacekeeper, risk, controversy and opposition were occupational hazards. In 1956 Hammarskjöld used a force of 6,000 from ten nations, UNEF I, to defuse the crisis over Suez when Britain and France needed a face-saver to enable them to withdraw from Egypt. A cease-fire was put into effect and maintained. Incidents threatening the fragile peace between Egypt and Israel were to be discouraged by a UN presence in desert locations. This was more of a truce to lower tension than any form of peacemaking and it was certainly not leading to settlement. Nevertheless, the creation of UNEF helped to plug a hole if it did little to build a foundation for peace. It established several useful precedents towards the desirable object of reducing inflexibility during the Cold War. The inevitability of P5 involvement was lessened, except that their support for a peacekeeping mission was necessary as was the consent of all involved in the conflict. The

Secretary-General was able to exercise control of the operation since his mandate came from the broad-based General Assembly rather than the narrower Security Council. The UNEF initiative demonstrated two desirable components in UN peacekeeping: the encouragement of peacemaking by all concerned rather than any attempt to impose a resolution by force; and, essentially, peacekeeping could only proceed following the securing of a cease-fire.

Three years later, in 1959, Hammarskjöld laid down conditions for the implementation of a peacekeeping operation that are still insisted on today. No unit from any of the permanent members of the Security Council or from an "interested" state might be fielded. (More recently, in the cases of Bosnia and Somalia and with the demise of East–West confrontation, this rule has been amended.) Overall, there must be a clear distinction between enforcement measures permissible under the Charter's Chapter VII and peacekeeping under any other heading. If a UN force was despatched, it must be given precise terms of engagement, and freedom of movement for its units must be secured. Finally, not all conflicts might be deemed suited to UN intervention. These principles seemed fine in theory, yet within 12 months the Congo operation (1960–4) was to throw them into a web of questioning that revealed their blurred edges in practice. At the outset the proposed action in the Congo aroused the support of the powerful strain of anti-imperialist sentiment in the General Assembly. Most certainly a black Congolese government menaced by neo-colonial intrigue must be upheld as a temporary measure until its own security forces had control.

Soon, however, indecision in New York about how to act to meet both external threat and deal with an internal power struggle ranged East and West against each other in vociferous quarrelling. The attempt of the mineral-rich province of Katanga to break away, supported by the former colonial masters in Brussels and by mercenaries, particularly inflamed an international rupture. Hammarskjöld, shortly to pay with his life for his thwarted personal diplomacy, was soon in the firing line at headquarters. He did not help matters in 1961 when he stressed that the whole undertaking was not to be used to bring about any specific political situation. Such a declaration struck few people as credible, throwing into sharp relief the paradox that an unarmed and neutral mission had to use force in an unco-ordinated and imprecise manner to bring about a settled form of law and order. There ensued a barrage of complaints from those who saw the UN exceeding its own fuzzy mandate, from the lobby that suspected the machinations of great-powers, and from all those who deplored Hammarskjöld's excess of zeal. "Gradualism", if not hesitancy, was henceforth to put brakes on what was thought to be a "dynamic instrument".

Subsequent Secretary-Generals have trodden carefully the path from Article 99, which empowers them to alert the Security Council to any matter that in their opinion threatens the maintenance of international peace and security. U. Thant (1961–71) strengthened the Congo force to 20,000 from 39 nations, threatened economic sanctions, and slowly descaled the military commitment. Rather late in the day, it seemed, the lessons of inadequate civilian-military liaison and uncertain overall policy had been learned. Kurt Waldheim (1972–81) and Perez de Cuellar (1982–92) found themselves responsible for an array of international forces in three continents, and for observers, mediators and Good Offices missions. "Appropriate measures" of peacekeeping were now more carefully considered.

FRESH PROPOSALS FOR UN PEACEKEEPING

In 1988 UN peacekeeping was awarded a Nobel Peace Prize about the time of evident conceptual shifts that eventually led to a phase (still with us) of experiment, conjecture, and ongoing suggestion. Fresh ideas were suggested by the present Secretary-General, Boutros Boutros-Ghali, in July 1992 in his *Agenda for peace*. Clearly, the main emphasis was now to be on programmes to reconstitute rather than merely to restore. A crisis was to be anticipated rather than mopped up after it had occurred. To this end, priority was to be given to fact-finding about social and economic malaise to determine the threat posed by large-scale migrations, famine and ethnic unrest. An early warning system should be set up relying on a system at headquarters and in regional centres to monitor and appraise situations likely to erupt into conflict. Confidence-building measures should take the heat out of the old sparring by the Eastern and Western Blocs through systematic exchange of military information, monitored arms agreements, and regional "risk reduction centres". "Preventive deployment" of a UN force should be used to deter hostilities instead of coming in after a battle had started. In New York there must be fuller General Assembly participation to support approaches and methods. There should be a greater reliance on the International Court of Justice. Reactivating the original concept of a Military Staff Committee in New York, or replacing it with an improved military control centre, would enable peacekeeping to be co-ordinated. Permanent units with contingents earmarked by member-states were thought highly desirable. Indeed, a control centre in New York, continuously manned and with all the latest technology to supply it with information, should be able to decide on a range of possible actions to meet evolving situations and problems.

Peacebuilding is to be the objective of UN peacekeepers in Boutros-Ghali's view. Anywhere war had raged there must be a regenerative scheme to remove the detritus, mines, fortifications and so on, followed by a programme to bring in relief supplies, improve transport and repair damaged resources. A veritable life-support system has to sustain people in safe havens or demilitarized zones. UN personnel must be protected (a problem with UNPROFOR in Bosnia, and with UNTAC in Cambodia). The training of peacekeepers needs to be improved. Soldiers sent out on UN missions require a repertoire of languages and mediatory skills rarely to be found in conventional manuals of military training. A multinational training programme would do much to bring staff college expertise to bear on the problem of devising standardization procedures for equipment and back-up logistics. The conventional military trinity of control, command and communication must be reassessed and knit together. The Secretary-General believes that to meet global demands on peacekeeping there should be a re-examination of the role and usefulness of regional infrastructures such as the OSCE and the OAU. In the case of Bosnia in 1992 there was a hesitant and ineffectual response by the European Community (EC).[2] What was plainly lacking then was any clear agreement over who was responsible for what. Three years later there is still confusion and rival factions have sometimes taken advangtage of this.

Financial difficulties have hobbled the progress of UN peacekeeping for many years. There are currently large arrears in the subscriptions of member-states. Some of the defaulting states, shamed perhaps by wide comment, are at last making amends for their financial slackness.[3] Recently, costs have doubled, yet they are relatively small compared to what individual nations spend on arms. Sir Brian Urquhart, a former UN peacekeeper, has estimated that the annual cost of UN peacekeeping worldwide is roughly the same as the cost of one and a half days of the 1991 *Operation Desert Storm* in Iraq. Few nations questioned that expense at the time, but they are always ready to criticize the expense of peacekeeping, now running at $3,200 million a year. Would not UN peacekeeping benefit greatly from a concerted effort to reduce the arms trade? The P5 supply more than 80% of the world's arms exports. The most that has been done to exercise restraint and control was the plan proposed at the UN in April 1993 to compile a voluntary register of arms transfers, but this has proved inconclusive and has done very little to stem the profitable trade in weaponry that goes mainly to areas of existing high tension.

UN INTERVENTION AS AN ISSUE

In what circumstances should collective intervention to deal with gross abuse of human rights, denial of need, or flagrant internecine hostilities be permitted? Already, the UN has gone beyond the excluding provisions of Article 2.7, for instance, in carrying out a search-and-destroy operation in Iraq against nuclear and chemical warfare apparatus and installations.[4] However, since 1993, the world has watched in frustration the dithering over stricken former Yugoslavia (see Chapter 14). UN peacekeeping is now recognized as something the international community must institute experimentally, but carefully and effectively. The thin line of Blue Berets is here to stay.[5] Five case-studies of UN peacekeeping follow. All these operations, in different ways, demonstrate the crucial role of the UN in action for peace. Not one of them, however, has escaped controversy.

NOTES

1. A very thorough discussion of the related peacekeeping techniques of "preventive diplomacy" and "preventive deployment" is found in Gareth Evans, *Cooperating for Peace* (Sydney: Allen and Unwin, 1993) Chapters 5 and 6. Mediation techniques are listed in Article 33 of the UN Charter.
2. The European Community (EC) is now the European Union (EU). For a note on the EC Bosnian "response" see Chapter 14 below.
3. Peacekeeping costs have increased dramatically this decade, partly because there are so many operations in the field. The chief defaulters in peacekeeping funding have been the US, Russia and China, that is, three of the P5. In early 1995 there is much earnest discussion of alternative means of fundraising, e.g. a tax on arms sales, borrowing from the World Bank or the International Monetary Fund, or a levy on the defence spending of member-states.
4. Article 2.7 of the UN Charter specifically does not authorize UN intervention in matters deemed to be "domestic". It follows that any peacekeeping "intervention" must only be at the invitation of a host state.
5. Peacekeeping as one of the areas benefiting from military (non-violent) skills is imaginatively considered in Michael Harbottle, *What is proper soldiering?* 2nd edn (Chipping Norton, Oxford: Centre for International Peacebuilding, 1992).

FURTHER READING

Bailey, S. D. *The United Nations and the termination of armed conflict 1946–64* [2 vols]. Oxford: Oxford University Press, 1982.

Berridge, G. R. *International Politics. States, power and conflicts since 1945*, 2nd edn. London: Harvester Wheatsheaf, 1987: see Chapter 12.

—*Return to the United Nations: UN diplomacy in regional conflicts.* London: Macmillan, 1991.

Boyd, J. M. *United Nations peacekeeping operations: a military and political appraisal.* New York: Praeger, 1971.

Evans, G. *Cooperating for peace.* Sydney: Allen & Unwin, 1993.

Goulding, M. The evolution of United Nations peacekeeping. *International Affairs* (July 1993) 69(3).

Haas, E. B. *Why we still need the United Nations: collective management of international conflict 1945–84.* Berkeley, California: Institute of International Studies, 1986.

Harbottle, M. *The Blue Berets.* London: Leo Cooper, 1975.

Higgins, R. *United Nations peacekeeping* [4 vols]. Oxford: Oxford University Press, 1969–81.

James, A. M. *The politics of peacekeeping.* London: Chatto & Windus, 1972.
—*Peacekeeping in international politics.* London: Macmillan, 1990.
Martin, P. Peacekeeping and the United Nations. *International Affairs* 40(2), pp. 191–204, 1964.
Norton, A. R. & T. G. Weiss. *Soldiers with a difference: the rediscovery of UN peacekeeping.* New York: Foreign Policy Association, 1990.
Parsons, A. The United Nations and international security in the '80s. *Millennium* 12(2), pp. 101–9, 1983.
Rikhye, I. J. & K. Skjelsbaek (eds). *The United Nations and peacekeeping: results, limitations and prospects.* London: Macmillan, 1990.
Rikhye, I. J., M. Harbottle, B. Egge. *The thin blue line. International peacekeeping and its future.* New Haven, Connecticut: Yale University Press, 1974.
Stedman, J. The new interventionists. *Foreign Affairs* 71(1), 1993.
United Nations. *The blue helmets.* New York: United Nations, 1990.
United Nations. UN Peacekeeping. *Survival* 32(3) (special issue), 1990.
Urquhart, B. *A life in peace and war.* London: Weidenfeld & Nicolson, 1987.
Wiseman, H. (ed.) *Peacekeeping: appraisals and proposals.* Oxford: Pergamon, 1983.

Chapter Three

PEACEKEEPING IN PRINCIPLE

Operations

1948 to 1995: 36
Currently under way: 17

1948–	UNTSO	United Nations Truce Supervision Organization
1949–	UNMOGIP	United Nations Military Observer Group in India and Pakistan
1956–67	UNEF I	First United Nations Emergency Force
1958	UNOGIL	United Nations Observation Group in Lebanon
1960–4	ONUC	United Nations Operation in the Congo
1962–3	UNSF	United Nations Security Force in West New Guinea (West Irian)
1963–4	UNYOM	United Nations Yemen Observation Mission
1964–	UNFICYP	United Nations Peacekeeping Force in Cyprus
1965–6	DOMREP	Mission of the Representative of the Secretary-General in the Dominican Republic
1965–6	UNIPOM	United Nations India–Pakistan Observation Mission
1973–9	UNEF II	Second United Nations Emergency Force
1974–	UNDOF	United Nations Disengagement Observer Force
1978–	UNIFIL	United Nations Interim Force in Lebanon
1988–90	UNGOMAP	United Nations Good Offices Mission in Afghanistan and Pakistan
1988–91	UNIIMOG	United Nations Iran–Iraq Military Observer Group
1989–91	UNAVEM I	United Nations Angola Verification Mission I
1989–90	UNTAG	United Nations Transition Assistance Group

1989–92	ONUCA	United Nations Observer Group in Central America
1991–	UNIKOM	United Nations Iraq–Kuwait Observation Mission
1991–	UNAVEM II	United Nations Angola Verification Mission II
1991–	ONUSAL	United Nations Observer Mission in El Salvador
1991–	MINURSO	United Nations Mission for the Referendum in Western Sahara
1991–2	UNAMIC	United Nations Advance Mission in Cambodia
1992–	UNPROFOR	United Nations Protection Force
1992–3	UNTAC	United Nations Transitional Authority in Cambodia
1992–3	UNOSOM I	United Nations Operation in Somalia I
1992–	ONUMOZ	United Nations Operation in Mozambique
1993–	UNOSOM II	United Nations Operation in Somalia II
1993–	UNOMUR	United Nations Observer Mission Uganda-Rwanda
1993	UNOMIG	United Nations Observer Mission in Georgia
1993	UNOMIL	United Nations Observer Mission in Liberia
1993	UNMIH	United Nations Mission in Haiti
1993	UNAMIR	United Nations Assistance Mission for Rwanda
1994	UNASOG	United Nations Aouzou Strip Observer Group
1995	UNCRO	United Nations Confidence Restoration Operation (to replace UNPROFOR in Croatia from 31 March)
1995	UNPREDEP	United Nations Preventive Deployment Force (established in Macedonia)

Two forces in particular are not regarded as peacekeeping forces:
1. UN Force in Korea 1950–3
   Under national rather than UN command; not based on consent of disputing parties; fully engaged in active combat.
2. Allied coalition against Iraq 1990–1
   The actual force in the field was not established by the Security Council and was not under UN command.

Additionally, Unified Task Force in Somalia (UNITAF), December 1992–May 1993, is not generally regarded as a UN force. Security Council had welcomed the US offer to lead a multistate force to re-establish a secure environment for humanitarian operations. Liaison with UN and with UNOSOM.

The UN and Korea, 1950–3

WAS KOREA THE FIRST UN FAILURE?

The previous chapter recalled expectations about UN peacekeeping widely aired in its early years. Collective resolve reluctantly employing force if necessary would deter an aggressor, aid negotiation of disengagement, oversee any resulting partition, and go on to encourage and furnish means of rehabilitation. Judged in this light, Korea, the first specific UN operation to re-establish peace, seems a lamentable failure. Deterrence was seen by some UN members as a need to block expansion of an ideology thought of as a political and military threat to the global interests of one of the P5, namely, the United States. A barrier put up to keep the peace came to depend on propping up an unpopular and autocratic regime in South Korea. Disengagement would centre on North and South Korea agreeing to face each other across a gulf rather than a bridge. If this maintained a tense armistice, it was hardly likely to make for peace with any degree of certainty or permanence. Only 16 nations responded in 1950 to the call by Trygve Lie, then Secretary-General, for a collective force. The lines along which the initiative might be conducted were confused, risking the fragmentation and collapse of the one organization in the world best able to secure an end to hostilities. The Korean story is considered in this chapter in several phases: the preliminary Asian scene; the UN involvement at New York; the onset of armed conflict; the search for conciliation; and, lastly, the settling through armistice into a splintered and uneasy coexistence of pacified rivals.

THE PRELIMINARY ASIAN SCENE

Four elements were significant as peace came to Asia with the war's end of 1945. Imperial powers – the British in India and Malaya, the French in Indo-

China, the Dutch in the East Indies — were clinging on to their possessions opposed by insistent nationalist sentiment. A shattered Japan had been flung out of its pivotal position between the homeland and a wide arc to the south and west. Evident everywhere was the military power of the US, which had won the war in the Pacific. Then there was the immensity of China's 500 million people split between a Communist movement growing inexorably and a corrupt, elitist, Nationalist regime. The Land of Morning Calm has never seemed an appropriate name for Korea. Historically loyal to the Manchu dynasty of China, Korea was forced to cede ports and trading rights to Japan after 1875. Commercial competition between Russia and Japan led to annexation by Japan in 1910. Peace in 1945 removed Japanese colonization but made peace hostage to the brooding presence of Communist China, backed by the USSR, and to US military power directed from a capitalist Washington and tactically operated from occupied Tokyo.

Superpower rivalry came to bear in the shape of dilemmas. Stalin appeared surprised by the Communist victory of Mao-tse Tung's People's Republic of China and uncertain how far to follow his agreement at Yalta to fight Japan and so be drawn into the politics of the Asian Rim. Both sides demobilized between 1945 and 1948. Washington had a twofold mission: to hold firm to an obligation not to desert a wartime ally, Nationalist China, now visibly crumbling; yet at the same time to maintain a US sphere of influence on the Asian perimeter in the destabilizing wake of Japanese removal. This dilemma would involve readjustment to the inevitability of Communist victory in China while ensuring that its Japanese base did not disintegrate. Korea was divided between north and south at the Yalta Conference of February 1945 when the 38th parallel of latitude was established as a purely military line of demarcation between the Red Army and that of the United States. Undoubtedly, Moscow could then envisage Korea as a buffer zone against a reinvigorated China. Whether the Americans dug in in Japan or reduced a Korean foothold by withdrawal, China would surely be dependent on Soviet support. Peking, however, was certain to regard Soviet penetration southwards as unwelcome.

The powers occupying Korea in August 1945 observed the agreed demarcation carefully as a provisional arrangement until the future of the country could be decided, but discussions went on inconclusively for some years. The general objective of the Allies was to restore independence to Korea and to establish a unitary state there. The USSR agreed that democratic groups within Korea should be consulted about a new constitution; meanwhile a four-power trusteeship could be exercised by the US, the USSR, the UK and France. China was not included. The notion of trusteeship was not at all popular in Seoul, the capital of South Korea, and while Washington might have been willing to modify its objectives, Moscow took a much harder line.

THE UN DISCUSSES KOREA

In September 1947 the problem of Korea's future was laid before the UN. The opposing positions of the major powers were soon obvious. For Moscow there could be reliance on four-power agreement and an appointed assembly to bring peace to Korea which was, after all, on its vulnerable eastern flank. This might provide temporary stability but was unlikely to please either Washington or Seoul. The alternative was to go along with a proposal endorsed by the USA and by a Western majority in the General Assembly, namely, to hold elections in two zones, under UN supervision, for a single national assembly and government. Occupying powers would withdraw after 90 days. The US and the General Assembly regarded decisions about Korea's future as a legitimate attempt by an international body to promote understanding and peace between two separate factions although the P5 expressed preference for unification rather than division. The opinion voiced by Washington that bilateral negotiations would only delay establishment of an independent united Korea suggested to Moscow that a solution was to be imposed by one side. Providing

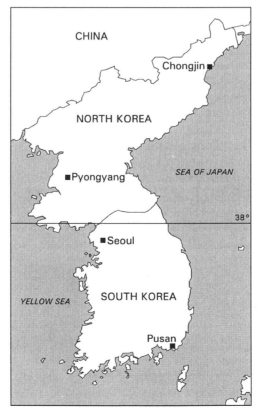

Korea

for elections and the despatch of a UN Temporary Commission to oversee matters were both opposed by the Soviet Union. Their client state, North Korea, refused to admit the representatives of the UN Commission to its territory.

Despite the anxieties of more than a score of UN members that prevailing conditions were unfavourable to a democratic process, Korean elections were to be held on 9 May 1948. Right-wing parties gained the upper hand in an electoral contest that was difficult for outside observers to monitor, and their leader, Dr Syngman Rhee, was to form a national government. The North also went to the polls and established the leadership of a veteran guerrilla campaigner, Kim Il-Sung. Inevitably, the two parts of Korea proclaimed their separate autonomies. American and Soviet forces now withdrew with some misgivings but without overlooking the need to supply their rival protégés with squads of advisors and some defensive equipment. North Korea was the more heavily armed. Both powers were uneasily aware that the two new governments were already asserting counter-claims to be the ruling body of all Korea. Washington no longer saw any possibility of reconciliation between North and South. Rhee's administration began to oust left-wing opposition ruthlessly and hawkish noises emanated from Sung's capital of Pyongyang. The UN Temporary Commission could only organize an array of observation posts along the North/South border. A General Assembly Resolution of 1949 authorized this device without in any way reconnoitring the possibilities of negotiation between major powers and their subordinate states. In the United States Senate the more "primitive" opinion now saw Korea as yet another example of Communist infiltration and expansion that must be contained, if not rolled back, by defenders of the free world. The impartial function of the UN as peacemaker did not seem to mean much to them.

WAR AND UN COLLECTIVE ACTION

Hostilities in Korea began on 25 June 1950, thought generally to be the consequence of North Korean forces attacking those of the South. The incident was laid before a hastily summoned Security Council. US President Harry Truman, however, acted independently without carefully consulting his allies. Air and sea support forces were ordered to Korea, and a military command set up reporting to the White House, not to the UN. This was to be the only UN peacekeeping operation when commanders of a UN force have not reported to the Secretary-General who, in fact, authorizes an operation but does not actually command it. (In this sense, it is suggested, he is more the "Secretary" than the "General".) Nationalist forces in Formosa were ringed around by the US 7th Fleet. Stalin, assured that the tasks were limited, decided to take no action. His representative in the Security Council, outraged that China was represented by the Nationalist rump element and not by the People's Republic, had absented himself and so was not able to veto any Security Council Resolution calling for an end to the fighting and for a North Korean withdrawal. Security Council Resolutions were not as impartial as had been expected. The first one of 25 June required all UN members to assist the UN and refrain from aiding North Korea. A following Resolution, two days later, recommended that members furnish assistance to South Korea to repel the attack and restore peace. Approval of a unified UN command of a military force was secured by 7 July 1950, but by the end of the month the Soviet representative was once more in his seat and vetoes and other tactics hampered decision.[1]

In Washington, President Truman was anxious to demonstrate his country's readiness to defend independence and guarantee the security of other states, and at the same time to enlist international aid to supplement pared-down US forces – and to give the enterprise a moral tone. US General Douglas MacArthur, distinguished by service in the Second World War, was appointed Commander-in-Chief on 8 July 1950. His multinational expeditionary force from 16 nations eventually included contingents from Australia, Belgium, Canada, Ethiopia, the Netherlands, Thailand, Turkey and the UK among others. Latin America was notably cool. The US provided 50% of the ground forces, 86% of the ships, and 93% of the air forces. It had not been easy to persuade veterans and victims of the war in Europe to make the long journey to Korea to enrol in a UN corps of peacekeepers whose terms of reference and of engagement were unprecedented and difficult to understand.

In autumn 1950 the whole purpose of the UN was in jeopardy as determined attacks by North Korea hit home, breaching defences and, in September, even capturing Seoul. The situation that month was only retrieved by General MacArthur daringly launching an amphibious operation behind the western flank of the North Koreans, which forced them to pull back. MacArthur, flushed with victories, determined to push northwards. His objective in crossing the 38th parallel went beyond non-political intervention: from a defensive action to restore the *status quo*, it became an offensive move to bring about the reunification of Korea. Chinese anxiety was represented by the US in late October as "defiance of the United Nations" and condemnation and sanctions were called for. The threat of intervention by Peking's army was discounted. Little effort was apparent towards any settlement of outstanding differences and the United States was particularly reluctant to work for the bridging of differences. It had never been expected that UN forces would go beyond the 38th parallel. Previously, in June, UN Resolutions, and indeed statements from the White House, had limited UN intervention to restoring South Korea to its status prior to the invasion and to the re-establishment of a violated peace. The mere possibility of such a bold move would change the objectives and conduct of the whole operation to a drastic and unjustifiable degree.

In mid September the General Assembly had listened with growing apprehension to an American case for making the most of a stand on the "threshold of victory" and thus working for unification. A Western resolution in September 1950 called for the securing of stability and representative government "throughout Korea"; this was seen by many as explicitly authorizing a move across a tenuous line of demarcation. Quickly, a counter-resolution from Eastern Bloc states indicted any frontier violation and demanded the pulling-back of the UN force to allow all-Korean elections under UN auspices. The Western majority in the General Assembly succeeded in getting their Resolution accepted, clearly aware that the Security Council's enforcement power was being bypassed.

The first week of November 1950 brought full-scale intervention by Chinese forces. Earlier exploratory probing of South Korean positions revealing defensive anxieties now gave way to a mass response to what Peking regarded as a deliberate drive north across the Yalu River. MacArthur's irresponsibility and Washington's mistaken assessments of the military and political significance of the new developments were to subject the Korean venture to nine months of bitter fighting and to a great deal of criticism from governments not deploying personnel in Korea. Disaster, in the fullest sense of that term, was only narrowly averted. China felt it was denied an ideological triumph in Korea, but in the eyes of the world was to stand tall in power and influence.[2]

Further constitutional precedents were established in New York on 3 November 1950 when a special measure, the Uniting for Peace Resolution, was passed. This was to provide for recalling the General Assembly at short notice if the Security Council reached deadlock by veto. In that event the General Assembly itself could call for the use of force to deal with a situation judged to be endangering world peace. This provision was emphatically not in the UN Charter. Moreover, the veto, for all its disadvantages, had the safety-valve function of keeping the P5 more or less in accord, yet it was now being jettisoned. The admittedly clumsy processes of negotiating and compromise among the major powers were now dangerously sidelined. A crucial exercise of political skills to bring about an end to hostilities was almost inevitably to take second place to the enlistment of military enforcement powers. It might well be thought that now was the time to stop. Wrongful aggression had been righted. It would surely have been better to have "frozen" the ideological elements in the conflict by negotiating a cease-fire, refraining from pressing on towards a "final" settlement, especially one provocative to Communist China. The yawning gaps between UN policies and those of General MacArthur were healed when the force commander, enraged at political restrictions on his campaigning, was relieved of his command by President Truman on 11 April 1951. Many now in Washington and certainly inside the UN building in New York agreed with the American General Omar Bradley that it was "the wrong war, at the wrong place, at the wrong time, and with the wrong enemy". The ideal of a unified Korea was a United Nations purpose: it was not a war aim.

THE PROCESS OF PEACE

Toe-to-toe stalemate in summer 1951 found all weary sides willing to discuss cease-fire and an armistice. This process was to last two years until final agreement was signed at Panmunjom, a hamlet in North Korea. It was to be an armistice without victory, a cessation of to-and-fro hostilities. At Panmunjom two peace-supervising bodies were set up. The Military Armistice Commission, made up of officers and observers from the UN Force, from North Korea and from China, would patrol a demilitarized zone. The other group, the Neutral Nations Supervisory Commission, was less effective in checking that the levels of armaments following the armistice were not being exceeded. They found it difficult to stem the continual flow of charge and counter-charge. That these bodies still meet today, after 55 years, attests to the difficulty the UN has had enforcing any lasting peace accord. At least these vestiges of UN peacekeeping have allowed the former warring parties to disengage and demobilize and they have afforded a modest degree of stability. Each side has been more anxious to prevent the opposing party from winning dominant control of the entire country than bringing about its reunification.

Much of the tortuous discussion of cease-fire terms was hampered by argument over the repatriation of prisoners of war. The issue at stake was whether all prisoners of war should be exchanged or only those who were willing to cross borders. The Communist contention was that all prisoners should be returned. The military delegates to the armistice talks, US army officers on the UN side, insisted that there was a duty to observe a humanitarian concern for prisoners' welfare and that nobody who was averse to returning to his original country should be forced to do so. When in April 1953 it was put to North Korea that only some 70,000 out of 132,000 Communist prisoners were prepared to return home, it looked as though no exchange arrangements would be acceptable to the North. At the General Assembly in October 1952 it proved harder still to reach any compromise over what was certainly a crucial point in negotiation. The possibilities of screening or of mediation by a third party were put forward without being taken up. It was not until mid April 1953 that some progress was visible with the Chinese and North Korean negotiators prepared to go ahead with an exchange of wounded and seriously ill prisoners. Both sides found favour with India's proposal that a neutral-nations commission look after all prisoners for a month and arrange for them to meet counsellors from both sides.

Free and frank discussion sessions, an imaginative notion, might have broken the impasse had not President Rhee sabotaged impending agreement. The armistice would prove an end to his hope of removing the hazards of communism to the north. He had little doubt that UN forces, after three frustrating years, felt able to accept a cease-fire based on the lasting partition of his country. Deliberately, then, the gates of a prisoner of war camp were left open and 25,000 North Koreans flooded out into the countryside. A bare 1,000 or so were recaptured. Somehow, the situation at Panmunjom was saved although the front line as a whole was racked by intense combat. Rhee agreed not to obstruct negotiations further., although he would sign no concordat.

A month after the signing of the Korean Armistice on 27 July 1953, the General Assembly met in special session to work out details of a peace conference. Unhappily, discussion froze on the question of inviting certain neutral states in addition to the obvious need for the presence of those nations that had fielded troops. Nobody opposed the attendance of the Soviet Union. Progress was only thought possible if those who had sacrificed most in the conflict were permitted to attend. Neutral nations such as India, Pakistan and Burma saw expediency triumph, narrowing international participation in peace establishment. Geneva was to be the location for talks in May 1954, which featured yet again the opposing positions of the two sides that had quarrelled in Korea. There seemed no alternative to a divided nation whose constituent parts would be jealously administered and protected. Battles had ebbed and flowed between 1950 and 1953. Inexperience and the unfamiliarity of terrain had dogged UN fortunes in the first year and they were almost eclipsed by massive Chinese attacks. Spring 1951 had featured decisive UN advance to the 38th parallel and across it and in the autumn, as armies became bogged down, the first tentative negotiations on terms for a cease-fire. Against a background of long-range bombing by the US Air Force, relative immobility on the ground and argument over prisoner repatriation, the years 1952 and 1953 had brought reluctant recognition that a definitive resolution of conflict was never likely to happen. Three years of warfare and eight years of negotiation had done nothing to bring about the tolerance and good neighbourliness for which the UN Charter called.

KOREA TODAY: DIVISION AND PROBLEMS

Today, the severed halves of Korea face each other across a highly militarized divide: peace has been enforced but never in any real sense made. South Korea has come out of it well, materially. There are towns with high-rise flats and office blocks, garish neon-lit prosperity and a booming electronics industry. The North, languishing for 41 years under the eccentric repression of Kim Il-Sung, until his death in July 1994, has been treated by most other nations as a diplomatic pariah. Despite this, an implacable Kim initiated a "gigantic struggle" to reconstruct the economy and build a self-sufficient industry and trading system. His calculated diplomacy played off Beijing against Moscow, securing aid from both. Latterly, the North's nuclear potential, which has alarmed so many other states, has been used as a bargaining counter for US recognition and following the exploratory visit of ex-President Jimmy Carter in June 1994 there is some prospect of resumed dialogue between the US, Russia and the suspicious South Korea.[3]

What took place in Korea 50 years ago and has happened since raises issues that UN supporters may still ponder. First, that of approach. Intervention exacted a dreadful toll in human lives, decimating the land that international action was setting out to save. Casualties in the international UN Force alone rose to 142,000. A peacekeeping mission turned into one of thankless war.[4] Could a more peaceful intervention along the 38th parallel, similar to that later used in the Middle East, have brought more productive results at far lower cost? Secondly, the ideological fixity of the conflict was all too obvious. There seems to have been no sustained search for negotiated means ending the dispute, such as those enumerated in Article 33 of the UN Charter. Policies were declaratory rather than exploratory, concerned most with defending entrenched positions. The earlier suggestions about UN trusteeship were not carefully scrutinized. Superpowers, with the support of their Korean clients, pursued objectives likely to lead only to permanent division. The UN appeared unable to forestall these adversarial tendencies. Indeed, the purpose of UN Resolutions to expedite the unification of Korea went in the face of very obvious political realities. Their laudable aim only strengthened refusal to compromise. A tight-lipped disinclination to consider tentative "feelers" by both sides and by neutral observers aborted what might have proved a gradual and concerted approach to conciliation. Thirdly, the structural components of any successful peacekeeping operation, that is, command, control, communication, leading towards disengagement and eventual rehabilitation, were never adequately co-ordinated. The overall control of military operations and, too, its monopoly of peace negotiations, were factors unlikely to reduce mistrust among other UN members.

It is easy in retrospect to brand the UN's first real initiative in the field as something that was insufficiently addressed and badly conducted, with members of the Security Council unable to comprehend and disentangle the ideological elements in the conflict. But it would be unhelpful to slight the memory of those thousands who paid for misunderstandings with their lives. The least, perhaps the most, that can be said of the Korean venture is that it has provided a case-study from which peacekeepers and others have learned much to aid the success of later operations. If Korea was a peace-enforcement rather than a peacemaking operation, the crucial question remains: how far can the UN *enforce* a peace?

NOTES

1. This unified command was the only time during the course of the Cold War that the UN was able to resort to enforcement action under Chapter VII of the Charter. The US appointed the commander and the force flew the UN flag.

2. Max Hastings in *The Korean War* (see Futher reading below) makes this point in the course of a detailed account of the whole operation.
3. See Chapter 9 below for an account of controversy over North Korea's nuclear "potential". Already, in early 1995, the situation has eased and there is some possibility of reconciliation.
4. It is possible to consider the Korean operation very much in terms of Cold War "containment" where defence of US interests in Japan and the stabilization of Asia called for a robust defence against Communist "expansion". This would have been ideological manoeuvring rather than aiding the UN to regain the *status quo*.

FURTHER READING

Goodrich, L. M. *Korea: a study of United States policy in the United Nations*. New York: Council on Foreign Relations, 1956.

Hastings, M. *The Korean War*. London: Pan Books. 1987.

Lowe, P. *The origins of the Korean War*. Harlow, England: Longman, 1986.

Lyons, G. M. *Military policy and economic aid: the Korean case*. Columbus, Ohio: Ohio State University Press, 1961.

Rees, D. *Korea: the limited war*. London: Hamish Hamilton, 1964.

Rees, D. (ed.) *The Korean War: history and tactics*. London, Orbis, 1984.

Chapter Four

THE UN AND KOREA, 1950–3

February 1945	Yalta Conference divides Korea into North and South along 38th parallel.
September 1947	UN proposes supervised elections for Korea.
May–August 1948	Elections appoint rival leaders in two Koreas.
25 June 1950	North Korea attacks South Korea. Security Council adopts Resolution calling on North Korea to fall back to 38th parallel. USSR absent.
27 June 1950	Security Council calls on member-states to aid repelling of Korean aggression. President Truman orders US forces to support South Korea. Landing of US forces following week and naval blockade.
7 July 1950	General MacArthur to be C-in-C 16 nations UN Force.
August–September 1950	Ebb and flow of warfare. Daring US amphibious landing at Inchon relieves hard-pressed UN Force.
3 November 1950	General Assembly adopts Uniting for Peace Resolution.
November 1950	Chinese enter war, massive attack imperils UN Force.
January–April 1951	Dogged battles with advantage tending to go to UN Force.
11 April 1951	MacArthur relieved of command by Truman.
June–July 1951	Tentative cease-fire enquiries consolidate in armistice talks.
January–April 1952	Confusion over prisoners. Disorder in camps. Truce talks in danger.

24 October 1952	Eisenhower announces that if elected US President he will visit Korea. He does so in May (after gaining 55% of the vote at home).
January–April 1953	Desultory peace talks. Exchange of wounded prisoners. US threatens intensified "action" if negotiations fail. Small-scale battles continue.
27 July 1953	Armistice signed at Panmunjom.
May 1954	Inconclusive Geneva conference fails to get Korean settlement. The country remains bisected but without occupying forces

Cyprus

A UN peacekeeping force was sent to Cyprus in spring 1964. Over 30 years later the Blue Berets are still there with a virtually unchanged mandate to keep the peace and to work for a return to normality. The cost of this operation and its failure to reach final settlement is now tempting participants in the United Nations Force in Cyprus (UNFICYP) to withdraw their personnel. Tensions have been dampened by an international presence, yet the tranquillizing of incompatible demands has been achieved only through carefully guarded partition. Is this success in peacekeeping? Is it a failure in peacebuilding? What has the world learned from the case of Cyprus? This case-study begins with an island rent by traditional divisions and unable to form a stable republic. A UN peacekeeping force arrives but is unable to do more than temporarily anaesthetize the situation. Intervention by two NATO powers adds to enmity. Various peacekeeping approaches are discussed. The UNFICYP mission, still deployed, creates dilemmas for Cypriots and for UN members.

A DIVIDED ISLAND

Cyprus has been torn by strife since Turkey took the island from Venice in the sixteenth century. Greeks colonized Cyprus in 1400BC and descendants of the early settlers have a strong bond of association with the parent country. Turkish ascendancy over Cyprus lasted from 1573 until 1878 when Britain acquired administrative rights and in 1914 it went on to annex the island from the Ottoman empire. As a base for asserting interests in the Levant it became a British Crown colony in 1923. Independence was won in 1960 and a year later Cyprus joined the British Commonwealth as a republican member. The relationship between Turkish Cypriots and Greek Cypriots has been volatile. The Greek community, 77% of the population, has a strong affinity to Greece.

It was Greece that in 1954 asked the UN to table a recommendation for granting Cyprus self-determination. To Turkey this Greek move was an assertion of the prime interests of Greek Cypriots and it was countered by Ankara championing self-determination for Turkish Cypriots. The initiative was ultimately negatived on strategic and constitutional grounds by the UK and the USA, the former feeling aggrieved at interference with its sovereignty, the latter anxious about ill-feelings between three members of the NATO Alliance. Turkish islanders (18% of the population) look for support towards mainland Turkey, visible some 40 miles away across the eastern Mediterranean. Insecurity arising out of their minority status has caused them to rely heavily on the security and safeguards that Turkey can provide.

Union with Greece, or Enosis, is for the Greek Cypriots an aspiration more than 100 years old. Strenuous support for this in the 1950s, led by conservatives, militaristic radicals and by Church dignitaries (notably Archbishop Makarios), excited communal disorders culminating in sabotage and sectarian assassination. Makarios, Head of the Greek Orthodox Church in Cyprus, was deported to the Seychelles by an irritated British Government, only to be brought back the following year when the Greek-officered independent movement, Ethniki Organosis Kypriou Agoniston (EOKA, National Organization of Cypriot Fighters), had promised to renounce violence. Possibilities of reconciliation were explored, as both the General Assembly and Greece deplored London's intransigence. In February 1959 conferences in Zürich and in London agreed a new deal for the island. Britain, Turkey and Greece were to guarantee that a new Republic of Cyprus would neither participate in political or economic union with either Greece or Turkey, nor resort to partition. There was to be a defence treaty between Greece, Turkey and Cyprus. Executive power would be vested within a year in a Greek Cypriot President (Makarios), a Turkish Cypriot Vice-President, and a Council of ten ministers, seven Greek and three Turkish. Britain would retain sovereign rights over its two military bases, 99 squares miles in all.

General Assembly pressures seem to have made the interested powers relax their claims. For the UK came the slow realization that its strategic interests in the eastern Mediterranean were improved if Cyprus became more stable through being allowed independence. For Greece it was politic to claim that "self-government" in Cyprus would respect minority interests more than the ambiguous alternative of "self-determination". Yet the settlement was essentially between Greece and Turkey rather than between two antagonistic groups of islanders scattered heterogeneously about Cyprus. For Cypriots it was above all the issue of municipal control that was to render the new constitution unpalatable to any minority considering itself outvoted. In September 1960 the Republic of Cyprus (ROC) was admitted to the UN as an autonomous member. The exercise of self-determination was fraught with uncertainties as constituent elements lived in a state of deep mistrust and tension. The issue of decolonization had been settled; an internal ethnic conflict was now developing in the shadow of direct interests by two external powers, Greece and Turkey. Violence was endemic in the island, even bisecting the capital, Nicosia, and in 1963 a "Green Line" neutral zone was set up, only a few metres wide in places, to be patrolled by British, Greek and Turkish soldiers. This temporary expedient was to become a permanent frontier and an obstacle to any "normalization". Widespread fighting, destruction of property and kidnapping flared up everywhere. The Cyprus Government formally requested UN help to replace British efforts to keep the peace.[1] There was a real danger that Turkey and Greece, then both NATO members, might be set on a collision course.

THE UN INTERVENES

The Security Council on 4 March 1964 unanimously adopted Resolution 186 recommending the creation of a UN peacekeeping force to be sent to Cyprus, initially for three months, to forestall conflict. Lieutenant-General P. S. Gyani, from India, who had UN peacekeeping experience in the Middle East and in the Congo, would lead a force of some 6,000 Blue Berets (some regulars, others volunteers or conscripts) and 174 civilian policemen. The UNFICYP was able to recruit from Austria, Canada, Denmark, Finland, Ireland and Sweden with a division of the island into six sectors. For the first time there was a contingent from one of the P5, the UK, in recognition of its historic role in the island. Apart from the soldier, the civilian policeman was limited to non-executive observation, advice and negotiation. The mandate charged the UN force to use its best efforts to prevent fighting, and contribute to the maintenance and restoration of law and order and a return to normal conditions. The guiding principles of the operation were acting with complete impartiality; interposition in areas where a recurrence of violence might be deterred; and the use of armed force only as a method of self-defence and then only to minimal extent. Military officers and political advisors were to work in harmony assisted by an international secretariat. There was no question of the UN helping a government to control a civil war. At the same time a UN mediator was appointed, as Special Representative of the Secretary-General, who would use "good offices" to find a long-term solution. Despite unremitting toil and inventive diplomacy these efforts were to prove fruitless.

The straightforward mandate given to UNFICYP did not augur well for the start of the operation. The Nicosian Government saw the operation as assisting it in ending a Turkish revolt and in restoring authority over the entire Republic. On the other hand, Turkish Cypriots regarded it as impregnable fortification against Nicosia's illegal denial of their status. U. Thant, UN Secretary-General, rejected both interpretations. A UN peacekeeping force was an impartial agency needing unimpeded access and with no responsibility for devising and imposing political solutions. In view of the precarious plight of many innocent civilians and the incessant terrorist nature of the conflict, the mandate was to be renewed every three months (from June 1965 every six months). As maintainer of peace, rather than enforcer of it, UNFICYP had to earn the trust and goodwill of Cypriots of all persuasions and in many respects it was gradually able to do that. By degrees an agreement was reached with Nicosia that the peacekeeping force should have right of access to most of the island and be granted immunity from irregular stop-and-search. Their enhanced effectiveness began to reassure much of the public.

The early years of UNFICYP were not without serious incident. Greek and Turkish trigger-happy "freedom fighters" harassed UN patrols, which some-times found themselves under cross-fire from nervous villagers. Nevertheless, they pressed on with such *ad hoc* tasks as escorting essential merchandise, food, medical supplies, personnel and civilians like members of the Turkish community in fear of abduction. Farmers were protected at harvest time and all movements of weaponry and suspicious traffic were vigilantly screened. A high degree of alertness contained armed violence, kept roads open and main-tained communication with local residents and representatives of local admin-istration. Patience, foresight and initiative were sorely tested and peacekeeping would have been set at naught had tempers been lost or threatening postures adopted. The UNFICYP also had to use a good deal of persuasion to restrain over-zealous enforcement by the Cypriot National Guard.

Fairly steadily, attitudes in Nicosia were hardening in a way difficult for any outside interposition to deal with. Greek Cypriots seemed determined to establish a unitary state in which Turks would have no clear minority rights. They were, indeed, unwilling to concede a Turkish wish for federal govern-ment to preserve security as this would pave the way for partition and lead to the eviction of many thousands of Greek families from Turkish areas. (This attitude was to be noticeable once again in 1983.) A unitary state would give the Greeks a monopoly of four to one over the Turks. Turkish Cypriots, on the other hand, were convinced that the growth of Greek autonomy was a greater threat than any desire for *Enosis*. Inevitably, both parties in Cyprus were to look to the UN for acknowledgement of their validity and support for their

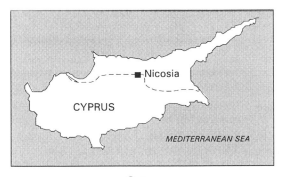

Cyprus

claims. Peacekeeping operations in Korea and in the Congo had suffered from the charge that a UN force was regarded by many as helping one faction in a civil contest against the other. The possibility that UNFICYP might be anything other than strictly neutral was strongly denied in New York and by the force itself. Most certainly, the international force could never take sides in the dispute. Its task to dampen down the equivalent of brushwood fires was ambitious, onerous and dangerous, with every outburst of hostility, however small, needing containment. Once again a peacekeeping venture had more success coping with short-term restoration than with the treatment of underlying causes of conflict. UNFICYP was fire brigade rather than medical practitioner.

GREECE AND TURKEY INTERVENE

The late 1960s featured a deterioration in relations between Greece and Turkey. In the New York forum of the UN, Greece and the ROC frequently cited evidence of Turkish plans for invasion of the island of Cyprus. Turkey denounced constitutional modifications made by Makarios, claiming that they violated international agreements, imperilled human rights, and menaced the safety of Turkish Cypriots, many of whom would have liked the UNFICYP to restore by force, if necessary, their status under the 1960 constitution. A return to any sort of normal conditions would never be possible, so each side pointed out, unless the guarantor powers were more vigilant and impartial. Thoroughly alarmed, the Security Council went on to stress the need for supervised disarmament measures. A stronger emphasis on mediation was desirable to attempt reconciliation of widely diverging ethnic claims. UN mediation was to struggle unavailingly. Progress was more likely to follow an understanding between Athens and Ankara than one between the two feuding elements in Cyprus.

There was little prospect of a real breakthrough since Turkey reserved the right to intervene to protect its kinsfolk in the island. Already dawning was the fundamental question that interposition for peacekeeping raises: how do intermediaries avoid forcing apart rival attitudes which then harden into confrontation? "Normalization", the approach to peacebuilding, is almost impossible unless disputants can be induced to drop their guard. (Korea should have taught the UN that.) The very task of dismantling fortifications and persuading forward units of Cypriots to pull back from combat was likely to bring a fusillade of bullets rather than compliance from both sides. Peacekeeping as maintenance rather than enforcement depends on trust, goodwill and lessened interference from outside. Notable irritants to the commander of UNFICYP were the intelligence reports of the smuggling into Cyprus of personnel, guns and tanks from both mainland Greece and Turkey.

A second phase of the conflict in Cyprus began on 15 July 1974 when a military junta in Athens sent an assassination squad to Nicosia to deal with the President. Makarios was airlifted to safety, taken to London and then went on to the UN to protest. In Nicosia a puppet government under an arch-terrorist, Nicos Sampson, took over. Fearful of *Enosis* being implemented, Turkey invaded Cyprus and occupied a large wedge of the island. Even though a cease-fire was agreed and the Athenian junta had collapsed, more than 30,000 Turkish troops advanced southwards as a "Peace Operation" until by mid August they occupied the northern third of Cyprus. This involved the immediate displacement of 225,000 Greek Cypriots to find refuge in the south while 40,000 Turkish Cypriots moved in the opposite direction. During the next few years most Turkish Cypriots moved north, while Greek Cypriots came south, making the island politically and culturally divided. The invasion extinguished any hopes of negotiation between the two sides. There were now two separate island zones: the ROC and the Turkish Republic of Northern Cyprus (TRNC). UNFICYP could only look on ineffectively at the time of the coup and the Turkish encroachment. In two respects its potential was hampered. First, its mandate related only to a dispute between Greek and Turkish Cypriots. It did not operate in the case of dispute internal to either community, as in the Nicosia coup, nor in the event of intervention by an external state such as Turkey. Its mandate had been drafted originally for an entirely different set of circumstances.

The operational emphasis in 1974 was different from what it had been ten years previously when tension and violent outbreaks needed handling. In later years the main concern was with reconciliation and rehabilitation and with civilian priorities rather than military ones. Should not modification of the mandate, or at least review, have been explored either in private in New York or in the forum of the Security Council? Secondly, UN Resolutions recognized the administration of Greek Cypriots as the only government in the island, which effectively isolated the other community forcing them to look to mainland Turkey for support. Again, as in Korea, rivals held apart by the UN sought the support of a larger power.

On 1 November 1974 the General Assembly took the initiative of summoning a Special Session on Cyprus. Months of disappointing discussion in Geneva had managed to achieve only a cease-fire on 16 August. New York called for mutual withdrawal of contesting forces, for the return home of people displaced from their homes, and for all to respect the independent sovereignty of the Republic of Cyprus. Six weeks later the Security Council endorsed this call. Ideally, a demilitarized zone should be interposed between hostile groups. Unilateral offensive actions by Turkey were condemned. Schemes of resuscitation for refugees should be put in hand at once. Numerous observers expressed their concern that in this crisis the UN seemed more of a talking shop than a convener of conference and an initiator of action.

Again, Korea comes to mind where the uniting of nations may be thought of as too detached and irresolute. In the UN Charter there is provision for urgent measures in Chapters VI and VII. Turkey, quite naturally, opposed any international attempt to impose sanctions against themselves or their Cypriot clients. It is not difficult to concede that the application of sanctions would have increased the vulnerability and isolation of the northern part of the island and would have led to even more resentment and hostility. It has been pointed out that while the population balance favoured the majority, the balance of military potential lay with the minority – which lessened the readiness of that minority to hold with the establishment of a unitary state.

THE CYPRUS PROBLEM TODAY

Notwithstanding all the negotiations that have taken place, the uncompromising positions of the ethnic groups remain poles apart. The Greek Cypriot government of the ROC has actually strengthened its assertion that it speaks for the entire territory of Cyprus. Other states at the UN acknowledge this claim, and the TRNC is still a diplomatic outcast, recognized by Turkey alone. Financial problems have encumbered the Cyprus operation for most of its life. The current deficit is $191 million and the cost each year is about $47 million. Some UN members, such as Russia, China and France, have never been prepared to accept the notion of an assessed levy. In consequence, states fielding contingents to UNFICYP, some 11 in all, have borne a disproportionate burden. Although the International Court of Justice ruled that funding for peacekeeping is in law to be a claim on the regular UN budget, no Secretary-General has been able to put this into effect. There have been suggestions from the states bearing operational costs that military observers might be more economically deployed than infantry units. These states have recently warned New York that they feel unable to delay planned troop reductions while waiting for any UN decision on the apportionment of funding. Of the 1,400 members of UNFICYP who remain (in itself a reduction from 6,411 in 1964) the majority are British and Australian. It is reckoned at headquarters that a minimum force of 1,500 is needed to keep peace along a demarcation zone stretching 110 miles.[2] Ominously, if the UNFICYP becomes too thin on the ground there is the danger of the gap being manned provocatively by units of Greek Cypriot National Guardsmen or from Turkey. There has been little progress over the last decade or so in working out a compromise, although from time to time leaders of the Cypriot factions have met and held exhaustive discussions.[3]

The reluctance of nations contributing to the peacekeeping operation to continue with funding and deployment has given the negotiations some momentum, but not enough to shift the log jam. The more drastic proposals such as those of the Soviet Bloc and a group of uncommitted states in 1983 calling for an immediate withdrawal of all occupying forces and then for complete demilitarization, have never found favour widely. Then, and frequently since, powerful Greek lobbies in Britain and in the US have preferred their sponsored community to stand its ground, reassured by UNFICYP protection against any move southwards. This sort of response has encouraged rival islanders in at least two unhelpful respects, namely, that they would not be prepared to negotiate from any position other than that of "strength", and they are unwilling to convene any conference in order to "fail".

Still being considered at length is a "set of ideas" that the present Secretary-General, Boutros Boutros-Ghali, put to Cypriot leaders in spring and summer 1992. Cyprus would enjoy "single sovereignty and international personality" in a "bicommunal and bizonal federation". There would be a wide measure of self-government for each of the constituent groups, with each enjoying a clear majority of population and of land ownership in its zone. Islanders who had been displaced by the conflict would be given the option of either returning to their original homes or receiving a compensation grant. This proposal, however, would not be easy to implement. Rival parties would have to agree to the shape of one form of sovereignty, one citizenship status, and one customs and financial union. A legislature in the capital would have Greek and Turkish Cypriot members in a 50:50 ratio in the upper house and 70:30 in the lower house. Lifestyles have changed among those who were forced to leave their homes; farming families are no longer predominant. Finally, the occupying Turkish army would have to leave and it would be required to relinquish control of a significant area of land. It is possible that these UN proposals have been studied with interest in Athens.

Government ministers in Nicosia, through President Glafos Clerides, have been quoted as believing that the UN ideas at least provide a possible platform for advance. They have described the existing partition as a violation of human rights when 250,000 Greek Cypriots are banned from returning to their homes. There is also the point that the unsatisfactory situation in Cyprus lessens the chances of its application to join the European Union (EU) being accepted. To begin with, Turkish Cypriots did not endorse the suggestions from the UN.[4] For some it was worth enduring a stalemate in the expectation that a better deal might eventually be forthcoming. The Security Council has spoken of their obduracy in severe terms: after 59 talks with the UN they had shown only "total opposition to all UN Resolutions, to the society of nations, and to the Security Council".[5]

UNFICYP remains in Cyprus, albeit not very happily, after 31 years. The operation has cost a vast sum of money and the lives of 165 UN personnel. Its function still is to man the 140 observation posts, to check any illegitimate movement into the buffer zone, to do their best to prevent any interference with water supplies or farming or communications, and in general to cool tempers and lower anxiety. There seems nothing to justify the opinion, sometimes heard, that a firm time limit on UNFICYP presence and a programmed withdrawal of the international peacekeeping force would bring disputing parties towards conclusive settlement. The work of resuscitation done by the UNHCR and by the UN Development Programme (UNDP) is vital to the restoration of normal life, security and material well-being and that needs a supervising, impartial presence. A stern verdict would be that while the UN no longer faces a dangerous military challenge in the island it does confront over 30 years of failure to solve a political problem. The *status quo* of partition is widely rejected in rhetoric most of the time, yet it has to be protected internationally.

If there is any truth in the observation that Cyprus is wired like a detonator to other, larger problems, the UN has with great skill and success prevented explosion. For all that, one can say that Cyprus is another example of the dilemma facing UN peacekeepers, namely, how to bring pressures to bear consistently and objectively in a search for conciliation while scaling down physical involvement.

NOTES

1. The slightest violation of peace and order by either "side" led to a ripple of lawless violence. Marauding bands of young Greek Cypriots imprisoned Turkish Cypriots in fortified enclaves. UN soldiers at first were often caught in the midst of indiscriminate fusillades and sabotage. In 1963 rural communities were resisting all reconciliation attempts.
2. In 1995 UNFICYP is financed by assessed contributions from all UN members rather than by voluntary contributions from states sending peacekeeping units. Russia initially vetoed the Security Council Resolution in 1993, pleading its expensive peacekeeping operations nearer home. Later, a financial compromise was agreed.
3. In 1991 US President George Bush and the then UN Secretary-General, Perez de Cuellar, each tried hard to talk over solutions with Cypriot leaders. Progress was blocked by Greek Cypriots being unwilling to recognize Turkish settlement rights in TRNC.
4. Rauf Denktash, President of TRNC, rejected the UN proposals in August 1992. The present Turkish holding in the north of 37% of land must not be whittled down to a suggested 28.2%. Possibly, 29% might be acceptable, he added. (The "bones of contention" seem minute ones!)
5. Desultory talks, styled "confidence building measures", continue in 1995. The Turkish Cypriot side in negotiation appears to be splitting into harder and more moderate elements.

FURTHER READING

Boyd, J. M. Cyprus: episode in peacekeeping. *International Organization* 20(1), pp. 1–17, 1966.
Camp, G. D. Greco-Turkish conflict over Cyprus. *Political Science Quarterly* 95(1),

pp. 43–70, 1980.

Crawshaw, N. Cyprus, a failure in Western diplomacy. *The World Today* **40**, pp. 73–8, 1984.

Harbottle, M. *The impartial soldier*. Oxford: Oxford University Press, 1970.

Higgins, R. Basic facts on the UN force in Cyprus. *The World Today* **20**(8), pp. 347–50, 1964.

James, A. The UN force in Cyprus. *International Affairs* (Summer 1989) **65**(3).

A long-lasting situation such as this and its developments can be followed in *Keesing's Record of World Events*, see Appendix: Where to find out more about the UN.

Chapter Five

CYPRUS

1914   Britain annexes island from Ottoman Empire.

1923   British Crown Colony.

1959   Zürich and London Conferences: Britain, Turkey, Greece
       guarantee independence of a new Republic of Cyprus.

1960   Cyprus becomes independent under President Makarios.
       Joins UN.

1963   Violence between Greek and Turkish Cypriots.

1964   UNFICYP recruited and despatched.

1974   President Makarios airlifted to London (and on to New York to
       UN) after coup.

       Turks invade northern Cyprus. Junta in Athens collapses.

       UN Special Session on Cyprus. TRNC becomes an outcast.

1983   UN call for Turkish withdrawal and demilitarization not heeded
       in Cyprus.

1992   UN "set of ideas". Intensive talks in Cyprus and in the US.

1995   UNFICYP pared down in numbers. Negotiations continue in "low
       profile".

The Palestinian problem

Anyone with a sense of humanity must sympathize with the Palestinians. Their lands are occupied, they have no political rights, and they are daily victims of a misguided policy which believes that the security of Israel must rest on closed universities, illegitimate settlements and even collective punishments.

These were the words of Britain's Secretary for Foreign Affairs, Douglas Hurd, in October 1990. No other issue has demanded so much of the UN's time and attention as the Palestinian problem. Nothing has sparked off and inflamed debate in the General Assembly or troubled the Security Council as much as Middle Eastern affairs centred on the Israeli/Palestinian disputes. Jews and Arabs have fought six wars since 1948. Since 1948 one in four of the Security Council's Resolutions has referred to these issues and for the rest of the UN, that is, the General Assembly and the Specialized Agencies, there have been well over a thousand Resolutions. The whole situation is a network of problems out of which many of the principles and practices of UN peacekeeping have evolved. Some of the units interposing and monitoring as a function of peacekeeping are still in the Middle East 45 years later. Altogether, on the ground some 21,600 personnel have been involved and this has cost 364 lost lives.

This chapter features the irony of a UN tirelessly working to advance the cause of the Palestinian Arabs yet being sidestepped as external negotiations bring the contestants together. The origins of the quarrel over Palestine are discussed first followed by an account of how the UN became involved. Inevitably, the emergence of a sovereign Israel pits Jew against Arab. UN peacekeeping forces are interposed and Resolutions passed. A long and difficult reconciliation process is discussed in outline. The UN has gone through a number of attitude changes during almost 50 years of concern. Initially, and in the tradition of the League of Nations, the UN was a forum and a listener to a candid and often heated exposition of a case and a defence. In the 1940s and 1950s the world watched the process of debate and took sides. In the 1960s the UN, together with non-governmental bodies, earnestly rallied support for a campaign against what was seen as violation of human rights and persecution. Apartheid in South Africa had a parallel in the discrimination and forced separation in Israel, once known as Palestine. At this time the UN was something of a detached arbiter; it very cautiously interposed a peacekeeping force only when judged absolutely necessary.

The past three decades have seen the UN moving forward and out into the area of deliberate intervention when the forces of liberation have been backed. Contacts were made with freedom fighters and liberation movements were accorded a representative place in New York. Inevitably, this placed the UN in a spotlight of controversy, with a sovereign state such as Israel feeling arraigned by a world tribunal that could no longer be considered impartial. Once more, the UN was placed in the position of standing by its Charter and then deciding to act as policeman as well as judge. Thus, 50 years of concern about the plight of the Palestinians have seen friends recruited, enemies made, and the role of the UN itself increasingly put under scrutiny. If this has been the UN in action, what has been achieved? Should events have been handled differently?

THE ORIGINS OF PALESTINE

Jews have thought of Palestine as the Promised Land. Arab and Jew had lived together in this land for 4,000 years but it was not until the later years of the nineteenth century that Jews in Europe, increasingly faced with discrimination and expulsion, began to turn towards their ancient home as a refuge. The First World Zionist Congress held in Basle in 1897 envisaged a home for Jewry in Palestine where settlement and new institutions would reinforce national consciousness. The First World War gave the Zionist movement its opportunity. Britain had enlisted aid from Arabs and Jews in campaigns against the Ottoman Empire of Turkey, which had allied with Germany and the Central Powers. Given slices of the Ottoman lands, including Palestine, a grateful Britain made promises to both Jew and Arab. The former would be given an assurance under the 1917 Balfour Declaration of a national home in Palestine. The terms of the Declaration, and later in 1923 those of the League of Nations mandate conferred on the UK, now read as a rather naïve assumption that promises made to both sides would enable them to live together without any competitive ambitions. Both Arabs and Jews differed as to whether a Jewish "national home" in Palestine constituted a Jewish state. The Council of the League of Nations presented Britain with the mandate on the understanding that Balfour conditions would be observed and saw clearly a strong Western power as the only possible administrator. Arab apprehensions mounted as immigration from a Europe ruled by dictators became significant and cast into doubt how far the mandatory power could promote the interests of the one and protect those of the other.

Further fuel was added to a smouldering fire when in 1937 London's Peel Commission recommended that the mandate be replaced by a treaty dividing Palestine into three, namely, Arab lands, a separate Jewish entity, and a mandated area smaller than the previous one to guarantee the inviolability of the Holy Places and access to the Mediterranean. "Partition offers a chance of ultimate peace. No other plan does", was the optimistic thought of the commissioners. What, though, would be the fate of the minority now to live in a majority area? Would they have to be "transferred", if not voluntarily, then by force? Such anxieties persuaded the British Government to send the report to Geneva hoping for an "understanding" between the parties rather than resorting to partition, which might involve force, and would dislodge populations, and damage relations with the Arab world. Whatever the government in London tried to do to play fair to both parties appeared to exacerbate the Palestinian problem. A White Paper in 1939, hoping for some sort of condominium and averting its eyes from a festering reality in Palestine, proposed a ceiling on Jewish immigration of 15,000 over the next five years and thereafter the quota to be agreed with the Arabs. This impracticable idea was put into cold storage by the outbreak of the Second World War.

If in some respects the course of the war in other parts of the world gave the people of the Middle East some respite, it also gave them time to think. Here were two dynamic movements living in territory over which they made conflicting claims. A compromise made by outsiders with promises to each party alienated both and made reconciliation most unlikely. Short of elimination of one or other rival, the possible solutions appeared to range over coercion or domination, assimilation, federalism, or partition to preserve minority rights and advance the cause of autonomy. As peace brought world hostilities to a close, momentum was most certainly accelerated by the revelation that the Jews of Europe had suffered grievously through the Holocaust, that nations felt both guilt and a sense of obligation, and that desperate Jewry would now look towards the Promised Land for succour and security.

THE UN ADDRESSES THE PROBLEM

Armed with the fine assertions of its Charter, the UN General Assembly resolved in 1947 that the Palestine mandate be superseded by an arrangement for partition. The Security Council was advised that world peace would be threatened if London was unwilling to continue with mandatory administration of a region where nobody was living in peace or seemed to want to live in peace. US partiality towards the Jews was marked, with a request that 100,000 immigrants be admitted through the port of Haifa. Fifty nations favoured partition. Arab spokesmen in New York were quick to declare that this violated the Charter, which gave people the right to decide their own destiny. More tangibly, they pointed to the unfairness of any partition that would give the Jews 56.5% of the territory although they were but 32% of the population and owned only 7% of its land. There was some doubt whether the UN could legally deal with the constitutional future of the territory since the British League of Nations mandate had not been transferred to the UN. A way out of the maze was to form a United Nations Special Committee on Palestine (UNSCOP) with members from 11 states other than the P5 and including Australia and Canada, previously British Commonweath Dominions. The General Assembly now approved partition by a two-thirds majority and went on to constitute a face-saving committee. This brought about resolute Arab opposition and refusal to co-operate with the Committee in April 1947. Why not, they asked, apply the principles of the Charter and declare that Palestinian independence was the objective? Was it not very significant that the agenda of this committee referred not to "future government" but to "the problem of Palestine"?

UNSCOP's report in August 1947 put forward the idea of separate Jewish and Arab states with a UN trusteeship for places such as Jerusalem and Bethlehem. Economic union would be desirable. A minority report opted for the alternative of a single federated state and the UN to oversee a transition towards this objective. The Arabs would not consider either plan, and Britain rather meekly declared that while it did not oppose either of the suggestions it could not see itself enforcing them on a reluctant community. Despite protest and reservation the General Assembly adopted the UNSCOP majority proposals at its November 1947 meeting. Arab and Jew would automatically become citizens of a state where full political and civil rights were enjoyed. If the Peel Commission had doubts about Arab–Jew co-operativeness, the UNSCOP plan envisaged marked trust and co-operation. Could partition ever succeed given the prevailing hostility? The question was never put into print. Would the proposed Jewish state be viable with a bare 60% Jewish majority? How would provisions for shared economic development, currency system and customs union between two states, be worked out? And what would be the position of minority interests in an Arab state with 750,000 Arabs and 10,000 Jews and a Jewish state with 500,000 Arabs and slightly more Jews? The latter would be surrounded by powerful neighbours sympathetic to the Palestinian Arab disadvantage. These neighbours rejected the plan as both unwieldy and unfair.

In February 1948 the security situation in Palestine was so bad that the Security Council met to consider enforcement of partition in Palestine if the earlier schemes were to bring about settlement. It was soon clear that nobody at the UN was prepared to use force. Washington now pitched the discussion elsewhere. It repudiated partition, suggesting that a temporary UN trusteeship for Palestine would be the best arrangement. Taken by surprise since there was no prior discussion with the interested parties, the General Assembly gave the idea short shrift (as did the Jews), half-adopted an American amendment to call for a truce and further all-party negotiations, and finally decided to appoint a UN mediator. A Special Assembly was to be convened for April, meanwhile further discussion on the public stage of New York might only prejudice objective settlement.

As the end of the mandate approached both parties steadily armed themselves for a confrontation. Neighbouring Arab states made plain their concerted readiness to oppose partition, if need be, by force. The US idea of trusteeship was not at all welcomed. The mediator appointed was Swedish Count Folke Bernadotte. It was soon evident that his priority was the rehabilitation of refugees from Jewish areas – for was it not a statutory responsibility of the UN to furnish relief to the needy and dispossessed? The need of human aid was to take precedence over the more theoretical notions of constitutional reform.

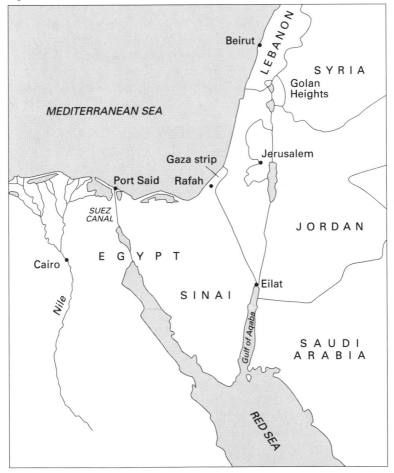

The Middle East

THE EMERGENCE OF INDEPENDENT ISRAEL

May 1948 brought the Palestinian problem abruptly to the world's attention. Britain laid down its Palestinian mandate. On 14 May 1948 the State of Israel proclaimed its independence. On 15 May the new state was attacked by its Arab neighbours. All was chaos; the UN had lost the chance of bringing about a satisfactory solution to "the problem of Palestine". Even so, a temporary expedient was to despatch a United Nations Truce Supervision Organization (UNTSO) force of 300 observers to the war area to monitor a truce called for by the Security Council and to observe that the provisions of a cease-fire were being maintained. A truce was devised and the enemies glowered at each other across a supervised divide.

Tragically, Bernadotte was assassinated; his successor, American Ralph Bunche, worked hard to develop principles, rules of conduct and strict impartiality that were to become characteristic of future UN peacekeeping operations. He continued Bernadotte's priority of helping refugees, working strenuously against Jewish unwillingness to cede land for refugee accommodation. For the Jews peace must precede repatriation; for the Arabs repatriation must come first. However it was viewed, the notion of separate existence (a type of apartheid) was to the Jews something that might have to be implemented by force and to the Palestinian Arabs something that would have to be prevented by force.

The war of 1947 led to large-scale Arab exodus. Now Israel had a Jewish majority at the expense of a repressed Arab minority living on sufferance. Most Arab refugees were not easily persuaded to emigrate – if they did so it would enable Zionism to triumph and signal fatalistic acceptance of lost lands. A large-scale relief operation was mounted by the UN. The United Nations Relief and Works Administration (UNRWA) had the task of providing tented camps for the first wave of 750,000 displaced people, and then of setting up clinics for basic healthcare, for measures of environmental health, nutrition, education and training. This mission is still very active today, depending as it does for 93% of its funds on voluntary contributions by governments. Trygve Lie, the UN's first Secretary-General, was to express a belief that if the major powers wanted to do something positive through the UN then Palestine was the place to do it. This might not be too obvious in the heated exchanges of New York: in the desert the earnest work of UNRWA brought fruitful and much appreciated dividends.

THE CONFRONTATION OF ARAB AND JEW

The 1950s and 1960s were an era of waiting on events and of preparations for unavoidable confrontation. The contest being played out by Israel, Egypt,

Syria, Jordan, Lebanon and in the mid 1950s by the United Arab Republic under Nasser in Cairo revealed digging in by both sides, with overall a sense of defeat and lost pride for the Arabs. The armistice agreements meant territorial changes in Palestine, as Israel secured control of all land provisionally allotted in the partition schemes. The Gaza coastal strip, held by Egypt, and the West Bank of the River Jordan assigned to the Kingdom of Jordan, were nominally non-Jewish but represented to chauvinists in each camp areas that must either be annexed or defended.

The Palestine Arabs lost no time in mustering a response to Israeli intolerance. The Palestine Liberation Organization (PLO) came together in 1964 to represent displaced people who now had little confidence in a pan-Arab ability to liberate them. PLO leader Yasser Arafat had skillfully evoked a worldwide response to the anguish of his fellow Palestinians – often of censure and sometimes of strong support. In his view, Israel was not a legitimate state and must be opposed by every means, not excluding violence. It was, of course, also obvious to observers that the leader had to contend with a good deal of dissension if not disarray in the ranks. The PLO was regarded by the Israeli government as a fifth column to be dispersed by security detachments. A deliberate ploy, too, was the establishment of Jewish settlements in the Arab lands, anchoring as it were satellite fortresses.

The situation exploded in 1967 with the Six Day War, in the course of which Israel put Arab forces to rout. Once again the Arabs had shown concern for the appalling plight of their Palestinian brothers. Once again the humiliating collapse of Arab power convinced the oppressed that their own backs must bear the burden. As the Jews took over the Golan Heights from Syria, the Gaza Strip, the West Bank and old Jerusalem, it became apparent that the Palestinians would rely on underground methods such as sabotage, hijacking and insidious harassment. It was not at all clear just what help the UN might be able to muster. Resolutions in the strongest terms called for withdrawal from occupied lands, for the cessation of discriminatory claims and actions, for the recognition of self-determination as a right and for the absolute need to relieve the sufferings of the mass of displaced people. Unfortunately, these verbal expressions of faith risked the veto of the great-powers on behalf of their client states, that is, the United States taking the side of Israel and the USSR espousing the Arab cause. Worse still, the UNEF brigade had to be withdrawn in June 1967 when the Secretary-General had to yield to Egypt's insistence on its termination.

RESOLUTION 242 AND ITS SIGNIFICANCE

The Palestine problem was underlined as a peace threat in 1967 when the Security Council agreed Resolution 242. This has become the bedrock of UN policy and a foundation for all negotiations by the Palestinian Arabs over the past 28 years. The brief wording unequivocally expresses continuous concern and emphasises the obligation of UN members to take action in working for a just and lasting peace for the entire region. Acquisition of territory by war is inadmissible. Peace in the Middle East depends on Israeli withdrawal, termination of all belligerent claims and actions, and respect and acknowledgement of the sovereignty, territorial integrity and political independence of every state in the area.[1] A just settlement of the refugee problem is needed. A Special Representative of the UN would proceed to the Middle East to initiate and maintain contacts for settlement.

Although greeted with acclaim, the Resolution understandably has been scrutinized word by word. Many commentators have found a looseness in the document. "Withdrawal of Israeli armed forces from territories occupied in the recent conflict" could perhaps be clarified by inserting the word "all", to denote the entire lands taken over from the Arabs since 1948. It has been suggested since 1967 that the wording was left deliberately vague when US and Arab diplomats were conferring so that minor adjustments could be negotiated.[2] If this is true, it seems unfortunate in view of Israel's expansion from an allocated 5,000 square miles in the 1947 UN partition plan to some 8,000 miles afterwards. There was further doubt about the phrase stressing "the inadmissibility of the acquisition of territory by war and the need to work for a just and lasting peace". Agreeing with the latter sentiment, the Israelis pointed out that the "inadmissibility" only applied to a war of aggression. In that sense the Israeli government would be loath to make specific commitments about withdrawal that to every thinking Israeli would mean lessening their national "security".

If interpretation of Resolution 242 was left to the two main parties, the parties' imbalance should be remembered: one was a rich and well-armed state, the other a fervent non-governmental group lacking resources and influence. Additionally, the Jews asserted that the territories were "disputed" and not "occupied". In that case, certain strategic and historically significant places such as Arab East Jerusalem were "not negotiable". It would be difficult to transfer and "sacrifice" land on which 100,000 Jews had recently settled without inviting argument and possibly retaliatory action. A point of some importance, finally, is that Israeli diplomats were quick to describe the objectives of this UN Resolution as desirable in the *final* stage of negotiations, meanwhile, in the transitional period, states should understand that a government (feeling beleaguered) must keep options open and, by implication, play for time and ground. The Arabs, of course, would have none of this. The Resolution stood firm on the promise of land, self-determination and peace.

Several years later, in 1973, on the holiest day of the Jewish calendar, Yom Kippur, Arab armies launched an all-out offensive across Israeli borders. Despite concerted tactics and being well-armed, Egypt and Syria were beaten back. This reinforced Israeli concern about "security" and their determination to stand four-square. The UN rallied all its forces to stop the fourth Arab–Israeli war. The General Assembly specifically nominated PLO as the legitimate point of contact on all Palestinian matters and it was given observer status in New York. Would the PLO now become a government-in-exile and so attain exalted diplomatic status? Although its extremist wings discredited the PLO in many places, the General Assembly received Yasser Arafat in 1974 as though he was a head of state and almost unanimously passed Resolutions supporting his liberationist struggle.

ARAB AND JEWISH ACCORD INITIATED

During the 1970s the UN's concern to effect reconciliation between Jew and Arab was misrepresented on all sides. Israeli hostility severely limited anything the UN might be able to do. Not surprisingly, many member-states considered Washington to be more partial towards the interests of Israel. No Security Council initiative would be entirely welcome if it thrust into the reckoning the substance (or the shadow) of US–Israel designs.

At this point US President Richard Nixon's Administration decided to take a deliberate gamble. As no direct negotiations were likely and UN mediation was not wanted, there could be scope for essentially bilateral diplomacy if it could be hoisted into place via a multilateral conference. Egypt, Syria and Jordan would find it easier to accept external negotiating principles than meet Israeli demands. Washington and Moscow would furnish co-chairmen. Secretary-General Kurt Waldheim was to be asked to invite the parties to Geneva for December 1973 and thereafter he would have a place at the top table.

In Washington's view the items heading the agenda would be the immediate Israeli evacuation of occupied Palestinian lands (including Jerusalem) and "the re-establishment of full national rights for the Palestinian people". Predictably, these twin points roused dissension. Argument ensued over the rights of Palestinian representation at Geneva. Israel appeared unco-operative, regarding Palestinian assertiveness as a direct threat to their sovereignty. For US Secretary of State Henry Kissinger, prime mover behind Geneva, several difficulties loomed large. First, the very identity of the Palestinians was disputable in 1973. They were:

> still treated as refugees in the UN, as terrorists [PLO] in the United States and Western Europe, as an opportunity by the Soviets, and as simultaneous inspiration and nuisance by the Arab World.[3]

Secondly, the strident Palestinian claim to statehood would be seen in much of the Middle East as "irredentist" and difficult to accommodate. Thirdly, the public positions of contending parties were in contrast to what they were

actually doing, for instance, Israel stressed the importance of the legal obligations of securing peace but rejected the concept of a Palestinian state. Conference members had to present themselves as constantly vigilant and firm to
their domestic hardline supporters in Tel Aviv, Damascus and Cairo. Was this
Geneva Conference a failure in not bringing settlement to the Middle East?
The UN saw it as the first time high-level Arab and Jewish delegates had been
persuaded to talk comprehensively face to face. As for the United States (in
Kissinger's opinion), belligerent oratory might have clouded inclination to
make concessions, but preconditions had not been obstinately insisted on.
Nobody had left the table. Doors to future negotiations had not been closed.
The needs of the Palestinians, so long standing and unmet, had now been
made very plain. Rhetoric was clearly "too greatly at variance with reality"
but the conference itself surely demonstrated the usefulness of the UN's moral
support for the realities approached through bilateral diplomacy.[4]

On 10 November 1975 the General Assembly in Resolution 3379 resolved
that Zionism was "a form of racism and discrimination"; 72 states supported
the charge but 32 abstained. The equation was strongly contested by the US
and by Israel.[5] Towards the end of the decade other significant events took
place. One was the resolve of the General Assembly in deeming the "changes"
in Palestinian territory resulting from Israeli expansion as "invalid". The satellite settlements must be dismantled. The second event, a notable achievement,
was President Jimmy Carter's initiative in September 1978 to bring together
at Camp David (the presidential "retreat" in the US) the former arch-enemies,
President Anwar Sadat of Egypt and Prime Minister Menachem Begin of
Israel, to sign a Declaration of Peace. Perhaps even more significant was
Sadat's daring visit to Israel the previous year when he had addressed the
Knesset, the parliament of Israel, and offered to recognize Israeli sovereignty
in return for their withdrawal from the occupied territories, including Jerusalem, and for the endorsement of the rights of Arabs in Palestine to live in peace
(which was, after all, in the spirit of Resolution 242). This might have heart-
ened the PLO had the Organization been acknowledged at Camp David. If the
intention and the achievement of this summit meeting was to devise an accord
between the Egyptians and Israel, it did nothing to ease Begin's intractability
in negotiation. As for Sadat, he was promptly accused by the Arab world of
betrayal and was to pay with his life some time later. Arafat was scathing in his
dismissal of statesmen content with "partial agreements and separate treaties". Nor did an attempt by Saudi Arabia to advance negotiations with a plan
for withdrawal and guarantees, all to be supervised by the UN, meet with any
success. There seemed little promise in the future for the PLO, now expelled
from Jordan by King Hussein: it found a new home in Lebanon, but was left
politically unstable with members doubtfully loyal to their cause.

The focus of quarrelsome engagement shifted to Lebanon in June 1982
when Israel launched *Operation Galilee* to flush out Arab terrorists and to
mark out a 40km "security zone". A successful operation may have obliter-

ated the bases but atrocities among the civilians and in refugee camps horrified the world, caused Israel to be pilloried, and reinvigorated the PLO image. The UN condemned what it saw as a retaliatory mission. Was this Begin's scheme to railroad negotiations since no Arab would consent to talk while the Jewish commandos were in Lebanon? The PLO came off badly and had to evacuate Beirut in rented Greek ships flying the UN flag shadowed by inquisitive warships.

Evacuating the Palestinians and reassuring Israel as to security northwards into Lebanon called for a delicate peacekeeping mission. This was not to be given to the UN since New York appeared too "soft" towards Palestinians. Once more the United States was to be the peacekeeper and in August 1982 the US Congress authorized the despatch to the Lebanon of 800 Americans to form with French and Italian contingents a multinational force (MNF).[6] Yet again, the imperatives were to co-ordinate the disengagement of adversaries and to work on bringing them to negotiation.

The following year the General Assembly sent out invitations for an International Peace Conference on the Middle East to be held in 1983 in New York. The major powers, other concerned states, and the PLO were all to attend. There was much discussion, some of it impassioned, regarding Israel's temerity in its annexations, evictions, dismissal of Arab mayors, closure of Arab schools and colleges, and interference with water supplies and transportation. Israel was accused of "gun Zionism", of violation of rights, of lack of co-operation and of denial of truth. It was well known that an Israeli premier had to take into account the hard urgings of the right-wing parties. By general consent the UN amplified its distress and its intent in a Declaration on Palestine and a Programme of Action for the Achievement of Palestinian Rights.

THE *INTIFADA*

The situation in the "occupied territories", namely, those Arab areas under Israeli control, was grim indeed. Twice as many people as 20 years ago were leaving the countryside for the town: some of these were Jewish "infiltrators"; half were under the age of 15; only one in three men had a job. This segment of the community suffered grievously, as had happened in South Africa. The UN General Assembly frequently declared that the rights, especially of young people, were being violated. Geneva Conventions and the 1959 Declaration on the Rights of the Child were of little account in the eyes of Israel. Again, as in South Africa, youth was at the vanguard of protest. The helplessness, despair and defiance of young people, the *intifada,* were featured in the world's media in accounts of the protest movement of the Palestinian Arabs since 1987. Stones thrown by youths at armed members of the Israel Defence Force were met by bullets and tear gas with little other result than increased bitterness on both sides. In PLO statements the trauma of youth was frequently mentioned – "a new generation is rising in streets of despair" was one such allusion.

Yasser Arafat, often surrounded by young people, had directed during the 1980s a deliberate appeal to the UN to work for the liberation of that generation. The point was made markedly in 1988 when Arafat, refused an entry visa to the US, was able to persuade the General Assembly to convene in Geneva rather than New York. "Tomorrow's young people will never be so intolerant", he told the delegates. Plainly put, the problem of Palestine was a moral one, not just land, flag and water but an invincible drive to keep hold of what was right, to oppose what was unjust and cruel. The young generation in Palestine wanted not abstract justice, but the chance to live collectively in a justly ordered system, ready to live amicably with others. The UN Charter and Resolution 242 were cited as illuminating precedents. In his concluding remarks to the General Assembly Arafat glossed over his earlier opinion about Resolution 242 – that it had not given the acknowledgement to the Palestinian Arabs that as a political entity they deserved and issued this invitation:

> I ask the leaders of Israel to come here, under the sponsorship of the United Nations, so that, together, we can forge that peace. . . . Come, let us make peace. Let us make the peace of the bold, far from the arrogance of power and the weapons of destruction, far from occupation and oppression and humiliation and murder and torture.

The present decade will be seen as the time of tentative co-operation between Jew and Arab brokered by the US rather than by the UN. Some have seen the United States as proudly acting the roles of judge, jury and policeman. Others have detected a tendency towards isolationist impatience and a desire to be rid at all costs of an irritating challenge to global security. The UN has continued to watch events closely and to work energetically in the field through UNRWA and the peacekeeping operations UNDOF, UNIFIL and UNOGIL still needed as much as ever. US Secretary of State James Baker brought together, in Madrid in October 1991, representatives of Israel and the Palestinians together with Syria, Jordan and Lebanon under the co-sponsorship of the US and the USSR. The UN (and others) were to be present as "observers", given that Israel was judged to be "sensitive" to certain outside bodies. Progress was uncertain and very difficult. The PLO as a formal body was excluded; its members felt ostracized and were morally and financially bankrupt; it had no major power as a backer.

For Israel, outwardly in a strong position, there was an impending election and the immediate problem was not so much a matter of opposing self-government for Palestinians as how best to deal with it without destroying Israel's democracy or compromising the advantageous position of the majority. There was a constant security danger for an isolated Israel. The meeting in

Madrid would be a balancing exercise where both sides would weigh up what was on offer in the way of guarantees to offset a period of turbulence. Living with the *status quo* would not be good enough. There were two stages in the Madrid design: first, that of bilateral discussion of particular grievances; and secondly, a reinforcing phase where regional states would talk over wider issues. Once again, direct negotiation was to be "hosted" by external, powerful sponsors who had the moral backing of UN Resolutions.

FURTHERING RECONCILIATION

The years after Madrid were a time of rather furtive diplomacy in several continents to see how far the Palestinian situation might be eased and improved. Official negotiations between representatives of Jews and Arabs ploughed on in New York, remarkable for a stop–start progress punctuated by "leaks" that were often deliberate and sometimes accidental. Each side made the most of prime-time TV and the morning editions of leading newspapers. The UN building was constantly visited by the official delegates and by crowds of loyal and disloyal supporters. UN officials were composed and discreet but ever ready to help. Eventually, it was revealed in summer 1993 that secret talks had been going on in Norway between the two parties. In September 1993 a Declaration of Principles was solemnly signed in Washington. This led to what was now the Gaza–Jericho Accord, conceived in Norway and born in Cairo in May 1994 before an admiring audience of 2,000. In the presence of the President of Egypt, the UN Secretary-General and foreign ministers from the US and Russia, Prime Minister Yitzhak Rabin of Israel and PLO leader Yasser Arafat solemnly sealed a binding agreement to grant the Palestinian Arabs a measure of self-rule over Israeli concessions in respect of land, settlement and administrative responsibility.

What seemed to be the possible gains from this peace progress? A slow movement in several directions was discernible: zero-sum (win–lose) attitudes shifting towards mutual recognition that security and peace were more important in the long run than narrow claims over land and water; incompatibility between sovereign state and revolutionary movement being replaced by that between state and would-be state; Israel's preparedness to recognize PLO moderation; the PLO acknowledging Israeli rights and needs; and Arab states now dealing with the recognized state of Israel. On the other hand, possible non-gains were evident or debatable. There remained a mismatch between the presumed intentions of the PLO to maximize progress towards statehood and the Israeli desire to maximize security and overall sovereign control. Would the religious, ideological hold of the orthodox on both sides ever relax?

The 1992 Declaration of Principles begs the question of whether the granting of "self-government" but not control of land, water, security and foreign affairs is "delegation" rather than "transfer". If the period of transition is to last five years will the PLO, "on probation", settle for less or demand more as the "final" phase draws near? What will be the response of those in the intrusive Jewish outland settlements who are already declaring in uncompromising fashion "Gaza and Jericho First: Gaza and Jericho Last"? If the statesmen in Israel assert that their dream of a Greater Israel is now replaced by a Secure Israel, what can that mean in practical terms? Questions and comment abound. To some Arabs the negotiators of Israel speak three languages: the generous one behind the scenes, the cautious one at the table, the hard-line, prescriptive one of documents. Unhappily for many Jews the two sides find it difficult to march forward together because they are, after all, intent on marching in different directions.

What, then, may the UN be able to do, even though it has been sidetracked from the negotiations on the Palestinian problem? First, the resettlement of refugees will be stepped up as an urgent task of enormous proportions. As with Cambodia, the programme will demand intensive preparation and resourcing. Then, the delayed election proposed originally for late 1994 (with no final date yet announced) will be a candidate for preparation, arrangement and supervision by the UN on the model of those successfully carried out in Namibia and Cambodia. Already, the International Labour Organization has carried out a survey of unemployment in the occupied territories, where it ranges from 30% to 50%. A first tranche of $135 million is being sought for job creation schemes among 500,000 camp "returnees". An ambitious Peace Implementation Programme has been launched by UNRWA, which will straightaway offer work to 15,000 Palestinian Arabs in the first phase. Large loans from the World Bank are being negotiated to rebuild a rundown infrastructure. A first budget of $2.1 million for the first five years will go into redevelopment schemes for transport, water supplies and agricultural improvement. The PLO has gone further in its estimates suggesting that eventually $14 million will be needed over the first seven years. There is, of course, discussion as to how far international investment can be attracted to rejuvenate a fractured but slowly healing economy. The Palestinian problem demonstrates dramatically that the furtherance of human rights depends on building a secure political and economic base. Over 50 frustrating years the UN has inched its way forward to reconcile the two halves of a community – now there is some hope that they will be able to advance together.

NOTES

1. This point was to lead to much controversy. As a precondition of negotiations, Israel contended that Arabs must acknowledge Israel's sovereign existence. The Arab precondition, demanded by most Arab opinion was acceptance of territorial

demands and recognition of Palestinian autonomy.

2. Henry Kissinger, who was party to so many Middle East negotiations, would scarcely agree. In his *Years of upheaval* (Boston, MA: Little, Brown, 1982) he believes that the Resolution text was definite enough: what went adrift were the interpretations. The Resolution he sees as more an expression of a stalemate than a means of resolution (cf. p. 197).

3. Kissinger, *Years of upheaval*, pp. 624–5.

4. Kissinger gives a full account of the 1973 Geneva Conference in Chapter XVII of *Years of upheaval* with references to the Palestinians which are not always sympathetic.

5. Reservations about Zionism were also aired elsewhere. On 11 November the World Council of Churches stated that it found no evidence that Zionism was racism, rather, it was a movement historically connected with liberating the Jewish nation from racist oppression, and thus it was an understandable, complicated expression of diverse aspirations.

6. There were precedents for this. Spring 1982, US personnel went to Sinai with a Multinational Force and Observers and are still active today. Similarly, in 1982–3 a group, MNF2, was deployed in Lebanese areas but was withdrawn in 1984 after harassment by irregulars.

FURTHER READING

Evans, G. *Cooperating for peace*. Sydney: Allen & Unwin, 1993: especially Chapters 7 & 8.

Howley, D. C. *The United Nations and the Palestinians*. New York: Hicksville, 1975.

Hudson, M. C. *The Palestinians: new directions*. Washington DC: Georgetown University Press, 1990.

Lall, A. *The United Nations and the Middle East crisis*. New York: Columbia University Press, 1970.

Sicherman, H. *Palestinian autonomy, self-government and peace*. Oxford: Westview, 1993.

Stein, K. W. & S. W. Lewis. *Making peace among Arabs and Israelis. Lessons from fifty years of negotiating experience*. Washington DC: US Institute of Peace, 1991.

Tessler, M. *A history of the Israeli–Palestinian conflict*. Bloomington, Indiana: Indiana University Press, 1994.

United Nations. *Prospects for peace in the Middle East: an Israeli–Palestinian dialogue*. New York: UN Department of Public Information, 1993.

Chapter Six

THE PALESTINIAN PROBLEM

1917   Balfour Declaration gives Jews national home in Palestine.
1923   Britain given League of Nations mandate.
1937   Britain's Peel Commission recommends Palestine partition.
1947   UN General Assembly prefers partition to continued mandate.
       UNSCOP formed, reports, suggests UN trusteeship.
1948   British mandate ends. Israel independent, attacked by Arab
       neighbours. UNTSO and UNRWA deployed.
1956   Suez Crisis: Anglo-French-Israel attack. UN and US mediation.
1964   PLO and Arafat become Palestinian "freedom fighters".
1967   Six-Day War. Security Council's Resolution 242.
1973   Yom Kippur War. PLO granted observer status at UN.
       Geneva Conference co-chaired by US, USSR.
1975   UN General Assembly brands Zionism as "racist".
1978   Camp David: Carter's initiative and Declaration of Peace signed
       by Israel and Egypt.
1982   Israel launches drive into Lebanon to oust Arab terrorists. PLO
       has to evacuate. US as peacekeeper fields MNF.
1991   *Intifada* protests reach climax in Palestinian areas, i.e. "Occupied
       Territories".
1993   Madrid Conference.
       Declaration of Principles signed in Washington (settlement
       envisaged).
1994   Middle East settlement outline signed in Cairo. Self-government
       for Palestinians a key item.
1995   Election scheduled for Palestinian areas. UN launches rehabilita-
       tion schemes. Continuing tension and controversy over final
       settlement details.

Afghanistan

TEN YEARS OF TROUBLE AND TRIAL

When Red Army tank columns rolled across the Soviet border into Afghanistan in December 1979 the political reverberations were far-reaching. A period of confrontation and unpredictability in international relations ensued, profoundly affecting superpower relations. Fissures were exposed in the Atlantic bridge between the United States and its European allies. The uncommitted Third World writhed in dismay. A number of disconcerting questions were raised as to motives and possible response. Was this naked aggression on the part of a mighty power against a small and remote country, an expansionist thrust born of overconfidence in nuclear superiority, or was it a clumsy and hasty defensive move? Why was it that the Soviet Union, ostensibly on an ideological rescue mission to offer succour to a threatened Socialist state (or so it claimed), was also willing to risk world censure? Was this an end to *détente*? What could the outraged world do about this act of aggression?

This was commonly agreed to be an opportunity for the UN. Nobody then could realize that the conflict would give UN members ten years of trouble, trial and some limited success. A decade later the invading force was out, superpowers were on better terms than ever and Cold War suspicions and hostilities were melting away. Once more, a case-study shows the UN in action as peacekeeper and mediator, stopping the externals of war where one state attacks another, but quite unable to reconcile internal disputes. The ten years of active UN diplomacy here can best be considered in four phases: the Soviet impulse to intervene in 1979; the first UN involvement in 1980 when the New York headquarters and its representatives in the field encouraged negotiation; the continuous UN mediation through a Personal Representative of the Secretary-General culminating in the Geneva Accords of 1988; and lastly, the peacekeeping carried out by the United Nations Good Offices Mission in Afghanistan and Pakistan (UNGOMAP).

SOVIET INTERVENTION

Conjecture as to Moscow's original impulse usually centres on that strategic hinterland of remote mountains, the Roof of the World, which occasioned so much ill-feeling between Czarist Russia and the British Raj. Instability here could menace the southern flank of the USSR, the so-called Muslim Threshold. Religious fundamentalism in Iran and elsewhere, together with what were conventionally seen as the evil-doings of capitalism and the CIA, wound up tensions that were stretched taut when a neighbour, backward surely, but still Socialist, was in apparent danger of counter-revolution. Its left-wing government was insecurely perched in the capital, Kabul. Brezhnev in the Kremlin must have been convinced that here was a case for going to the aid of a client state, although in so doing his reputation as a man for *détente* would be endangered. We now know from Soviet archives made accessible recently that Brezhnev was unhappy at expressing his duty of solidarity in this way. The prospect, though, of the Afghan leader, Hafizullah Amin, paying court to such as Pakistan, possibly China, and even the US, was more than Moscow could stomach. Eighty thousand troops (Asian regiments in the main) would quickly establish firm political ground and fortify the tenancy of a puppet, Barbrack Kamal. Amin was shot in his own palace and a host of Soviet "advisors" clamped down on a tendency to counter-revolution. They also aroused passionate resentment among Afghans, traditionally not the mildest-mannered of men.

Several days after the occupation of Kabul the UN Security Council met at the insistence of 52 UN member-states. At its meeting on 3 January 1980, the USSR and also Afghanistan's puppet government lost no time in asserting that consideration of the intervention by the Council was invalid since the movement of Soviet troops in response to an "invitation" from Kabul was a "domestic" matter. Germane to this, they said, was a bilateral treaty of friendship and co-operation signed in 1978, which justified all efforts to preserve the sovereignty of Afghanistan. Ignoring this plea, the Security Council went on to frame a Resolution condemning an unlawful act and calling for a Soviet withdrawal as soon as possible. Inevitably, this Resolution bit the dust with a Soviet veto. The General Assembly was the obvious next forum for discussion. An emergency session ten days later had no option but to accept the intervention as a *fait accompli*, although delegates were loud in their censure. Blatant aggression was sharply rebuked as something that went counter to those fundamental Charter principles of respect for sovereignty, territorial integrity and political independence. A Resolution similar to the defunct Security Council one was passed and the Secretary-General was asked to keep members informed of the situation. It was noticeable that this Resolution contained no provision for restitution or enforcement by counter-action other than an insistence on an immediate, unconditional and total withdrawal of foreign troops. Both Moscow and Kabul thought the statement peremptory and unlikely to ease negotiation. They foresaw its only effect would be to lend some legitimacy to armed struggle to reverse intervention.

Away from the UN building attitudes towards the Soviet intervention hardened considerably. In the White House, President Jimmy Carter, facing an election, could not afford to appear irresolute. Sanctions against the intruder must be applied. America's grain exports were to be suspended. No right-thinking state should be represented at the 1980 Olympic Games to be held in Moscow. While Soviet–American relations were consigned to the deep-freeze and an arms build-up initiated, there was a notable lack of accord in European capitals, particularly in Paris and Bonn. In the European press was speculation about the principles of the Carter Doctrine. Although in its call for retributory action it was a pale shadow of the Truman Doctrine of 1947 (pledging US assistance to "free peoples" menaced by Communism), was this a positive approach to something that the "quiet diplomacy" of the UN might be engaged in more fruitfully?

THE UN INITIATES NEGOTIATION

In response to impatient urgings within the UN and in governments outside, the Secretary-General, Kurt Waldheim, appointed representatives to investigate the chances of peaceful resolution along with delegates from the main parties to the dispute. Soundings were taken in Moscow, Geneva, Kabul, Tehran and in Pakistan's capital, Islamabad. In February 1981, since tentative exploration was getting nowhere, Perez de Cuellar, Undersecretary-General and soon to follow Waldheim in the top post, was given the title of Personal Representative and charged with the task of furthering intensive discussions. This was an interesting move since a Personal Representative acts on his own authority and not solely on delegated authority from New York. The "pivotal difficulty" (to use UN jargon) was to get the Red Army out and away from a situation that was already proving impossible for it tactically and politically. Twelve months of verbal exchange had not shifted Soviet forces one kilometre.

However, in Afghanistan itself, a harsh winter and difficult terrain had immobilized Soviet tanks and transport, garrisons had been besieged, aircraft shot down by guerrillas, supplies and reinforcements endangered. Morale was diminishing week by week and Moscow's embarrassment was plainly visible. How could the USSR prevent this unfortunate escapade from becoming their Vietnam? For all parties to the dispute a settlement needed to be comprehensive in removing the unauthorized occupation, in providing for non-interference in the government of Afghanistan, and in arranging the rescue of large numbers of refugees. Above all, some form of guarantee of security by outside powers would take the heat out of the political chaos, or so it was assumed.

Eleven months later as de Cuellar took over the directorate of the UN a fel-

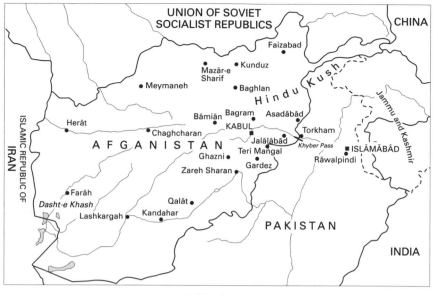

Afghanistan

low Latin American, Diego Cordovez, was brought from his post as Undersecretary-General for Special Political Affairs and given the brief of dealing with
Afghanistan. Six years of spadework were to follow, made difficult by the
impatient promptings of Western nations, and by a torrent of suggestion and
equivocation from countries in the Third World. Most of these professed not
the slightest support for Moscow's aggrieved stance of coming to the aid of a
state menaced by reactionary and foreign interests. Only India, Syria, Libya
and the PLO gave some qualified support and all four thought withdrawal was
essential. Common to all was grave unease at the swift and brutal way in
which a state's leader had been "liquidated" and replaced by a Moscow
stooge. In most countries, East and West, there was strong support for the
Afghan guerrillas, the Mujahadeen, who were taking on the might of the Red
Army and effectively nullifying military conquest. Weapons were supplied to
them by Egypt, Saudi Arabia (sensitive to the threatened Muslim Threshold),
China and the United States. Iran now offered asylum to one million Afghan
refugees. Pakistan assumed the role of guerrilla staging-post and capital for an
exile government. The cherished good relationship between Moscow and
countries in the "uncommitted" world dived into rapid decline. Throughout
these frustrating years, Cordovez's plodding progress was made more difficult
by the diffidence and obstruction of the main parties. The UN's chief negotia-
tor had to shuffle from capital to capital and in Geneva had to await the depar-
ture of one delegation before inviting the other as they refused to meet at the
same time in the Palais des Nations.

A SOVIET CHANGE OF DIRECTION

Early Soviet negotiating ploys in the days of Brezhnev had featured an appeal for withdrawal by "external powers" from the entire area of the Persian Gulf as a means of enhancing regional security. This would be traded against a Soviet withdrawal from Afghanistan. Not surprisingly, this proposal found scant favour in Washington and London. The real breakthrough came in spring 1985 with the coming to power in Moscow of Mikhail Gorbachev. After only one month in post he was regularly communicating with the UN. There had been, he said, a hard and impartial examination of an exit strategy despite some resistance from his hierarchy.

Two needs were self-evident: to persuade the apprehensive Marxists in Kabul to face up to political compromise and removal of tangible support; and to negotiate a time-frame for leaving when the original clear inclination was to wait for a political settlement. Towards the prime aim there would be a replacement of the Marxist Kamal by the moderate Mohammed Najibullah. The Soviet leader would attempt dialogue with opposition forces, although rebuff was likely. And so it proved. Assessment by the UN mediators found a disunited opposition front, a quarrelsome mix of "trigger-happy" Mujahadeen (also variously divided) and a coterie of journalists, schoolteachers and others who yearned to get their economy out of dependence on basic-wage peasants living on a dollar a day (a World Bank estimate), and to develop a modern social and cultural independence. The old Communist line of popular development was now discredited, but there was no credible plan for progress as an alternative. There must be some other way than a fatalistic reliance on the growing and marketing of 700 tonnes of opium a year to line the pockets of traders in Kabul.

UN talks in Geneva provided a new emphatic focus with lines out to Washington and European capitals. Gorbachev's contribution to these talks proved vigorous and inventive. First, he struck an ethical note with the admission that intervention in Afghanistan had been "immoral", even a "sin". To step across the frontier with force had been "wrong" and a mistake. Secondly, he offered pragmatism. In what ways could a moderate coalition be set up in Kabul, with or without Najibullah, if the Red Army support was withdrawn? Was there not a place for a proper UN peacekeeping body to go in to monitor a cease-fire, investigate border violations, and prevent any more weapons being delivered from outside? In any case, Najibullah's People's Democratic Party of Afghanistan (PDPA) would need to be legitimated eventually through an electoral process, which the UN ought to supervise. The culmination of exploratory discussions could be for the UN to convene a general conference to attempt to secure a neutral and demilitarized Afghanistan.

Another realistic suggestion was that any mediation set in motion by the UN could be materially assisted by a background of guarantees from major external powers, in this case the United States and the Soviet Union. The harmony envisaged here preceded the definitive setting aside of Cold War hostilities.

Undoubtedly, Gorbachev saw this linking of mediation and guarantee as a possible model for the settlement of other regional conflicts. In his view, "when the Afghanistan knot is untied it will have the most profound impact on other regional conflicts too". Within 18 months, indeed, Soviet untying of knots by putting pressure on client states was dramatically assisting UN-brokered reconciliation in South West Africa and in Cambodia.

As the momentum of peace discussions mounted in 1987 and 1988 a firm UN position was declared. This was that the final status of the unhappy country must be determined by the Afghan people themselves. Cordovez, the UN Personal Representative put it in these terms:

> Throughout negotiations it has been consistently recognized that the objective of comprehensive settlement implies the broadest support and the immediate participation of all segments of the Afghan people and that this can best be ensured by a broad-based Afghan government . . . any questions relating to government in Afghanistan are matters within the exclusive jurisdiction of Afghanistan and can only be decided by the Afghan people themselves.

To some this would have been a gloss derived from the Charter's high-sounding principles; to others it would have signified improbable optimism. Yet within a week of that declaration, on 14 April 1988, a meeting of representatives of all interested parties was to witness signature of a four-part agreement to be known as the Geneva Accords. This seemed to be a fine and fitting climax to years of tension and halting advance. If the future was not at all clear, the steps by which progress just might be possible were to to be discerned and were agreed by all.

THE GENEVA ACCORDS

The four Genevan components were an accord between Afghanistan and Pakistan on mutual non-interference and non-intervention; an agreement between the same two states about the voluntary return of refugees; a Declaration on international guarantees; and a general agreement on "the interrelationships for the settlement of the situation regarding Afghanistan". It should be stressed that the accords were not those between Afghanistan and the violating state of the USSR. What was given particular attention was that Pakistan had been the main provider of solace, funds and weaponry to the opposition inside the country and it was in a concerted attempt both to dry up these sources and, more positively, to provide for better and peaceful relations, that a bonding must be engineered. In other words, the chief objective of diplomacy, while not overlooking the nature of the first injury, was to underwrite a peaceful and controlled outcome.

In this spirit, the first of the accords set out to remind signatories of the elemental principles in the UN Charter to do with respect for a nation's sovereignty, its political independence and territorial integrity. In conformity with this, the contracting parties must refrain from hostile activities and other forms of intervention, overt and covert, as well as support of rebellious activities, employment of mercenaries and all forms of harmful propaganda. Secondly, the problem of refugees was to be addressed by allowing their free return to the homeland, their freedom of movement and domicile, and the right to work and to take part in civic affairs. Voluntary repatriation was to be co-ordinated by UNHCR. Thirdly, the Declaration on International Guarantees was a brief and clear undertaking between the USSR and the US to refrain from any form of interference and intervention in the internal affairs of both Afghanistan and Pakistan. They urged other states to do likewise. They supported the negotiated settlement between the two countries designed to normalize relations, promote good neighbourliness, and strengthen regional peace and security.

One of the clauses in this Declaration that might be thought rather ambiguous was the wish "to contribute to the achievement of the objectives that the Republic of Afghanistan and the Islamic Republic of Pakistan have set themselves"; to any critical observer this begged a number of questions. Finally, a detailed Agreement on Interrelationships went on to acknowledge the successful conclusion of the UN diplomatic process by tracing the steps that had been taken, noting also the concordance of the treaty provisions with the appropriate principles in the UN Charter and providing for a continued role for UN supervision and monitoring of progress by the UN Personal Representative and others.

Eight and a half years after the Soviet army crossed the Afghan borders a treaty was signed to finish one chapter and begin, so it was hoped, a more peaceful one. The Geneva Accords did not attribute blame to a transgressor (in contrast to most public opinion and the stated views of governments). The matter of intervention was approached as it were from a tangent. It was quite clear that $70,000 million worth of war had achieved little and certainly nothing by way of definite political reconciliation. To elaborate the practical mechanisms of working out the settlement a Memorandum of Understanding was added to the fourth part of the Geneva Accords. This filled out some of the provisions agreed earlier in setting up a UN peacekeeping operation together with continued mediation. The Personal Representative lending his "good offices" to ensure implementation would be assisted by a body, small in number, of unarmed officers who would deal with complaints, and go out to inspect, visit and report where there were suspected irregularities or violations. All this would be performed by the UNGOMAP with their headquarters in Kabul and in Islamabad. Fifty officers from ten countries, detached temporarily from other Middle East peacekeeping operations, would take up their duties as UNGOMAP from May 1988 with a budget of $14,000 million. Considering the difficulties and dangers in their work this was a remarkably small complement and quite slender funding. Essentially, priority had to be given to a phased withdrawal of the occupying army provided this could be done smoothly within a nine-month period. There were approximately 80,000 Red Army soldiers in 18 main garrisons who would need efficient and safe evacuation after they had cleared the detritus of war from more than half of Afghanistan. Soviet liaison was readily effected and within three months half of the Soviet units had left. There was to be a pause during the winter but by February 1989 all would have gone home.

THE UNGOMAP MISSION

The mandate accorded to UNGOMAP must have seemed clear and purposeful to its originators. In practice it was very different. The slim group of officers found themselves impossibly stretched in terrain that was hostile and strewn with thousands of mines. In any one week they would hurry to a border crossing and find it encumbered with a flood of starving and sick refugees. Back in town, having dodged ambush on the way, they would have to take shelter from aerial bombing and rocket attacks. The supervised evacuation of Red Army units had to be done by somehow escorting apprehensive soldiers without extra ammunition, air cover or guaranteed food and shelter. It was never quite clear just which faction of the Mujahadeen was behind the shooting, and it was rarely possible to secure an assured passage for those who were still seen as foreign invaders. If the physical tasks were difficult enough for UNGOMAP, it was the political responsibilities that became almost impossible to handle.

The ambiguity in the guarantee Declaration springs to mind. What objectives had Afghanistan and Pakistan "set themselves"? Would Kabul, uncertain now of any Soviet backing, ever cease to upbraid its Pakistani neighbour for illicit support of the "terrorist" Mujahadeen? Were there any grounds for hope that one day Islamabad would grow out of its obsessional belief that after a Soviet withdrawal Afghanistan would present a serious threat to their north, which they would have to meet with troop emplacements and spy planes? Inevitably, the UNGOMAP mandate was disparaged by each side unwilling itself to concede anything significant, blaming the other, and seeing the "weakness" of the UN mission as justifying the need actively to "defend" its own interests. Moreover, governments not only disagreed; they impeded UNGOMAP's arrangements in the field. Contacts with Iran and Pakistan to try to effect the safe return of five million Afghan refugees proved unavailing, partly because of obstructive bureaucracy, but largely because few of these hapless people wanted to return to insecurity and deprivation.

In May 1988 an emergency relief operation was mounted with the UN appointing a co-ordinator for all assistance programmes, yet again a web of UN and non-governmental agencies. In the October *Operation Salaam* was given a first tranche of $900 million for first aid rather than systematic reha-bilitation. Three years later, funds ran out. This operation to help the biggest ever spontaneous repatriation of refugees, 70,000 each week, had to be sus-pended temporarily.

In 1990 the future of peacekeeping in Afghanistan came under scrutiny; January was the end of the schedule. The UN had been massively involved in diplomacy that had begun inauspiciously and after a decade had pacified the situation though not finally settled it. Should the involvement continue? And in what shape? Several general developments brightened the picture. There was now more respect for UN peacekeeping. Where peacekeeping within a state had rarely been possible during the Cold War, its practicability and value were now more than ever acknowledged. Both superpowers, one of them directly involved, were now able to guarantee arrangements for peace.

Was, then, the UNGOMAP mandate to be renewed? Kabul and India saw UNGOMAP as a useful watchdog over Pakistan. Washington and Pakistan pre-ferred it to fold. Seven out of the ten contributing states reminded the Secre-tary-General of the anticipatory spirit of the Geneva Accords, namely that settlement should be a "strictly Afghan process". A compromise was devised: UNGOMAP would be given two more months. At last, in March 1990, UNGO-MAP was withdrawn, except for the residual presence of the UN Personal Rep-resentative and a small military staff. In the background both guarantor powers began to explore the chances of elections that would be administered by the UN. How, though, would the Kabul Government react to the result if it proved less than enthusiastically supportive? What would be the responses of the disunited Mujahadeen groups?

AN UNCERTAIN PEACE

Movement has been slow and unpredictable since 1990. There seems today scant prospect of the turmoil subsiding. New directions in negotiations were put in hand in 1991–2 when a new Personal Representative, Benon Sevan, started intensive discussions looking for a formula for a broadbased Afghan government. This was not to be understood as any form of external interven-tion: it was an attempt by a neutral body to "facilitate . . . a comprehensive political agreement" as a General Assembly Resolution had requested of the Secretary-General. To this end Sevan drafted a five-point plan in early 1992 whereby a Governing Council fully representative of diverse political parties would implement measures for legislative reform, economic improvements and proposals for better education, health and welfare. This promising scheme was unfortunately hamstrung by political in-fighting in Kabul. In

April 1992 President Mohammed Najibullah was toppled amid ferocious discord. The moderate leader who found a way of working with the UN had clung to power for three years, not so much on account of his own strength or that of a Soviet backer, as by the chronic incapacity of the opposition to join forces to oust him. The UN was faced with the ruin of reconciliation attempts and a relapse into a chaotic pattern of tribal fiefdoms.

What does the future hold for the land where good offices and good intentions have made such uphill progress? Was the mandate given to the UN mission an impossible one? Should the UN have sought authority for a peace-keeping operation several thousands strong to delineate and patrol demilitarized zones and to maintain "green lines"? If the internal powers are at each other's throats a number of external powers are now more willing to offer help. In spring 1993 three states, Pakistan, Iran and Saudi Arabia declared that they would no longer support the Mujahadeen guerrillas. Pakistan then and since has worked hard to allay the suspicions of a Kabul administration as to its "objectives" and its behaviour. Towards the end of that year, Russia, the successor to the USSR, publicly acknowledged the injury done to Afghanistan. Moscow was now ready to lend help for resettlement of refugees and for the reconstruction of grievously damaged towns and communications. The slow business of repair and rejuvenation is currently in hand, much of it being undertaken under the auspices of the UNDP. Neither success nor failure can be the verdict on the UN's achievement in Afghanistan. But what might have been the consequence of the UN *not* trying to do something?

FURTHER READING

Klass, R. *Afghanistan: the great game revisited*. New York: Freedom House, 1987.
Newell, R. S. International responses to the Afghanistan crisis. *The World Today* 37, pp. 172–81, 1981.
Rubin, B. A. Afghanistan: the next round. *Orbis* 33(1), pp. 57–72, 1989.

QUICK REFERENCE

Chapter Seven

AFGHANISTAN

1978 USSR and Afghanistan sign treaty of friendship and co-operation.

1979 December: USSR invades in response, it claims, to invitation. UN General Assembly deplores, Security Council urges withdrawal.

1980 US–Soviet trade embargoed, relations soured, no US athletes to go to Moscow's Olympic Games. UN representatives explore negotiation chances.

1981 UN appoints Personal Representative of Secretary-General to oversee situation in Afghanistan.

1982 Intensive mediatory attempts by UN's Special Representative.

1985 Mikhail Gorbachev, now in power, works closely with UN searching for settlement and Soviet withdrawal.

1988 Geneva Accords propose four-part comprehensive settlement (Pakistan particularly involved).
UNGOMAP set up. Emergency relief put in hand. Red Army begins withdrawal.

1990 UNGOMAP stands down. Small UN presence remains.

1992 UN five-point rejuvenation plan hamstrung by Kabul's political turmoil.

1993 Moscow takes the blame for 1979 invasion. UNDP slowly gets to work.

The Gulf conflict, 1990–1

Sixteen weeks of anxiety, argument and fierce battle held a world breathless before its TV screens between November 1990 and late February 1991. Not since the Second World War had there been seen the disruption and carnage represented by almost 30 nations fielding over one million men, and the death and destruction raining down on military emplacements and inhabited towns and villages. A coalition, seeing itself as authorized by the UN Security Council, confronted a dictator who had annexed a neighbouring state, stopped his forces in their tracks and reversed the hostilities decisively. The coalition was able to launch a Hot War in consequence of unanimity achieved by the melting away of the Cold War. Yet the operation that proceeded under such phases as *Desert Shield*, *Desert Sword*, *Desert Storm* and *Desert Sabre*, and accomplished with military flair, has thrown up many questions during the onrush of the undertaking and ever since. Could the eruption of the crisis have been better foreseen? Was it not likely that combustible elements in the Middle East, so readily apparent, would burst into flames unless preventive measures were thoughtfully and carefully implemented? At what points did misinterpretation and lack of objectivity cause appraisal and discussion to go off the rails and so precipitate situations that could not be retrieved? What was to be the function of the UN in dealing with threats and disputes at that time and in that place? Were the alternatives to using military force adequately considered? Was this a war that should and could have been avoided? Was a final "victory" an objective that the UN Charter could underwrite as the restoration of peace and security or was it the culmination of a win-or-lose mission that had to destroy in order to reach a conclusion? How far in maintaining and restoring international peace and security can the UN legitimately resort to force?

The Gulf conflict is worth studying briefly in several respects: the significance of its location; the way in which the UN got involved; the linkage particularly with the problem of the Palestinians; the violation of minorities; and the political aftermath in the region. Public scrutiny of these aspects has subjected the UN's action and inaction to intense controversy. Altogether, the Gulf conflict was not a peacekeeping mission: it was a peace enforcement operation, similar to that in Korea 40 years previously.

THE GULF: A SIGNIFICANT LOCATION

The cliché of a disaster waiting to happen was surely true of the Arab lands east of the Mediterranean. For thousands of years dynastic rivalries have produced turbulence in what are now two dozen states, rich in culture, diverse in their ambitions and disunited in their scramble for those essential ingredients of life, land and water, and access to them both. This wide region was in the grip of the Ottoman Empire until its dissolution in 1918. Western nations with "an irreducible interest", namely, oil and the guardianship of international trading routes exercised a "protective" surveillance until the 1960s. The League of Nations gave Britain a mandate over Palestine and what is known today as Iraq, while France gained Syria and Lebanon. Arab nationalism demanding independence was blunted by mandatory powers manipulating the loyalties of kings and aristocratic chieftains, so that today the Middle East is an uneasy mixture of dynasties and socialist republics. Autocratic rule, religious fundamentalism, a yawning gap between vastly rich sheiks and impoverished peasants *(fellahin)* are all characteristic of a region that has twice as much oil as the rest of the world. In a very direct sense "energy security is national security" as President George Bush told US troops in Saudi Arabia in November 1990.

Iraq and Kuwait, the main players in the Gulf drama, have coexisted uneasily since a charismatic Saddam Hussein in the mid 1970s replaced a republican clique, which 15 years earlier had ousted a British puppet king from the capital, Baghdad. The ruthless organizer, Hussein, soon had the Baath Party, a socialist and revolutionary group, aiming at spearheading Pan-Arabism and challenging the conservative al-Sabah sheiks of oil-rich Kuwait. The new leader was able to muster a huge force in a bid to crush the Khomeini regime in Iran. UN efforts brought a cease-fire to that quarrel in 1988 after almost eight years of war.[1] Hussein's determined stand against the expansion of Islamic fundamentalism, seen as a threat to other nations' security, earned him the respect and material assistance of Arab neighbours such as Saudi Arabia and Kuwait, and also of the United States. Moscow also backed Baghdad. Arms poured in mainly from P5 suppliers and mobilization put 1 in every 12 men into uniform. Military values, discipline, patriotism and even martyrdom were the cardinal virtues, and even if approaches by the UN over Hussein's aggression against Iran or over the harsh treatment of minorities were not rebuffed they met a fiercely defensive arrogance. By July 1990, when US ambassador April Glaspie unwisely assured the Baghdad dictator that the US had "no opinions on the Arab/Arab conflicts, like your border disagreement or Kuwait", the crucible was about to boil over.

THE UN BECOMES INVOLVED

When, on 2 August 1990, Saddam Hussein's forces crossed into Kuwait, few observers can have been surprised. That is not to say that they knew what to do about it. Iraq claimed that it was responding to support a group of young revolutionaries in Kuwait. It was not immediately obvious why Hussein had not contented himself with occupation of certain border areas or one or two disputed islands, unless he felt that only a grand stroke could establish his reputation among brother Arabs. A meeting of the Security Council, hastily summoned, condemned the invasion with Resolution 660 and called for an unconditional withdrawal. At the same time, the US leaned heavily on Saudi Arabia with photographic "evidence" of Iraq's hostile intent in their direction.[2] Surprisingly, there was no determined approach to the Arab League, as the Resolution suggested, to enlist its support for a negotiated process. Within the week two UN Resolutions followed the first, 661, requiring member-states to impose mandatory sanctions in the light of Iraq's non-compliance, and 662, declaring the Iraqi annexation of Kuwait "null and void", obliging members to refrain from any action that might give the annexation any indirect recognition.

The audacity of Iraq's claiming Kuwait as "the nineteenth province" was somewhat softened on 12 August 1990 when Baghdad sent a peace plan to the UN. There were three parts: Israel was to withdraw from the Palestinian occupied territories; Syria was to leave the Lebanon; and, in consequence of Iraqi and Iranian troops being pulled away from the contested area, the situation in Kuwait could be "arranged" in line with UN Resolutions. Hussein was clearly linking the situation over Kuwait with associated problems especially that of the Palestinians. If this was an attempt to widen the field of play it met a frosty reception in the White House. Several things happened quite quickly. Washington's telephone lines were humming with calls to European ministries. "Phoney deterrence" was held to be useless: there must be a scheme if all else failed for an aerial deterrence phase of "persuasion" to be followed if necessary by a concerted land operation. A *Desert Shield* might need ultimately a *Desert Sword*. Iraq's divisions would exercise a stranglehold on much of the world's oil, something that the West could not tolerate.

At this point it became obvious to those who followed media reports that the United States would rely on its own muscle to deal with an illicit annexation rather than wait for the UN's cumbersome and lengthy processes of negotiation. *Izvestia*, the Moscow newspaper, saw the reality in stark terms: "While Moscow is relying on the UN and collective action, Washington banks on its own strength and independent action". There appeared to be a double edge to American policy, that of playing up the notion of "war is imminent" and then of turning on the "diplomatic tap". If this confused the enemy, it certainly bemused much of the public and those in the UN building. Was the heavy-handed approach to the crisis passing the point of no return? What principles lay behind the increasing personalization of the quarrel where the quarrel was not with Iraqi people but with their leader, the "madman", "murderer" and "liar"?

There was no possibility in the American view of parleying with a power that had moved from occupation to annexation, was completely averse to withdrawal and did nothing to prevent its soldiers from committing atrocities. In the eyes of UN Secretary-General Perez de Cuellar, as he was later to admit, these were elements of the problem enormously difficult to resolve but they were issues for negotiation based on objectivity, restraint and law. It was fairly clear that brandishing the sabre without careful exploration of all aspects of the problem could hardly bring worthwhile and lasting resolution. A possibility advanced with some caution by the financially embarrassed UN was that prompt despatch of a sizeable peacekeeping force to the Iraq/Kuwait border might prevent or reduce armed conflict. This suggestion seems never to have been seriously entertained by P5 politicians now being recruited by telephone for a proposed coalition force in the Gulf.

Meanwhile, as the prospect of forceful encounter grew the political divide widened, as had been forecast by UN advisors. Although the USSR broadly supported a firm stand by the UN, China generally abstained in the Security Council and France had reservations. Members of the Arab League either supported a possible coalition undertaking (these were Egypt, Saudi Arabia, Syria and Morocco), or they showed sympathy for Iraq (Jordan, Sudan, Algeria, Mauritania, Yemen and the PLO). Sanctions and blockade were measures advocated at the UN and elsewhere in the hope of a peaceful resolution. Iraq was thought to be more vulnerable than most to blockade. Usually, 70% of goods had to be imported and 90% of exports consisted of oil. Lost oil income alone would be $62 million each day. There were many who were later to declare that mandatory sanctions were never given a chance to take grip. The Security Council imposed a maritime blockade on 25 August with Resolution 665, and three weeks later with Resolution 666 strove to permit "appropriate humanitarian agencies" to send in a controlled supply of food and medical supplies for children and invalids.

Towards the end of September 1990 the UN faced increasing politicization of the conflict, which might have been avoided if an international organization had been allowed to negotiate rather than merely reiterate resolutions through a loudspeaker. Iraq now began to intone the injured quasi-religious note of the American "infidel" defiling the holy places that all Islam must hold sacred. There were those in the US Congress who now urged that "democracy" be reinstated in a part of the world where few acknowledged that such a system would even be recognized, let alone practised. Further UN Resolutions, 669 and 670, imposed an embargo on air space in Iraq and Kuwait and at the same time tried to provide help to those states facing hardship as a result of economic sanctions.

A PEACEFUL RESOLUTION IS SOUGHT

It was also in September that some chinks of light appeared. Libya proposed a seven-point peace plan after a show of voting against five UN Resolutions. Iraqis withdrawn from Kuwait would be replaced by a UN peacekeeping force. Arab and other Muslim troops, not Western contingents, would protect menaced areas such as Saudi Arabia. Negotiations under UN management would discuss matters such as the nature of Kuwaiti government, the possibility of a unified and equable oil policy, and arrangements for debt repayment and compensation. Sadly, these proposals were given scant attention. However, Presidents Gorbachev and Bush met in Helsinki and agreed that "Our two states and the UN have a huge arsenal of means at our disposal to resolve the situation through political means". President François Mitterrand of France put forward a peace plan echoing this sentiment. At the UN General Assembly, on 24 September 1991, he spoke of moving from "the logic of war" to the "logic of peace". Simpler than the Libyan proposals, the plan envisaged four stages: an Iraqi declared intention to withdraw; then evacuation monitored by the UN together with the freeing of civilian hostages; Kuwaiti sovereignty restored; and the future decided through a UN-supervised plebiscite. Next, the linked problems of the Palestinians, the Lebanon, and Israeli security must be addressed. Finally, there would have to be a concerted approach to arms reduction in the region. This mixture of realism and breadth of vision appealed to China and even to Iraq. Despite these promising signs the package was not taken up and the French, while disappointed, signalled their determination to continue probing the possibilities of a peaceful settlement.

There was not much that the UN could do that autumn or, indeed, was allowed to do, against the machismo paraded by a coalition with over half a million men digging in, accompanied by a rationale that presented them as defensive one minute and in an offensive posture the next. From Baghdad was trumpeted intent to deal for all time with the invader and menace to Islam. Resolution 678 of 29 November 1990 expressed the UN's intention to uphold the Charter, and to adopt the robust meaning of Chapter VII, which is headed by the word "Action". The Resolution noted that Iraq, in flagrant contempt, had refused to comply with international resolutions. All members were now authorized "to use all necessary means" to uphold and implement UN Resolutions and to restore international peace and security to the area unless Iraq had fully complied with the Resolutions on or before 15 January 1991.

A shift in general attitude in New York and most capitals was becoming clear. It was now too late to keep the peace: all that could be done was to try to enforce it. The UN did not have the means to do this and the task was to be subcontracted to the US. The Security Council, well aware that the "means" was the coalition force-in-waiting, would rely on national command structures (again, as in Korea), not that of a UN Military Staff Committee, which the Charter had long ago hoped for but never managed to obtain. The Resolution was adopted with the USSR in agreement, Cuba and the Yemen dissenting and China abstaining. Whether or not the White House had leant on certain of the P5 members was arguable but at least President Bush now had a mandate with which to enlist Congress support for despatch of an expeditionary force from the US. (Some units were, in fact, already in the Gulf area.) The American press was now able to talk of "New World Warriors" and "World Orderists" embarking on a legitimate mission.

A major UN initiative was attempted in January 1991. The Secretary-General flew to Baghdad feeling, as he later admitted, that he had been sidelined and that however objective his stance, he would be given little room for manoeuvre and not much credit at the end of it. He had nothing much to bring with him and there would probably be little to take away. Minds appeared to have been made up on all sides, even so, Perez de Cuellar was to continue with exhaustive discussions on his return to New York. Some days later the Security Council met in an atmosphere of foreboding, if not despair. A revised peace plan was handed to it by France. It was an improvement on the earlier proposals in that, first, UN observers and an actual peacekeeping force would replace the evacuated Iraqis; secondly, a group of Nordic states were keen to make up the force; and further, the coalition would proffer a guarantee of non-aggression and once more there would be a promise from the Security Council to convene an international conference on the Middle East. There seemed some hope that the plan might be acceptable. Endorsing it, the Secretary-General stressed that the UN sought not the surrender of the aggressive power but some means of resolving a crisis through respecting all legitimate interests and the rule of law. Interestingly, at this time seven out of ten of the non-permanent Security Council members came from Third World states. However, hopes were dashed when the US and the UK opposed the plan, disliking, as they put it, the possibility of "rewarding" Iraq. Once more they rejected the wider linkage of the Iraqi problem with general Middle East discussions. In the end, to the dismay of France and other members of the Security Council, these two powers called for unconditional surrender on the part of Iraq.

DESERT OPERATIONS ARE MOUNTED

The air campaign of the US-led coalition, *Operation Desert Storm*, thundered into action on 16 January 1991. In the next three weeks there were 49,000 offensive sorties, an astounding number approximating the total amount of explosives used in bombing raids during the Second World War. The Secretary-General, with a clutch of cease-fire proposals in his hand from the USSR, India and Algeria, was unable to reach Baghdad through the shattered telecommunications systems. The momentum of enforcement was now irreversible. When a cautious enquiry was received from Iraq on 15 February it was treated with some contempt. Would the allied coalition be prepared to lay aside 11 out of 12 of its Resolutions following that significant one, Resolution 660 (calling for unconditional withdrawal), if it was now accepted by Baghdad? If both sides then fell back from the disputed area negotiations could begin to work for a comprehensive settlement of Kuwait's future. The White House reply was dismissive with the added hope that the people of Iraq would rise and force the deceitful leader to step aside. There was now a good deal of anxiety at the United Nations that "the logic of war" urged the coalition to go beyond Security Council Resolutions, aiming at the overthrow of Saddam Hussein and the decimation of his forces and his country. France, Italy, India,

The Gulf

Germany, Pakistan and Algeria made their discomfiture and alarm very plain. They felt that there was insufficient restraint, for instance, when in Moscow Mikhail Gorbachev had come forward with an imaginative peace plan, not too different from the French proposals, only to have it cast aside by President Bush as a rather useless "compromise".

Operation Desert Sabre, the land phase of the allied action, was launched on 24 February 1991 with an immense artillery barrage and advance on several fronts. Heated opinion in the Security Council about the needless "irresponsibility" and "recklessness" of the weight of the operation was somewhat placated when news came in of obvious preparations by the dazed Iraqis to disengage their forces from Kuwait. Hussein's "Mother of all Battles" had become the "Mother of all Retreats", it was remarked. After 100 hours of savage land war a cease-fire was effected on 28 February. The air bombardment phase of *Desert Storm* had been expected to last a few days: it had taken six weeks to accomplish. The land thrust of *Desert Sabre* had been forecast as a dogged advance taking weeks and very likely incurring heavy casualties. In fact, this last phase lasted four days and overall fewer than 400 of the coalition force lost their lives. Relief at the prompt ending of the land war was nevertheless much soured by the reports that retreating Iraqi forces had been savagely blasted for 40 hours on the "Highway to Hell". No UN mandate could ever have lent itself to this.

CEASE-FIRE AND PEACE NEGOTIATIONS

In New York on 2 March 1991 the Security Council put together a Resolution 686, which set out steps to consolidate the provisional cease-fire. All 12 UN Resolutions were to be unconditionally accepted by Iraq. Hostile and provocative actions must cease immediately. Prisoners were to be exchanged and released. The following month, Resolution 687 was issued as a detailed document in 34 sections outlining in stringent terms the conditions on which sanctions would be lifted, and a military presence by the allies ended. The sovereignty and territorial integrity of Kuwait would be guaranteed through respect for frontiers and the provision of a demilitarized zone to be under the scrutiny of UN observers. Liability for loss, damage, and injury in Kuwait was to be accepted and compensation paid. Particularly, remaining stocks of nonconventional armaments such as chemical and biological weapons had to be listed, and destroyed or removed. Due to reports that Iraq had a nuclear weapons capability, Baghdad must within 15 days notify the Secretary-General and the International Atomic Energy Agency in Vienna of any nuclear material in their possession suitable for weapons and stand by to receive urgent IAEA inspection and, if necessary, confiscation and destruction. The last measure was seen as a step towards the establishment in the Middle East of a zone free from weapons of mass destruction.

In addition to the implementation of this Resolution the Specialized Agencies would put into effect a major mobilization of resources to deal with the "deep crisis" of severe shortages of food, housing, medicine and water as well as a drastic dislocation of transport and distribution facilities throughout Iraq and Kuwait. By mid April 1991, 1,440 members of a United Nations Iran–Kuwait Observation Mission (UNIKOM) were in position to make sure that cease-fire conditions were being honoured.

IRAQ'S TREATMENT OF MINORITIES

The Gulf conflict sent shock waves round the world not only on account of its military intensity but because of Iraq's barbarous treatment of two of its minorities, the Kurds in the northern hills and the Shia Muslims who were mainly in the south. As fierce reprisals were aimed by Saddam Hussein at people he regarded as "unreliable", an ambitious UN relief plan was initiated in mid January 1991. Meeting in the Geneva office of the United Nations Disaster Relief Co-ordinator (UNDRC), 70 governments and representatives of Specialized Agencies and NGOs, together with the Red Cross, began to assemble a package of relief aid for stricken communities and for the reception of many thousands of displaced people from Iran.

The flood of refugees and the protest of many still trapped by the forces of Saddam Hussein soon acquired political importance. Security Council Resolution 688, condemning Iraq's repression of the Kurds, brought a quixotic reply from Hussein himself, namely, that he would pardon the Kurds in order that they might return home in "full security and dignity". At the time 1.5 million homeless people were in need of sustenance in areas harassed by Iraqi forces. Soon Kurdish guerrillas, *peshmerga*, were in control of 10% of Iran and from Hussein's own army some 100,000 Kurdish auxiliaries had deserted. The coalition could hardly intervene in the matter of Iraqi fratricide as no UN Resolution would countenance internal interference within the borders of a sovereign state. Despite this there were loud calls in the media and in the US Congress for an allied push "all the way up the road to deal with the Beast of Baghdad". Could members of the UN stand by and watch a progressive violation of human rights amounting to genocide?

In April 1991 the question was being asked in unusual and frustrating circumstances. Allied forces had withdrawn for the most part, leaving some 500 UN unarmed "guards" and teams of aid workers under the protective umbrella of US Air Force units flying out of Turkey. There was an obvious need to act quickly without waiting for an invitation from Baghdad, or even expecting one. In fact, statements from Saddam Hussein that the Kurds would not be harmed were ambiguous, perhaps deliberately so. Relief drops of food from the air were seen by him as unwarranted interference. On the other hand, Iraqi and UN officials agreed that a chain of UN Humanitarian Centres (UNHUCs), staffed by UN civilians, could be set up to provide food, medicine and shelter. The European Community and the German Government each contributed substantial funds.

The US and UK governments decided to act – and they did so without too close liaison with the UN Secretary-General. *Operation Provide Comfort* would set up what were termed "safe havens". This time armed men would guard the camps and the temporary accommodation contrived in shattered villages. A patchwork agreement was somehow negotiated with a very reluctant Baghdad. Over a groundswell of protest about violation of national sovereignty from many Iraqi politicians (a sensitive issue for the UN), there was put in hand an understanding that those Kurds who wished to return home (they soon numbered 250,000) might do so. Perhaps this was not so much that Iraq was willing to allow access as the realization that they had no alternative given the superiority of allied power.

Towards the end of May there were 16,000 allied troops guarding the humanitarian mission in a security zone for Kurds of some 3,600 square miles. Eventually, this garrison would be replaced by personnel from the UN and from UNHCR. Would pressure on the Kurds now be lifted? Would Saddam Hussein do this in return for the removal of sanctions that were hurting his people? Or would the Iraq government, sure that it could make its compliant populace tighten their belts to the *nth* degree, continue with dictatorial repression? Within a month or two it was evident that Baghdad would turn to flush out "renegade and adventurous traitors" in its midst – and it found them among the Shia Muslims in the south, many of them rather poor peasants who had for centuries lived in marshlands. Artillery raked their villages, the marsh vegetation was burned to smoke out 30,000 people who, if they survived, were herded into trucks and forcibly evacuated.

A UN response to pass Resolutions and despatch 50 or so monitors was considered too tame by most observers. Precedents needed to be set and maintained. "Forceful intervention" to safeguard basic human rights within another state and without their permission was an innovation, but seemed the only possible action in dire circumstances. Allied threats of air strikes were made. A "no-fly" zone was to be created south of the 32nd parallel of latitude "putting the lid on" Iraqi movements by air. What, though, would happen on the ground? Could armed intervention, going beyond a palliative of rescue, be effective and justifiable? In the end, no ground expedition was ever mounted and the strafing of the Shia Muslims went on.

Was it a crucial mistake not to have included very firm measures for respecting human rights in the extremely detailed Resolution 687 of April 1991? Most other contingencies relating to cease-fire and withdrawal and restitution were addressed in that document. The position was complicated in that there was no occupying force to oversee and underpin new constitutional safeguards. The dispossessed were extra vulnerable in that their protest was divided by allegiance to rival Kurdish parties. Saddam Hussein was able to take advantage of these divisions at the same time as he protested to the UN over the "fabricated furore" in New York and, nearer home, over the "protective interference" of an international relief mission. There was nothing much in the UN stance that was decisive either on the ground in shifting Iraqi intolerance or in the various discussions that went on. When in August 1991 the UN permitted Iraq to sell oil worth $1,600 million to buy food and other humanitarian supplies under strict UN supervision, Saddam Hussein was to oppose this, seeing it as interference in Iraq's internal affairs. The use of the money, he thought, would be controlled by the UN.

IRAQ'S NUCLEAR CAPABILITY

One more bone of contention between Iraq and the coalition was the issue of nuclear weapons capability. Certain UN member-states had information that Iraq had tried to acquire materials for a nuclear programme. This would be entirely contrary to obligations under the 1968 Non-proliferation Treaty (NPT) (see Chapter 9) to which Iraq was a signatory. Resolution 687 had called for destruction of non-conventional weapons. Was Iraq devious enough to deny or disguise illicit nuclear work, even though no nuclear weapons had been brought into the desert war? The Iraqis were reasonably co-operative at the beginning and supplied information relating to chemical, missile and civilian nuclear programmes. Inspectors from the IAEA toured the area in April 1991 and established that Iraq's entire stockpile of 98 pounds of uranium reported to them was in fact radiation-safe, some of it in bombed-out and deserted nuclear reactors, while other materials that were not assembled lay in bomb-proof bunkers.

The information about nuclear stocks, filed from Baghdad, was neither reliable nor comprehensive. The Security Council decided on 15 July to give the Iraqi Government ten days to provide full details of its weapon facilities. If it did not, renewed air strikes would be mounted by the coalition. There was a delay, followed by ugly scenes in Baghdad when UN monitors and IAEA inspectors were ordered to surrender their reports. Although they were held at gunpoint for three days they refused to give ground and eventually Iraq relented. There was great relief in the West when the IAEA final reports showed that Iraq would need at least four or five years to produce even a small arsenal of two to three weapons each year.[3]

THE CONFLICT APPRAISED

The Gulf conflict cost at least $70,000 million.[4] Regionally, the ecological consequences were disastrous. Argument over reparations and compensation was endless. The flow of oil from the Middle East declined and resulted in economic difficulties for many nations. Where the military outcome was relatively clear-cut the political and social consequences have proved turbulent. The Arab states among the 21 nations in the UN coalition have not found it easy to align themselves in peace and regrettably consider they must race for armed advantage by buying the means of war. *Shield, Sword, Storm* and *Sabre* won back desert sands, but these operations inflamed many moderate Middle East views; they reinvigorated government and public attitudes in Israel; and they condemned the PLO to despair and self-blame.

The UN was put in an embarrassing position, figuratively kicking its heels. Demonizing the conflict had clouded issues and jerked understanding into pugnacity. "Let us at him!" was scarcely a rational sentiment for dealing with an errant state. Mixed ethics, outrage and *realpolitik* on many occasions led observers to believe that a swift and heavy blanketing action to repress a delinquent would deal finally with complex political issues and somehow confer security where it was lacking. It is easy in retrospect to cast doubt and find scapegoats – yet official pronouncements from the UN have done neither. More positively, what has been learned from the 1990–1 Gulf encounter?

If the UN had been enabled in *practice* to underwrite collective and regional security through conflict resolution as *theoretically* outlined in its Charter, a number of responses might have been possible given that the Gulf operation was one of collective, enforcing intervention.

Initially, perhaps there should have been:

1. more concerted preventive diplomacy (given that intelligence from the Middle East was surely pointing to the likelihood of flashpoints);
2. possible preventive deployment of peacekeeping units to areas perceived as tense and explosive; and
3. a system of sanctions appropriately designed and consistently applied.[5]

And later, if, as suggested, earlier enforcement was seen as the only possible course of action, a coalition acting under a franchise from the UN, should have paid rigorous attention to such points as:

(a) advance goals clearly identified in the mandate (their nature, the reason for them, their timing);
(b) specific terms of engagement outlined unambiguously and adhered to by national contingents and their supplying member-states;
(c) as far as possible, the stages of the operation defined in terms of effecting cease-fire, armistice, withdrawal, disarming, safeguarding human rights through dealing with evasion and violation;
(d) indication of when an "exit strategy" could be contemplated following evaluation of the success of the operation;

(e) the terms on which the delinquent government would henceforth be regarded by the UN.

If this was action authorized by the UN then, as far as possible, full policy control had to be maintained by the UN to underpin legitimacy and credibility. There is clearly an urgent need to think out how a maxim like "forewarned is forearmed" can be applied peacefully.

NOTES

1. See R. P. H. King, *The United Nations and the Iran–Iraq War (1980–6)* (New York: Ford Foundation, 1987). G. R. Berridge, *Return to the UN* (London: Macmillan, 1991).
2. Accurate data from intelligence sources seems not to have been supplied to the UN by those powers possessing it. In any case, the UN does not have the sophisticated, round-the-clock evaluation unit that fed-in data surely requires at headquarters.
3. IAEA reports in 1995 persistent reluctance by Baghdad to disclose all activities on-site and in commercial dealings with other nuclear-supply states. The IAEA is becoming increasingly worried about the possibility of illicit nuclear development in Iran, a near neighbour to Iraq.
4. The US cost was not less than $60,000 million.
5. UN sanctions limited Iraq's capacity to re-arm. Unfortunately, they have also provided a focus for resentment and much international concern about the inevitable distress of innocent civilians.

FURTHER READING

Bullock, J. & H. Morris. *Saddam's war: the origins of the Kuwait crisis and the international response*. London: Faber, 1991.

Hiro, D. *Desert Shield to Desert Storm: the second Gulf war*. London: Paladin Books, 1992.

Johansen, R. C. The UN after the Gulf War. *World Policy Journal* 8(3), pp. 561–74, 1991.

Lewis, B. Rethinking the Middle East. *Foreign Affairs* 71(4), pp. 100–19, 1992.

Miller, J. & L. Mylroie. *Saddam Hussein and the crisis in the Gulf*. New York: Random House, 1990.

Parsons, A. The United Nations after the Gulf War. *The Round Table* 319, July 1991, pp. 265–73.

Sfiri, M. L. & C. Cerf (eds). *The Gulf War reader: history, documents, opinions*. New York: Times Books, 1991.

Stedman, J. The new interventionists. *Foreign Affairs* 71(1), pp. 1–16, 1993.

QUICK REFERENCE

Chapter Eight

THE GULF CONFLICT 1990–1

1920   Iraq under British mandate from League of Nations. Kuwait a
        dynastic sheikhdom under British protection.
1930   Britain and Iraq sign 25-year term Anglo-Iraqi Treaty to protect
        the Iraq Kingdom.
1941   Anti-British coup ousts regent and young king; Britain restores
        order after two months.
1958   Military coup overthrows pro-Western royal regime.
1963   Arab Baath Socialist Party takes over. Long-standing bad
        relations with Kuwait.
1969   Saddam Hussein moves into prominence.
1980–8 Iraq–Iran War. Kuwait leaned on by Iraq. Increasing repression
        of minorities. Iraq becomes a significant military–industrial
        complex.
1990   2 August: Iraq invades and occupies Kuwait. UN Security
        Council imposes sanctions on Iraq, declares annexation null
        and void. UN Secretary-General's inconclusive talks with Iraq.
        September: peace plans from France and Libya.
        November: US troops in Gulf now to number 430,000. UN
        Security Council authorizes "all necessary means" to uphold
        earlier Resolutions and restore peace and security unless Iraq
        fulfils before 15 January 1991.
1991   16 January: *Desert Storm* air campaign begins.
        23 February: Gorbachev peace plan eventually fails.
        24 February: *Desert Sabre* ground offensive launched.
        28 February: Cease-fire.
        April: UN peacekeeping force monitoring cease-fire. Resumed
        Iraqi repression of minorities. Relief operations mounted by UN
        and by coalition partners using safe havens and air drops.
        September: IAEA inspections under great difficulty and evasion
        by Iraq.

PART THREE

Nuclear questions

Nuclear proliferation

Briefly surveyed in this chapter, first of all, is the extent and nature of the global nuclear arsenal. Measures devised at the UN to contain nuclear spread are then outlined. There follows a description of the steps taken to fashion a non-proliferation treaty culminating in the establishment of the International Atomic Energy Agency. Next, there is discussion of problems that dog progress. Successful regional treaties are mentioned. The five-yearly review conferences from 1970 to 1990 throw light on debatable issues and the possibility of consensus. Finally come the prospects for an auspicious 1995 Review Conference. In May 1995 delegates from 175 UN member-states will converge on Geneva for the final review of the Treaty on the Non-proliferation of Nuclear Weapons (NPT). Delegates have reviewed this UN-sponsored treaty every five years since 1970 and this time they will be taking a long, hard look at the track record. Proliferation of nations' nuclear capabilities has been a fact of contemporary life since 1945. Expressed in terms of the haves and have-nots, this is a problem that will not easily go away.

THE NUCLEAR WEAPONS ARRAY

The world statistics are formidable. Military uses of nuclear energy are indicated by around 50,000 weapons of mass destruction in an armada of ships, submarines, aircraft, and in missile silos. Strategic missiles with a range of 8,000 miles and tactical ones capable of 10 miles are an intercontinental and intracontinental menace. Commercial proliferation is represented by more than 600 power and research reactors in well over 50 countries. All too obvious are the dangers of radiation, hazardous waste, malfunction, sabotage, and the diversion of the essential element, plutonium, into undesirable usage. Nuclear weapon states (NWS) are so termed if before 1 January 1967 they were in a position to test such weapons.[1] These states are the P5 members who additionally have military bases in 20 foreign countries together with some 14 other nations: India, Israel, South Africa, Pakistan, Egypt, Libya, South and North Korea, China, Argentina, Brazil, Taiwan, Iran and Iraq. Non-nuclear weapon states (NNWS) include nations with potential who might be persuaded "to go nuclear" for a variety of political and technical reasons. The facts have engendered fear for half a century. Fear is compounded by an atmosphere of secrecy ("Who's moving in next door?"), duplicity and evasion. How is this proliferation to be contained? Has the UN a cardinal responsibility and function in this area, or should it be left to bipolar negotiators? Is there a place for unilateral gestures?

The international approach to management to date reveals a number of contradictory elements.

(a) The P5 impose obligations on others yet their own enterprise is barely restrained. Indeed, they firm up nuclear commitment and their dependence on its hardware in the belief that it will underpin their security. The posture appears to be rationalized as a custodial role rather in the vein of Roosevelt's Four Policemen. After all, the motto of NATO is Peace through Strength.

(b) There is an ongoing dispute as to whether possession of nuclear capability has prevented conflict by deterring potential peace-breakers or has led to greater tension and encouraged the nuclear arms race. Those who hold the former view include the P5 peace-maintainers; those who incline to the latter are disarmers (multilateral and unilateral) on the whole. For both, viewing the problem from different ends of the telescope, the nostrum might well be "better active today than radioactive tomorrow".

(c) A mix of political and technological motives may persuade NNWS to cross the nuclear threshold. They may seek security through enhanced military standing (unfortunately this leads others to compete) or calculate that the improvement of energy sources, science and transport is clearly to their advantage. Developing states, poorly resourced, will see this as an inalienable right.

(d) Control of proliferation becomes a guarded reduction or limitation of what there is (NWS) rather than a vigorous and progressive elimination of what there might be (NNWS). An instance of this is the July 1991 Strategic Arms Reduction Treaty (START), which reduced strategic weapons by 20% but stocking, trials and emplacement continued.

(e) Proliferation is increasingly understood not so much as a failure to manage or abort a global spread but as a failure to deal with its incidence in politically sensitive areas such as the Middle East, Latin America and Eastern Europe, where regional instability is growing.

(f) Control may actually increase danger as nations, prohibited from spreading horizontally, resort to trials and tests and modification, which is a form of vertical proliferation. This is a charge often levelled at NWS.

MEASURES TO CONTAIN NUCLEAR SPREAD

Nuclear proliferation spreads like a rash. Over 40 years ago US President Dwight Eisenhower proclaimed the need of "atoms for peace". Undoubtedly, harnessing nuclear energy confers great benefits that should be denied to no nation. The obvious problem is to contrive vigilant and progressive means of verification and control to which all may subscribe. After years of intense discussion two great steps towards control of proliferation have been taken through the agency of the UN: the 1957 foundation of the IAEA and the 1968 Non-proliferation Treaty.

In July 1957 the IAEA was set up to cope with two important tasks. First, to seek to organize control of atomic energy and regulate its contribution to peace, health and prosperity in global terms, secondly to prevent "seepage" or misapplication of nuclear knowledge into military and unauthorized channels. The first responsibility is addressed through establishment of standards for radiation protection, and codes of practice to do with laboratory research, production, transport, storage of materials and equipment, management of waste, and health and safety of personnel. A databank at the IAEA headquarters in Vienna has information on almost every aspect of nuclear science and technology. Liaison is maintained with Specialized Agencies such as WHO, UNESCO, FAO, the World Meteorological Organization (WMO) and a host of research institutes, governments and commercial plants, libraries, universities and hospitals. The second responsibility, that of preventive control, is put into force through safeguards devised and applied to forestall illegitimate "diversion" into harmful channels. The safeguards system is based on audit, report and on-site inspection by IAEA staff. By the end of 1988 there were 168 safeguard agreements with 99 nations. Yet, somehow, this system of incentives and penalties had to be built into a treaty that would demand the agreement of signing nations.

Following the detonation of two atomic bombs over Japan in 1945 the possible threat of nuclear warfare exercised the minds of General Assembly delegates on numerous occasions. Understandably, while the P5 were all stern in their condemnation of illicit nuclear activity, it was conceded that the US would be unwilling to relinquish its monopoly of stock unless it was sure that no other state would ever pose a threat. Correspondingly, the USSR, already anxious about the armed might of a capitalist world, sought also to narrow the distance between actuality and potential and called for nuclear-free zones to be scheduled for strategic areas in Europe and Asia. Western Powers, that is, the US, the UK, France and Canada, preferred the conclusion of a treaty to ban the dissemination of nuclear weapons by NWS and any acquisition of such weapons by NNWS. Unhelpfully, on every occasion that one of the superpowers or any other state – such as France, UK, Ireland, India or Sweden – proposed measures to limit existing nuclear arsenals and to contain the spread to other countries, there intervened ideological arguments and the vexed question of who belonged to which alliance.

TOWARDS A NON-PROLIFERATION TREATY

In 1959 the General Assembly proposed that a Ten Nation Disarmament Committee work out possibilities of international agreement where NWS would refrain from transferring nuclear weapons or materials to NNWS who, in turn, would desist from manufacture. Once more the USSR was to block a resolution fearful that the US might retain nuclear arms within the NATO alliance. Two years later, the Secretary-General was asked to investigate the conditions under which NNWS might enter into reciprocal arrangements. Inevitably, pressure grew for a non-proliferation treaty that would be not just an end in itself but an integral component of a wider disarmament programme. Non-aligned states, most of them NNWS, were in favour of this step. However, three obstacles to acceptance of such a treaty remained. In the first place, the USSR always feared that the US nuclear monopoly would persist; it had little confidence in the readiness of its American rival to halt production and testing. Secondly, some NNWS were looking for assurance that by renouncing these arms they would not then be disadvantaged militarily and so be vulnerable to nuclear threat, and further, that they would not be bereft of the regional benefits of armed alliance. Even more importantly, such states craved acknowledgement of their right to employ atomic fission for peaceful purposes, otherwise they would suffer industrial and commercial handicap. They had strong reasons for doubting whether the NWS would be willing to share their "know-how", but rather would exploit their monopolistic position.

In the mid-1960s the great-powers attempted to clarify differences as to the acquisition, transfer and deployment of nuclear weapons and the associated problems of verification and standardization of civilian and military procedures. Draft treaties were tabled one after another in an effort to reduce loopholes. Proliferation endangering peace should be prevented through the principle of allowing all to have free access in good faith to nuclear knowledge and to technical expertise. To this end the IAEA in Vienna would employ its safeguards to underpin the obligations of a treaty and to deal with malpractice without curbing legitimate economic and technical development in the NNWS. Indeed, such progress could be facilitated through information exchange and technical co-operation.

By 1968, after a decade of discussion and speculation, the outline of a non-proliferation treaty (the NPT) was clear; it was opened for signature on 1 July 1968 (eventually coming into force on 5 March 1970). First to sign were three NWS (the US, the UK and the USSR) and more than 50 other nations. Gradually, the number of signatories was to build up to 175. Fundamentally, the NPT was to have two clear objectives: to prevent nuclear proliferation and to encourage the peaceful use of atomic energy. (These are in reversed order of priority to those of the IAEA Statute.) The NWS undertook not to transfer nuclear weapons to others, nor to receive such a transfer, nor to provide fissionable material to any NNWS save under strict IAEA safeguards. Inducement was the other side of the coin. Nothing was to affect adversely the "inalienable right" of states to develop nuclear energy for peaceful purposes. Moreover, all signatories were expected to go further in sharing information and equipment "with due consideration for the needs of the developing areas of the world", thus reducing the incentive to act arbitrarily. Article VI of the Treaty is crucial: it links members' intention to negotiate a cessation of the nuclear arms race with a general commitment to pursue complete disarmament.

The text of the NPT in fact contains two points that might offer loopholes in general control of proliferation. First, nothing in this Treaty is to be held to affect the right of any group of states to conclude regional treaties to deal with the presence of nuclear weapons in certain areas – this is reminiscent of the Article in the UN Charter that concedes the right to self-defence precautions by a state. Secondly, Article X of the NPT allows that, "Each Party shall in exercising its national sovereignty have the right to withdraw from the Treaty if it decides that extraordinary events, related to the subject matter of this Treaty, have jeopardized the supreme interests of its country". Could not this right, if so exercised, negate the whole purpose of the anti-proliferation agreement? Finally, member-states were to meet every five years at a review conference. After 25 years (i.e. in 1995), there must be a decision as to whether the NPT should continue in force indefinitely or should be extended for a certain period or periods.

THE IAEA AS A CONTROL MECHANISM

Central to the effectiveness of the NPT was the IAEA responsibility to conclude safeguards with the NNWS. For the application of these safeguards and the inspection of a state's facilities by inspectors four main steps were envisaged.

(a) IAEA experts were to scrutinize existing and projected installations testing for effective control.

(b) The IAEA would examine detailed day-to-day records of plant operation, inventories, and the use of materials, which each state must keep and submit.

(c) Periodic reports would also be called for from states.

(d) IAEA inspectors were to carry out site checks.

The NPT has changed its role in 32 years. At the outset each superpower sought a means to prevent its rival from disseminating nuclear information and weaponry to allies and satellites. On the other hand, developing nations hoped to see the treaty helping to disarm NWS while facilitating their own access to peaceful applications of nuclear energy. Gradually, for the superpowers, the treaty would rein in the supposed nuclear ambitions of certain states by castigating their failure to observe an international norm. More recently, as old security patterns have changed dramatically, the NPT is seen as reinforcing stability and as a bulwark against unregulated proliferation. What seems to be the most useful approach with a treaty such as the NPT is to work for consensus on the undesirability of nuclear proliferation, rather than hold the negative line of discriminating between states and attempting to deny materials, technology and production facilities. After all, these components and skills can be employed for legitimate civil purposes and, on the brink of developing alternative energy resources, few states are likely to tolerate external embargo.

A particularly difficult problem is that of the IAEA dealing with such undertakings in the nuclear cycle as marketing of uranium, reprocessing spent fuel rods and developing breeder reactors for producing plutonium. These are operations that a state might legitimately and profitably carry on, but that lend themselves to illicit export and acquisition by "irresponsible" third parties. Meanwhile, the nuclear industry in a number of countries has bridled at international restrictions on the export of technology, fuel and components where investment, contracts and sales are endangered. Thus, a non-proliferation treaty has somehow to discriminate across a spectrum of activity where some facets are illegal and threatening to peace and others are held to be necessary for industrial progress. Collateral agreements of a political nature seem to be more effective than mainly technical criteria. One ingenious suggestion occasionally heard at Geneva is that if access to nuclear energy is being made more difficult for developing countries, the NWS might offer economic and technical assistance to aid their expansion in non-nuclear areas.

PROLIFERATION CONTINUES TODAY

After 25 years the sad fact is that nuclear proliferation is still very evident. It is true that the IAEA has been supported politically so that no violations by NNWS have been reported, and the existing safeguards are better than nothing at all. On the other hand, we have a group of nations ready to cross the nuclear threshold. The NNWS are critical of the hegemony and hypocrisy of the P5 and they deplore the hesitation of the NWS to work conclusively for the cause of general disarmament as called for in Chapter VI of the NPT. They rely on the inadequate 1963 Partial Test Ban Treaty (PTBT, see Chapter 10). Doubts about the effectiveness of verification are constantly being voiced, as is the assertion, mainly by NGOs, that all fissile processing, peaceful or military, endangers the quality of environments. The disastrous happenings at Three Mile Island in 1979 and at Chernobyl in 1986, which had led to significant leakage and radiation fallout, and uncertainty about some installations in Europe are very much in mind.

Especially worrying is the fact that some states possessing nuclear weapons, or in the stages of developing them, have not ratified the NPT, and among these are India, Pakistan, Israel, North Korea, Iran and Iraq. However, the first two are considering setting up a nuclear-free zone. Safeguards instituted by the IAEA have a clear meaning on paper; in practice they have to rely on selective monitoring where quantification is erratic and not very dependable. In no way does violation of safeguards bring severe sanctions as a consequence. Safeguards, after all, are only technical attempts to verify; they cannot punish transgressors. There is an ever-present temptation to conceal "diversion" of material assigned to peaceful use into weapons-grade stock.

Adequate verification is, of course, at the heart of controlling proliferation. UN conferences frequently present this operation as comprising three stages: monitoring-observation, followed by analysis of recorded data, then judgement as to capacity, trends and intent. The entire weapons cycle has to be examined, namely, testing, procurement, deployment, maintenance and obsolescence. Short-, medium- and long-term objectives must be clear and agreed. Stages of readiness in delivery systems, launch programmes and arming of missiles must be logged. Unannounced on-site "challenge inspections" may verify effectively the state of production facilities and deployed weaponry. Much more troublesome is an audit of finance, training and the deployment of employed personnel. Given the intricacy of determining significant noncompliance with the NPT, the problems of establishing confidence in detection, and of dealing with evasion, the most the UN can hope for is a realistic reduction of risk rather than idealistically expecting watertight elimination. Recent technical advances in satellites and electronics have made clandestine enrichment and recycling of nuclear materials easier to detect. Summit negotiation between Washington and Moscow has led to cut-down weapon stocks and withdrawal of armed weapons between former adversaries.[2] Among smaller nations what is not adequately safeguarded is the extent to which potential rivals may be tempted to adopt a nuclear weapons posture.

NON-PROLIFERATION TREATIES: INNOVATION AND REVIEW

Despite very real perplexities in the limitation of nuclear proliferation much has been achieved through patient negotiation at the UN. The 1959 Antarctic Treaty applied a denuclearization regime to an uninhabited area. Prohibition there has been observed scrupulously. Five years later 17 Latin American states adopted a similar measure for a densely populated area. Since then, 23 nations have signed the Treaty of Tlatelolco, although ratification of the process has been tardy in some cases. Fissile material was to be processed for peaceful purposes only. A supervisory agency would ensure that in no circumstances could the edict be evaded. A further safeguard was that a number of extra-continental states, mainly NWS, pledged to respect and guarantee the military denuclearization of Latin America. In 1985 the Treaty of Rarotonga established a huge nuclear-free zone in the South Pacific. Unfortunately, France has not acceded to this Treaty because of its testing programme on a Pacific atoll, nor have Britain and the US, whose warships visit the area.

An international regime to govern the uses of the seabed beyond territorial waters (generally, outside a 12-mile offshore limit) was initiated in 1972. On this occasion 102 states promised to keep these areas nuclear-free by desisting from emplacing nuclear weapons or any means of mass destruction there. The principle of ensuring safe access to what today would be termed "global commons" was similarly applied to outerspace. In the mid 1950s there was heightened concern about the race for management of outerspace where exploration and experiment might easily degenerate into unbridled military proliferation. Nuclear powers already committed to vastly expensive space programmes were reluctant, understandably, to abort them, despite their obvious dangers to world peace. Two decades of discussion centred on the twin objectives of preventing violation yet encouraging scientific and economic enterprise. The NPT had similar aims. By the end of 1984 the Treaty on the Peaceful Uses of Outerspace, which had come into force in 1967, now had 113 states acceding to it.

A brief look at the review process associated with the NPT highlights achievements and points to issues still unresolved. Meeting in Geneva for a month every five years the review conferences appear to have been most occupied with three major obligations bearing on member-states: working for disarmament, examining compliance and maintaining IAEA safeguards, and providing for members' security. If, it was asked in 1970, the NPT were to help strike the right balance between obligations and responsibilities, how was it that NWS appeared satisfied with a measure of arms limitation when NNWS saw them as still possessing and refurbishing their exclusive nuclear armouries? There was an element of self-righteousness in the NWS concern to recruit adherence to the NPT by the have-nots and to put safeguards into position when, in the eyes of many non-aligned states, there was an urgent need to plug gaps and to deal more firmly with evasions.

At the 1975 conference disquiet was voiced as to the vague definition of just when proliferation menaced a nation's security. At what point in the weapon cycle was a threat so critical that it would justify the strongest measures to combat it? Could this be done always by the IAEA? This anxiety surfaced again at the 1980 Review Conference when it became clear that a lack of universal adherence to the NPT lessened its credible implementation. There were too many nations with nuclear capabilities "on the outside". In addition, those countries in the magic ring were still insufficiently vigorous in slowing down the nuclear arms race. Dissatisfaction focused above all on the extent to which IAEA safeguards were lagging behind the fast-growing complexity of nuclear fuel cycling. It was vital for the IAEA to be able to distinguish accurately between peaceful and military production. Putting a blanket embargo on nuclear exports was a clumsy way to limit proliferation and would benefit nobody.

Once more, in 1985, the Geneva conference pointed to steady nuclear pro-liferation sabotaging the assurances offered by the NPT and making nuclear disarmament even more remote. Members were reminded of a Security Coun-cil Resolution of June 1968 declaring that aggression with nuclear weapons or its threat should be met by a firm response from the P5, all of whom were NWS. In what respects could this still be taken as a form of positive guarantee? Sev-eral NNWS, while hailing such a firm assurance, preferred a "negative" guaran-tee – a pledge by NWS that they would never use nuclear arms against a NNWS. Surely, the NNWS argued, in renouncing nuclear weaponry they were entitled to expect an effective system of security guarantees. Was a wide-ranging con-centration on general prohibition not possible? Progress since then in this re-spect has proved disappointing. The United States and other Western nations have preferred to issue their own statement of assurance rather than collec-tively affirm a general Declaration. In their view, many varied circumstances, locations and politics influence security perspectives and that cuts the ground away from any universal set of principles. This narrowness of viewpoint is at odds with UN ideals of working for collective security.

The last point occasioned a lively debate at the 1990 Review Conference. Nigeria and some other nations expressed yet again the anxiety of NNWS that forgoing the nuclear option as a consequence of NPT membership might expose them to nuclear intimidation. This was as much in the minds of certain European states, formerly components of the USSR, as it was for African and Asian members. The extent of any wide-ranging security guarantees that Brit-ain and the United States might be willing to offer was uncertain, as neither power had opposed the NATO admission that nuclear weapons might have to be used as "weapons of last resort". It was proposed that in Geneva the UN Conference on Disarmament should give this whole matter its fullest, urgent attention. Also at the 1990 meeting different interpretations of the NPT resur-faced. The Treaty should make it easier for developing countries to extend their energy resources under safeguard. But was the Treaty basically restricting this resource as a vital means of stemming proliferation? Some 70 non-aligned states detected contradictions in the NPT and deplored its ineffectiveness. On the other hand, while in the past non-alignment signified neutrality in the con-text of armed East and West, the recent fragmentation of the old Cold War po-larity had disposed some states towards fresh assertiveness of their "inalienable right" to exploit peaceful uses of nuclear energy despite the tre-mendous costs and possible environmental damage.

The meeting was further regarded as the eleventh hour for airing disillu-sionment over the NPT's failure to effect tangible nuclear disarmament. Not surprisingly, the conference was unable to agree on a final Declaration. The final review in 1995 would be concerned with strategy rather than with tac-tics, as well as the burning question: should the NPT be extended? Finally, at the 1990 Review Conference political controversy flared. Arab states con-demned Israel for building a nuclear stockpile and France and the US for reputedly assisting this process. France and Israel, they said, should sign the NPT. It was not lost on delegates that Israel feels secure in its own nest, as it were, surrounded by Arab states who have acceded to the NPT. On the other hand, there was great relief and satisfaction that South Africa, criticized at previous review conferences, now felt able to sign the Treaty. Provided other states in southern Africa acceded, South Africa would initiate negotiations with the IAEA in February 1991 and also look at the feasibility of a nuclear-free zone in the region.

PROSPECTS FOR FUTURE CONTROL

What are the prospects for the NPT Review Conference in 1995? Certainly, in Geneva, there will be intensive discussion about how to deal with states such as Iraq and North Korea who have been dilatory in concluding safeguards agreements with the IAEA. These two cases illustrate how the UN and the IAEA attempt to deal with proliferation. Iraq has been a party to the NPT since October 1969. It is generally assumed that while Iraq did not have the means to produce a significant amount of nuclear material, it may be able to do so by 1996 having combed the world for uranium. Inspection by the IAEA has been impeded on several occasions. The IAEA and the Security Council have been pressing hard for the admittance of inspectors, for Saddam Hussein's compliance with NPT obligations, and for the destruction of any weapons-producing installations. Speculation and unease continues.[3]

North Korea has also signed the NPT (on 12 December 1985), but reneges on the clear obligations of the Treaty. The government in Pyongyang has recently refused to conclude a safeguards agreement with the IAEA unless the US formally guarantees not to use nuclear weapons against it and on condition that US holding forces in the region are withdrawn.[4] Even more than in Iraq, there is a history here of evasion and duplicity. Nobody seems to know how the North Koreans originally acquired their nuclear knowledge and materials. IAEA inspectors visited the area frequently and found evidence of activity that could be transformed from civil to military applications, although the state has denied this intention. Pyongyang from time to time has conducted discussions with the UN and has even suggested that a nuclear-free zone be established, guaranteed by China, the US and South Korea.

In March 1993, North Korea, exasperated by IAEA inspections and by the proximity of US forces on large-scale manoeuvres, notified the IAEA of its intention to withdraw from the NPT. In summer 1993, President Clinton, visiting South Korea, warned the North that if it persisted in its nuclear weapons programme, the United States was ready to take "appropriate countermeasures". These, at least, would be sanctions in conjunction with the UN. In summer 1994 there was more ingenuity as well as stringency in the negotiations with an errant regime. Former US President Jimmy Carter and UN advisors, visiting Kim Il-Sung in North Korea, held talks that featured an offer by the US, Russia and South Korea to provide technology for, among other things, a nuclear electricity grid, in return for an unambiguous commitment by North Korea to abide by the NPT. Characteristic of the nuclear age is the political manoeuvre of angling for diplomatic recognition by posing a nuclear threat, which in this case is of some concern to neighbours such as South Korea, Japan and China.

The chief issue in respect of nuclear proliferation, and most aspects of disarmament negotiations, is the mutual exploration of security guarantees. The 1995 Review Conference will have this prominently on its agenda. The problem of offering negative guarantees might be met with a model scheme for security assurance that could be modified if necessary by member-states to suit the circumstances of diverse regions. To lend substance to such assurances some form of demilitarized zone might be set up, along the lines of the Treaty of Tlatelolco, in "sensitive" areas such as Africa and the Middle East. A programme using mainly technical safeguards has to go beyond the inspectors' first objectives of "transparency" and verification. Prediction of future behaviour is naturally beyond the reach of customary safeguards. Yet there will have to be experiments with early warning systems and confidence-building measures if the NPT is to be solidly underpinned.

One other problem for those conferring in 1995 will be the growing smuggling of plutonium and, also, the brain-drain of scientists and technicians from the former USSR. The old monolithic bogey of the Communist bomb has given way to an insidious form of proliferation, less apocalyptic, but very difficult for any international body to detect and control.[5]

Perhaps in the twenty-fifth year of the NPT the crux of review will be seen as the matter of nuclear testing. Too much time has been spent on engineering short-term and partial measures, moratoria and other intermediate steps. Fresh thinking is required. A comprehensive test ban (CTB) would signal the determination of the negotiators to concentrate their energies on definitive and lasting forms of arms control. It would do something to allay the fears and resentments of NNWS. It could do much towards advancing the intentions of the NPT and, while not necessarily prolonging the Treaty indefinitely, it could make possible, say, another 25 years. But the whole business of nuclear testing is the concern of the following chapter.

NOTES

1. The official distinction between nuclear weapon states (NWS) and non-nuclear weapon states (NNWS) uses state of potential in 1967 as criterion. For the sake of brevity in this chapter the acronym is used even in reference to the position of

states before 1967.

2. Nuclear disengagement in 1995 is taking the form of "detargetting" where Russia, the US and France no longer have strategic nuclear missiles aimed at targets in any other country. Also, the dismantling and removal of land-based strategic missiles proceeds under START I and II of 1992 and 1993.

3. In April 1991 the Security Council authorized creation of a special commission with mandate to destroy and render harmless all weapons of mass destruction in Iraq. Monitoring of nuclear potential was done in collaboration with IAEA. Iraqi compliance with inspections and report findings remains erratic, but the nature and extent of Iraq's nuclear potential is now reasonably verifiable.

4. Dialogue continues in 1995 between North and South Korea, the US and IAEA. Inspection rights and monitoring accuracy are still not satisfactorily assured.

5. Following disintegration of the USSR, the brain-drain remains a difficult problem. In 1995 an international science and technology centre is at work in Russia to fund and co-ordinate peaceful employment of former Soviet military scientists. The EU, Russia, US and Japan are the sponsors.

FURTHER READING

Boskey, B. & M. Willrich (eds). *Nuclear proliferation: prospects for control*. New York: Dunellan, 1970.

Bundy, M., D. J. Crowe, S. Drell. Reducing nuclear danger. *Foreign Affairs* 72(2), pp. 140–55, 1993.

Carpenter, T. G. Closing the nuclear umbrella. *Foreign Affairs* 73(2), pp. 8–14, 1994.

Deutsch, J. M. The new nuclear threat. *Foreign Affairs* 71(4), pp. 120–34, 1992.

Dunn, L. A. & H. Kahn. *Trends in nuclear proliferation 1975–95*. New York: Hudson Institute, 1976.

O'Neil, R. & D. N. Schwartz. *Hedley Bull on arms control*. London: Macmillan, 1987.

Simpson, J. Nuclear non-proliferation in the post-Cold War era. *International Affairs* 70(1), pp. 17–41, 1994.

Chapter Nine

NUCLEAR PROLIFERATION

1945   Atomic bombing of Japan.
1946   UN sets up Atomic Energy Commission.
1957   IAEA instituted in Vienna.
1959   Ten-Nation Disarmament Committee at work on control of nuclear proliferation.
        Antarctic Treaty.
1963   PTBT.
1967   States able to test nuclear weapons now NWS; those not able are NNWS.
        Treaty of Tlatelolco.
1968   In July NPT. Comprehensive measures of nuclear weapons control.
1970   IAEA convenes NPT Review Conference – to be held every five years until 1995.
1967   Treaty on Peaceful Uses of Outerspace.
1972   Treaty to keep ocean beds nuclear free.
1985   Treaty of Rarotonga and a nuclear-free zone (NFZ) in South Pacific.
1991   START I Treaty signed.
1995   NPT Final Review Conference in Geneva: 175 UN member-states expected to attend in May. Crucial decision as to NPT extension.

CHAPTER TEN

Nuclear testing

At the Non-proliferation Review Conference in 1990, several states, parties to the NPT, intimated that they would oppose any lengthy extension to the Treaty if the issue of nuclear testing remained unresolved. While the increase in radioactive fallout was now considerably less than hitherto, the spread of nuclear weaponry, or the spread of its potential, was clearly discernible. States such as North Korea and Iraq were certainly seen as contenders for a place in the nuclear circle. Research and development were going ahead whether in the laboratory or out on the proving grounds. Nuclear testing must be checked. In 1990, 27 years had elapsed since a partial test ban treaty. Testing in the atmosphere, in outerspace, under the sea, had all been prohibited under the terms of the 1963 Treaty but not testing underground. Half a century of talking had not brought any definitive end to nuclear testing and the likelihood of proliferation. How had this state of affairs come about? What had delayed decision? Who had been participants in the disputation – at the UN and elsewhere? And was the UN the forum best suited to the resolution of the problem of testing? In 1995, these questions still need answering.

A description of an early attempt at test control opens this chapter. The following decades each had a distinctive hallmark, such as growing public concern met by earnest UN involvement, the interlinked bluff and crisis of superpower "brinksmanship", the cautious progress of trials and treaties, and the equally careful resort to moratoria. In conclusion, a long, hard look is taken at the difficult approach to a comprehensive test ban.

EARLY ATTEMPTS AT CONTROL

The stop–go saga of international efforts to deal with nuclear testing is disheartening but instructive. The issues are dramatic. When in 1946 US statesman Bernard Baruch addressed the UN, he spoke of the choice we all must make between "the quick and the dead". Granted, the use of nuclear energy would confer great benefits, but against nuclear weaponry there was no defence. We must reach beyond initial terror to a programme of enforceable sanctions. International law must have teeth. Nor must we be fobbed off by considerations of narrow sovereignty. This impressive declaration addressed the need of disclosure and control in the widest sense: it did not mention testing the product. The stakes were high: peace or war. President Truman had thanked his God for a device that would replace the old diplomatic gamesmanship with the new "brinksmanship" armed with a peacekeeping and freedom-ensuring deterrent. The negotiating process was stern but varied. At the UN there was public wrangling, earnest argument, evasion, propaganda posturing, and what J. Robert Oppenheimer termed the evident reluctance of the powerful to share their power and their secrets.[1] The participants were diverse – the Presidents of the US and France, the British Prime Minister, the leaders of China and the Soviet Union, flanked by their advisors, UN delegates, clergymen, philosophers, a phalanx of scientists, and non-governmental groups representing the man in the street.

THE UN SCENARIO: CONCERN IN THE 1950s

Seen from the UN building in New York, the attempt to deal with nuclear testing is a scene of confrontation, *détente*, renewed confrontation, further *détente* and accommodation. As the 1950s dawned, Hiroshima had already demonstrated that a comparatively small weapon could unleash the equivalent of 20,000 tonnes of TNT. The ongoing nuclear testing at Bikini Atoll and in Australia clearly proved the damage to health and to the environment, with the prospect of greater hazards as weapons entered the megaton range. In 1954 Prime Minister Jawaharlal Nehru of India appealed to the UN Secretary-General for a standstill agreement on testing. Twelve months later, at Bandung in South East Asia, a group of Third World leaders endorsed this call. As if in response, the Soviet Union proposed the banning of tests with emphasis on prohibition. The West emphasized security as the prime need with a move then towards reduction and eventual prohibition.

The UN General Assembly of 1957 listened uneasily to a wealth of scientific advocacy for a test ban. Afro-Asian nations clamoured for firm action. A voluntary ban was put into effect, albeit reluctantly, by the nuclear powers accompanied by an orchestration of tripartite talks, General Assembly reverberations and private discussions in UN corridors. In New York and in Washington there was an all too public collision of science and the military.

Geneva was to be the venue for talks scheduled for 1958 between the US, Britain and the USSR under UN auspices. Motives among participants were mixed, yet there was an obvious wish to explore the grounds for agreement. The West, this time, was dropping its insistence on a test ban as an integral part of a general disarmament measure. Was this a hard-faced negotiating position, waiting to see how far the other side would move, or did it reflect domestic pressures? Again, the USSR gave priority to a test ban, although both it and the US had accelerated a testing programme ahead of the moratorium they were to observe. A particularly difficult problem was deciding who should monitor high-altitude tests needing aerial surveillance. A foolproof control system was the objective for Western nations not trusting Moscow. The possibility of 180 control posts manned by expert observers was greeted with little warmth by the Russians. Differences in the approach of the two superpowers could be deduced from the make-up of their expert delegations. Washington sent mainly scientists and technocrats; those from Moscow were much more politically briefed. Ideological differences made the going over four years exceedingly rough despite the mediating role of the UN Secretariat. What finally caused an impasse was, first of all, US "decoupling" work, which was to use low-yield explosive devices detonated in large underground chambers (surely an obvious loophole that could be exploited by both sides?). Secondly, the cautious optimism of President Eisenhower and his contingent meeting in Geneva was embarrassingly shattered for all by the U2 spy plane incident which enraged the Kremlin. Added to the anger of the Soviet Premier Nikita Khrushchev over the UN enterprise in the Congo and the West's position in Berlin, this was enough to wreck any prospect of a test ban accord for 1960.

BLUFF AND CRISIS IN THE 1960s

The Administration of a new US President, J. F. Kennedy, began hopefully in 1961 with a strong commitment to a test ban linked to a general disarmament move. For the Russians a verified ban alone would never be enough. More suspicious than ever, the USSR dug itself into an unmoveable position and both sides put aside the procedure of a moratorium and resorted to testing once more.[2] UN initiatives were now deemed urgent and the General Assembly formed an 18-nation Disarmament Committee to meet in Geneva as a new multilateral forum. Inititally this body was uncertain about the accuracy and reliability of any complicated monitoring arrangement that would be internationally manned. It was reassured, to some extent, by the opinion of a group of eight uncommitted nations, who echoed, in fact, the conclusion reached by the US and USSR that monitoring systems installed separately on national territories and supported by conventional intelligence activity were an adequate safeguard against violation of a ban. Two speculations especially haunted the minds of Western delegates, namely, that the USSR was seeking by any means to delay US testing while preparing a programme to compensate for its own technical inadequacy and that, in any case, the USSR would be firmly resistant to the notion of "capitalist" observers entering its territory.

Stalemate might well have lasted had it not been for the 1962 Cuban Missile Crisis. This brush with death and the "eyeballing" of two Presidents seems to have been a powerful impetus for discussion. Bluff and mistrust took second place to a show of compromise that had the USSR at last agreeing to on-site visits, say, three or so, and to the installation of "black boxes" (automatic seismic detectors). The West replied in a series of number-swapping exercises that failed to resolve gaps. For Washington technical aspects of the testing problem were uppermost; for Moscow the necessity was still political provisions. Unhelpfully, the missile programmes of both sides began to accelerate. However, apart from their contacts at the UN, direct communication between Washington and Moscow was improved markedly the following year with the provision of a "hot line". A test ban was attained finally in August 1963. The first signatories of the Partial Test Ban Treaty (PTBT) were followed by 116 others, although both China and France stayed away. Most of those present that August must have sensed that bluffs were being called even though the exclusion of underground weapons testing was a concession to the military. The monthly *Bulletin of the Atomic Scientists* always printed on its cover a "doomsday clock", a symbolic warning of the shortness of time before mutual destruction might ensue. Now the PTBT, so the *Bulletin* said, set the clock hands back to 12 minutes to midnight. Any failure to realize the promise of the Treaty would once more bring the hands back to four minutes. President Kennedy saw the Treaty as "a shaft of light cut into the darkness". He and UN Secretary-General U. Thant earnestly conferred about the possible conversion of a partial treaty into a full one, although sadly that was not to be. It was true that the preamble to the treaty in banning all explosions save those underground went some way towards discourage testing in all environments. Slowing down the arms race must surely pave the way for further control agreements and definitely reduce proliferation. Nonetheless, the optimism of the moment was soured by underlying mistrust and the evident determination of the Treaty principals to hold on to (and even strengthen) their nuclear monopoly. While delegates in the UN building might cheer, there was concern in Washington (and distantly in allied London) that the US Senate might delay the PTBT ratification in the hope of an eventual comprehensive treaty. A partial treaty was not an impregnable safeguard. (The treaties so resoundingly accomplished by the UN between 1967 and 1972 on outerspace, non-proliferation, Tlatelolco, biological weapons and the seabed, were all to prove hostage, in fact, to renewed nuclear weapons testing.)

THE 1970s: TRIALS AND TREATIES

The phase of the-morning-after-the-party has lasted 32 years. The public may have been reassured, even lulled into complacency. Yet if fallout were reduced amid signs that common interests dispelled hostility and encouraged compromise, the nuclear arsenals continued to grow. In some quarters it was thought that the rapid accession to the treaty meant that strategic realism prevailed over humane considerations and feathered the caps of leading politicians and their compliant nuclear experts. Both East and West, if this were so, could accumulate political capital with scant technical loss. Limited in name and in nature, the PTBT might be seen as largely a holding operation. Nations could use the theatre of the UN General Assembly to stage ritualistic acts of support or condemnation while the real drama was acted out elsewhere.

A number of geopolitical facts diminished the effect of the Treaty's shaft of light. For the US there was a "lead" to be kept in Europe where "miniaturized" tactical weaponry and the 96% "clean" bomb of Edward Teller would be of use to NATO. The USSR, on the other hand, looked westwards to the fear of revanchist Germany and eastwards to a dissenting China. In each case a permanently disabling ban would freeze advantage in a military sense, although politically it might recruit hostile public opinion. Scientific technology also raised intrusive elements. Seismic detection instruments located externally could now distinguish weapons tests from earthquakes and keep tabs on a nation's observance of the Treaty. Even so, it was possible to get significant information from legitimate, underground testing, and in that process to use relatively low-yield materials. In the United States the Chiefs of Staff and some voices in Congress approved large subsidies for research into the hydrogen bomb. Finally, there were domestic "difficulties" that beset a national leader whether democratically he has to enlist the support of Administration or Parliament or whether dictatorially he may take more risks. In this connection there were those who regarded open encounter at the UN as something too public, if not irreversible, and who would have preferred secretive dealings between diplomats and soldiers. The PTBT required member-states to be accountable even if it did not restrain strategic impulses. Hardline advisors in the White House and Kremlin seemed to accept their masters' need to play to the UN gallery in New York, most particularly to take account of the fairly steady pressure of Third World countries. Keeping powder dry to meet the exigencies of an unstable world consigned a comprehensive test ban to the pending tray (where it has languished for more than 30 years).

Two points, above all, lent force to the arguments outlined above. Even in the UN chamber they were frequently and explicitly stated by nations. In the first place, most states with responsibility for effective defence (a duty endorsed, after all, by Article 51 of the UN Charter) thought it prudent to maintain and increase strong conventional capabilities as a prerequisite to substantial nuclear reductions. (This to some presented the paradox of a measure of nuclear disarmament being conditional on a thrust of rearmament.) Secondly, given that there was no possibility of returning to a pre-nuclear Golden Age, it was the duty of "responsible" governments to provide resources to enhance security even if this involved the stocking of nuclear arms in a grand effort to persuade "irresponsible" governments to act sensibly. Negotiations, although long drawn-out, and certainly if they had the patronage of the UN, were means to a distant end. The slim logic of this position was too often confounded by the artifice of testing weapons that were retained and denied to others while proclaiming an intention never to use them or, at least, never to use them first. From every angle the PTBT was clearly a scheme of negotiated arms control (in a very literal sense) without at all being a provision for disarmament. What seemed all too obvious, again at the UN, was that the major powers resorted to posture and feint in order to secure and maintain strategic advantages. Even a short moratorium was not disadvantageous in that scientific personnel and expertise were not displaced. Politically, this state of affairs had a "geotechnical" spin-off, namely, that keeping the lead necessitated a redefinition and redirection of effort into more sophisticated weapons and launching systems as well as the supporting research and development. The nuclear powers were best able to afford the extra costs and retraining; thus their monopoly position was strengthened.

During the 1970s and 1980s, whenever there were signs of *détente*, negotiations for a more complete test ban ran through two channels: that of the UN and that of turbulent bilateral negotiation. In 1970, for instance, with the disconcerting frequency and extent of underground testing plainly seen, there was a sustained campaign by the UN Disarmament Commission to table a proposal for a Comprehensive Test Ban Treaty (CTBT). This body, representating all member-states and meeting each May in New York, examines General Assembly Resolutions and decisions and reports back to its parent body. At the same time, a less unwieldy group, the UN Conference on Disarmament, resident in Geneva for six months, was given the task of searching for possibilities of agreement. The 40 members of this conference, the P5 and 35 others, have the sole multilateral authority to negotiate disarmament measures. Both bodies call expert witnesses or visit plants and military installations.

Two treaties were to emerge from intensive UN brainstorming in rival capitals and at the UN Conference on Disarmament in Geneva. In 1974 the Threshold Test Ban Treaty (TTBT) limited the size of US and Soviet test explosions to 150 kilotons. Parties to these treaties were to exchange verification data and not to interfere with the verification procedures of the other. Critics were quick to assert that this threshold had been set too high and would hardly restrain activity at lower levels. In 1976 the two superpowers signed a complementary accord, the Peaceful Nuclear Explosions Treaty (PNET). The PNET was designed to ensure that a supposedly peaceful programme of nuclear explosions (such as the major engineering projects both countries then had on the drawing-board) did not, in fact, breach the Threshold Treaty. Excavation for canals, harbours and the storage of natural gas would be permitted with the added safeguard of on-site inspection. Many firmly believed that the 1976 accord should have preceded the 1974 one; others held both treaties to be counter-productive, concealing issues under a mass of technicalities. However, neither of these treaties is yet in force, ostensibly because neither party can see its way around certain problems of verification. Most other observers at the UN have seen the failure to implement these treaties as more evidence that the superpowers are unable or unwilling to halt the nuclear armaments race.

Apart from activity at the United Nations the major powers began to show preference for bilateral management of discussion and decision in the mid 1970s. President Carter, influenced perhaps by recommendations from a specially convened UN working party, put forward in March 1977 a proposal for tripartite talks to begin in Geneva. Discussion eventually went to the UN Committee on Disarmament with a scheme for relying on detection instruments and on challenge inspection to override the inhibitions over verification. Any disagreement would be taken to the Security Council for arbitration. This promising notion was not acceptable to the hardliners in the superpower capitals. Within three years all hope of reconciling viewpoints was squashed by the succeeding Reagan Administration, which broke off talks asserting that there were unbridgeable gulfs over verification. Although the Soviet invasion of Afghanistan caused an outraged President Carter to sever contacts with Moscow over treaty exploration, it seems that both Carter and then Reagan waited to see whether the Strategic Arms Limitation Treaty (SALT II) would be ratified at a time of eroding *détente*. Once more the ball was passed specifically to the 40-nation Conference on Disarmament in Geneva. In 1980, at a time of despondency and frustration, China and France rejected the mild suggestions of the UN working party. Sabres were ominously rattling in both camps. For something like four years, urged on by a fairly desperate set of General Assembly Resolutions (some of which the US opposed), the Conference concentrated on a set of substantive proposals for converting a partial ban into a comprehensive one. Acceptance by the great-powers would be seen as the acid test of their willingness to collaborate.

THE 1980s: CAUTIOUS CO-OPERATION

Heightened activity, much trumpeted by the media, saw in 1985 the USSR unilaterally proclaiming a moratorium on testing to last in the first instance, if it were reciprocated, for four months. Washington responded with more testing. Gorbachev, the Soviet leader (and a man very conscious of enlisting UN support), twice extended the moratorium until the end of 1986. Despite the moment of hope occasioned by the Reykjavik Summit of October 1986, testing by both sides resumed. It was now commonly agreed that verification problems were not perceived as the main obstacle. For Reagan's Washington the chief needs were to proof-test a new generation of Trident missiles and to subject to trials the components of the Strategic Defense Initiative on which so many hopes were pinned. A corresponding military concern in Warsaw Pact circles was to confound, if not abort, US/European militarism.

Amid the gloom some light was visible. Multilateralist enterprise was to re-emerge in 1987 with the setting up of a Missile Technology Control Regime (MTCR), at first an understanding outside the UN between the UK and six allies (France, Japan, Canada, Italy and West Germany). It did not pass notice that these states included those with strong attitudes to nuclear weaponry (for and against) and within five years 22 states, all members of the European community, were showing that it was possible to embargo illegitimate export of missiles and missile-related technology and, by implication, to put some control into research and development. This was, after all, along the lines of the embargo-and-control arrangements that proponents of a test ban regarded as essential preliminaries. The following year, 1988, saw a return to bilateral transaction.[3] It was the twenty-fifth anniversary of the PTBT and by a fortunate coincidence linked to the stipulations of both the TTBT and the PNET joint verification experiments were devised for sites in the Soviet Union and in the US. This was an unprecedented exchange of data, and a trial run for calibration and evaluation. Site monitoring was a leading feature of the ploy.

THE 1990s: TOWARDS A COMPREHENSIVE BAN

The phase of the hope of the 1990s has its roots in fresh thinking about comprehensive control by Canadian and Australian delegates to the General Assembly in 1988. The underlying impulse seems to have been the thought that if improved superpower relations reduce global tension, they could perhaps reduce anxiety about taking arms control initiatives. Nuclear testing was now in partnership with trials of a new brood of chemical and biological weapons some of which might be coupled effectively with thermonuclear warheads. Ominously, too, it was becoming easier for small, private groups to get access to sources of destructive force. Improved intelligence facilities and early warning systems had to be co-ordinated if a comprehensive ban was proposed. Strength was put into this proposition by one-third of the PTBT signatories, 40 states altogether, recognizing an opportunity to call for a conference to amend the PTBT. Although the P5 did not view this move with warmth they did at least suspend their testing for periods varying from 9 to 12 months. France, even China, dampened down test activity by 1992, as did the Commonwealth of Independent States (CIS). On all sides was a willingness to suspend and an equally clear determination to resume the testing should "the other side" renege. Argentina and Brazil, meanwhile, signed a full-safeguard agreement proscribing testing.

That the path towards comprehensive test banning was strewn with obstacles was proved by the lack of consensus at the 1992 meetings of the General Assembly and of its First Committee. In November, the new Secretary-General, Boutros Boutros-Ghali, spoke powerfully in support of a move to achieve a comprehensive ban by 1995, the fiftieth anniversary of the UN's founding. There was much support; equally there were reservations – France stated that, "our nuclear arsenal is already at its strictly essential level". This looked like self-sufficiency at its most unhelpful. For the governments of the UK and the US the attainment of a comprehensive ban was a "long-term objective", while they regarded a "minimal programme of nuclear tests" as the best means of ensuring the safety and credibility of the nuclear deterrent whether it was deployed in the field or laid on a stockpile elsewhere. It seemed a return to the conferred responsibility of defending freedom of the 1950s and the retaliatory litany of the Cold War era. The PTBT had, after all, contained in its Article VI a specific pledge to work for test renunciation.

In summer 1993 President Clinton embraced the objective of ending US testing in 1996, his re-election year. He hoped, too, that by then the US Senate might have been able to ratify both the TTBT and the PNET. Tentatively, an existing US moratorium was to last for another 12 months, as was that of the other P5 members on the understanding that any breach would lead to resumption of testing. However, states such as Iran, North Korea, India and Pakistan who had not signed the NPT, might have regarded this as the green light to their unhelpful attitude towards cessation of testing. As for Washington and London, this sets a disappointing precedent. Despite the alleviation of East–West tension, but perhaps because of unproductive efforts to persuade former Soviet republics to disarm, both countries feel they must keep a lead. The British Government has lobbied hard for test resumption in Nevada. Nuclear possession has always given that State a ticket to the "top table" – an anachronistic prestige factor that has been expensive financially and environmentally. The US State Department has proposed that Britain should pick up the multimillion dollar bill for clearing up the Nevada site, having carried out some 90 of the total 900 tests there. The opinion has been voiced at the UN that a moratorium would be a forward step rather than a breathing period required to prepare for the next test series. An adequate moratorium serviced by the UN Secretariat would keep negotiators eyeing the need, say, to ratify the TTBT and the PNET as linked elements in progress towards a CTB. Already, some nations in their frustration are threatening to take a firm stand at the 1995 NPT Review Conference. They will declare their unreadiness to extend the NPT unless the essential CTB component is either operative or ready for the table. Otherwise they believe the entire NPT is ruined by the onset of proliferation.[4]

THE CRUX OF A COMPREHENSIVE TEST BAN

Put simply the prime objectives of a CTB would be:
  (a) prohibition of any nuclear weapon explosion in any environment;
  (b) a protocol differentiating peaceful and other explosions;
  (c) specific provision for verification, data exchange and non-interference
      with permissible monitoring by others; and
  (d) consultation and review procedures controlling violation of agreement
      and proliferation.

Generally speaking, such an approach would discourage NNWS from going ahead with untested and so unpredictable weaponry, either existing models or envisaged new types. Public fear of the apocalypse would be greatly reduced. Science and industry would redirect enterprise more towards beneficial civilian use. There are, of course, many problems. In what way would states violating a CTB be "punished"? If warhead testing is forbidden is there not a risk of experiment with alternative delivery systems? Supposing that flight testing of missiles and underground testing are both disallowed, would it be easy to check and control small-scale laboratory trials? However comprehensive the arrangements for control might be, would it not be feasible and useful to give regional systems some responsibility for exacting compliance?

For many years debate has covered a range of political and technical aspects of nuclear weapons testing. The moral dimension has not been neglected. From time to time in the UN and other forums the question has been asked: is the possession and threat of a nuclear bomb morally justifiable? In view of the fact that strategic missiles are massively indiscriminate and environmentally ruinous, surely their very existence is contrary to all humane principles? Two representations reaching the UN General Assembly in recent years are worth recording, both emanating from the International Peace Bureau in Geneva in alliance with the group International Physicians for the Prevention of Nuclear War. (Both organizations are Nobel Peace Prize winners.)

In May 1992 the International Court of Justice was to be asked for an advisory opinion as to whether the use and threat of use of nuclear weapons might be prohibited under the canons of international law. In other words, this would legally underpin the stipulations of any CTB. The proposers of this move were encouraged by the decision, a unanimous one, of the General Assembly to declare the 1990s the Decade of International Law. The court opinion would not bind states but it would give time for sustained enquiry and work on codification, and it would add authority to legal and moral arguments for reducing and ultimately eliminating nuclear weapons.

The second suggestion is that the UN Security Council might use its powers under Chapter VII of the UN Charter, citing Article 39, and rule that continued nuclear testing constitutes a threat to the peace and is henceforth forbidden.[5] Such a ruling would be binding upon all UN members, but to be effected it would need the affirmative votes of the P5 and sufficient votes of non-permanent members to total nine positive votes. Recourse to this legitimate provision of the Charter is thought simpler than trying to secure the approval of all NPT signatories. A prohibition along these lines might be adopted either for a fixed period as a norm and be renewable, or it might be indefinite. Measures such as these two are seen by their sponsors as appealing both to moral criteria and to the broad bases of common sense. They affirm, with all the power of UN advocacy, that the proliferation of nuclear weapons and nuclear testing is a complete violation of man's right to survive.

NOTES

1. The US had a nuclear monopoly in Soviet eyes. Basic control was extensively discussed without final agreement.
2. A partial treaty might very likely encourage "redirection" of warhead development from large thermonuclear to smaller tactical devices.
3. Several transactions took place. In 1987 "nuclear risk reduction centres" in Washington and Moscow were to exchange data. Also in 1987, the Intermediate-range Nuclear Forces Treaty aimed to eliminate intermediate and short-range missiles through mutual verification. Agreement on notification of any strategic missile launches followed in 1988.
4. Article VI of the NPT pledges NWS to work towards a CTB. Reluctance by the P5 is condemned by NNWS. See also Note 5 below.
5. The British Government officially regards testing as necessary "to ensure we can maintain the highest standards of safety for nuclear weapons" (this is a constant refrain in the Foreign and Commonwealth Arms Control and Disarmament Research Unit quarterly reviews). There is also a firm commitment "to work hard" for a CTB. NNWS see these policy statements as incompatible. Reports from Geneva in mid-1995 indicate that the outline of a draft CTB Treaty is slowly emerging. A moratorium on testing is at present still being observed.

FURTHER READING

Barton, J. H. & C. D Weiler (eds). *International arms control: issues and agreement.* Palo Alto, California: Stanford University Press, 1976.

Dahlitz, J. *Nuclear arms control.* Boston: Allen & Unwin, 1983.

Jacobson, H. K. & E. Stein. *Diplomats, scientists and politicians: the United States and the nuclear test ban negotiations.* Ann Arbor: University of Michigan Press, 1966.

O'Neil, R. & D. N. Schwartz. *Hedley Bull on arms control.* London: Macmillan, 1987.

SIPRI. *World armaments and disarmament.* London: Taylor & Francis, 1980.

United Nations. *Disarmament, a periodic review by the United Nations* (Autumn 1988), XI(3); (Summer 1989, XII(2).

Chapter Ten

NUCLEAR TESTING

1945 UN and Atomic Energy Commission intensively debate nuclear weapons control and factor of testing.

1955 Bandung Non-aligned Conference appeal to halt testing.

1958–62 Geneva talks: superpowers discuss test halting among other nuclear issues.

1962–8 18-nation Disarmament Committee (name changed to Committee on Disarmament 1979, to Conference on Disarmament 1984. Now regular meeting of at least 40 states).

1963 PTBT.

1970 Negotiations on CTB in process including "official" and "non-official" approaches to governments.

1974 TTBT.

1976 PNET. *Ad hoc* Group of Scientific Experts established at UN.

1978 Conference on Disarmament (P5 and at least 35 others) meets in Geneva for six months. Negotiating forum.
Disarmament Commission (all UN members) meets in New York for four weeks, reports to General Assembly. Monitoring, research body.

1987 MTCR (Missile Technology Control Regime) to aim at control of technological transfer before and during test programmes. Data exchanges.

1995 NPT Review Conference to consider proposals for CTB among other nuclear issues.

PART FOUR

Human rights

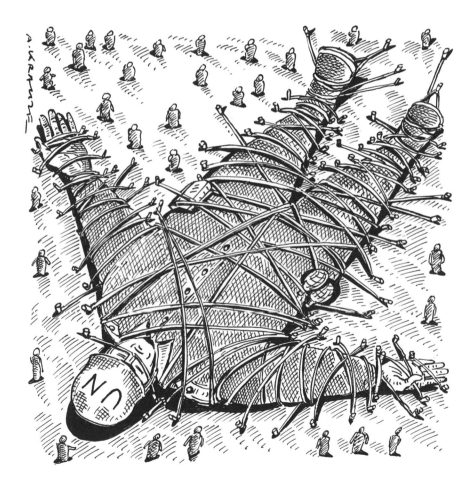

Human rights

Vienna, in mid June 1993, greeted the arrival of 5,000 delegates from 160 nations and 1,000 non-governmental organizations. There was to be a World Conference on Human Rights to review progress after 50 years of work proclaiming and implementing human rights. Vienna reverberated with intense discussion and persistent questioning. Why, it was asked, was there so little progress being made in the attainment of fundamental freedoms? In what specific areas was the contemporary world still a disordered and grotesquely unjust place for many of its inhabitants? What were the circumstances that forced 20 million desperate people to leave their homes to find some crumbs of liberty? Was the North/South divide moral as well as economic? Were delegates satisfied merely to recite the 1948 Human Rights Declaration and to draw up a well-meaning agenda when all around new difficulties and reservations were crowding? Despite their scepticism and the objections from some quarters, delegates did undertake a comprehensive review of principles, legislation, implementation and future prospects. Twelve days of deliberation were given over to reviewing the efforts of half a century.

First of all, in this chapter, we look at the Universal Declaration of Human Rights and at some of its interpretations. An account follows of the momentous work of the UN in framing human rights Covenants and other statutory measures. There is a summarized overview of UN work for the rights of women, children, minorities and refugees, and finally, some scrutiny of problems that remain.

THE UNIVERSAL DECLARATION OF HUMAN RIGHTS

It was an American President's wife, Eleanor Roosevelt, who in 1948 vigorously piloted the work of a committee to draw up an International Bill of

Human Rights for submission to the General Assembly. The principles in the Bill would not be the product of any one ethical tradition, rather, they represented the lowest common denominator of human values understood as a reaction to the horrors of the Second World War. The Bill would reflect aspirations, declare goals, and set down moral norms. Its legal and moral force, it was believed, would blaze a trail condemning violation and offering protection. The Bill would be shaped in three parts: a Universal Declaration, Covenants to support the Declaration and an Optional Protocol. The General Assembly adopted the Universal Declaration on 10 December 1948 (now Human Rights Day) and work commenced on drafting the other two sections.

Thirty Articles in the Universal Declaration attest that all men are born free and equal in dignity and rights and that they are entitled to rights and freedoms "without distinction of any kind". They have the freedom *to* life, liberty, security, equality of protection under the law and the right to a free trial, to move freely, to marry, inherit, think without censure, worship, work, rest, associate, be educated and receive welfare. To these fundamental rights are added the freedom *from* servitude, degrading treatment and punishment, arbitrary arrest, detention, exile and racial discrimination. These are civil, political, economic, social and cultural rights girded in universality. Even cynics are heard to endorse this universality by pointing to the number of governments that never fail to invoke these rights when accusing others of violation.

It is an impressive list, but there are several points worth remembering. In the first place, entitlement is no guarantee. The rights are laid down, but Article 29 points out that everyone has duties "to the community in which alone the free and full development of his personality is possible". Linking rights with duties is a venerable humanistic tradition for the individual to observe. Community and citizen have mutual responsibilities. If this relationship is thought less than satisfactory there is no provision in the Declaration, or even in the UN Charter, for the UN as an institution to intervene beyond application of systematic sanctions in some cases. The stipulation in Article 2.7 of the UN Charter forbidding interference in matters that are "essentially within the domestic jurisdiction of any state" could well provide an escape clause for rogue governments. A second difficulty arises with the admirable principle of self-determination, which includes the right of a person to an adequate standard of living for himself and for his family. Unfortunately its application in practice may fall grievously short of expectation, especially where nations attribute the gap between the theory of rights and its implementation to unfortunate political and economic "realities".

For most observers the Universal Declaration does two things and does them well. It effects, primarily, a transformation from the horizontal plane (where rights are conferred by states in a comity of nations) to the vertical plane (where rights reach down to individual men and women). Where the UN Charter of 1945 was largely states-centric, the Declaration and the other documents in the Bill of Human Rights distinguish moral rights as the legitimate expectation of the common man. Not all rights are there in detail. There could be more explicit acknowledgement of the right of minorities and of women and children – areas of great concern that have welled up powerfully since 1948. It is probably true that too specific a document would never have gained the wide assent of members whose cultural, political and religious traditions were so diverse. The Declaration principles are understood as expressions of moral value rather than as norms requiring compliance, but it is interesting to see how many have been incorporated into the customary law of nations, including new states emerging from old empires.

Political forces soon blunted the edge of a number of the principles. The Soviet Bloc quite firmly held that while the UN might certainly profess these rights, the enforcement of them remained a domestic matter. Similarly, the colonial powers of the day, such as Britain, France and the Netherlands, maintained walled-in jurisdiction in their dependent territories. There was, in fact, a degree of option and discretion in the human rights documents, enough to allay some of the fears certain governments had about anyone else appraising their behaviour at home. Especially in regard to economic and social matters it was not too difficult for a government to reason that it had still some latitude as to when and how to use its resources to enable rights to be enjoyed.

THE FRAMING OF COVENANTS

Listing the principles of human rights was the easiest task in the process of legislation. What had to be done next was frame the Covenants that bound the signatories. The conversion of Declaration principles into treaties and the elaboration of procedures for their implementation was to take 18 years in UN committee rooms. Two Covenants were designed: an International Covenant on Civil and Political Rights and an International Covenant on Economic, Social and Cultural Rights. The first was the most probable step towards adoption in international law, the second seemed more difficult to monitor and attain. Ready adoption of these measures was only likely if they were kept separate from each other. They both took ten years from launch to ratification.

The International Covenant on Civil and Political Rights (1966) is chiefly a prescriptive measure in that the 90 ratifying states are obliged to report on their implementation to a Human Rights Committee. They have to stand up to be counted where their policies are visible to the rest of the world. Exposure of a violation or neglect of human rights will not often lead to speedy compliance but as in the case of South Africa's apartheid, or the "disappearance" and torture practices of certain Latin American states, international publicity, censure and pressures have exerted a leavening effect on recalcitrant regimes. Fifty-three Articles lay down in very great detail what is required of states obliged to recognize, respect and facilitate the full, free and dignified exercise of civilized living.

The International Covenant on Economic, Social and Cultural Rights (1966) is, as one might expect, difficult to implement in any standard fashion. Even so, close on 100 nations have ratified it and in so doing subscribed to its progressive realization by appropriate means, in policies and legislation. Quite clearly, some rights may be conferred or earned quickly; others only slowly and perhaps imperfectly. Large-scale reforms may not tangibly benefit the individual. Thirty-one Articles enumerate what any self-regulating community would understand as steps towards ordered and productive co-existence of an administration and its dependent citizens.

Linking these two Covenants was considered unfeasible in the 1960s. Their separateness was vindicated during the harder days of the Cold War when the West stridently labelled civil and political rights observance as inadequate in the Communist world, while the East lambasted the West as uncaring about rights to do with employment, housing and health. Even so, it was never easy to see how rights in either category could be exercised legitimately in isolation from each other. What was then mainly a political polemic can now also be regarded from a sociological standpoint. One view is that economic and social rights are not so much human rights as goals or aspirations of societies. They represent positive attainment of (or failure to realize) civil policies and programmes. Those who hold this opinion would see the UN not as an ethically judgemental institution, but as a body empowered and able to advise and encourage material betterment; and while the Covenants have common ground in recognizing the right to self-determination and in the prohibition of discrimination, there is a difference in the way they operate. Implementation of civil and political rights is observed by a working committee considering situations in various countries; economic and social rights are surveyed using national reports that demonstrate how far it is possible for resources to be used specifically and productively. The common political and economic rights of mankind are essentially defined in UN Charter Articles 55 and 56, so that Human Rights Declarations and Covenants are designed to energize these objectives. The Covenants were drafted and published assuming that competent Specialized Agencies such as WHO, UNESCO, ILO, FAO would take up the means to put them into effect. Agencies such as these would report to the General Assembly.

It is now possible to file a complaint with the United Nations for a violation of a right protected by treaty. Previously it was almost unthinkable that an individual citizen could complain to an international body against his own government. Under the Optional Protocol (1976), which is an ancillary instrument to the Civil and Political Rights Covenant, the 45 ratifying states agree to allow any citizen to lodge a complaint provided the state has ratified both the Protocol and the Covenant on Civil and Political Rights. (The UK has ratified only the Declaration and the two Covenants but not the Optional Protocol.) A complaint will be examined by a Human Rights Committee to ensure that it is *bona fide* and not an anonymous grievance and that all "available domestic remedies" have been tried and found unavailing. Clarification of the matter is then sought with the offending state with a view to resolution within six months. More than 500 complaints are submitted every week to New York. Similar complaints procedures are being operated under the Convention on the Elimination of All Forms of Racial Discrimination and under the Convention against Torture. Moreover, it is possible for a grievance to be heard even though the nature of the case is not covered by a UN treaty. The so-called "1503" procedure (originating from Resolution 1503) submits a case to working groups who carry out a thorough study in confidence. Few members of the public are aware of this painstaking and perhaps rather cumbersome procedure, although it is known that some 50 states are currently under scrutiny for alleged rights violations.

Fifty years have elapsed since the pioneering committee work that was to produce the innovative legislation of Declaration and Covenants. There has been a wealth of agreement placed in statute form since then. General Assembly Declarations and Conventions have dealt broadly with the rights of children, women, disabled persons, refugees, slavery, prostitution and apartheid. There is now wide acceptance of principles to do with colonial independence, racial and religious intolerance and territorial asylum. In Geneva, the ILO has been active as a UN Specialized Agency in the field of labour legislation. Conventions, recommendations and supervisory procedures have been designed since 1919 to enunciate rights, to examine complaints, to provide advice and assistance to governments and to employers' and workers' organizations. The focus of effort has been on developing social policies, laws and institutional bodies.

Those 50 years, however, have seen the emergence of a dramatically changed world. In contrast to the bold fine phrasing in statute form and the public acceptance of government spokesmen, we see a world rent by war, dissension and appalling need. New nations confidently coming into being in the 1940s and 1950s now find themselves victims of indiscriminate "free market" forces with no moral basis. They gloomily contemplate liability for immense debt repayments, vulnerable economies and internal political rivalries. Apart from the blocs represented by the G7 (economically powerful states) and the Group of 77 (mainly Third World developing states) there is an indefinite pattern of nations unable to give full expression to the rights and freedoms so hopefully ascribed to in less confused times. Implementation of rights is the crux of the whole matter of human rights and this is what we must examine next.

UN BODIES FOR HUMAN RIGHTS IMPLEMENTATION

Two UN bodies spearhead implementation of human rights legislation. They are the UN Commission on Human Rights and the Human Rights Committee. Based in Geneva, the 43 states' representatives on the Commission on Human Rights monitor worldwide observance using special rapporteurs. These are specialists on either particular issues or specific countries. They communicate with governments, interview victims and witnesses and when invited visit as fact-finders, not judges. Where dispute becomes violent they may have to withdraw or attempt to mediate, say, between El Salvadorean guerrillas, the Red Cross and the Government. Back in Geneva a report is compiled to be embodied in approaches to the offending government. The UN believes that steady pressure methodically applied "saves lives in a quiet manner". The two bodies each recruit experts from various fields to function as watchdogs and as investigating workshops. Recommendations from these groups then go to their UN parent body, the Economic and Social Council.[1] This UN activity is only the tip of the iceberg. There is a profusion of supportive agency work from specially convened groups who report, study, prepare programmes and action years, research, train personnel and arrange funding and trusts.

Several hundred international NGOs have now received consultative status enabling them to liaise with the UN and to sit as observers at public meetings of the Economic and Social Council. The "nuisance role" and image-building of concerned groups has a long Western tradition and the corporate force of such bodies as the World Council of Churches, of Amnesty since 1961, of the Society of Friends, of Oxfam, the World Jewish Congress, and the International Commission of Jurists, to name only a few, is very great indeed. Most nations are very wary about having their reputations questioned and facing a groundswell of protesting public opinion.

Also to be taken into account is the growing credibility and effective human rights maintenance of regional institutions in three continents, which have modelled much of their constitution and their procedures on the example of UN legislation and conference. Europe has had its own Human Rights Convention since 1953 together with a Human Rights Commission and a Court. The Organization of American States succeeded in persuading 19 states to ratify a Declaration and support an Inter-American Commission and Convention. In Africa a Charter on Human and People's Rights and a Commission with the same brief have acquired a more pronounced political emphasis than elsewhere, doubtless because nations of recent origin are sensitive about authoritarian tendencies in their political and constitutional development. There is no judicial review process as there is with the other two regional bodies and little evidence of success in overturning the denial of rights here and there. Africa today, as the media presents it, is scourged by disasters both natural and man-made; UN and other agencies struggle to cope with famine, displaced peoples, civil war and the pressing follow-up need to rehabilitate.

Human rights principles are vividly in the minds of relief personnel coping with immediate physical priorities and seeing for themselves the truth of the adage that "human rights begin with breakfast".

Delegates at the World Conference on Human Rights in 1993 stressed that implementation of human rights must rely on programmes and campaigns to promote, protect, protest, disturb public conscience and rock apathy and fatalism. Tremendous energy has been concentrated on the rights of women, children, minorities and refugees. A brief look at each will demonstrate the direction of human rights activity by the United Nations.

WOMEN'S RIGHTS

Women's rights need to be taken a long way beyond the limits of the Universal Declaration on Human Rights, it is often suggested. This is dealt with more fully in Chapter 12. Progress has to be made on two fronts: *protection* against discrimination and exploitation, and *promotion* of equality in such areas as education, employment, inheritance, ownership of property, nationality and suffrage. For almost half a century, as Chapter 12 relates, the UN and a network of NGOs have worked intensively to bring about an improvement in the acknowledged role of women.

CHILDREN'S RIGHTS

The 1990s have been described as the "decade of doing the obvious" when there has to be a resolute effort to save the lives and rescue the blunted development of millions of children. The child has no political power: dependence is easily and often abused. Almost 40 years ago the UN Declaration on the Rights of the Child (1959) had the dual purpose of defining adults' obligations as well as children's rights. Progress has been erratic and uncertain. The connection between the individual's rights, masked so often by maltreatment and exploitation, and the rights of parents has only slowly been acknowledged. Where such links are recognized controls are loose and imperfect. Sophisticated communities marginalize children, many developing nations violate universal values by overlooking abuse or even by practising it. Overall, perhaps 30 million young people are "children of the street", existing somehow in the slums of Mexico City, Calcutta and New York. Their childhood is "stolen"; often their parents and relatives do not know how best to help them.

A World Summit for Children was convened by the UN in September 1990 to be co-chaired by Canada and Pakistan. The event brought 70 world leaders and Prime Ministers to the UN building in New York. At the forefront of all discussion was the interdependence of factors in developing talents and personality. The child had a right not only to live but to live fully. Speaker after speaker on this occasion called for a co-ordinated policy to "network" the efforts of UN Agencies such as UNICEF and ILO and of non-governmental bodies and governments. Even the most carefully drafted legislation would need international and informed public support. Time was short. By the Year 2025 eight out of ten children would be living in Asia, Africa, Latin America – continents of need – and more than half would be under the age of 15. A broad front of action was called for to provide a basic right to schooling for 120 million young children still not in primary school, and for healthcare for 14 million children under the age of five, dying from malnutrition and a handful of common, preventable diseases.

Children's rights have been given a breath of life by the Convention on the Rights of the Child (1989), which has gained careful ratification by 139 states. There were instances of delay and reservation from those states whose cultural mores and social conventions did not make full acceptance feasible. Four main areas provide the foundation for a system to codify existing laws and tighten new ones: the right to survive, to develop, to be protected and to participate fully in the community. It might be thought that these rights are self-evident and to be taken on trust, but experience shows that they have been either neglected or implemented erratically. Explicitly stating children's needs in enforceable terms, and insisting on states regularly reporting to the UN, reveals an underlying priority – a "first call" for children on society's concerns, capacities and resources. The 1993 Vienna World Conference on Human Rights set the target that all UN member-states would have ratified the Children's Convention by 1995.

THE RIGHTS OF MINORITIES AND INDIGENOUS PEOPLES

Minority peoples are the victims of a loophole in the UN Charter. Article 2.7 strikes many as conservationist of the *status quo* in forbidding intervention in states' domestic affairs. Neither this legislation nor that of many human rights measures can effectively deal with the glaring injustices meted out within some states to minority groups. Tamils in Sri Lanka, Indians in Peru, Moslems in Bosnia, Roman Catholics in Ulster are all in conflict where a General Assembly can do little to prevent gross denial and abuse, however horrified it may be at violence and violation. A particular difficulty for an inter-state organization like the UN is that minority interests may often be led by irregular guerrilla leaders and factions not generally represented in the General Assembly. An interesting exception in this respect is the case of the Palestine Liberation Organization leader, Yasser Arafat, who was shunned at first in many quarters, and was at length invited to address the General Assembly. Harsh treatment of minorities often seems to operate at two levels: sustained discrimination and in the hideous form of genocide. An international Convention on Elimination of all Forms of Racial Discrimination, launched in 1969, took 11 years of insistent persuasion and some careful manoeuvring before 108 states felt able to ratify and approve the setting up of a monitoring committee to survey and report.[2] Despite this legislation and the force of public outrage, thick-skinned leaders of an offending state can still plead that the affair is "essentially within the domestic jurisdiction of any states".[3]

Minority discrimination, where it takes the form of apparent genocide as does the abhorrent "ethnic cleansing" witnessed in today's former Yugoslavia, is resistant to prompt prevention by any external force. Although 100 UN members ratified with earnest conviction a Covenant on the Prevention and Punishment of Genocide (1948) following the Nazi Holocaust and its toll of perhaps 15 million *Untermenschen* (inferior, subhuman people – in the Nazi view), this vicious crime still characterizes the twentieth century. The outside world has writhed in frustration at its inability to forestall inhuman behaviours in Bosnia, Kampuchea, Ethiopa, Rwanda, Zaire and, to a lesser extent, in Iraq, South Africa, Tibet and Georgia. Punishment through tribunals or sanctions may be ineffective or indiscriminate. Some violations may perhaps be prevented by using early warning systems to deflect or scale down excesses, followed by attempted mediation and rehabilitation. But again, some states regard this as unauthorized intervention. The happenings in former Yugoslavia, discussed in Chapter 14, are a case in point.

One minority problem is that of 300 million indigenous people. These are non-dominant groups, usually descendants of the original inhabitants of a territory overcome by invasion and conquest. Among them are the North American Indians, the Australian Aborigines and the Maoris of New Zealand. Mostly they live in a state of unreliable dependence on the patronizing goodwill or non-concern of later comers, perhaps in some type of "reserved" area. Others are urbanized and deprived, second-class citizens lacking respect and recognition of inherent rights. An International Year for Indigenous People in 1992 pressed the need of their right to preserve, develop and transmit to future generations a sense of ethnic identity and their cultural and social patterns. There had to be an end to forced integration, eviction and displacement by intensive agriculture and mining concessions. Self-determination was one of the absolute principles of the UN Charter and of subsequent legislation.

THE RIGHTS OF REFUGEES

In the perception of those who drew up the UN Charter, refugees were a transitory feature of Europe recovering from wartime chaos and displacement. Tragically, 50 years later, Europe again has a refugee problem of disconcerting extent and complexity. Throughout all continents there are something like 20 million victims of intolerance, persecution and violence and many thousands more displaced by natural and man-made calamities. Nearly 10,000 people become refugees every day; their desperation is seen worldwide in newspapers and on television screens. Amid discussion of relief, however, there are misunderstandings about terms. In international law a refugee is defined as a person who has a well-founded fear of being persecuted in the homeland for reasons of race, religion, nationality, social grouping or political opinion. In Africa, Asia, and now in Europe, this definition has been extended to include people obliged to leave their own country on account of war, internal conflict and civil disorder. The crucial point here is that of protection: the refugee is unable to rely on the protection of the home state and thus must seek the protection of the outside world.

All these people are the responsibility of the United Nations High Commissioner for Refugees, which has twice been awarded the Nobel Peace Prize for its work (1954 and 1981). With its headquarters in Geneva and representatives in more than 80 countries, UNHCR relies on charitable contributions and some government funding to offer sanctuary to those desperately in need and to search for lasting solutions. The 1993 Vienna Conference saw the establishment of a budget as a priority; UN members could be expected to have more adequate contributions levied upon them. Protection of refugees as the UN understands it takes three forms:

(a) *voluntary repatriation* or a return to the place of origin when conditions have improved and safety is assured;

(b) *reception* in a host state for a limited period and for a determined quota; and

(c) *resettlement* where long-term programmes are set up to give them a fresh start in life either in the country of first asylum or in a second.

What must never be countenanced is a process known as *refoulement*, or forced repatriation.

Geographically, the spread of refugees has altered dramatically. In the 1950s European displacement and Arab/Israeli partition were the main problems. Ten years later sub-Saharan Africa was in a post-colonial state of flux. People scattered in millions. Then followed a decade of volatility in South East Asia, in Vietnam, Cambodia, Bangladesh and Pakistan. The 1980s saw the numbers of refugees swelling hugely in Africa and also in Central America. In Europe in the 1990s thousands have been displaced at gunpoint in Georgia, Tajikistan, Turkey, millions in Bosnia and Croatia, and further afield expulsion is endemic in Somalia, Ethiopia and Angola, Bangladesh and Sudan. Disinheritance, separatism, leadership rivalry and scapegoating occur widely in Rwanda, Burma, China, Nigeria, Lebanon, Iraq, Haiti, El Salvador, Mozambique. Quarrels are settled with bullets, mines and fire.

Against the 100 violent conflicts today the tidy assurances of UN Declarations and Covenants seem light years away. Two aspects of this confounded the delegates in Vienna in 1993 at the Human Rights Conference. One problem was to think out the possibility of UN preventive action to forestall exodus. An effective system of rapidly deployed personnel, highly trained in counselling and mediating skills, a breed of Blue Berets, in fact, might marshal political and technical skills to reduce ethnic tension and spillover. The entire concept of "intervention" would have to be looked at afresh.

The second stage must be reconsideration of just what means of sanctuary could be offered to the displaced *within* their own territory, partly to reduce or stem panic, and partly because relief is most effectively applied *in situ*. Should we use camps? (Some Palestinian refugees have lived in camps for more than a generation.) Are safe havens (as in Iraq and Bosnia) a tenable proposition? How are they to be supplied and safeguarded? As for resettlement, again, *in situ,* these are now being tried in Mozambique where 6,500 Blue Berets are restoring rights and life to 1.5 million "returnees" from six neighbouring states. In Cambodia the United Nations Transition Assistance Group (UNTAG), as we shall see in Chapter 17, restored the franchise and got 90% of the people to the polls in 1993. After two decades of war there a series of reintegrating programmes is turning "scorched earth" into self-sufficient rice-farming communities with secure homes and livelihoods. Restoring human rights in each locality is termed a "quick impact project".

For the majority of "host nations" resettlement has been the least preferred solution to refugee flow. Governments, wanting to be generous, have encountered immense difficulties in identifying vulnerable (maltreated) individuals and members of divided families among 700,000 Vietnamese, or 200,000 Hungarians or 40,000 Ugandan Asians. Over-generous offers of places may trigger fresh economically motivated outflows, and in the case of today's Bosnia, for instance, suggest an acceptance of "ethnic cleansing". From reception to eventual provision of material essentials resettlement has to be steered by carefully appraised needs rather than by demands and this needs an interlocking structure of national resettlement programmes.

Displacement of people and denial of rights is partly a moral problem and an increasingly embarrassing political feature in Western Europe. A disturbing element is emerging in the public "globality of concern". A number of states are more and more differentiating between "political refugees", perceived as victims of circumstances beyond their control, and "economic refugees" or "migrants" who move to another country solely to elude poverty and better their way of life. It is the latter who are frequently regarded as a threat to the stability and prosperity of the nation to which they migrate. Indeed, public opinion, hard hit by recession, may brand them as undeserving cases, deny them rights, and even resort to violence. The stress shifts from protection of refugees to protection from them. Europe, backing up against what are seen as problems of reception, accommodation and transit, is then tempted to override the criteria of individual and group rights and impose stringent immigration controls.

PROSPECTS AND PRIORITIES

Finally, what are the prospects for human rights taking hold comprehensively and firmly? There are glimpses here and there of progress in an acclaimed Convention, in instances of a state's ill-treatment and discrimination ending because of international condemnation and in governments modifying legislation because of adverse reports to the UN Committees. On the other hand, there are no "quick fixes" and very little "quick impact". Exploitation, torture and violence are commonplace. Iraq guns down its Kurds. Moslem houses are burned in Bosnia. China's professed regret over Beijing's Tiananmen Square incident is suspect. Britain, the US, France and Germany ratify UN legislation for the most part, yet interpret and practise some rights most unfairly in employment practices and nationalization laws.

Are the standards set 50 years ago unrealistic? Delegates at Vienna in 1993 did not come up with a definite reply, rather, the sombre mood was one of continued enquiry, a listing of problems in achieving implementation, and some difference of opinion about ways of working and establishing priorities. A number of crucial issues were raised.

(a) *Intervention.* When does a state's internal violation of rights entirely justify humanitarian intervention on the ground? What form might this take?

(b) *Interference.* May not General Assembly denunciation of practice in a named state be regarded by that state as intolerable trespass and so be refuted? And so the victims are not helped?

(c) *Universal values.* How far can these be translated into appropriate measures for different cultures, for example, sex equality, franchise, labour laws, religious freedom? Islamic and Western attitudes will be very different.

(d) *Assistance rather than censure.* What is the best approach to states such as Guatemala, Iraq, China and Cambodia, where political factors are complex?

(e) *Deliberate or incidental abuse.* Is it easy to distinguish between deliberate abuse and indirect effects such as those resulting from macroeconomic schemes, where farmers may be forced to grow cash-crops for a multinational corporation and not food for their families? How can rights be retrieved from such "market forces"?

(f) *Public awareness.* Is it possible in the work for general enlightenment about fundamental freedoms to avoid dogmatism and indoctrination that may be offensive to some cultures?

(g) *Costs and funding.* Promoting human rights and follow-up relief work is exceedingly expensive. What resources do many poor nations have to counter unfairness and neglect? As with peacekeeping funding, should there be a specific human rights work levy on all UN members?

(h) *"Trading" human rights.* Western nations occasionally have made political and economic aid conditional on improvement in human rights observance, for example in the Soviet Union, in China, and in many developing countries. Isn't this leverage intrusive and rather hypocritical?

Central to UN activities on behalf of human rights is the individual – as beneficiary of rights proclaimed and as the key actor in their realization. Eleanor Roosevelt, some years after working on the International Bill of Rights, reflected on its meaning:

> Where, after all, do universal human rights begin? In small places, close to home. . . . The neighbourhood he lives in; the school or college he attends; the factory, farm or office where he works. Such are the places where every man, woman and child seeks equal justice, equal opportunity, equal dignity without discrimination. Unless these rights have meaning there, they have little meaning anywhere.

Ultimately, it can only be through the responsive action by governments aided by informed and active support of individual men and women globally that UN efforts to protect human rights will bear fruit.[4] The UN Year for Tolerance, 1995, could be an excellent opportunity to look at where we stand.

NOTES

1. Two other committees, each of 18 members, periodically report to the Council on the implementation of the two Human Rights Covenants adopted in 1966 and which came into force in 1976.
2. States party to this Convention undertake to eliminate racial discrimination and also to promote understanding among ethnic groups. The monitoring committee reviews the progress of implementation and may also consider individual and group complaints provided the state concerned has recognized the committee's competence to receive them.
3. For many years South Africa disputed UN "interference" in what were declared internal affairs. See Chapter 13 below.
4. Comprehensive legislative norms and improving procedures for implementation have accumulated over 50 years. There is still a great need of information and education on human rights. The UN in 1988 launched a 10-year programme by the media and various institutions to promote awareness and understanding of human rights and fundamental freedoms.

FURTHER READING

Alston, P. (ed.) *The United Nations and human rights: a critical appraisal.* Oxford: Oxford University Press, 1992.

Best, G. Whatever happened to human rights? *Review of International Studies* 16(1), pp. 3–18, 1990.

Davies, P. *Human rights.* London: Routledge, 1988.

Dominguez, J. I. *Enhancing global human rights.* New York: McGraw-Hill, 1979.

Donnelly, J. *The concept of human rights.* New York: St Martin's Press, 1985.

Forsythe, D. P. The United Nations and human rights. *Political Science Quarterly* 100(2), pp. 249–69, 1985.

Gordenker, L. *Refugees in international politics.* London: Routledge, 1987.

Johansen, R. C. Human rights in the 1980s. *World Politics* 35(2), pp. 286–314, 1982.

McDougal, M. S. *Human rights and world political order.* New Haven, Connecticut: Yale University Press, 1980.

Moscovitz, M. *International concern with human rights.* Leyden: Sijthoff, 1976.

Mower, A. G. *The United States, the United Nations and human rights.* Westport, Connecticut: Greenwood Press, 1979.

Ogata, S. The evolution of UNHCR. *Journal of International Affairs* 47(2), pp. 419–28, 1994.

United Nations. *United Nations reference guide in the field of human rights.* New York: UN Centre for Human Rights, 1993.

Chapter Eleven

HUMAN RIGHTS

1948	International Bill of Human Rights goes to General Assembly. Universal Declaration of Human Rights adopted 10 December. Covenant on Prevention and Punishment of Genocide.
1954	UNHCR given Nobel Peace Prize.
1959	UN Declaration on the Rights of the Child.
1966	International Covenant on Civil and Political Rights. International Covenant on Economic, Social and Cultural Rights.
1969	International Convention on the Elimination of All Forms of Racial Discrimination.
1976	Optional Protocol. The 1966 Covenants now in force.
1981	UNHCR given second Nobel Peace Prize.
1989	UN Convention on the Rights of the Child.
1990	World Summit for Children: UN in New York.
1993	UN World Conference on Human Rights: Vienna. International Year for Indigenous People.
1995	UN Year for Tolerance.

Women's rights

Today 185 nations are joined together in an attempt to "develop" a fairer and more peaceful world. From the beginning, 50 years ago, when there were only 51 UN member-states, it was realized that women are crucial partners in this attempt. Allied with this has been the concern to demonstrate that what were formerly thought of as the rights of male citizens should be seen as the rights of all human beings. Women's groups and political parties the world over have approached the cause of women's rights in two chief ways. First, maintaining that civil and political rights apply to men and women equally. Secondly, securing the same access to the same opportunities as men and recognizing that economic, social and cultural rights as listed in the 1948 UN Universal Declaration of Human Rights must be granted to women fully and unconditionally. Kurt Waldheim, UN Secretary-General in 1975, insisted that "unless we make a joint effort, we risk condemning half the human race to mark time in the march of humanity".

This chapter surveys the work the UN has done for women's rights, first by outlining some of the general principles emanating from the 1948 Universal Declaration of Human Rights, and then briefly referring to the disadvantage of women in employment, education and suffrage. The function of the Commission on the Status of Women and its Covenant and Declaration are looked at in some detail. The achievements of three great International Women's Conferences are described, with reference to the UN Decade for Women, which resulted from conference recommendations. There are several examples of projects to promote women's rights in developing countries. The chapter ends in anticipation of the fourth World Conference on Women.

OUTLINE OF PRINCIPLES

Women's rights came into the limelight in the early days of the UN; clearly if an effort to build a new world with better conditions for mankind was to succeed, the equal contribution of men and women was needed. The reality was different: women – half the human race – were not participating fully in public life, they were not given equal rights and opportunities in many countries, and so they were not in a position to use their skills and talents fully. In many countries women's organizations have worked hard to extend the role of women in public life ever since the late eighteenth century, concentrating particularly on universal suffrage for women and men alike. These non-governmental organizations were very active in many Western countries at the time when the UN came into being and the Universal Declaration of Human Rights was drafted. They lobbied and urged their countries' representatives to adopt measures that at last would enshrine the rights of women in international law.

Developing appropriate legal instruments by the UN in order to promote women's rights has not gained women total equality; the struggle for a fairer deal and clear acknowledgement of women's rights remains central to much that the UN and its supporters have to do. The Universal Declaration of Human Rights, as noted in Chapter 11, has many articles that specifically concern women, women's work and obligations, but of course all articles apply equally to women, even Article 1, which says: "All humans are born free and equal in dignity and rights. They are endowed with reason and conscience and should act towards one another in a spirit of brotherhood"! However, Articles 16 and 17 deal with matters of marriage and family as well as property. Articles 22, 23 and 24 deal with economic, social and cultural rights as well as work, equal pay and leisure. Articles 25 and 26 refer to an adequate standard of living for all, protection in motherhood and childhood and everyone's right to education. Article 29 refers to everyone's duty to their community.

It has not been easy to legislate for women's rights according to need as their needs are so different across the world. Some are university professors and national presidents, others are underpaid factory workers. Many are burdened by large families, dependent relatives or they may themselves be ill, undernourished or without adequate means of subsistence. As pointed out above, the objective of early UN legislative work for women was to seek their freedom from, among other things, arranged marriage, serfdom, prostitution, ineligibility in voting and professional entry, and unequal remuneration. Much more firmly the UN now requires member-states to declare and pursue national policies promoting, for instance, equal access to education and equality of treatment in regard to occupation and employment. That progress in securing women's rights is slow is very much due to the fact, to quote the International Labour Organization, that "discrimination is subtle but brutal". It is not easy to deal with a male response that considers the affirmation of women's rights as unrealistic or exaggerated because of inherent differences between the sexes and results in grudging and largely symbolic concession. There is now a greater awareness among men of the need for a fairer approach to women's equality and the UN work for women's rights is generally considered to have been both determined and helpful.

Catching up. Twelve countries have lifted female literacy by 30 points in 20 years.

| | % women literate | | % point |
	1970	1990	rise
Saudi Arabia	2	48	46
Jordan	29	70	41
Kenya	19	59	40
Tunisia	17	56	39
Zaire	22	61	39
Libya	13	50	37
Turkey	34	71	37
Algeria	11	46	35
Ghana	18	51	33
Indonesia	42	75	33
Iraq	18	49	31
Syria	20	51	31

The big 10. Female literacy rates for the 10 most populous countries of the developing world (representing almost three quarters of its total population).

	% women literate 1990
Philippines	93
Mexico	85
Vietnam	84
Brazil	81
Indonesia	75
China	68
Nigeria	40
India	34
Bangladesh	22
Pakistan	21

Source: Statistical yearbook 1993, UNESCO. Population: *World population prospects: the 1992 revision*, United Nations Population Division, 1993.

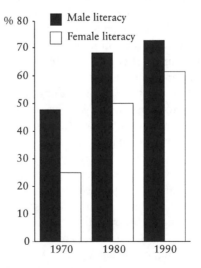

League table of equality in literacy. Female literacy as a percentage of male literacy. Average for the Developing World is 76%. The tables are intended as a guide to gender inequality – not literacy levels. In countries with near-universal literacy this criterion is less revealing.

150

EMPLOYMENT

A Chinese proverb has it that women hold up half the heavens. If this is so, they do it very unevenly and equilibrium must be in danger. The inequity that overshadows all others is economic. One in three of the world's workers is female. Many of them are drudges working in general for two-thirds of human working hours. For this they earn only 10% of the world's income and they own 1% of the world's property. Domestic work, heavy and lasting long hours, is usually regarded as a duty and is unpaid. In the EU women constitute 36% of the workforce but only 11% are in well-paid jobs with managerial responsibilities. Britain has the second widest earnings differentials between men and women in the EU (they are wider still in Luxembourg). In 1990 women in the UK received 69% of the gross earnings for male manual workers and 55% of the gross earnings for male non-manual workers. Many women are in low-paid, part-time or temporary employment where job insecurity is marked. In Britain today women are the only wage-earners in roughly one-third of all households.

EDUCATION

If economic disparity holds women at a disadvantage so also do educational opportunities. Of the 800 million illiterates in the world, 500 million are women. For every 5 women judged illiterate in Europe, there are 2 in North America, 27 in Latin America, 57 in Asia and 84 in Africa. In their crucial teen years, 95% attend school in North America, 47% in Latin America and only 20% in Africa. These are the women and mothers of tomorrow whose role and influence in every aspect of family life will be decisive. Leaders in developing countries have long realized the link between education and progress. "Educate a woman and you educate a family" has been rephrased as "educate a woman and you educate a nation".

SUFFRAGE

In 1945 women were denied the vote in one in three of the UN's 51 member-states. Today, they are eligible to vote in 150 of the 185 member-states. Yet the percentage of women in policy-making positions at local, national and international levels is still remarkably small, and this is reflected in the balance of representation in the General Assembly and the Security Council. Women outnumber men in the European Union (EU), comprising 53% of the population, but decisions affecting their futures are made by parliaments such as that in Britain where female MPs in the 1992 election increased to 60, but this was still only 9% of all MPs in the House of Commons. Women's role in law-making in some Islamic states is particularly small.

THE UN COMMISSION ON THE STATUS OF WOMEN

In 1946 the Economic and Social Council established the Commission on the Status of Women. Meeting each year the Commission carries out a watchdog function observing the statutory rights enunciated by the rulings of the General Assembly, such as that in 1952 regarding women's entitlement to vote and hold public office on equal terms with men; the 1957 Convention safeguarding a wife's nationality on marriage; and the Declarations in 1962 and 1965 upholding the principle of free consent to marriage. Many of the Conventions mentioned above were brought together in one Declaration on the Elimination of Discrimination Against Women in 1975. This is a classic case of the thorough but slow work that drafting international legal instruments in the UN involves. Four years were spent discussing this Declaration (which of course had no legal power), then, after the Declaration was accepted by the General Assembly in 1976, the work began on drafting a single Convention that included what the Declaration said but was not limited to it. This was the Convention Against All Forms of Discrimination Against Women. The General Assembly adopted it in 1979 and it came into force in 1981, when the required number of states had ratified it. The UK signed its intention to ratify it in 1981, but did not actually do so until just before an End of Decade Conference for Women in Nairobi in July 1985.

The Convention requires signatories to submit reports on the measures they adopt to improve the status of women. Members of the General Assembly, earnestly framing a Resolution and seeing it embodied in a Convention such as this, are well aware that ratification permits 100 or so states to adopt and interpret that Convention in ways suited to culture, and economic and social structures. When asked by reporters why it had taken so long for the British Government to ratify a UN Convention that fundamentally granted equal rights to women, something that already was happening within the UK, albeit slowly, the answer by a minister was that they generally reckoned that seven years was the norm before the UK was ready to ratify any legally binding UN Convention!

Each year the General Assembly hears the Commission on the Status of Women submit a progress report. With the clauses of the 1981 Convention in mind, the Assembly can then judge what advance has been made and how much remains unrealized. While gender stereotyping and practices that reflect a concept of the inferiority of one sex are to be eliminated, special measures that take into account gender differences, for instance, as concerns pregnancy, maternity or segregated accommodation are to be allowed as long as they do not result in loss of status or dismissal. Above all, equality before the law is to be ensured in respect of marriage and its dissolution, family circumstances, ownership of property, taxation and mortgages and loans – all matters that traditionally have incorporated a "gender bar".

Another UN body, Committee on the Elimination of Discrimination Against Women, complements the work of the Commission. Made up of 23 members, who are lawyers, experts on women's matters, teachers, diplomats, sitting in their personal capacity, the Committee spends two weeks in New York each year at an investigative workshop sifting the reports governments are required to submit and interviewing their authors. These discussions help the Committee to appreciate what (and how) governments think, and they bring home to government ministers what the outside world thinks of them. This ongoing monitoring process attempts to bridge the gap between equality *de jure* and equality *de facto* by increasing awareness of women's legal rights.

WOMEN'S INTERNATIONAL CONFERENCES

The UN has taken a bold lead in advancing the cause of women's rights in the last 20 years. It was the General Assembly that voted for the 1975 International Women's Year. There would be three commanding aims, those of equality, development and peace. Marking 100 years of struggle for women's liberation, the year was not seen as a global extension of a movement spearheaded merely by the world's richest states. All states, rich and poor, would campaign not simply for "equality" but to prepare women for equal roles in partnership "freeing them to share both the tasks and the fulfilments that are the birthright of all humankind". The hub of activity was Mexico City in 1975 with the first international conference on women to be sponsored by the UN. Eight thousand women from 133 states and 113 NGOs were there. The presence of 1,200 journalists attested to its significance. Several days of intensive discussion saw two measures adopted: the Mexico Declaration on Equality of Women and their Contribution to Development and Peace and a World Plan of Action for the implementation of the objectives agreed. Once more the agenda for action was moving from protection to promotion: equal educational access, a greater emphasis on literacy and civic education, coeducational training in industry and agriculture; in employment, less discrimination in conditions and terms for female workers and improved welfare services for women and their families; explicit recognition of the value of women's work in the home and in other unpaid activities; and eligibility to vote and hold office and greater participation in policy-making.

This tremendous list of points in the World Plan of Action was endorsed by the General Assembly who then declared the years 1976–85 to be a UN Decade for Women. In brief, the objectives of the Decade were to "transform fundamental relationships within society to ensure a system which excludes the possibility of exploitation", a system with "set targets and priorities . . . for equitable representation of women at all levels of policy and decision making". Two practical steps followed. A Voluntary Fund for the Decade was instituted, to continue as a UN Development Fund for Women as part of the UN Development Programme (UNDP), in itself the world's largest multichannel programme for economic and social development, active in 150 countries. Also created was an International Research and Training Institute for the Advancement of Women (INSTRAW). Here research and training would be done in collaboration with UN Specialized Agencies, governments and NGOs with the central idea of promoting the role of women as key agents of development. INSTRAW was located in the Dominican Republic and funded by voluntary contributions from UN member-states and from many private sources. One of its leading concerns was to devise strategies to put to employers where a common response to the claims about women's equality was an evasive "Yes, but", where the claim might receive acknowledgement but preparations for male promotion still went ahead.

Copenhagen was the venue for the second international meeting in 1980. There was disappointment with progress in emancipation at this halfway point in the Decade for Women. There was some dissent, too, over the universality of women's rights when representatives of certain Socialist states pinpointed women as a political vanguard, where 93% of them at the workface were "active builders of Communism". Yet delegates reported that in nations where ideology conferred egalitarian status it was the male intentions and attainments and prerogatives that were given priority. Apart from this the main task of the conference was to decide how to channel into action the objectives of improved provision for education, employment and health. Workshops, projects, seminars, courses and study groups were all devised. It was pointed out with some force that emancipation of women also involved freeing men in less well-off countries to take a more active share in community development, and to this extent it must be a liberated partnership. Neither sex should feel locked into its gender.

It was argued that real progress in improving the status of women and of men depended not only on changes in contemporary social structures, but on changes in the complacent mentality that tolerated those structures, Delegates at Copenhagen spent some time examining the contribution of UNESCO to the UN Decade for Women. This took the form of two medium-term plans, one for 1977–83, the next for 1984–9. Initial concentration on women's status and their participation in development work was beginning to move towards identifying obstacles to equal access to education and employment and to determining how best to cope with them. A significant concern of UNESCO, naturally, was over media sources that were thought often to reinforce unhelpful stereotypes.

The General Assembly meeting in 1982 highlighted women's issues by adopting a Declaration on the Participation of Women in Promoting Peace and Co-operation. Women should contribute equally with men to international efforts to secure peace and progress. This seemed a splendid sentiment, one delegate pointed out, until you looked behind those Assembly representatives nodding through the Declaration and saw that in most of the nations they came from it was men who were the legislators, executives and planners. If this was true of most developed states, it was poignantly apparent in the Middle East where religious dogma was used to justify male dominance.

WOMEN'S FORWARD-LOOKING STRATEGIES

With the end of the UN Decade for Women in 1985 there had to be a major review exercise. The third international women's meeting took place in 1985 in Nairobi, where over 2,000 workshops discussed every topic of interest to women. As at all other international conferences organized for women by the UN, a great number of NGOs actively participated, representing women's and youth groups, trade unions, religious groups, political parties and community groups. Many radical views were expressed from Islamic fundamentalism to advanced positions on women's liberation. An exhibition of tools and technology from many parts of the world demonstrated how women's lives could be improved at little cost and with some elementary skills.

A set of guidelines was adopted termed Forward-looking Strategies for the Advancement of Women to the Year 2000. Taking up the movement in the UNESCO medium-term plans the aims were twofold: to enumerate obstacles still needing removal if the goals of the decade were to be overcome; and to concentrate on priorities. It was agreed that issues needing urgent attention were the inadequate remuneration of female labour, and the position of women who were elderly, young, destitute, rural, immigrant or refugee. Women should have a greater say in decision-making. Special attention was given to the problem of violence against women and general questions of women's vulnerability. These strategies were to be reappraised every five years.

The Nairobi conference featured particularly a long and detailed look at the economic issues relating to women's emancipation. The case of Africa afforded a useful lesson. In that continent between 60 and 90% of all food production, processing and marketing was in the hands of women. Therefore the crisis of food in Africa should be addressed through women and they should be involved all the way up to the highest level. Mobilization of women in the fullest sense was related to three main areas of concern. First, there was the *capacity* of women to participate in development. Significant factors here were literacy, care of children and facilities in the home. Secondly, there was *opportunity* to participate, dependent to a large extent on what the local culture preferred, allowed or denied women. Thirdly, there was the *will* of women to participate, which depended on an increasing sense of their own worth and dignity.

There was ready acceptance at the Nairobi conference of the fact that among uneducated and less fortunate women what must come first are a meal and a home for the family – abstract ideas and rhetoric are hardly useful to them. Meeting direct needs and interests is an indispensable prerequisite to social and economic advance. Possibilities of altering the conventional shackles of dependency, and asserting women's rights, will lie in the hands of the younger men and women in developing countries. Education may build the capacity, open up the opportunities and stimulate the will. In the discussions at the 1985 conference it was immediately realized that the maxim "women and children first" does not only apply in an emergency. Specialized Agencies of the UN such as UNICEF, WHO, UNHCR know that for many in developing nations life is a series of emergencies and priority must be given to those vulnerable sufferers who will form the nation's future. In at least 100 countries today women's rights only emerge out of straightforward sustenance of life.[1]

There are many examples, at the moment, of the action-oriented approach to asserting women's rights, that women are to be considered partners in enterprise. In the Philippines UNESCO is encouraging vocational schools *not* to teach traditional female skills such as handicrafts, home economics and beauty care. More technical subjects normally taught only to men will train female electricians, engineers, carpenters and plumbers. Similarly, there will be women building reinforced concrete water tanks in Fiji, overseeing fish farming in Nicaragua and new irrigation schemes in Indonesia and Malawi. Papuan women will enter intensive courses in business management. Women agricultural advisors will assist the UN Development Programme (UNDP) in Upper Volta endeavouring to persuade families to leave nomadic ways for settled farming, which will be less risky and will treble their incomes. Women planners at senior level are being offered fellowships to institutes in the Caribbean, Latin America and East Africa.

WOMEN AT RISK

Physical and mental violence against women has preoccupied the 45 members of the Commission on the Status of Women. European recession has made women often the first victims. Armed conflict in Bosnia, Sri Lanka, South Africa and Central America has caught them up into vicious turmoil. The UN Committee on the Elimination of Discrimination Against Women in 1993 despatched a team of medical experts to former Yugoslavia to investigate rape allegations and they reported strong evidence that Muslim women especially had been victims. Elsewhere, in such countries as Saudi Arabia, Kuwait and Iraq, conflict is not alone responsible for the lack of esteem in which women are held.

The Commission currently has launched enquiries into four major areas: the education of women as to their legal rights; the structural causes of extreme poverty among women in affluent states; the concept of women-at-risk (social and cultural discrimination); and women's involvement in peace-keeping operations. Women-at-risk are now highly visible in the media. They are half of the world's 20 million refugees. They are deprived of normal family and community support. Widowed, evicted, abused, such gravely trauma-tized individuals may need special resettlement opportunities.

It is with such women in mind that preparations are now in train for the fourth World Conference on Women, to be held in Beijing in 1995. Women will meet in a vast country, where the enormous population of 1,200 million (census 1990) is fed adequately through the policies of a socialist government, without any UN aid, and where compulsory limitation of family size has been in force since the late 1970s, leading to the current predominance of men. No special treatment has been thought necessary for women. Women's problems exist both at work and in marriage. It is said that the Chinese language does not yet have a term for sexual harassment. Urgent rescue missions for the dis-possessed and the violated will head the agenda but several other matters will receive heightened attention. Family related problems will be much consid-ered, following the 1994 International Year of the Family. The position of rural women will be taken further since its public airing in 1992 when the wives of 50 heads of state met in Geneva to draw attention to it. Much thought is likely to be given to the dramatic spread of AIDS among women in Africa and Asia. One other topic of growing importance is the plight of elderly women, 70% of whom live in developing countries. Above all, the Confer-ence will set its seal, it is hoped, on the goal of universal ratification of the 1981 Convention on All Forms of Discrimination Against Women. By the end of 1993, 130 nations had signed approval including all states in Latin America and the Caribbean, the first region to attain 100% endorsement.

It has taken half a century for the UN and, of course, informed world opin-ion, to push forward the movement for women's rights inch by inch. There have been setbacks but much has been achieved in developed states. In some parts of the world, however, among developing nations, progress has been in-finitesimal. Nevertheless, there is encouraging agreement among the sexes that it is less urgent to define new rights than to persuade states to adopt exist-ing instruments and apply them effectively. The UN Commission on the Status of Women has set down priority themes for women for the years 1991–6 under the areas of equality, development and peace:

1994   Equal pay for work of equal value.
         Women in urban areas; population, nutrition and health factors
         including migration, drug consumption and AIDS.

Risking death to give life Twelve nations have estimated maternal mortality rates of 800 or more. The average rate for Western Europe is 6.

	Maternal mortality (per 100,000 live births)	Lifetime chance of dying in pregnancy or childbirth*
Guinea	800	1 in 15
Nigeria	800	1 in 16
Zaire	800	1 in 16
Burkina Faso	810	1 in 16
Nepal	830	1 in 18
Congo	900	1 in 15
Papua N. Guinea	900	1 in 19
Chad	960	1 in 15
Ghana	1000	1 in 14
Somalia	1100	1 in 11
Bhutan	1310	1 in 11
Mali	2000	1 in 6

*Affected not only by maternal mortality rates but also by the number of births per woman.

Maternal deaths Maternal death rates for the 10 most populous nations of the developing world.

	Maternal mortality (per 100,000 live births)	Lifetime chance of dying in pregnancy or childbirth
China	95	1 in 400
Philippines	100	1 in 210
Mexico	110	1 in 240
Vietnam	120	1 in 180
Brazil	200	1 in 150
Indonesia	450	1 in 60
India	460	1 in 45
Pakistan	500	1 in 30
Bangladesh	600	1 in 30
Nigeria	800	1 in 16

Low birth weight Prevalence of low birth weight in the 10 nations with the largest numbers of births each year (representing almost 60% of all the world's births).

	% babies born below 2.5 kg
United States	7
China	9
Brazil	11
Mexico	12
Indonesia	14
Ethiopia	16
Nigeria	16
Pakistan	25
India	33
Bangladesh	50

Sources: Maternal mortality: *Maternal mortality: a global factbook*, WHO, Division of Family Health, 1991. Total fertility rate: *World population prospects: the 1992 revision*, United Nations Population Division, 1993. Low birth weight: *Low birth weight: a tabulation of available information*, WHO, Maternal Health and Safe Motherhood Programme, 1992.

Measures to eradicate violence against women in society.
1995 Equality in economic decision-making.
Promotion of literacy, education and training, including technological skills.
Women in international decision-making.
1996 Elimination of stereotyping of women in the mass media.
Child and dependent care, including sharing of work and family responsibilities.
Education for peace.

NOTE

1. The UNICEF 1989 State of the World's Children Report illustrates the double disadvantage of being born poor and female. For every social indicator, be it literacy, life expectancy, infant mortality, school enrolment, immunization levels or maternal deaths, there is a wide gap between industrialized and developing worlds. Some 500,000 women die of "maternal causes" (related to pregnancy and childbirth) every year leaving behind over one million orphans.

FURTHER READING

Acker, S., J. Megarry, S. Nisbet, E. Hoyle. *World Year Book of Education: women and education*. London: Kogan Page, 1984.

Braidotti, R., E Charkiewicz, S. Häusler, S. Wieringa. *Women, the environment and sustainable development: towards a theoretical synthesis*. London: Zed Books (for INSTRAW), 1994.

Byrnes, A. Women, feminism and international human rights law. *Australian Yearbook of International Law* 12, pp. 205–40, 1992.

Grant, J. P. *The state of the world's children*. Oxford: Oxford University Press (for UNICEF), 1994.

Sullivan, D. J. The implementation of women's rights: the effectiveness of existing procedures. In *In brief: human rights at the UN*. New York: UN, 1990.

United Nations. *Women: challenges to the Year 2000*. New York: UN Department of Public Information, 1991.

United Nations. *The world's women: 1970–1990, trends and statistics*. New York: UN Department of International Economic and Social Affairs, 1991.

United Nations. *The progress of nations*. New York: UNICEF, 1994.

Chapter Twelve

WOMEN'S RIGHTS

Since 1945 the UN has been dedicated to promotion of women's rights and economic, social, cultural and educational equality. There have been appropriate legal instruments, conferences and public information work worldwide. Much work has been done in liaison with NGOs and interest groups building on many years' intensive campaigning by women's groups.

1946 ECOSOC: Commission on Status of Women.
1948 Universal Declaration of Human Rights incorporates specific articles on women's rights.
1951 ILO: Convention on Equal Remuneration of Men and Women Workers.
1952 ECOSOC: Convention on Equal Rights of Women.
1957 ECOSOC: Supplementary Convention on Abolition of Slavery, the Slave Trade and Practices similar to Slavery.
General Assembly: Convention on Nationality of Married Women.
1962 General Assembly: Convention on Consent to Marriage, Minimum Age for Marriage, and Registration of Marriage.
1975 Mexico Women's Conference: Declaration, World Plan of Action.
1976–85 International Women's Decade.
1979 International Year of the Child.
1980 Copenhagen Women's Conference: Medium Term Plans 1977–89.
1981 General Assembly: Convention Against All Forms of Discrimination Against Women; Committee on Elimination of Discrimination Against Women, standing function.
1982 General Assembly: Declaration on the Participation of Women in Promoting Peace and Security.
1985 Nairobi Women's Conference: Forward-looking Strategies.
1992 Summit meeting of wives of heads of state, Geneva.
1994 International Year of the Family.
1995 The fourth World Conference on Women in Beijing scheduled.

CHAPTER THIRTEEN

Apartheid

South Africa had never known a day like Tuesday 10 May 1994. In the presence of 80 heads of national governments, some 6,000 foreign dignitaries and the UN Secretary-General, the country's first black President was inaugurated. The man tumultuously applauded by a great crowd was Nelson Mandela, released several years previously after 27 years in prison. This was the man who in prison and on his release had symbolized to the world an unswerving opposition to apartheid, the crime against human rights that had gripped his country for the best part of half a century and subjected it to condemnation and relative isolation. The world's media now saw this occasion as both a funeral, despatching a hated ideology into oblivion, and as a marriage, cementing the union of white and black in a country where no union, not even association on equal terms, had ever been allowed. It was all the more remarkable that both Mandela and the white President de Klerk he was succeeding had been awarded a Nobel Peace Prize in December 1993 for their painstaking work for accord. The mood was of reconciliation, not triumph. The first impulse of the victor over apartheid, declaring, "I stand before you filled with deep pride and joy . . . free at last", was followed by the noble acknowledgement of his predecessor:

> Mr Mandela has walked a long road and now stands at the top of the hill. A traveller would sit down and admire the view. But a man of destiny knows that beyond this hill is another and another. The journey is never complete. After so many centuries we will finally have a government which represents all South Africa. All South Africans are now free.

Never again, the new President declared, would his country "suffer the indignity of being the skunk of the world".

This account of the UN and apartheid explores, first, ideological origins,

161

and then goes on to trace the beginnings of an anti-apartheid campaign. Much polemic is stirred up as the UN espouses a "liberation" movement. Censures lead to rejection. The slow, experimental collaboration of black and white South Africans is described as it brings experiment, a new franchise and representative government for the oppressed, and dismantling of the old separatism.

THE ORIGINS OF APARTHEID

Apartheid as an ideology pervading South Africa for many years seemed irreversible to victims and onlookers. Literally meaning "separateness", it had its origin in the care taken by Dutch settlers in mid-seventeenth century Cape Province to erect a ring-fence against surrounding negro tribes. The British came 150 years later to establish garrisons and farms, bringing with them more humane readiness to disregard notions of colour. Many of the earlier Dutch, known as Boers, trekked north into the hinterland and set up independent republics. Contest over access to land and to minerals led to Anglo/Boer hostilities between 1899 and 1902 and resulted in a Boer defeat. Inevitably, feelings of vulnerability hardened among the Afrikaner Boers and they soon adopted a *laager* (defensive camp) approach to coexistence with the black majority.

The Union of South Africa in 1910 adopted a deliberate strategy of colour discrimination and separateness. White freedom, for which the Boers had fought, had to be preserved. Blacks lost their rights to land, work and residence, becoming second-class citizens of a country in which they were denied any responsibility. Discriminatory policies set hard. Racial elements were to be identified to create a structure where six million whites were at the top with 18 million Africans at the bottom and in between 4 million Indian and "coloured", that is, mixed-race. These four elements were to be kept separate in provision for tenure, housing, healthcare, education, employment and leisure.

The discrimination was enforced obsessively after 1948. Nationally the result of this was gross disparity in the extent of poverty, infant mortality, life-expectancy and monthly income. Locally, colour determined who was served first at post-office counters, who was allowed in the hotel, the bus, the public park, the beach and the swimming pool. "Mixing colour" was not tolerated. There was a geographical separation, too, in the move to force Bantu to live in black homelands where, it was said, they could "develop" in distinctive fashion. They were expected, in fact, to develop the poorest 13% of South Africa's land. Those blacks who serviced their white employers were denied the suburbs and assigned to the shanties of black townships.

After the Second World War came the growing realization outside South Africa that fascist racism was extant. The uncompromising affirmations of premiers in Pretoria such as Daniel Malan (1948–54) and of Hendrik Verwoerd (1958–66) sounded ominously like the racial doctrines of the Nazis that the new United Nations emphatically set out to expose. A belief in racial "purity" and superiority was dressed in the protective armour of legislation. Arrest and detention without trial was resorted to. There was a ban on mixed marriages. All blacks over the age of 16 were to carry a passbook, to be produced on demand by the police. Two hundred legal statutes biased in racial terms indicated that apartheid was not just parliamentary policy but an institutional device bearing on every sort of political, economic and social relationship. Ironically, the severity and extent of imposed apartheid was to create a group of middle-class blacks, professional and intellectual, who resented discrimination bitterly. In association with many like-minded whites they set out both to oppose Draconian measures in their own land and to appeal to the world for sympathy and help. While the mass of the population ingeniously cultivated survival skills, these potential resistance leaders wrote, spoke, travelled abroad and, for many, dodged scrutiny and imprisonment.

APARTHEID AS A UN CAUSE

For almost 50 years apartheid has been a particular concern for the United Nations, briefed as it is to safeguard and promote the observance of human rights. The concern has taken different forms at various times; the initial attempt to draft norms and Resolutions in the 1950s was succeeded in the following decade by more vigorous and direct campaigning for betterment; in the 1970s and 1980s, as white South Africa dug in its heels and black South Africans reacted with more frustrated anger and violence, members of the UN rallied to target specific violation and impose sanctions. This has represented a move from the general and abstract to the specific and concrete. The General Assembly, at first somewhat timidly and then with resolve, has thundered its denunciation.[1] Newer states lately released from colonial dependence have been most vociferous. To many the Security Council has seemed to pussyfoot, in that members of the elite P5, traders in the main and some with imperial records, voiced reservations at the outset, which dulled the edge of any forcible pressure on a delinquent state. Pretoria was quick to protest that what it did at home was an internal matter not to be interfered with by the world organization. Time after time the rogue regime hid behind the exclusion clause of Article 2.7 forbidding UN intervention in matters deemed to be within a state's domestic jurisdiction.

Apartheid appeared on the agenda at the General Assembly's very first meeting in autumn 1946, when India complained about South Africa restricting the residence and trading of Indians in the Cape. Majority opinion urged that measures be implemented in accordance with Charter principles to affirm inalienable rights and freedoms. Fruitless talks between the aggrieved parties and others anxious to mediate eventually shifted UN involvement from an attempt at reconciliation to the graver step of passing judgement on the direction of South African policies. When the South African delegation walked out of the General Assembly in 1955, the possibility of any non-contentious discussion and solution appeared remote. A watching world was now viewing apartheid as a crime and as a policy, originally domestic, which could surely lead to international conflict. The judgemental role of the UN did not find favour with former colonial powers such as Britain, France, Belgium and Portugal although they did not dissent from Resolutions, "deploring" and viewing with "deep regret and concern" a deteriorating situation. To require a drastic change of policy by one member was considered a dangerous precedent; others believed that it might be more dangerous *not* to require a change of policy.

The Sharpeville Massacre of March 1960, when police gunned down 69 demonstrators, sent shock-waves around the world and jolted the General Assembly into passing a Resolution of historic importance. South Africa was told to abandon the practice of apartheid. Dag Hammarskjöld, then UN Secretary-General, was to take "appropriate action" to uphold the Charter. Apartheid was no longer merely a domestic "difficulty" – it was now everybody's business. Hammarskjöld decided that he must go to see for himself the possibilities of negotiating specific betterment proposals rather than somehow requiring the overthrow of what was, after all, a sovereign government and UN member. Progress was slow. Even if "preventive diplomacy" could have yielded some small alleviation, the Secretary-General's death that year aborted all initiatives. The idea that the UN is a place where men meet either to settle a problem or to make resolution more difficult gained substance from debates facing a blank wall of contempt and rejection from South Africa. It was clear that bringing outside pressure to bear carries the risk of increasing an offender's stubbornness to conform. What was the UN to do about that? Action by an international organization judged ineffectual leads to other *ad hoc* groups orchestrating a protest campaign. This is seen by the offender as non-institutional, suspect, and as propaganda to be resisted rather than ignored. Could the UN then legitimately act as a clearing-house for protest and add further to the charge of unwarranted interference? Encouraging resistance from within the violating state might lead to tightened repression, torture, even death. Was moral responsibility endangered here?

The 1960s ushered in an era of fairly desperate enterprise on the part of those who stood against apartheid, in New York and elsewhere. In 1960 the General Assembly listened to a passionate appeal from Albert Luthuli, a Zulu chief and leader of the African National Congress (ANC), the resistance vanguard. He argued that an economic boycott of his country would hit the oppressors where it hurt and it was the only chance of aiding a peaceful transition to democracy. Impressed by Luthuli, the first African to receive a Nobel

Peace Prize, the Assembly set up a committee to examine the practicability of boycotting ports and airfields in South Africa. This was not too audacious a shift from promulgating human rights to enforcement. Nor was it particularly effective. The UK, a main trading partner with 650 companies represented in South Africa, opposed the move and 21 other nations retained representatives in Pretoria. New York had not clearly thought out how an external agency might persuade a state to promote economic and social rights as well as the traditional liberal values of free speech, religion, press and association. To provide equitable distribution of the former might strike a conservative government as more revolutionary a challenge. It would be unwise to expedite changes threatening the foundations of state power. The Universal Declaration of Human Rights calls for the legal realization separately of economic and social rights and civil and political rights. In the case of South Africa's apartheid framework the conceding of one category of rights by no means guaranteed the implementation of the other.

Something of a side issue, but associated with apartheid, was the extent of South Africa's unfriendly attitude to the "frontline states" in the vicinity. In the case of Botswana, Angola and Mozambique this partly involved political differences, but in the case of Namibia, the former South West Africa (as Chapter 16 describes), there was an insistent claim and attempt at take-over of the territory. This was in defiance of UN rulings and it led to a General Assembly Resolution putting its admonition in very strong terms.

UN opposition to apartheid gathered momentum in the 1960s. The South African liberation movement was badly mauled in 1963 when eight of its leaders were sentenced to life imprisonment. Nelson Mandela, facing 27 years behind bars, told the court from the dock that the struggle for the right to live was an ideal for which he and others were prepared to die. "Charge us, ban us, jail us, you can't silence the truth" was the rallying call of his acolytes outside. The UN General Assembly, inspired by an ANC Freedom Charter broadcast around the globe, now called on South Africa in 1963 to convene a national Convention to represent all ethnic interests. Prisoners must be released; a general amnesty declared. The Security Council took up the cudgels and called for a voluntary arms embargo in the same year (although it did not become mandatory for 14 years). There followed in 1964 a boycott of South Africa on behalf of the world's sportsmen and the International Olympic Committee sorrowfully expelled the nation. A year later the UN established a large trust fund for apartheid victims. A further ban came in 1968, this time prohibiting educational, scientific and cultural exchanges with South Africa. Many people began to wonder whether cutting off an erring state could be anything other than punitive, and was scarcely productive. It would not be easy consequently to detect any feelers for negotiation, even though that possibility seemed remote.

ANTI-APARTHEID MOVEMENT AS "LIBERATION"

An International Convention on the Elimination of All Forms of Racial Discrimination was signed in 1969 and in time it was ratified by 128 states. This was a trumpeted edict against apartheid. In New York a committee of nine nations was to provide an information bank, carry out surveys (at arm's length) and deal with complaints and petitions. The wording of the measure plainly expressed the double-edge of racism – it harms not only those who are its objects but those who practise it. Within months and into the 1970s the UN had moved from report, recommendation and censure to espousing and facilitating "liberation". This was a sea-change putting punch into Charter principles; it was a movement out of the declaratory stage of attempting to shape values via Resolutions and published principles to trying to realize those values by means of active intervention.

Practically, however, the demands of this more onerous concept and politico-economic considerations induced certain major powers (France, Britain and the US) to resort to veto in the Security Council. Apparently these nations could not bring themselves to agree that there was a threat to international peace. A "fresh approach" to Pretoria was their stated preference, arousing the fury of other African states such as Zambia and Tanzania. Where was the "solidarity" with the oppressed? United Nations action was now unambiguous, at least at source. An International Convention on the Suppression and Punishment of the Crime of Apartheid predictably incurred the wrath of Pretoria. Twelve months later the General Assembly recommended the expulsion of South Africa from the UN and blacklisting by the Specialized Agencies. Once more, there was dissent from France, Britain and the US, who clung to a belief that it was better to keep the delinquent state in UN suspended membership and continue with attempts at some form of persuasion. Reinstatement would be an easier process than readmission. In fact, the General Assembly excluded South African delegates from debates and they then went home. No contributions would be paid by the South Africans and they were either expelled or suspended by the Specialized Agencies. Final judgement against apartheid was evident in 1976 with a carefully framed Programme of Action to be mounted from a UN Centre against Apartheid. It was perhaps questionable how effective "action" might be thousands of miles away given the adamant refusal of South Africa to initiate even preliminary negotiations.

If the force of opposition was now enhanced, so was the argument over methods. When the UN vigorously sought to apply mandatory sanctions in 1977 it met equally strong opposition from Britain and from Washington. How could sanctions be enforced?[2] Who would they hurt most – the white South Africans, the blacks dependent on a buoyant economy for their employers, or frontline states also dependent on their powerful neighbour? If, for all sorts of reasons, sanctions were likely to prove ineffective, was their symbolic function really worth the trouble? Would not sanction-breaking greatly erode their grip as had happened elsewhere? Sanctions that were not sufficiently deterrent or coercive in leverage would almost certainly lend force to a siege mentality in the target state. Moreover, should the UN not reach beyond punishment to encourage a deprived state to prefer the process of dialogue and negotiation?

The issues surrounding the practicability of sanctions were given extra prominence when the Security Council in the same year, 1977, determined that the sale of arms to South Africa constituted a threat to peace (under Charter Article 39), and so it followed that measures not involving armed force had to be taken. Only sanctions of an economic or diplomatic nature could be used. This presented certain of the P5 with a dilemma. If they acquiesced to applied sanctions (so the cynics said), anxieties about other drastic options would be allayed. Could active trading nations interrupt and suspend normal commercial and consular relations and encourage disinvestment when the consequences of placing out of contact the embargoed client were so uncertain? On the other hand, if they did not endorse sanctions, and especially if they applied a negative veto, they could be charged with safeguarding a policy deemed criminal and so be acting contrary to Charter purposes and principles. An embargo on arms sales to South Africa, a voluntary measure in 1963, was made mandatory in 1977. Any nuclear arms dealing was also proscribed.

The story of the campaign against apartheid would not be complete without a reference to the Herculean efforts of many NGOs. An impressive array of groups that are political and non-political, religious and charitable, have kept up a round-the-clock vigil as the Anti-apartheid Movement for more than four decades. Some 400 NGOs have consultative status within the UN's Economic and Social Council, indicating its belief that in matters of world importance the involvement of states alone is no longer adequate. Through gathering information, hosting and aiding victims, and by mounting protest action, their objective has been to make South Africa realize that a reputation for being unjust to a majority of your own people is internationally demoralizing and internally corrosive.

CHANGING ATTITUDES AMONG SOUTH AFRICANS

It was in the 1980s that many South Africans at last began to appreciate what UK Prime Minister Harold Macmillan had described in Cape Town 20 years previously as the winds of change sweeping their continent. The maintenance of apartheid was increasingly seen not as a protective device that furnished economic well-being and security but as a threat to existence itself. Neglect by government of black education, housing, sanitation and preventable disease fuelled violence, drop-out from schools, and drug dependence in a population likely to double in the next 30 years. Reluctance to even up prosperity and reverse environmental decline would steadily erode the economic and social fabric. South Africa would only have a future if it began to dismantle the tradition of apartheid.[3] The old myths, confidently held, were now giving way to something approaching despair. The earlier optimism, shared by people in many countries, that a strongly growing prosperity would bring gains that in due course would "trickle down" to the less fortunate, was clearly misconceived. So, too, was the allied hope that some sort of economic osmosis could be achieved without radical upset of the social order, whereby "stability" would be maintained, outside investors reassured and the process of evolution rather than revolution accommodated.

Uncertainty within and pressure from without shook South Africa's complacency and brought tensions to an unendurable pitch. Inevitably, the Government sought to screw down dissent and opposition by recourse to a state of emergency in 36 areas, to the use of the armed police posse, detention and censorship. The original ANC claim that a struggle for liberation could be peaceful was no longer credible. South Africa's military budget, increased 12 times between 1960 and 1980, indicated mobilization for civil war. Three great protests had severed the nation and angered the world: Sharpeville in 1960, Soweto in 1976, and the national strikes of 1984. It was obvious that the flailing efforts to silence the oppressed only made the voices of protest more audible.

A highly visible aspect of the liberation struggle against apartheid was the participation of young people in South Africa. One in two detainees was 18 or younger. The so-called "children" were the most deprived and the most assertive (as they are in reports from the Palestinian conflict). There was great poignancy in 1985 when the UN proclaimed the year International Youth Year and from South Africa came the cry, "Nothing demonstrates the utter bankruptcy of apartheid as the revolt of our youth. Never on our knees! Victory is certain!" This was a poignant message from Nelson Mandela, smuggled out of Robben Island Prison in 1980.

After 40 years of a consistent stand the UN found itself faced with the issue of supporting violence as a legitimate vehicle of protest against apartheid. If the opposition persistently resorted to violent tactics as the contest burst out in virulence, what moral position should the outside world adopt? What, for instance, were the ultimate implications of the Rev. Allan Boesak's statement before the UN Special Committee on Apartheid in January 1988 when this South African freedom campaigner declared: "Apartheid is so wrong, so indefensible, so intrinsically evil that it cannot be modernized, streamlined or reformed; it can only be irrevocably eradicated"? The UN's lawyers had found that a legally permissible right to use violence arises only in extreme situations as the final response to systematic violation. Furthermore, means used to resist violation of rights of individuals or of peoples should be "proportionate" to the gravity of that violation. But is the right to violent combat legitimate only if it is accorded to a responsible group? Is it disproportionate to allow any individual guerrilla the option of violent tactics, perhaps irresponsibly?

With some impatience another question was being asked in South Africa: if our active resistance becomes violent can the international community really sit on its hands and take refuge in the non-violent liberalism of the Charter while our persecuted community and its oppressors are exploding? The General Assembly, after all, had challenged Pretoria in establishing the "inalienable right" of the anti-apartheid wing to use all available means "including armed struggle". The ANC lost no time in blessing the militaristic efforts of its armed guerrilla force, *Umkhonto we Sizwe,* the Spear of the Nation – and it felt justified on hearing such last-ditch statements as that of President P. W. Botha in 1986, "If we respect minority rights, we won't have black majority rule".

THE CRUMBLING OF APARTHEID

Apartheid began to disintegrate very visibly in February 1991, more or less as the floodgates of democracy were swinging open in Eastern Europe. In February of that year President de Klerk promised to repeal three of the noxious laws that had inflamed protest, namely, the Land Acts (1913, 1936) restricting black farming; the Group Areas Act (1950) confining blacks to "townships"; and the Population Registration Act (1950) dividing the nation into racial categories. Segregation in public places was ended. The previous February Mandela had been released from imprisonment amid scenes of euphoria.

Although there were government concessions contending groups remained partisan and suspicious. Right-wing factions deemed de Klerk a traitor and began to agitate for a *Volkstaat* (a white people's state) around Pretoria. ANC activists became locked in bloody feuds with a powerful Zulu group, the *Inkatha.* Mandela, urging restraint, warned the international community at the UN not to be too hasty in jettisoning sanctions until full enfranchisement was secured. He went on to point out that repeal of the Land and Group Areas Acts would not guarantee either comprehensive transfer of land rights or access to desirable suburbs in the near future without a drastic redistribution of wealth. There was a surmise here and there among black nationalists that the reforms were more theatre than reality. Apart from the expected public posturing in preparation for electoral battles there was doubt whether established echelons in the bureaucracy, the police and the army could ever learn to make promised reforms attainable on the ground. Was it possible that whites would rid themselves of the more outrageous elements of apartheid legislation and then hang on to power without fear of serious repercussions? Should such a government not be presumed guilty until proven innocent?

Whatever the extent of reservation and uncertainty, in 1992 de Klerk and Mandela conducted a series of very thorough discussions as a working party on eventual transition. Now not only was apartheid to go but a new constitution was to be brought into being with the expressed aim of transferring power to the erstwhile victims of the discrimination. Outside observers have been intrigued by the skilful way in which the leading participants steered towards consensus. Mandela himself was adroit enough to enlist world backing for his position when he began extensive tours abroad and to the UN. He was at pains to stress that "to let bygones be bygones", as he put it, was to temper magnanimity with realism. Black "domination" was not his objective, he stressed, and he frequently implied that a swim-or-sink coalition with white parliamentarians was the only way forward. Orchestration of harmony such as this was fully in accord with Charter principles. At home both Mandela and de Klerk had the task of delivering an acceptable compromise deal to activists. Government in black hands had to be modified by structural guarantees for the white minority. Agreement on a "Government of National Unity" would not be possible if each side claimed the power of veto. Yet somehow the white minority must be eased out of monopoly into a situation where the population ratio of 22 million non-white to 6 million white would ultimately be reflected in majority dominance. That would indeed be a transition to democracy. Everybody's question was: how long can the transformation be delayed?

Twelve months or so of exhaustive parleying brought agreement in February 1993 that a government of national unity would go into office until the turn of the century. Mandela's advisors counselled that a party emerging as a majority at any election (to be held in April 1994) would invite other parties to join the government of its own free will, not because it were forced by the constitution. Mandela's own conviction was that negotiations would progress only if whites were rid of the fear that a majority (and certainly a landslide one) would be used to coerce the minorities. An imaginative "sunset clause" was proposed. Whites would concede something of their share in power at the centre in return for a federal system where regional autonomies could be enjoyed.

SOUTH AFRICA'S FIRST FREE ELECTION

The heady brew of proposed reform was not easy for unschooled blacks to swallow. In addition to vociferous claims and counter-demands abundantly aired in a press now free there were preparations afoot for 22 million people to vote for the first time in their lives. Mandela was heard to remark to the UN's Secretary-General when in New York that he would be entering an election booth for the very first time at the age of 75 in company with youths of 18. To help in the process of public relations the UN sent a neutral Observer Mission in South Africa (UNOMSA), which had the sensitive task of calming over-expectations by some and reassuring the long-accustomed circumspection and disbelief of others. Blue-garbed field workers watched at rallies and marches and encouraged the setting up of regional and local Dispute Resolution Centres. Their "quiet diplomacy" was to try to build trust over six months, to assist mediation not lead it. They reported to New York and liaised with fellow observers from the EU and from the British Commonwealth.

Important assignments for all these international observers were to work for understanding with the security forces and with members of the coloured community, many fearing their future was trapped between white and black interest groups. The election held in April 1994 was accomplished with surprising peacefulness. The difficulties of getting people to the polls and physical administration of the ballot were enormous and on the whole not too satisfactorily achieved. Yet it was a victory over discrimination and despotism. Two-thirds of the electorate gave the ANC a commanding lead (although not quite the overall predominance they had hoped for) and one in five re-elected the Government's National Party. A coalition then took office: South Africa was free at last.

SOUTH AFRICA'S FUTURE

If the unshackling of apartheid represents "liberation", two questions especially need to be addressed. Liberation from whom? Liberation for what? Black South Africans have lived not in a nation but in an occupied territory. The prime need is to seek restoration of rights of access to land, to other resources, and to opportunity. Repossession and redistribution are both complex problems. The succeeding phase must demonstrate that in a very literal sense the victimized will have to be helped to escape from their past if they are to be united with a future. Liberation as release from constraining elements and factors will demand examination of fresh targets, new methods and experiment in communal redesign. How will the priorities be determined?

Will the UN turn its back on South Africa now that its watching brief is diminishing with the toppling of the apartheid system? There will be an urgent need for programmes of rehabilitation on a massive scale to fill in inadequacies in the social framework where seven million people live in chronic poverty, are undereducated and underhoused; one in three are jobless and generally in a state of need. This is where the skills and resources of the UN's Specialized Agencies could be of immense help. Then there is the economy of South Africa, once so vibrant, which has been upset by isolation and sanctions. This could be assisted by the World Bank helping to fund short- and long-term programmes of resuscitation and renewal. Such programmes would be best approached and undertaken in a regional context and not solely within the parameters of one nation state. The UN with its long experience of aiding regional co-ordination and security will surely have an important job to do as South Africa is reinstated in the General Assembly, becomes a member (but not a domineering one) of the Organization of African Unity, and the Southern African Development Community, and after 33 years is readmitted to the British Commonwealth.[4]

Speculation is widespread as to the extent to which the collapse of apartheid was brought about by unremitting efforts and influences from outside or by the heroic persistence of the opposition inside South Africa. In the last few years the weight of influence from converging forces was quite remarkable. The question, however, is academic. The underlying prejudices and mistakes that engendered racial discrimination will take a long time to disappear. In Mandela's words, "the time for the healing of wounds has come. The time to build is upon us!". Eased in conscience, the world can utter the traditional South African greeting, "Go well!".

NOTES

1. On 28 November 1961 the General Assembly resolved that apartheid had "brought about international tension and [that] its continuance constitutes a serious danger to peace and international security". The voting was 97 for and 2 against (South Africa and Portugal). In November 1962 reservations (if not timidity) were reflected in voting to break diplomatic relations with South Africa, boycott its exports, and impose an arms embargo. There were 67 for, 16 against and the 27 abstentions included the US, the UK, the Federal Republic of Germany and Japan – all main trading nations.

2. Security Council sanctions are mandatory, for instance, the arms embargo against South Africa in 1977. General Assembly sanctions are only recommendations depending on voluntary compliance, for example, the 1985 oil embargo and the 1975 Resolution on sport participation. More weight was applied by a number of international and national bodies from time to time such as the British Commonwealth, the Organization of Arab Petroleum Exporting Countries (OPEC), the OAU and the EC. Above all, financial measures resulting in numerous banks and companies pulling out of South Africa in the 1970s and 1980s had a great and lasting effect.

3. Representatives of 124 states, NGOs, liberation movements, economists and sociologists met in Paris in 1981 to express profound concern over human rights violation in South Africa, the arms build-up, and transgressions against neighbouring states. Unless apartheid was soon dismantled every effort would be applied to bringing the pariah state to its (economic) knees.

4. In 1995 South Africa has been readmitted to a whole range of bodies including those mentioned. The Government has both white and black members and represents a wide range of political groupings. Former President de Klerk is now a Vice-President.

ΓURTHER READING

Hirson, B. The struggle for a post-apartheid society in South Africa. *Third World Quarterly* **12**(2), pp. 159–65, 1990.

Meredith, M. *In the name of apartheid. South Africa in the post-war period.* London: Hamish Hamilton, 1988.

Ozgur, O. A. *Apartheid: the United Nations and peaceful change in South Africa.* New York: Dobbs Ferry, 1982.

Southall, R. The new South Africa in the new world order: beyond the double whammy. *Third World Quarterly* **15**(1), pp. 121–38, 1994.

Chapter Thirteen

APARTHEID

1899–1902	Britain fights second Boer War.
1910	Union of South Africa adopts colour discrimination.
1946	India accuses South Africa at UN of racial discrimination in regard to Indians at the Cape.
1948 & 1958	Apartheid affirmed at inauguration of successive administrations of Presidents Malan and Verwoerd.
1955	South Africa walks out of UN General Assembly.
1960	Sharpeville Massacre.
1961	UN condemns apartheid (also in 1962, 1966, 1968).
1963	UN General Assembly Resolution on voluntary end to arms trading with South Africa.
1969	International Convention on the Elimination of All Forms of Racial Discrimination.
1976	Soweto Massacre; UN sets up Centre for Apartheid with a Programme for Action; International Convention on Suppression and Punishment of all Forms of Apartheid.
1991	Racial segregation in public places ended. Mandela freed.
1992	Government in discussion with working parties on eventual transition.
1993	Mandela and de Klerk awarded Nobel Peace Prizes.
1994	10 April: Mandela inaugurated as South Africa's President. May: South Africa's first universal suffrage election, observed by UN and others.
1995	Multiparty government in office with reconstruction programme.

Former Yugoslavia (Bosnia)

"Bloody Bosnia" in today's media represents the sort of horror that Europe thought it had consigned to the archives in 1945. The blood-spattered play-ground and market-place bread queue raked by snipers and pounded by mor-tars, the burned-out villages, the systematic pillage and rape, are a savagery that the Second World War seemed to have denounced and swept away. Apart from the chaotic society and ruined economy of "former Yugoslavia", there is a flagrant disregard of civilized relationships and a primeval emphasis on the slash-and-destroy of genocide. The pictures and reports in the media reveal the UN in desperate activity and, in some respects, powerless. Violent outrages are reported every day to an aghast world. In New York the Security Council wrestles with the politics and the logistics of a humanitarian relief operation. In two busy months in 1993, for instance, as peace proposals littered the table, the Security Council met 18 times, adopted 13 Resolutions, and issued six statements. In the severed provinces of former Yugoslavia 38,500 Blue Berets have been at work ever since February 1992 on 12-month stints, several times renewed, and the cost is running at $1,900 million a year.[1]

This case-study of the former Yugoslavia considers the UN as protector of human rights rather than provider of a military interpositioned force. The is-sues are humanitarian. The questions to be examined are, first, how is it that the conflict has become an "ethnic contest"? Then, in what ways is the UN attempting to help a flood of displaced people? Thirdly, what are the argu-ments current in the world community for some type of forcible intervention? Finally, and in brief, we take a look at the prospects for reconciling the war-ring factions and reasserting human rights.

ORIGINS OF COEXISTENCE AND DISSENSION

The part of Europe known as the Balkans has long been viewed as a pressure-cooker. Yugoslavia was carved out of remnants of the Austro-Hungarian and Ottoman empires after 1918, ultimately to comprise six constituent republics after the Second World War. After the trauma of occupation by the Axis Powers and internecine guerrilla fighting during the war when 10% of the population was destroyed, Yugoslavia became unified under the strong hand of Marshal Josip Tito, partisan leader and Communist who ruled until 1980. Dominance was exerted by Serbia from the nation's capital of Belgrade. In the last 15 years tension and rivalries have taken on a more political complexion as the Communism of three and a half decades has been modified from a one-party system to a multiparty democracy, and as the economy has shifted from centralized nationalization to a market economy. Serbia alone among the six republics has retained a strong Communist Party whose leaders have adopted nationalistic clothes. Their political pre-eminence monopolizes power in only one republic rather than five. They are not too secure, even so, for 100 opposition groups emerged in the election of December 1993.

The former Yugoslavia

While Serbia is proud of the fact that its population is 80% Serb and Ortho-dox Christian (with 14% Albanian), it is possessively concerned about the 2.5 million Serbs living elsewhere in other republics. There is a mission pro-claimed by Serb leader Slobadan Milosevic to "rescue" those who are outside, not by bringing them home but by expanding to envelop them in areas that must be "cleansed" of non-Serb elements. Communist zeal has given way to a narrow, chauvinistic creed generally amplified in apocalyptic terms. The fan-tasy of greater (purer) Serbia smacks of megalomania as Belgrade expresses it, and as the army (taking two-thirds of the budget) thrives on it. Particularly in Bosnia among the Serb communities there is a reverberating call for assertion and deliverance from "enemies".

Croatia, to the northwest, is centred on its capital of Zagreb. Originally it was a buffer zone against the Ottoman Empire for the Hungarians. Croats, Catholic in the main, make up 75% of the population with an 11% Serb minority. These people have strong ideals of defensive patriotism and separa-tism, somewhat skewed by their wartime puppet regime under Nazi Germany. The excesses of that era, when Serb partisans were ruthlessly hunted, were scarcely healed when Tito, himself a Croat, tried to reconcile Croat and Serb. Not surprisingly, when the Communist *diktat* fell apart it was towards suspect Croatia that the rescue mission launched a thrust.

Bosnia-Hercegovina straddles the space between Serbia and Croatia. Seized by the Austrians in 1908 and until 1918 a province influenced by Vienna, Bosnia has since held itself proud as a cohesive unity. It has an ethnic mix of fair proportions: Muslims 43%, Croats 18% and Serbs 32%. President Alija Izetbegovic is Europe's only Muslim head of state. There is a long-standing tradition of harmony and intermarriage. The present Bosnian Cabi-net has eight Muslims, six Croats and six Serbs, with a democratically elected parliament in the capital Sarajevo, and a constitution that deems ethnic dis-crimination an offence against the law. It is a cruel irony that Bosnia and the most northerly republic of Slovenia, both proud of their reputation for ethnic coexistence, were the victims of rapacious elements in Serbia. "We pay in flesh," a Slovene philosopher has said, "the price for being the stuff of others' dreams."

It is misleading to present the former Yugoslavia as a place where ethnic distinctions run riot. The unfortunate origin of the troubles, which have now lasted five years, lies in the illegitimate invasion of Slovenia, then Croatia, and finally Bosnia by Serb extremists who in Belgrade have pointed to numbers of outlying Serbs as in need of liberation. The smaller units of forlorn Serbs were in Vojvodina (54%) and Kosovo (13%) and these were soon annexed to Bel-grade. Slovenia held the Serb push at bay for ten days in summer 1991 and then the main campaign lunged at Croatia and Bosnia. The expression "ethnic cleansing", or forcible expulsion of rival groups, seems to have been coined not by its perpetrators but by observers. Political, and to some extent reli-gious, differences have been the chief discordant themes rather than those of ethnic affiliation. On the part of a few there has been resentment at loss of power and a fierce search for a new image and a stamping-ground.

Before the UN became involved European politicians were generally inclined to acknowledge the disparity of the constituent parts of former Yugoslavia and in a sense, although not deliberately, to facilitate their standing apart. Thus, the proclaimed independence of Croatia and Slovenia in June 1991 received the endorsement of Germany in December 1991 together with that of Bosnia, and the three republics were recognized as sovereign states by the EC in early 1992, later to be admitted to the United Nations (along with Macedonia) in spring 1993. Was the acknowledgment of a desire for autonomy by constituents of a state rather premature? Much controversy surrounds this question. Has outside interference "ethnocized" internal political differences? Whether or not this is the case, sadly it is now clear that partition is unlikely to rejuvenate a divided nation. Mandela's "rainbow nation" did refer to people who had not virtually destroyed each other, but such harmonization is surely the essence of a collaborative and unified approach to coexistence and rebuilding. The notion that "I can't share this with you so we'll both destroy it together" seems the last word in anarchy.

UN AS PROTECTOR AND MEDIATOR

The UN attempt to reconcile what was being seen as an ethnic contest was the despatch of a UN Protection Force (UNPROFOR) in February 1992. Its mandate was essentially twofold, namely, to safeguard four zones in the Serb areas of Croatia that were in dispute, and, further, to supervise the withdrawal of the invading Serb force.[2] Almost predictably, opposing sides interpreted this mandate differently. Belgrade, feeling outraged, saw protection as demonstrating the impermanence of frontiers. Zagreb saw the UN arrival as holding a line that the Serbs had failed to acquire. The UN position was fragile and pleased few people. The Serb forces in Croatia and later in Bosnia showed no hesitation in breaking the numerous cease-fires that were obtained under difficult circumstances. It was never clear how far contravention and atrocities were ordered from Belgrade or whether they represented the senseless extremism of local warlords. Beleaguered Croats and Bosnians soon expressed their frustration at not being allowed to hurl back the invading force. The Muslims in particular resented a UN embargo that denied them arms and they frequently broke a negotiated cease-fire. Did not Article 51 of the UN Charter declare that "nothing shall impair the inherent right of individual or collective self-defence if an armed attack occurs"? There was, of course, in the same sentence of the same Article the rider, "until the Security Council has taken measures necessary to maintain international peace and security".

The measure that the Security Council had taken was to put UNPROFOR in as a restraining barrier and as a protection-and-relief force. Political flavours coated even this when the General Assembly considered it. Some Islamic states, such as Pakistan, Iraq, Egypt and Senegal, were vocal in condemning oppression of Muslims in Bosnia. In proscribing armed support, wasn't the UN covertly backing Belgrade? Bosnia's Muslims were Europe's Palestinians also without homes, resources and friends. After all, one in three of the world's refugees was Muslim. There were two choices before Zagreb and Sarajevo. One was to negotiate under the flimsy shield of the UN umbrella on the basis of something neither wanted. The other was to go on fighting with, as it were, their hands tied. All the time that battle waxed and waned in the field the contesting parties talked in New York and Geneva under the auspices of chairmen from the EC and from the UN and, once again, the ethnic component of quarrels was in the ascendant.

Inevitably, the issue of war crimes was raised. Nearly 50 years earlier the International Military Tribunals at Nuremberg and Tokyo had carefully enumerated codes dealing with major criminals and a number of tribunals had tried minor offenders. Then, as now, there were two crucial questions of significance to what might be termed crimes against ethnic origin. First, did a suspect defend his action as obedience to a superior or to regulations? Secondly, did a senior disclaim responsibility because of the unauthorized behaviour of subordinates? Nuremberg clearly established that neither assertion would constitute a defence, but either might be put forward in mitigation of punishment. The true test was whether "moral choice" was possible for the individual, although inevitably there would be circumstances in which it might be suicidal to attempt such judgement.

These and other questions were asked in May 1993 when the Secretary-General proposed to the Security Council that a tribunal be set up. There would be two trial chambers, an independent prosecutor, arrangements for defence counsel, and an appeals bench of 11 judges. Only individuals would be tried, nobody *in absentia*, and there would be no capital punishment. Over 1,000 suspected violators from all three warring groups had been named since January 1991. Even so, the problems were legion. How would suspects be arrested and physically brought to the court? What about witnesses and documentation? In what light would a confession be regarded? Supposing politicians were listed as politically accountable, as was President Milosevic, then how could fruitful negotiations proceed, for they were main actors? Would they demand immunity in exchange for a settlement deal? If they were granted immunity what credibility would any tribunal then have? Conventionally, "war crimes" have been categorized as offences that can be harmful when they occur *between* states. Here was the UN endeavouring to act as a court exercising jurisdiction *within* a state. It could well be that national backing of an alleged criminal would both deny the right of the court to hear the case and to level judgment, and, most certainly, it would very likely refuse to extradite named suspects.

It is not yet clear just how far this extra-national judicial process might be able to go. The International Court of Justice at The Hague has ordered the former Republic of Yugoslavia to prevent flagrant violation such as sniping at civilians, shelling of towns, detention in prison camps and interference with relief convoys. The crime of genocide is above all proscribed. Another UN measure has been to despatch teams of forensic investigators to excavate sites where there is evidence of executions. Generally, the investigation of possible breaches of international humanitarian law by a UN Commission based in Geneva is making very slow headway. UN member-states have never got round to establishing an international criminal court, police force and prison to deal comprehensively with human rights violators.

THE WAR ON CIVILIANS

The war in this part of Europe is pounding civilians to dust and despair. All Europe knows the havoc and cruelty associated with Dubrovnik, Vukovar, Osijek, Sarajevo, Mostar, Srebenica, Gorazde and Tuzla. Although much of the world's press blames Serbia for its descent into barbarism, all contending parties have committed atrocities and shown little compunction or restraint. Almost two million people have fled the Balkan turmoil, the largest displacement of population since the last world war. They have no clear idea of their destination and are uncertain whether they can ever return. Two out of three are less than 20 years old. More than four million are trapped by the fighting, often penned in detention camps. Thousands have been killed, many thousands wounded. Hospitals, schools and food supplies have all been destroyed.

European governments, faced with a flood of refugees, are divided in their response. Some nations, notably Germany housing 425,000, Switzerland 85,000, and Sweden 70,000, have been outstandingly hospitable. There are others who call for an allocation of quotas to parcel out the homeless. A number of countries, the UK among them, urge that refugees should be the responsibility of the first country they reach, forcing Austria, Hungary and Czechoslovakia to absorb disproportionate numbers. Britain, among others, has found it difficult to decide whether those seeking refuge were "immigrants" or "asylum seekers" and the first response was niggardly both in easing visa restrictions (a mere 8,000 have been allowed in) and in advancing any assistance to the countries of "first asylum". Many Western states are not considering any immigration applications, a stage beyond seeking asylum, hoping for an improvement in Bosnia. Even asylum applications are left pending or refugees are granted an uncertain and temporary protection status, which is hardly in the spirit of the 1951 UN Convention on the Relative Status of Refugees. Refugees in the first phase of their flight are the proper concern of UNHCR, which has the tremendous task of supplying young and old with

180

clothes, food and medicine. There are orphans, cripples, and traumatized individuals by the thousand and the combined work of UNHCR, UNICEF and Médecin Sans Frontières is as much psychiatric as socio-physical.

This onerous mission, so graphic in the world's media, raises the question of how to help, and when and where. Is it best to staunch the outflow of refugees by bringing relief supplies to besieged civilians inside Bosnia and by opening up human land corridors to expedite and protect this relief? In some European capitals this is a plausible argument for the policy of dealing with refugees as near as possible to their place of anguish. More positively, most UNHCR staff would prefer to render first aid, in its fullest sense, either near an area people know and where families may be reunited or, where this is not possible, in neighbouring host countries for temporary asylum. It is necessary to conserve staff energies and funds when the undertaking is costing $420 million a year.

Two very pressing circumstances make relief work arduous and dangerous. One is that relief workers' hands are somewhat tied by UN embargoes on medicine, petrol and cash flows. Sanctions hit ordinary people. Relief agencies have asked the UN whether it is possible for them to be exempted from stringent controls. The second problem is that relief convoys are regularly impeded and often shot at. At least 700,000 Bosnians depend for their lives on a small corps of anxious and fatigued aid workers who have to dodge snipers and navigate mined routes. Perhaps only half of the designated supplies are getting through. "Robust protection" of convoys with lightly armed UNPROFOR escorts risks the banning of relief columns. In January 1993 British escorts did in fact hit back at Serbian mortar positions.

Reports such as this and the sight of exhausted relief workers in flak jackets has led to more than one impassioned public appeal for stronger military support to create an environment in which effective humanitarian action is possible. Oxfam has declared that no principle of sovereignty should block the protection of human rights. On the other hand, the Red Cross and the Red Crescent, to preserve their neutrality, have consistently refused to accept UNPROFOR escorts. All three warring parties in the Bosnian conflict have at times regarded UN efforts as a legitimate military target as it is prolonging the war and feeding the enemy. Relief aid becomes part of a war economy. If to accompany the food package with a gun jeopardizes the handlers and is liable to provoke a military response, then how and when is intervention necessary and practicable to get relief through? Some air surveillance is possible. There has been an earnest attempt to use the rather uncertain alternative of food drops from the air. *Operation Provide Promise* has flown out from Rhein-Main in Germany and Ancona in Italy in a co-ordinated enterprise using American, French and German aircraft. Slow-moving transports are vulnerable to ground fire and safe and effective delivery is difficult from either low or high altitudes. Much more reliable is the use on a continuous basis of such airports as Sarajevo and Tuzla. Unfortunately local militia have rendered air operating impossible and thus have most certainly increased starvation and suffering. In so many respects UNPROFOR personnel have been seen as hostages.

The UN mandated UNPROFOR in 1992 to protect a number of "safe areas" in Bosnia. These have been only lightly safeguarded compared with the "safe havens" for Kurds in northern Iraq protected by allied fire power on the ground and the wings of the US Air Force scrambled from northern Turkish airfields. That the policy of safety has not been successful can be illustrated by three examples. Srebenica, in April 1993, had 50,000 sick and famished people, and was denied water and electricity for 11 months as Serbs attempted to "cleanse" the town of Muslim presence. Mostar, to the southwest, had a similar crowd of terrified citizens in a community transformed from peaceful ethnic variety into one splintered by hostile zealots, Muslim and Croat, who not long before had allied themselves against Serbian intrusion. Gorazde, in April 1994, locked Muslims into a grossly overcrowded ghetto. A Serb refusal to lift a punitive siege brought a NATO air strike of dubious effectiveness. Here were three instances, it was alleged in the West, of lack of political will to deal with a human crisis and flat repudiation of the UN. Argument both in the press and in the Foreign Offices and parliaments asserted that this was a no-win situation, but one that could not be left. If the UN evacuated these helpless people it would be carrying out the ethnic cleansing objectives of Serb fanatics. By keeping them penned in glorified prison camps the UN would be reinforcing those notions of ethnic difference that would almost certainly lead one day to eviction.

The UN has overseen resettlement of refugees in places where there has been wholesale displacement of inhabitants such as in Vietnam, Cambodia, Kenya and Uganda. Circumstances in their homelands have not often favoured repatriation but it has been attempted in small numbers. Bosnia is a dismal case on its own. The final shape of settlement is not at present discernible and major resettlement is not a firm option. Once more, it is argued, removal of residents would be seen by both "winners" and "losers" as underpinning discrimination and would hardly be acceptable to the negotiators on any side. Resettlement would have to bring "returnees" to areas that peace treaties assigned to them, again, in accordance with the criteria of ethnic identification and dispersal and concentration.

The Bosnian government (not yet having entirely forsaken its old tolerant traditions) would like to see the majority of its 1.2 million temporary expatriates back to develop a peaceful and prosperous society. While one in five of those who have fled are sheltering not far away, in Croatia, perhaps hoping for a passage home, the Muslims among them are worried about Croatian prejudice and an uncertain place in what has emerged after much wrangling as a projected Croat–Muslim federation. Many families would be reluctant to return to villages from which they were hounded and where the future administration might not be sympathetic. UNHCR has already researched the practicability of resettlement where a quota of those returning would be located in areas controlled by the same ethnic group. This would be a delicate jigsaw puzzle, and it would certainly raise ethical questions. Transit camps are not a welcomed suggestion. Apart from its protective role in a pacified Bosnia UNHCR would be taking on a major rehabilitation exercise (something on the same scale as that undertaken in Cambodia). Among UNHCR staff special attention is already being directed to the best ways of helping those who have suffered forms of violence and horrific experience, the many thousands of women and children who are in the category of "vulnerable refugees". These people will need careful reassurance and further counselling.

THE CASE FOR INTERVENTION

"Something must be done for the Bosnians. It's no good just telling them to be brave" has been the keynote of more than one newspaper leader. There appear to be three options ranging from minimum to maximum intervention. International effort could continue its reliance on relief and on diplomacy, there might be limited military support, as UNPROFOR expressed, or full-scale intervention could be mounted to separate the contestants and perhaps turn Bosnia into a UN protectorate. It would be a gamble given the terrain, and more than 70,000 troops would be needed.

The first enterprise is seen increasingly as an expensive expedient not a very effective mercy mission. Meetings in Geneva, New York and London of participators and mediators have frequently degenerated into what Harold Nicolson once termed "exercises in forensic propaganda". In 1991 and 1992 military intervention to some degree would have been easiest but political will was wavering; now, when the political edge is keener because of their constituents' urging, the military difficulties are judged pre-eminent. Yet, how compelling for action was genocide? While the United States and Europe argued and delayed any concerted effort, the Serbs knew that time and winter were on their side. Belgrade saw no reason to stop fighting until it could ratify through negotiation what it had won by aggression. Newspaper leaders put a rationalization on this: "Stick in and do everything we can. But no more illusions. The UN can't stop a war that the Serbs (or the Muslims) decline to end", said *The Guardian* in April 1994. At the same time the same paper reported the ominous toll of UN personnel in Bosnia: 93 killed and several thousand wounded, many of them in times of nominal cease-fire.

Throughout, the US, Britain and France, tried to broker peace deals and cease-fires and when these were ignored and ruptured the forceful threats they issued were seen as empty. Intervention in support of humanitarian relief as aired in public has lain on two planes, the principled and the militarily pragmatic. UN intervention should be positive in calling for support of multi-ethnic communities in Bosnia as a political and moral objective. No truck with apartheid in South Africa should mean no approval of separation in the Balkans. There should be no compromise on the general ethical and civilized principle of co-operative living.

But how was this ideal to be enforced? The schemes for enforcement much discussed by armchair strategists and by recognized experts stressed that if military force were authorized to achieve resolution of a threat to international peace and security, it must be certain that peace could be maintained without permanent application of this force. This seems an obvious conclusion, but it was something that worried governments. It was proving difficult to maintain through rotation an adequate UNPROFOR force, as numbers were stepped up from the initial 14,000 in February 1992, to almost 30,000 just 12 months later. Denied "close air support" of any real significance, somewhat insecure in terms of readily available material resources and funds, the UN force has appeared more of a *presence*, and a residual one at that, than a protective *power*. The protective role of UNPROFOR has to stop short of making it in any way a party to the conflict. Such a thin blue line could hardly ever be expected to advance along a continuum from peacekeeping to peacemaking to peacebuilding. All too clearly the UN in action is being restricted by the necessity for inaction.

PROSPECTS FOR RECONCILIATION

What are the prospects for peace and settlement in Bosnia? Apart from the diplomatic probes and missions and experiments there have been five main peace proposals. When the Yugoslavia Peace Conference was convened in London in August 1992, the basic assumption seemed to be that Yugoslavia as an entity was finished and that it would be best to recognize separate sovereignty for each of a set of ethnically based "cantons". Brought in to mastermind the diplomacy were the former British Foreign Ministers, Lord Peter Carrington and Lord David Owen, who both acted for the EC, and then Cyrus Vance, retired Secretary of State in Washington who came in at the request of the Security Council. The EC had tried to sort things out before an appeal was made to the UN.

The second attempt to resolve the rapidly deteriorating and inflamed situation was that of Vance and Owen to accommodate the Serbs' wish for partition and the equally determined resolve of Croats to oppose division. Croat and Muslim objections, gathering the sympathy of most UN members, were not so much to the actual claims made on land, which, after all, might have yielded to negotiation, but to the savagery with which terror and massacre were used as a means of eviction and displacement. Not surprisingly, what came to be known as the Vance-Owen Plan (VOP) by summer 1993 was unlikely to be acceptable to fierce protagonists. Ten semi-autonomous provinces comprising three each for Serbs, Croats and Muslims, would give the

Serbs 53% of Bosnia (they had taken 70%), the Muslims 31% and the Croats 17%. UNPROFOR would supervise demilitarization. Human rights would be safeguarded with a court, commissioner, and ombudsman.

Apart from the vacillation of the contending parties, now moved to accept VOP, then ready to reject it, there was in wider Europe a great deal of controversy. Was this settlement, with its maps and figures, an anti-pluralist measure out of line with what justice and civilized living ought to require? Did it not ignore the role of external aggression in altering the earlier population mix? Were the Serbs rewarded and the Muslims punished? How many UNPROFOR troops would be needed to impose apartheid in the Balkans – 25,000, or 50,000, or 75,000? How could population displacement on this scale be justified? Looking ahead into a peaceful future, was it possible that separated and no doubt fractious groups would ever come together to rebuild a shattered economy? Steadily, VOP sank in the water (given a good push by Washington).

A third plan materialized in August 1993. Its authors, Lord Owen and Torsten Stoltenberg, the latter a Norwegian ex-Foreign Minister and experienced UN man, tried hard to devise a solution that did not just juggle the ethnic composition (although this did happen) but went further to place the fragile, bomb-blasted cities of Sarajevo and Mostar respectively under UN and EC control provisionally for two years. Partition zones would be fairer, it was thought, with access to the Adriatic and 40,000 Blue Berets to oversee the transition. Again, the plan was thrown out. Bosnians wanted a sovereign state still and not a UN protectorate. It was conjectured that Belgrade would be pleased if Croats and Serbs approved the plan thus demonstrating their "good intentions" and clearing the way for the lifting of sanctions. Undoubtedly President Milosevic tried to soften the hearts of the Bosnian Serbs, but failed to do so.

The fourth and fifth plans were manufactured elsewhere by political artisans. In Washington the Clinton Administration worked hard for six weeks early in 1994 to get Muslims and Croats in Bosnia to lay down arms and work out a form of Croat–Muslim federation. With the Cold War out of the way, Moscow and Washington were able to collaborate in moving beyond ethnic sorting. A joint legislative council would negotiate with Belgrade to reduce the holding of territory it had gained by force to 49%. There would be a UN Representative of the Secretary-General in UN-protected Sarajevo. The Central Council, composed of delegates from the three factions, would have to prepare for "free and fair" elections, draft a new constitution, and set up co-ordination with UNPROFOR and international aid agencies. Safeguarding of human rights and restoration of a free press were vital aims. UN personnel would continue escorted relief work, disarm the militia, man "confidence patrols" and arbitrate in disputes. A fragile peace was holding towards the end of 1994, but there is as yet no guarantee of any real progress with a rather ambitious agenda for collaborative action. Nor is Serb agreement a prospect. Initially, the Serb reaction was a feeling of isolation and, ironically, of being discriminated against by "outside forces".

In July 1994 there were signs of fatigue and perhaps fatalism among "donor" and "protector" countries, who were unwilling to keep supplying soldiers for an ineffective UNPROFOR of 20 states. Funds were dwindling. Bosnian affairs were now relegated to the inside pages of newspapers. Among politicians there has emerged a "take it or leave it" sense of frustration. Five states – the US, the UK, Russia, France and Germany – in summer 1994 decided to form a "contact group" to keep in close touch with negotiators among the Bosnians. Meeting in Geneva and then being represented at the G7 heads-of-state meeting in Naples in mid July 1994, they drew up proposals that would involve the Serbs having to be satisfied with 49% of their Serb tract in Bosnia. In return for a cessation of fighting and territorial adjustment, sanctions would be lifted and several million dollars would be pumped in to revive the Bosnian economy and infrastructure. Europe's impatience was very clearly made known, as was the threat that if no agreement was reached there might well be a reconsideration of the embargo on arms being supplied to the Muslims. Then, UNPROFOR would have to withdraw.[3]

The imbroglio over Bosnia has shown that the promotion and protection of human rights is an undertaking of vast complexity and uncertainty. The contest for power in former Yugoslavia has exploded into an unmanageable situation where what are thought to be significant ethnic differences have become justifying criteria for obsessive struggle. The UN has been faced with the problem of trying to translate Resolutions, Conventions and Declarations about human rights into practice. Overexpectation has meant that international action is almost certainly falling well short of target.[4] In regard to the UN under-reaching its aims, UN Secretary-General Boutros Boutros-Ghali has spoken of a "crisis of credibility". A world that was fatalistic during the days of the Cold War now wants to dump its problems on the UN and to await a promised resolution. But when an underfunded international body cannot "deliver" a definite solution it is open to blame, perhaps by irresolute members, for lack of active "response". If the case of Bosnia and its wholesale violation of human rights jerks members into exploring the implications of what the French term *droit d'ingérence* (the right to intervene), perhaps something has been achieved.

NOTES

1. The British contribution has generally been about 2,500 troops with a varying amount of service and civilian support.
2. The mandate has been amended from time to time. By 1995 the range of extra components covers UNHCR relief work in Bosnia-Hercegovina, securing clearance of Sarajevo airport as a main entrance point, and protecting UN personnel espe-

cially in six "safe areas" in Bosnia. UN Charter Chapter VII has legitimated these tasks. Many observers believe that the mandate lacks the clear guidelines needed where emergencies call for prompt, direct redress. In December 1992, 700 military observers and police were sent to Macedonia to give early warning of threatening developments and to assist in maintaining law and order. Seven months later, the force was increased to 1,000.

3. The 52 members of OSCE (the name was changed from CSCE in December 1994) meeting in Budapest in December 1994 completely failed to agree a solution to the Bosnian conflict. A "pull-out" of UNPROFOR remains a contingency plan. In December the US offered to send a substantial force to cover such an exit if it was found necessary. This offer brought very strong criticism from those Western states who deplored the US refusal to contribute ground troops earlier in the conflict.

4. In fact, UNPROFOR has an authorized strength of 45,000. Serbs are still unwilling to make territorial concessions. Cease-fires rarely hold. The new Republican majority in the US Congress threatens to approve lifting the arms supply embargo on the Bosnian Government. Independent war-lords still hold sway and impede negotiations. Croatia shows signs of preparedness to resume military operations. In early 1995 a four-month cease-fire is still obtaining following agreements at the end of December 1994 between Bosnian and Serb leaders. Former President Jimmy Carter served as mediator, heading an UNPROFOR negotiating team. Security Council resolutions on 31 March 1995 reconstituted UNPROFOR in Croatia as UN Confidence Restoration Operation (UNCRO). In Macedonia there was established a UN Preventive Deployment Force (UNPREDEP). By such means the UN hopes to negotiate overall peace settlement using the Contact Group's peace plan as a basis.

FURTHER READING

Ali, R. & L. Lifschultz. Why Bosnia? *Third World Quarterly* 15(3), pp. 367–402, 1994.

Bell-Fialkoff, A. A brief history of ethnic cleansing. *Foreign Affairs* (Summer 1993), pp. 110–21, 1993.

Glenny, M. *The fall of Yugoslavia: the third Balkan war*. London: Penguin, 1992.

Guttman, R. *Witness to genocide*. London: Macmillan, 1993.

Meron, T. The case for war crimes trials in Yugoslavia. *Foreign Affairs* (Summer 1993), pp. 122–35.

Roberts, A. Humanitarian war: military intervention and human rights. *International Affairs* 69(31), 1993.

Stedman, J. The new interventionists. *Foreign Affairs* 71(1), pp. 1–16, 1993.

Thompson, M. *A paper house: the ending of Yugoslavia*. London: Vintage Books, 1992.

Vulliamy, E. *Seasons in hell. Understanding Bosnia's war*. London: Simon & Schuster, 1994.

Chapter Fourteen

FORMER YUGOSLAVIA (BOSNIA)

1991

27 June:	Serbs attack Slovenia.
September:	Croatia: Croats and Serbs fight.
15 October:	Bosnia-Hercegovina proclaimed independent.

1992

15 January:	EC recognizes independent Croatia. UN sends Vance to broker peace.
21 February:	UN Security Council to send 14,000 Blue Berets to Bosnia for 12 months.
29 February:	Bosnian Serbs proclaim independence.
6 April:	EC and US recognize independent Bosnia.
26 August:	Yugoslavia Peace Conference. Abortive EC peace plan.

1993

January:	Vance–Owen Plan (VOP) tabled.
March–April–May:	VOP signed by Muslims. Bosnian Serbs reject, sign, reject, with referendum. Successive negotiations.
6 May:	5 "safe areas" designated by UN.
August:	Owen and Stoltenberg plan for partition, Sarajevo care of UN, Mostar care of EC.
December:	all parties considering EU (EC) proposals. US pressure exempts Muslims from arms embargo, opposed by UK and others.

1994

January:	Security Council reaffirms "all necessary means" to protect convoys, safe areas.
February:	US plan for Croat–Muslim Federation signed.

	NATO now ready to employ air strikes.
10/11 April:	NATO airstrikes. Desultory peace talks. UNHCR/ UNPROFOR airlift over 21 months now surpasses 1948/49 Berlin airlift.
June:	Tentative cease-fire in Bosnia.
July:	Five-nation Contact Group: partition, truce plan.
August:	Bosnian Serb referendum at 96% given as peace plan rejection. Spasmodic heavy fighting in Bosnia. Safe areas harassed.
September:	Stop–go mode in fighting and peace talks.
December:	Bosnians and Serbs negotiate a four-month cease-fire.

1995

	Desultory fighting in Bosnia. Possibility of Moslem counter-offensive. No firm prospect of settlement yet achieved by Contact Group.
March:	Security Council modifies mandates for Croatia and Macedonia.
April:	Contact Group continuing efforts to bring about overall settlement. Apparent Serbian intransigence and Croat-Muslim resentment and impatience – both likely to lead to further sectarian conflict.

PART FIVE

New nations

West Irian, 1962–9

This is another example of the UN carrying out a transition operation to bring a people through to self-determination. Here, for the first time, the UN took on complete responsibility for the administration of a territory. The case of West Irian successfully illustrates the usefulness of peacekeeping combined with mediation in easing the task of decolonization, where legal and political criteria both need to be satisfied. This has been the only UN peacekeeping mission to leave the field promptly and with its mandate entirely fulfilled. At the time, in the mid 1960s, the operation was considered as a triumph for democracy. In subsequent years there has been speculation about the nature of its success and a good number of questions have remained unanswered. It is worth looking at this enterprise in some detail to judge how far high hopes might have soured.

First, the emergence of West Irian from the Dutch Empire is described. It became a disputed pawn, and rival interests appealed to the UN. Mediation proved fruitless. The UN carried through an ambitious transition programme whose objectives and fulfilment are considered here. In conclusion, the possibilities and problems encountered by the UN in steering a people towards self-determination are explored.

EMERGENCE OF A SUCCESSOR STATE

West Irian, formerly West New Guinea, had been a Dutch colony since 1828. An area twice the size of Holland, its 750,000 people, often referred to as Papuans, lived for the most part in rainforest and one in five led a primitive existence. In 1945, with the capitulation and evacuation of Japanese troops who had occupied the island since 1942, there arose a dispute over sovereignty between the Netherlands, the colonial government, and the new state

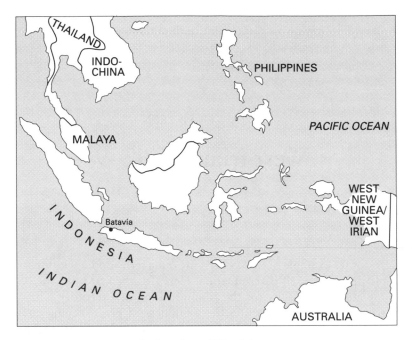

Indonesia and West Irian

of Indonesia, successor to the Dutch in the Dutch East Indies. British soldiers reoccupying the island had had to wait in the wings pending resolution of the national dispute. Fervent nationalists proclaimed a new state to be known as the United States of Indonesia, repudiating 320 years of Dutch rule. Batavia, the former capital in Java, was renamed Djakarta. Dr Achmed Sukarno, an engineer, formed a left-wing government, which the Netherlands refused to recognize. The task of introducing new rule to a confederation where more than 90 million people spoke 26 languages and were scattered over 3,000 volcanic islands and 750,000 square miles, was immense. Communal tensions and armed rebellion forced Sukarno into less liberal policy and persuaded him to look around for a diversion in a bristling nationalist atmosphere. He seized on the uncertainty over West Irian as an ideal issue to substantiate an image of patriotic leadership and call for unity.

President Sukarno was not short of allies in the first years of the Cold War. The Ukrainian representative tabled a complaint at the Security Council's first meeting in London in January 1946. The conduct of British forces ashore in West Irian had been reprehensible and merited a special enquiry. Britain was meddling in Indonesian internal affairs by hoping to bring back Dutch imperialists and endeavouring to oust the laudable principle of self-determination. Colonial peoples were being cheated of their right to independence. The UK rejected this accusation and defended its role in holding the ring until amicable and final settlement was achieved. Soon enough, however, the partisan nature of colonialists and anti-colonialists and the Cold War polarity of East and West became entrenched.

Twice the UN stepped in to bridge the gulf over sovereignty in South East Asia. Resolution 31 in autumn 1947 sent a Good Offices Committee to Indonesia. Clearly the Security Council was leaning towards the notion that no colonial power should exclude a UN effort merely by pleading that it reserved autonomy of domestic jurisdiction. There was every chance that warfare might result unless outside assistance was forthcoming. The frequent resort by the Royal Netherlands Navy to coastal "police action" and the rounding-up of "guerrillas" indicated that the Dutch no longer acknowledged Indonesia as exercising even *de facto* authority.

Two years later, in January 1949, Resolution 67 reconstituted the Good Offices Committee as a larger Commission for Indonesia with a mission to confer with all parties in Indonesia about the establishment of a federal interim government to take office in the spring. This ambitious Resolution set a daring precedent. Here was a Security Council moving in firmly to build a constitution for a new community. Indonesia was confident that Dutch recalcitrance had alienated its earlier Western supporters, especially those in Washington. Eventually, The Hague would be nudged into recognizing the inevitability of Security Council pressures. When, in 1949, the Netherlands reluctantly recognized Indonesia as an autonomous state it was agreed that the future of West Irian should be left open for later negotiation but that its status must be resolved without too much delay.

It is significant that the two parties drew back from the contentious term "sovereignty", preferring to use "authority" to describe continuing control. There were those in Djakarta and even in The Hague who would have preferred West Irian's destiny to be decided immediately. Inevitably, differences of opinion arose over who should exercise sovereignty during the interregnum; Indonesia pointed out that in its opinion the Netherlands had merely been granted administrative rights and not those of absolute sovereignty. Much of the exasperation on both sides derived from Security Council Resolutions 27, 30 and 31 of 1947, which had expressed members' anxieties about a breach of international peace and denial of human rights by the Dutch in Indonesia, and had called for a cease-fire and the speedy implementation of self-determination for the islanders. In Indonesia, for both nationalists and reluctant Netherlands officials waiting to leave, West Irian was a bone in the throat.

WEST IRIAN AS A UN ISSUE

A disgruntled Indonesia put the matter of West Irian squarely before the General Assembly in 1954 as an issue in decolonization, then a process understandable and acceptable to most UN members. The alternatives for a colony of full independence or of self-determination did not appeal to the fiercely nationalistic government because either of these solutions might have led to the loss of its northwestern region. The General Assembly was told that further delay in settling the future of West Irian would rob its people of the freedom that had been earned by the rest of Indonesia and that ill-feeling over this would threaten peace. Time and time again Netherlands representatives reminded the Assembly of the Charter principle that the interests of the inhabitants of non-self-governing territories were "paramount" and that their "political aspirations" (those of the Papuans and not of Djakarta) must be taken into account. Accordingly, the Netherlands would seek to promote the "political, social and educational advancement" of the territory in the course of time and in discharging this obligation it was most certainly not prepared to countenance West Irian being annexed by force.

Other Western nations sympathized with this position. Third World states preferred some form of UN arbitration. Indonesia's case for a direct transfer of territory between the Netherlands and itself never quite secured the needed two-thirds majority in the General Assembly. Three times discomfited in international debates, in 1954, 1956 and 1957, Indonesians increasingly resorted to retaliatory behaviour against Dutch interests and property all over the islands. Dutch nationals were sent packing and their properties expropriated. A movement for the "liberation" of West Irian now secured support from officials and public alike. Tensions ran high.

In the General Assembly of those days few states showed concern over the decline of the Dutch imperium. Powerful factions even in the Netherlands itself and in the US were calling for a speedy end to colonial rule and for self-rule to be given priority. Indonesia's pleas for decisive change, and its confrontational posture, found favour among uncommitted new nations in the Third World and in the Socialist Bloc. Mindful of support in the seats around him, the Indonesian delegate argued that no transitional arrangement under UN auspices could compare with an orderly, straightforward transfer of sovereignty from the Netherlands to Indonesia, blessed, by all means, by the Secretary-General. The alternative to a peaceful and agreed transition, he added, would be warfare in West Irian, which could then become a "hot spot" of escalating hostilities in the South Pacific.

THE UN ATTEMPTS MEDIATION

In October 1961 the Netherlands took up a General Assembly Resolution calling for independence to be granted to the remaining non-self-governing territories or Trust Territories. It suggested that the UN assume administrative responsibility for West Irian pending transfer of sovereignty. A UN commission would investigate the situation, and a plebiscite might be arranged. President

Sukarno was contemptuous of this proposal, maintaining that his state would be denied legitimate territory. He ordered the despatch of a small invasion force to West Irian and he was furious when it was repulsed by Dutch marines. The possibility of some basic and constructive engagement might have crumbled had not U. Thant, UN Secretary-General, stepped in to propose that his "Good Offices" be enlisted to explore conciliation. In so committing the UN to the objective of settlement Thant was fairly sure that Washington, worried about Communist inroads in South East Asia, would back him.

In early summer 1962, Thant asked former US Ambassador to India, Ellsworth Bunker, to devise a mediation scheme. Bunker already knew that the embarrassed Netherlands and insistent Indonesian Governments were cautiously testing the water in secret New York meetings and that they were unlikely to object to UN mediation. Bunker proposed that a body acceptable to both parties, to be termed a "temporary executive authority", should go to work under the eyes of a nominee of the Secretary-General. This body would be given full responsibility for administration in West Irian; its tasks would be maintaining law and order and ensuring uninterrupted normal services and basic civilian rights. If the programme were put into effect, say, in October 1962, by 1 May 1963 the temporary executive authority would hand over the administration to Indonesia. A UN security force would be needed to safeguard the operation.

Bunker had proposed for the UN the twin function of peacekeeping and of furnishing an infrastructure for national development. A programme such as this would enable decolonization to proceed reasonably smoothly and methodically without putting the colonial power in an humiliating pillory. Provided the programme was not rushed or disrupted, each of the rival parties could see their way towards compromise. Once administration was in Indonesian hands, there must be preparations for a plebiscite in West Irian to be held in 1969, which would give the islanders the opportunity to vote on their future.

To the surprise of the General Assembly in September 1962, the plan proved acceptable to both disputants. The negotiations had not proved at all easy. Sukarno, it seems, had received a number of appeals to show moderation from Thant at the UN and from US President J. F. Kennedy. His readiness to procrastinate was eventually overcome, and quite quickly arrangements were put into effect. The cost of the United Nations Temporary Executive Authority (UNTEA) would be shared equally between the Netherlands and Indonesia. A United Nations Security Force (UNSF) was to go six weeks in advance to supervise a ceasefire and generally to make things safe for the administrative group to move in. Commanded by a Pakistani, Major-General Said Uddin Khan, the force was to be made up of a substantial contingent from Pakistan, 1,500 in all, with aircraft and crews from Canada and the United States. There would also be a unit of Indonesian paratroopers together with civilian policemen and a militia group, the Papuan Volunteer Corps, officered from other lands.

It was necessary in the first instance to send advance parties into the rain-forest to notify an estimated 1,500 scattered Indonesian troops of the cease-fire. These men would then be escorted back to base camp areas. The Secretary-General's own military advisor, the Indian General Indar Rikye, and a staff of 21 officers from six nations did their best to co-ordinate the preliminary operation. Five hundred political prisoners who had been detained by the Indonesian soldiers were located, set free with an amnesty and rehabilitated. All objectives were achieved on time and without any serious incident. Soon things were clear for the arrival in October 1962 of the civilian wing of the operation, led by the Secretary-General's Representative José Rolz-Bennett and a staff from 32 nations. This was a brief visit and a new Representative, this time an Iranian, came to Djakarta the following month.

A UN TRANSITION PLAN GOES AHEAD

Nothing could go forward without the replacement by seasoned UN staff of those senior Dutch officials who had left. It was also crucial to train junior ranks of Papuans and Indonesians. UN and Netherlands flags were raised and the departing Dutch Governor wished UNTEA and UNSF well and appealed to the people to give their utmost support. Altogether, there was a tremendous task of rehabilitation in a land neglected by the Dutch and since 1942 occupied by a repressive Japanese army. Urban services had to be reconstructed by building surveyors, telephone engineers and medical personnel. Access to villages and living conditions needed urgent attention from road and construction engineers, agriculturists, foresters and irrigation experts. Technicians such as these recruited labour teams from the large number of unemployed. A whole town's population would need bringing into tented clinics for advice on infant rearing or for inoculation against typhus and cholera.

Fresh constitutional procedures needed to be devised and a system of local government had to be regenerated by lawyers and local government advisors who had the onerous task of preparing paperwork for the projected administrative transfer. Qualified Indonesians were enlisted to help man the judiciary and also to serve as a secretariat for the New Guinea Council (the old name was kept) and for 11 regional councils. It was necessary to explain the terms of the UNTEA mission to Papuans, people living in one of the world's most backward regions. With a great deal of difficulty and much improvisation this was effected through public meetings and a simple poster campaign. While the restructuring was being undertaken by UNTEA, the steady and peaceful withdrawal of all Netherlands land and naval forces had to be co-ordinated.

The long-range objective of this UN transition programme was self-determination for West Irian. With the aid of the UN Representative and his staff, Indonesia had to make arrangements to give the people of the territory a chance to express freedom of choice. In a plebiscite to be conducted no later than 1969 the inhabitants were to decide whether they wished to "remain in Indonesia" or to "sever their ties with Indonesia". As if to make a point about urgency and determination, the Netherlands flag was lowered from buildings on 31 December 1962 to be replaced with the flags of the UN and of Indonesia side by side. Three months later Netherlands and Indonesia restored normal diplomatic relations after a number of very frosty years.

At the end of April 1963 Djakarta announced the installation as Governor of Irian Barat (the Indonesian name for West Irian) of a Papuan member of the New Guinea Council. He would have an Indonesian deputy to head an administrative structure where Papuans outnumbered Indonesians by five to one. The handful of Dutch officials still there would give up their posts on the final vesting day. At last, on 1 May 1963, full administrative control was transferred peaceably by the UN to the Indonesian Government. The period of Indonesian administration was to be a "period of preparation". Then would come "self-determination" or "the free choice". This distinction was viewed with doubt by some UN staff in New York.

As UNTEA's main field staff and the Pakistani units of UNSF began to leave for home in May 1963, the UN transition programme was shifting from peace-keeping to administrative transfer and finally to assisted social and economic development. Experts in various fields were to come out from New York to collaborate on development projects. There was much work to be done both by Indonesian and UN advisors to prepare the regional councils and voters all over the island for the plebiscite that was finally conducted in July and August 1969. An overwhelming majority of the population expressed through delegates to the regional councils their wish to remain with Indonesia. This act of free choice was duly reported to the Secretary-General and then to the UN General Assembly at its meeting in November 1969.

TRANSITION: ITS PROBLEMATIC ASPECTS

The transition operation in West Irian was judged a great success at the time of its accomplishment. In retrospect, a number of questions arise that are also of significance to later UN ventures. What right has the UN to intervene in states' "domestic affairs"? What do UN members understand by "self-determination"? In regard to the first, the issue was addressed in quite different ways by the Netherlands and Indonesia in the West Irian dispute. The Hague asserted that the UN could have no interventionist role in an affair related to Dutch sovereignty. Indonesia, on the other hand, claimed that the jurisdiction of the Netherlands had never been re-established after the Japanese occupation in 1942. Neither party, at this stage, sought to clarify what constituted "intervention", although it was plain in this case and in other contests for independence that those who "have"(in political terms) resent outside intrusion and possible enforcement, while those who "have not" may welcome it.

In the UN some regarded the whole operation as less than idealistic and as smacking of realist compromise, given Washington's fear that a lengthy crisis might strengthen communism in Indonesia. However, several positive results distinguish the dispute over West Irian. Both parties welcomed UN intervention steering towards compromise. UN action secured a cease-fire and then went on to influence a settlement. A steady process of third-party conciliation reduced friction and averted hostilities between contestants. UN "good offices" enabled the possessing power to relinquish its hold with some dignity and without violence or confusing haste. The Netherlands was obliged to accept the existence of Indonesia as a newly independent state. Above all, in this case, the UN showed that without any significant military input it could intervene on the basis of moral authority alone.

As for the term "self-determination", when it cropped up in General Assembly rhetoric it was usually in the context of anti-colonial protest or understood as a demand for transfer of power. As noted previously, there is often a readiness to treat this concept as an absolute, inalienable right while others stress that the principle must be considered within the context of the people or the group demanding its exercise. Where a place like West Irian has been deemed primitive or unsophisticated (in factual rather than pejorative terms) colonial powers frequently delayed the process of territorial loosening. In the case of West Irian, after all, there was the problem of whether a right to "self-determination" permits secession of any part of state territory and, if so, to what degree. It is possible that for many Indonesians in 1969 it was an urgent matter to put the seal on a transfer from colonial rule to independence by contriving assured incorporation in the Indonesian federation. In their view, the backward Papuans, given a free choice, might have chosen to sever links. Anarchy could result. Certainly for some members of the General Assembly the root question was whether West Irian should belong to the Netherlands or to Indonesia, not whether it should belong to the people of West Irian themselves. Two other questions are worth considering.

How free was the "free choice" permitted in West Irian? Did the Charter principle of "sovereign equality" apply to both states disputing over West Irian? When the plebiscite was agreed to in 1962, the need for a carefully organized programme of public information during the seven year run-up to the process of decision must have been obvious. It was not going to be easy, clearly, to explain to people unused to democratic ways just what was entailed, and even more difficult to convince them that they could choose alternatives. Nonetheless, a similar undertaking was set in hand later in Namibia (as Chapter 16 relates) and in the end it bore fruit.

Among many observers of the contretemps over West Irian there was the feeling that the West had been dilatory in maintaining contact with the less opportunistic and corrupt elements in Djakarta. As 1969 approached it seemed more and more likely that West Irian might be absorbed by a regime whose ambitions were being discredited (certainly in Washington and in London). Free choice might not be free of "inducement". The actual wording of the plebiscite suggestion to be put to voters asked them to decide whether they would "remain" with Indonesia rather than "become" part of the federation. Was there a hint of a proprietary interest here? Should the UN have worked out safeguards preventing the people of West Irian being steamrollered into a new and unregarding form of tutelage? Again, a point mentioned earlier seems relevant here. If people choose to end existing ties and go for self-determined freedom, will they have the economic viability necessary for independence?

The doctrine of the equality of states must have been in the minds of those debating the issue of West Irian's sovereignty, when they considered, for instance, a Resolution in the General Assembly from nations such as Australia, India and Egypt, calling for an end to hostilities in Indonesia and the use of some form of arbitration. It was implied in such a Resolution that the UN would be dealing with two parties of equal and self-determined status, both of whom were sovereign entities. Steadfastly, the Netherlands held to the position that the UN had no business to intervene since Indonesia remained under Dutch sovereignty. Predictably, the new state of Indonesia vociferously laid claim to equality of sovereign status. There were occasions in the debates over decolonization when certain territories had been deemed "micro-states" because their limited territory and population were thought to impose practical limits on capacity to conduct external relations. That, at least, was how international lawyers saw it. Even so, this depiction did not bar such countries from admission to statehood. This was the view of the International Court of Justice and of the Secretary-General when the point was put to them. Of course, Indonesia was a major entity in respect of both land area, population and resources and it never ceased to smart from a feeling of invidious distinction and (so it could be inferred) was likely to seek compensation by making claims on neighbouring areas whose status was not yet finally determined.

It has even been thought that the result of the plebiscite might have gone by way of default where Western powers and, above all, the United States, were more concerned not to alienate a powerful and strategically important southeastern nation than to stand completely by the letter and the spirit of the Charter in regard to self-determination. Did expediency, in this case, rule after all and help to create a precedent encouraging larger powers to make claims on small, unequal and non-self-governing areas? The concepts of equality and of free choice have had a chequered career in the cases of Netherlands and Indonesia, Argentina and the Falkland Islands, China and Hong Kong, India and Goa, Ethiopia and Eritrea, and France and Algeria. These are all areas of contention where UN members in the General Assembly or gathered in the august reaches of the Security Council have laboured hard to realize the Charter's call for "appropriate procedures or methods of adjustment".

The midwife role of the UN in easing the birth of new communities such as in West Irian, Namibia and Cambodia was likely to be a difficult and painful process. Standing proudly in the text of the Charter, the concept of aided self-determination has inevitably been unpredictable and multifaceted in practice. There is absolutely no alternative, it seems, to the obligation the Charter imposes on UN members in Chapter XI "to promote to the utmost" the transition from dependence to independence.

FURTHER READING

Henderson, W. *West New Guinea: the dispute and its settlement.* New York: Seton Hall University Press, 1973.

van der Kroef, J. M. The West New Guinea settlement. *Orbis* 7(1), pp. 120–49, 1963.

van der Veur, P. W. The United Nations in West New Guinea: a critique. *International Organization* 18(1), pp. 53–73, 1964.

Chapter Fifteen

WEST IRIAN 1962–9

1945	West New Guinea liberated from Japanese. Dispute between Netherlands and Indonesia. Now West Irian.
1946	Controversy over self-determination at UN.
1947	Security Council Resolutions on West Irian. UN sends Good Offices Committee to Indonesia.
1949	Good Offices Committee becomes Commission for Indonesia with ambitious mission.
1949	Netherlands recognizes Indonesian sovereignty.
1954 1969 1957	Controversy at UN over "decolonization" of West Irian.
1961	General Assembly calls on UN to move West Irian step-by-step through to independence.
1962	Ellsworth Bunker invited by UN to devise transition scheme for West Irian. UNTEA set up.
1963	Restructuring and rehabilitation work of UNTEA to effect transition to independence. Full administrative control transferred by UN to Indonesia.
1969	Plebiscite confirms West Irian wish to stay with Indonesia. Many questions remain as to the nature of this transition exercise.

Namibia

In the past four decades 1,000 million people have achieved freedom globally and more than 100 new states have joined the UN. But never has the UN undertaken – with outstanding success – such a deliberate and difficult task as the making of Namibia. This was not just peacekeeping. It was an operation to facilitate the transition of a country from the subjugation of an illicitly occupied colony to self-determination as a sovereign state. It was not just a decolonization exercise. It involved the meshing together of elements, civilian and military, to bring about social, political and constitutional change among people without either democratic traditions or experience. Seventy years of determined effort have gone into this great UN achievement. Each step has been taken in the glare of public attention and often disputed interest. Namibia's story is a unique demonstration of what careful planning, full collaboration, international support, and adequate finance, can achieve.

However, the UN hopes of transition to independence for Namibia were thwarted by South Africa's stubbornness and by political developments in nearby Angola. Most probably, there would have been no movement at all had not diplomacy initiated by the US brought enough reconciliation to permit a UN task-force to go into Namibia. This chapter shows the UN taking up the Namibian cause, and describes the country's struggle for freedom, the UN drafting of a transition scheme, US intervention, and finally, the task-force operation culminating in a supervised election and independence Declaration.

THE UN AS MIDWIFE

Namibia became reality despite years of fierce protest and non-cooperation on the part of South Africa. When in 1945 the League of Nations was replaced by the UN, South Africa, the mandatory power, attempted to incorporate

South West Africa fully into the Union of South Africa. Pretoria even handed into New York a plebiscite return, which purported to express black willingness for a continuance of white rule. There was intense lobbying of the General Assembly, particularly by champions of the Herero tribe who had been almost exterminated by the German settlers before the Second World War. December 1946 saw nations in the General Assembly rejecting South Africa's request for the incorporation by a vote of 37 to 0 (including the US but with the UK abstaining). Former German colonies in Africa were now to be put under UN trusteeship, where development towards self-government and independence must be on the basis of non-discrimination. South Africa was unwilling to be "accountable" to the UN. It regarded itself as under no obligation to do other than continue its mandate. Eventually, South Africa decided to discontinue sending regular mandate reports to New York, declaring that facts in the reports were being used against it.

It looked as though the 1960s was to be a time of setback. In 1960 a UN Committee on South West Africa, one specially formed, was prevented from entering the disputed territory but it did manage to do so two years later when its inspection report struck many observers as rather tame, apart from finding things "unacceptable" and "repugnant". Nor was there any sign of agreement among Western nations to sever diplomatic relations with South Africa or to impose meaningful trade sanctions. Moreover, a test-case taken to the International Court of Justice in 1966 by Liberia and Ethiopia shocked world opinion when the ICJ reserved its judgment on trusteeship purely on technical grounds. Africans felt betrayed. International rhetoric in favour of ethical principles was impotent against the realities of power. There were, however, signs of movement as in 1968 the UN got to grips more plainly with a programme for transition for South West Africa, now to be known as Namibia. Internally, nationalist groups converged and consolidated, welding together old campaigners and young radicals. Enthused by slogans such as "Fortune becometh the Daring" and "Work in Solidarity for Justice and Freedom", a National Front prepared for struggle, if need be, by force of arms. Inevitably, the mandatory power regarded this as "terrorism". South Africa's Defence Force (SADF), wrestling with ambushes and sabotage, despatched some of the "freedom fighters" to join Nelson Mandela in the Robben Island penal settlement. In New York the South West Africa People's Organization (SWAPO) was granted Observer Status and voiced their protest in the General Assembly.

The response from Pretoria to "interference" from the UN was decisive and uncompromising. Namibia would be partitioned into 11 self-governing "Bantustans" (homelands). A "Transitional Government of National Unity" would in fact apportion 43% of the territory to white settlement. The attitudes of South Africa were seen by the General Assembly as making for ambiguity and delay and in no way meeting the needs of the dependent black society. There would be resistance to forced removals, to be met by imprisonment and shootings. Whites would arm themselves. Impelled, no doubt, by considerations such as these, and strongly deploring the failure of South Africa to act as it should, the General Assembly had terminated already, in 1966, the South African mandate and replaced the territory under direct UN responsibility. Eleven members of a Council for Namibia would be the legal administrators (from afar) headed by a UN Commissioner. No state must recognize the continuation of the mandate.

This initiative of the General Assembly was not received with acclaim by all UN members. South Africa itself, citing Article 2.7 in the UN Charter, was quick to accuse the UN of supporting a national liberation movement within the Republic's boundaries and thus intervening in matters essentially within its domestic jurisdiction. There were uncommitted nations who again were conscious of a rhetorical flourish and a mainly symbolic gesture that would have little meaning given South Africa's non-compliance. Terminating the mandate from across the Atlantic and even the well-intentioned provision for Council of Namibia conferences, trust funds and training schemes would do virtually nothing to shake the apartheid system of flagrant oppressors. Nor would the lack of agreement about the imposition of sanctions against South Africa do other than demonstrate UN weakness and partiality. Elsewhere in the UN building there was some anxiety that differences over Namibian trusteeship were being treated as a threat to international peace and security. Whatever the extent of condemnation in the General Assembly, this issue was now within the legitimate remit of the Security Council. Were we now moving towards a rule that states had a duty not to recognize any territorial or other situation brought about in breach of international law? This could easily constitute a precedent that could lend itself to many interpretations and even the possibility of manipulation.

In 1971 a breakthrough occurred when an Advisory Opinion asked for by the ICJ confirmed the General Assembly revocation of South Africa's illegal mandate. South Africa must withdraw its administration from Namibia. Members of the UN must refrain from any support or assistance to South Africa in Namibia. This Advisory Opinion may be thought of as a landmark in international law. The Court had ruled that the Security Council's primary authority and responsibility for maintaining peace entitled the Council to make a binding determination. The Security Council was adopting the view that a question ceases to be "essentially" a matter of domestic jurisdiction if, in its considered opinion, it raises an issue of international concern transcending state boundaries. As a means of furthering transition for Namibia the Security Council, in fact, was putting a political interpretation on what many, certainly in South Africa, held to be the inviolable legal statement of Article 2.7 in the UN Charter. Yet the ICJ had upheld the Council's responsibility. At its subsequent meeting the Security Council reaffirmed two essential points, namely, that continued South African occupation flouted UN principles and encroached on the authority of the UN, and, secondly, that the situation was likely to create conditions detrimental to the maintenance of peace and security in southern Africa. Members, apart from France and Britain, were able to go along with a Resolution elaborating the determination of the Security Council.

In the same spirit the General Assembly, also in 1971, went further in authorizing the Council for Namibia to represent the territory in the UN Specialized Agencies and in the international community as a whole. Understandably, Namibians leaders felt bound to declare that no court could really do justice in a political case unless it understood the suffering of litigants. Independence would never be a legal or a political gift either from the UN or, most definitely, from South Africa. Namibians would have to strive for their freedom.

NAMIBIANS STRUGGLE FOR INDEPENDENCE

The struggle of Namibia's subject people in the 1970s featured intense campaigning by SWAPO representatives at the UN, at the congresses of the Organization of African Union, at Commonwealth Heads of State summit conferences headed by the British Queen and at conferences of the Non-aligned Movement. A UN Institute for Namibia was set up by UNESCO to train administrative skills in future government civil servants. More critically, and within Namibia itself, resistance of a disenfranchised people now flamed into a war of liberation. SWAPO guerrillas, buoyed by a loosening of the Portuguese hold over neighbouring Angola, used bases there to infiltrate South African positions in Namibia. Intimidation and terrorist tactics led to appreciable military and civilian loss of life and revealed to the visiting UN Secretary-General, Kurt Waldheim, the full significance of the liberationist claim that "always politics leads the gun". There had patently been a shift in the mode of transition, namely, from an early acceptance of the concept of trusteeship to the full demand for independence and that as soon as possible. A thrust for direct action superseded any reliance on petitions. Namibian leaders lost no opportunity in urging the Security Council to act responsibly and urgently. The Advisory Opinion would remain a mere 20,000-word testimony unless action was taken.

A cat-and-mouse engagement was obvious by 1977. There had been a rather vague set of proposals from South Africa, the Turnhalle Proposals (named after the meeting place where they originated), designed to initiate exploratory talks between nominated African representatives. Elections would be held in Namibia but clearly on terms far too narrow to gain the approval either of SWAPO (who saw it as "the eve of political storms"), or, indeed, of the UN. The response of the UN was to call together a Contact Group of Western Nations (the USA, the UK, France, Canada and the Federal Republic of Germany) whose brief would be to promote dialogue between South Africa and SWAPO.[1] This step did not please certain members of the UN.

South Africa was seeking to perpetuate control of what was already theirs illegally. In their view the Contact Group would be anxious to reach a peaceful settlement, but also to avoid radicalization of South Africa because armed liberation struggles menaced the safety of continued economic investment. They recalled that the United States and Britain had vetoed mandatory sanctions three times. Nonetheless, the Contact Group began talks with the principals, that is South Africa and SWAPO, and took the precaution of widening the debate by inviting delegates from surrounding African nations, known as the frontline states.

THE PROGRESS OF TRANSITION

Real progress was discernible on 10 April 1978, when the Contact Group brought to the Security Council a negotiated "working arrangement" for Namibia's independence. This Settlement Proposal revealed that South Africa accepted the notion of elections supervised by the UN, although it did so reluctantly. Further, it had agreed to a staged withdrawal of the SADF. In the course of these negotiations SWAPO had insisted on earlier withdrawal and gone on to question South Africa's sincerity in assenting to an electoral process. Internal elections for a constituent assembly with any strong South African representation by whites would have been an obstacle to Namibian autonomy and a humiliating defeat after years of effort. The gulf in agreement was bridged and

Namibia

confidence strengthened by the twofold establishment of a Special Representative to the UN Secretary-General and by the setting up of a special task-force, the United Nations Transition Assistance Group (UNTAG), to supervise elections and oversee transition. Security Council Resolution 435 followed on 29 September affirming that, "the key to an internationally acceptable transition to independence is free elections for the whole of Namibia as one political entity with an appropriate United Nations role".

The Secretary-General's Special Representative appointed was Martti Ahtisaari, an experienced UN mediator (and, today, the President of Finland). He would spearhead UNTAG.

The Special Representative would work together with an Administrator-General, appointed by South Africa, whose responsibility would be to carry forward the objectives of Security Council Resolution 435. The Contact Group very plainly made the point that the working arrangement should "in no way constitute recognition of the legality of the South African presence in and administration of Namibia". Moreover, the work of the South African appointee must proceed one step at a time in a manner satisfactory to UNTAG.

Ahtisaari began by carrying out a survey mission in the territory and submitting a detailed report to the Secretary-General in New York to be laid before the Security Council. Agreement had been reached by all parties in Namibia, it was said, for UNTAG to carry out its mandate for a period up to 12 months, in the expectation that this would be done effectively and impartially. Further, all had agreed the lines of an election process establishing a Constituent Assembly. This Assembly would draft a Constitution for Namibia for adoption by a two-thirds majority.

South Africa accepted the UN plan in spring 1978 and spent another ten years raising issues to do with arrangements for transition. Delaying tactics took several shapes. For Pretoria, the prime irritant was the Marxist-inclined SWAPO. This movement was to be harried through SADF forays into neighbouring Angola where the SWAPO headquarters had taken refuge. A psychological attack was also mounted on SWAPO by infiltrating and influencing cadres in other political parties who might be persuaded to challenge the popular appeal of a far-left political front. A Democratic Turnhalle Alliance had already been set up in 1975 (with suspected South African support) to coax Namibians into other allegiance with a rather ambiguous slogan, "Take our hand and save our land".[2]

PEACEFUL TRANSITION IN DANGER

One factor in South African delay had much graver consequences. Angola, to the north of Namibia, a territory wrested from Portugal in 1975, had since then been largely in the hands of Marxist guerrillas, the People's Movement for the Liberation of Angola (MPLA), supported by an estimated 50,000 Cuban troops. Unless those Cuban allies were removed from Angola the Government of South Africa would never agree to Namibia's independence. There was a very real danger that southern Africa would be completely destabilized and the possibility of great-power involvement.

Competing for power in Angola were the National Union for the Total Independence of Angola (UNITA), a right-wing group backed by South Africa, and the MPLA, supported by SWAPO and the Cubans. The fighting was dogged and inconclusive during 1987 and early 1988, and the chief participants increasingly ready to consider a way out of their burdensome commitments. Fortunately, governments in Washington, Moscow, London, Pretoria and Havana were all feeling their way towards some sort of reconciliation process, a pacific approach to reducing conflict. Political developments by way of Namibian independence and Angolan settlement were on the UN agenda but had been stymied on the ground.

There seemed a possibility that a single power from outside Africa – the United States – might be a more useful intermediary than the Contact Group. In May 1988 there began a series of informal talks, 12 in all, chaired by US Assistant Secretary of State for African Affairs, Chester Crocker. London and the OAU were kept in close touch. The objective of the talks, bringing in South Africa, Namibia, Angola and Cuba, fell short of any resolution of civil war in Angola; more directly (and of relevance to this chapter), it was to effect a Cuban withdrawal from Angola in return for South Africa leaving Namibia. Thus, Namibian independence from South Africa (the UN's ideal) would be "linked" to a political "trade-off" by external diplomacy. The UN would meanwhile take a back seat although the Secretary-General set out for Pretoria and Windhoek, Namibia's capital, to take soundings.

It has been suggested that the US more or less *imposed* its mediation, partly to demonstrate US indispensability in the settlement of regional conflicts.[3] Whatever the case, it is almost certain that the UN scheme needed the persuasive influence of a great-power now able, also, to talk amicably with the Soviet backer of left-wing elements. Progress for the UN Contact Group was doubtless helped by other considerations: US President George Bush, newly in office, and more amenable to the UN than Ronald Reagan, his predecessor; the readiness of Chester Crocker to acknowledge Contact Group guidelines as trailblazing elements; and the significance of superpower guarantees of settlement. Each side had something to gain: nobody wanted to incur the odium of wrecking participation. Dogged and inventive discussion among a group of officers and officials avoided risks of high-profile ministerial summitry.

In the end it was the UN, in New York in December 1988, that brought signatories together to endorse two accords setting out a timetable for the staged and total withdrawal of Cuban troops from Angola. South Africa would honour its side of the bargain in relinquishing its hold over Namibia. All was now ready for the inauguration of the transition operation.

UNTAG GOES AHEAD

UNTAG's mammoth task of implementing UN Resolutions was scheduled to begin on 1April 1989 and to be completed within 12 months. It had taken ten years for parties in dispute to give formal assent to carrying through the plans. The high point of the transition operation was the organization of an election for November 1989. A military component in the task-force, trimmed eventually to 4,500 soldiers from 21 states and commanded by an Indian general, found itself deployed in 200 locations, monitoring a fragile cease-fire and attempting to demobilize reservists and irregulars. Infiltration of armed men across borders had to be curtailed. Overseeing the phased withdrawal of 30,000 SADF men involved ensuring that most of them returned to South Africa apart from 1,500 who were to make up a basic security group confined to specified camp areas.

Civilian personnel were responsible for a range of duties. To begin with, Namibia was divided into 23 electoral areas and the first wave of UN staff manned dispersed information points where over 700,000 Namibians had to be registered for the poll.[4] This was not an easy matter and it depended on effective collaboration between the UN and a skeletal staff of South African administrators. Country people crowded into 70 or so booths to face puzzling questions through an interpreter. Almost half the men were away from their families as migrant mine-workers. Namibians had always been denied both democratic representation and unbiased information. UNTAG decided to launch an ambitious political education (or re-education) programme through a network of people from local churches, trade unions, farmers' associations and trade. A multimedia campaign used daily TV and radio broadcasts, exhibitions, posters, leaflets and T-shirts. Progress was relayed back to Ahtisaari in Windhoek. Liaison between UN volunteer staff and representatives from UN Specialized Agencies such as UNHCR, UNICEF, WHO and FAO, put in hand the transport, reception and rehabilitation of 42,000 Namibians returning to their villages from exile. Those who were suspected of arms-bearing or of involvement in terrorist activity were scrutinized and afforded amnesty. White-painted UN Land-Rovers cruised the villages reassuring people that the police were no longer counter-insurgency "hit-squads". The actual setting up of almost 400 polling stations, many in remote semi-desert areas, the time-consuming business of collating and checking the documentation, training support staff, and ensuring the safety of people and paper, was all the responsibility of 1,300 specially recruited UN supervisors, clerks and interpreters. By the end of a week given over to voting 97% of those registered had voted. Fewer than 2% of the voting papers had to be rejected.

The whole UNTAG programme, a tremendous transition operation, depended on the hard work and improvisation of some 8,000 people from more than 109 states (including, for the first time, Switzerland). The cost of the whole exercise was at least $383 million. When, on 10 November 1989,

Ahtisaari told a jubilant crowd of the results, he declared that the world's youngest democracy had given the whole world "a shining lesson in democracy, exemplary as to commitment, restraint and tolerance". "Many people are calling this a success for the United Nations, which it is," he told his listeners, "but we who worked so closely with Namibians in every corner of this country . . . know that the real success is yours." All seemed set fair for Independence Day on 21 March 1990. Transition for Namibia had needed a peacekeeping element, but the year-long enterprise, one without precedent, had gone smoothly and a new nation had emerged. UNTAG could now disband. The liberation movement, SWAPO, achieved a majority in the election but not the overriding two-thirds, and so negotiations had to go ahead for convening a broad-party Constituent Assembly of 72 men and women from seven political parties.

FINAL SUCCESS

This "constructive engagement" throughout 1989 has been described as one of the most cleverly engineered diplomatic achievements of recent years. Namibia had been "freed" although Angola faced an uncertain future. The full co-operation of all parties concerned showed a way forward for the resolution of interlocked disputes. The UN was able to acknowledge the leverage that others had exerted. An operation to bring about political calm had begun with carefully safeguarded demilitarization and proceeded through elections supervised by the UN to full, equable and final settlement. At the capital Windhoek, a distinguished crowd saw a new state born, soon to become the 160th member of the UN. A little after midnight on 21 March 1990, the Secretary-General of the UN, Perez de Cuellar, invested a veteran freedom campaigner, Sam Nujoma, with the presidency. All eyes watched the South African flag lowered and the flag of Namibia, blue,white, black, red and green, fly proudly for the first time. President de Klerk of South Africa was there, an advocate for peace after three generations of struggle between the two neighbouring states. Perez de Cuellar voiced the wider meaning when he declared that "the international community has played an unprecedented role in the establishment of your state. The struggle of your people has been our struggle".

Peacekeeping and political transition are the legitimate objectives of international collaboration. The Namibian enterprise was a success story; the Angolan venture a probable failure. The making of new nations inches forward only if we learn from our misjudgements and our mistakes.

NOTES

1. The authority was Security Council Resolution 385, adopted 30 January 1976, which called for the release of all Namibian political prisoners, abolition of racial discrimination in law and practice, return of Namibian exiles, withdrawal of South Africa's administration, and for the holding of UN supervised elections.
2. SWAPO spokesmen wondered whether the hand to be grasped was South African rather than Namibian.
3. See Berridge, 1991, pp. 78–80.
4. Each district, headed by a UNTAG District Supervisor, set up permanent and temporary registration centres in towns and mobile registration teams for rural areas. Registration took 12 weeks for those who were over 18, were native-born or resident for the last four consecutive years.

FURTHER READING

Asante, S. K. B. & W. W. Asombang. An independent Namibia? The future facing SWAPO. *Third World Quarterly* 11(3), pp. 1–19, 1989.

Berridge, G. R. Diplomacy and the Angola/Namibia accords. *International Affairs* 65(3), pp. 463–80, 1989.

Freeman, C. W. The Angola/Namibia Accords. *Foreign Affairs* (Summer 1989), 68(3), pp. 126–41, 1989.

Karns, M. P. Ad hoc multilateral diplomacy: the United States, the Contact Group, and Namibia. *International Organization* 41(1), 1987.

Katjavivi, P. H. *A history of resistance in Namibia.* Letchworth, UK: J. M. Dent, 1988.

United Nations. *A trust betrayed: Namibia.* New York: United Nations Office of Public Administration, 1974.

United Nations. *A summary of twenty years of effort by the Council for Namibia on behalf of Namibian independence.* New York: UN Council for Namibia, 1987.

United Nations. *Objective justice* XXII(1), pp. 1–54. New York: UN Department of Public Information, 1990.

Urquhart, B. *A life in peace and war.* New York: Harper & Row, 1987.

Chapter Sixteen

NAMIBIA

1920	South West Africa League of Nations mandate to Britain administered by South Africa.
1946	Union of South Africa request for incorporation of South West Africa rejected by UN General Assembly.
1953	UN Committee on South West Africa set up to report each year to UN General Assembly.
1961	South Africa now a republic, no longer Union of South Africa.
1966	General Assembly terminates South African mandate for South West Africa (now to be called Namibia). Reserved judgement on ICJ test-case on South Africa's mandate violation.
1968	UN designs transition programme for Namibia.
1971	ICJ advisory opinion confirms actions of UN General Assembly and Security Council. Council for Namibia now to represent the country.
1977	South Africa frames the Turnhalle Proposals and tries to retain a hold on Namibia.
1978	UN Contact Group formed and Settlement Proposals issued.
	UNTAG established.

1988

May: US mediating diplomacy begins. Angola the problem.
December: accords signed at UN providing for Angolan/Namibian trade-off.

1989

April: UNTAG operation launched.
November: UN supervised elections.

1990

21 March: Independence Day in Namibia.

CHAPTER SEVENTEEN

Cambodia

REBUILDING: A DAUNTING PROSPECT

In two years UN efforts would rebuild a country torn apart by civil war. At a meeting in Paris in October 1991, 19 Asian and European nations drew up an agenda for an enormous scheme of conflict settlement and national renewal, outlined strategies for implementing it, proposed the deployment of a force of 22,000, and put the whole thing into effect. Peacekeeping in the normal sense of prising the disputants apart was to be followed by peacemaking in the defined stages of cease-fire and demilitarization, the preparation and supervision of an election, and refugee rehabilitation. This was to be the UN in action after the traumatic disunion of the Cold War era. An unprecedented package would demonstrate international faith, compassion and resolve – and it would be worth every cent of a $1.9 million budget. It would create a wide role for the UN in setting up administrative structures to aid transition from intra-national divide and conflict to a regularized and self-determined state. From conflict management to conflict resolution to promoting communal stability, the process would show what the UN could and should do as it approached its half-century. The laboratory for this huge experiment was Cambodia in South East Asia.

This case-study shows the UN involved in a territory with a long imperial history, succeeded by conflict and chaos, especially during the Khmer Rouge infamy. The implementation of the UN reconstruction effort is seen as an exercise, first, in dealing with complex political factors, and then, in implementing a carefully phased programme to restore administration, physical infrastructure and democracy. In regard to its success, we cautiously record an open verdict.

Yet in advance of the launch of the programme in October 1991, during its two-year operation, and in retrospect since the undertaking was disbanded in December 1993, controversy has been insistent. The whole idea was seen by many, both within the UN organization and outside, as too idealistic and too ambitious in requiring as indispensable a footing of a "neutral political environment". "Difficult to achieve and impossible to maintain" was a frequent criticism. As soon as the UN left there would be reversion to corruption and intimidation. How could the inalienable right of self-determination ever be promoted in a country used only to autocracy and the persuasiveness of force? National rebuilding was so multidimensional an undertaking that it was unrealistic to think of it being started, let alone achieved, by 22,000 earnest outsiders in 24 months. The careful advance in democracy brought about by the UN as midwife in places such as Angola, Namibia, Mozambique and perhaps soon in western Sahara, had all been fragile, in some respects questionable, but all were lesser-scale than the one projected for war-torn Cambodia. An international organization coming in to help create a new government system, because none of the existing parties could be trusted to do that either alone or in concert, was an "imperial" mission. If any success was gained because Cambodia and the rest of South East Asia accepted it as non-imperialistic, would it not be obvious that in a conflict situation the hardest struggle is to keep *out* of the arena?

Most of the controversy, often heated and shrill, centred on the military and political partisans, the Khmer Rouge, led by Pol Pot, whose unspeakable crimes of genocide had terrorized Cambodia and appalled all nations between 1975 and 1979. This evil faction would realize that the gentle UN presence was a paper tiger, disrupt everything, and terrify every Cambodian with the prospect of its hideous return. In spite of doubt, criticism and prejudice the national renewal of Cambodia was put in hand between 1991 and 1993.

THE ORIGINS OF CAMBODIA

Cambodia's history had twice been dynastic, first, in the glorious age of power and opulence in the tenth and thirteenth centuries, and then as a French colony from 1863 to 1954, allowed to have its own king and court. The French *mission civilisatrice* never really understood a surge of nationalism in its dependencies and its arrogance of power was finally shattered in 1945. Three decades of violence ensued as political allegiances were fought over by Left and Right. The country was variously called Kampuchea, the Khmer Republic, or Cambodia. With some substance of order, however, the Kingdom of Cambodia was admitted to the UN in 1955. Today the population, mainly Buddhists, numbers seven million; 85% are Cambodians, 7% Vietnamese, and 5% Chinese. Four out of ten are 15 years old and younger. Only one in ten live in townships, the rest are villagers in rice lands and forested hills. If the current violent conflict is dampened down, there will still be competition for resources in the 18 provinces of the country, a struggle for better lands and water, and an estimated population growth of 30% by the Year 2000, when over twice as many country people will have gone to the towns. The dispersal of people and the tensions aroused by disputed access to natural resources have made the task of the UN rebuilders difficult in many respects, particularly in the aftermath of strife.

Historically, yet again, Cambodia has suffered from its proximity to zones of contest in Indochina and later in Vietnam. The post-war US commitment to "containing" communism by "hanging in tough" brought devastation and resentment to South East Asia in the 1940s and 1950s. Cambodia was agreeable to being considered "neutral" by Washington but because its remoter areas became staging-posts for the Vietcong guerrillas in Vietnam it was inevitably exposed to the ferocity of B52 bombing raids (carried out with no regard for the stance of neutrality). If, it was asked, the guerrillas moved like fish, how otherwise do we drain the water? The people of South East Asia today, at least the older generation, live with memories of terror from the air and of numbing fear on the ground. Forty years ago an effort was made to lift them out of this paralysing situation by setting up International Commissions for Supervision and Control in Cambodia and for its neighbours Laos and Vietnam. The institutional title conveys patronage as well as concern, a flavour that the latest UN renovation programme has deliberately sought to avoid. In those day the great-powers were worried that the ill-defined borders of states emerging from European rule reflected neither ethnic reality nor equable distribution of natural resources.

If the politicians saw contesting claims as likely to create the domino effect of communist encroachment, and so necessitate supervisory investigation and guarded control, the UN anticipated that some countries would press for disinterested assistance, not that of superpower "balancing" nor of being drummed into a defensive alliance like the South East Asia Treaty Organization (SEATO). Already, by 1966, King Norodom Sihanouk of Cambodia, although something of a capricious autocrat, was prepared to convince the UN of his country's democracy (a slight misnomer), its right to self-defence, and its pledge never to enter an alliance that didn't conform to the principles of the UN Charter. For the Cambodians the General Assembly was preferred to the P5 calculations of the Security Council, a preference that is still favoured today.

THE KHMER ROUGE ERA

The year 1970 brought a coup and chaos. General Lon Nol, a disaffected military commander in the capital Phnom Penh, ousted his king, it was said, with the covert aid of the CIA. Whatever the truth of this, the Pentagon welcomed a man likely to co-operate with South Vietnam in clearing out the Vietcong bases in the Cambodian forests. President Nixon secretly authorized the bombing of the reserve areas in April 1970 and South Vietnamese forays burned their way across the paddy fields of the Khmer Republic. Sihanouk retreated to Beijing and from there fanned a campaign of protest and sabotage that established him as resistance leader *in absentia* with, as a matter of expediency, the ruthless Khmer Rouge as his ally, image and cause. For five years the tide of battle ebbed and flowed until in 1975 the Khmer Rouge swept across the entire country and captured Phnom Penh. Subsequent events were to horrify the rest of the world. Led by Pol Pot, "Brother Number One", the Khmer Rouge set out to reorganize society on lines that were a skewed form of Marxism and highly chauvinistic. Brutal oppressors rooted out the Western-educated elite and despatched all town dwellers to labour camps. The "new people" (peasants) were to replace the "old people" (intellectuals who were literate, spoke a foreign language, or wore spectacles). Money, markets and schools were all abolished. Genocidal control "cleansed" the people, causing 620,000 to flee across the border, and it executed perhaps one million Cambodians in the "killing fields". Terrifying memories of the Year Zero lie deep in the psyche of Cambodians still. The foreigner is respected and welcomed now, as he has had the morbid task of raking over a charnel house and rebuilding civilized structures.

The monstrous shadows of the Khmer Rouge were dispelled at last in November 1979 when Vietnam invaded Cambodia and installed Heng Samrin as President of the People's Republic of Kampuchea. The country soon became something of a shuttlecock. When Vietnam turned to Moscow for aid the traditional hostility between China and Vietnam soured further as Beijing suspected Soviet hegemony thrusting southwards. Brigades from the People's Republic of China locked horns with 200,000 war-tested Vietnamese but they had to retreat after a month. The Phnom Penh government, spurned by Beijing and Washington and barely tolerated in Moscow, felt increasingly isolated and pugnacious. Samrin especially took to heart the unconcern of the world in what was, after all, a mild Socialist recreation of normal life from the chaos left by the Khmer Rouge void. Urban infrastructures had to be rebuilt. Many wondered why the UN did not help them in the major task of recruiting, training and educating, and furnishing basic resources and care. Was the United States so savaged and embittered by the Vietnam experience that dollars could not fund the resuscitation of a victim of war?

THE UN DECIDES TO HELP CAMBODIA

Changes in world attitudes were evident by 1981. That year the UN arranged a conference on Cambodia, which opened badly. Moscow and Hanoi refused to attend. Beijing, Washington and London argued that the invasion two years previously had anchored an illegitimate republic in Phnom Penh. More moderate opinion in the General Assembly suggested that if Hanoi had joined this occasion it would have brought a solution to the crisis and so prompted Vietnamese withdrawal from illicit occupation of Cambodia. Vietnam's credibility as liberator of Cambodia from the noxious clutches of the Khmer Rouge might then have acquired plausibility. Did it have ulterior motives? The most that New York was able to do was to confer on Prince Sihanouk in 1981 the mantle of coalition leader and a seat in the General Assembly. Unfortunately, the delegation included ex-Khmer Rouge members, a circumstance, it was said, to which Western powers were ideologically blind. On the other hand, did UN votes in favour of that delegation express disapproval of the Vietnamese rather than endorsement of the Cambodian representatives?

Another eight years were to elapse while the Phnom Penh Government went about its solitary, halting reconstruction. Some professional Cambodians from this epoch were to complain, as the great contingent of UN rebuilders arrived, that their painful efforts ten years previously went unremarked and unappreciated by the blue berets and laboratory coats of their guests. What the UN advance party did detect were signs of corruption and mismanagement accumulated during the 1980s when rival Khmer factions struggled for power. In those eight years for example, the Khmer Rouge was transporting in from the Thai border some 40,000 guerrillas who eventually were to haunt UN personnel. In the wider world there was growing concern about a destabilizing crisis in the making. UN Secretary-General Perez de Cuellar began to blaze a trail in 1985 suggesting means towards full settlement, enlisting as he did the help of the Association of South East Asian Nations (ASEAN) to shoulder the burden of assuring security.

Cambodian interest was slow to form and three years of probing discussion passed before the process of negotiation quickened. The possibility of enfranchisement, the disarming of rival bands, the enactment of a new legal system, the supply of experts, materials and funds – all these possibilities were aired. Moscow and Beijing now applied pressure. Mikhail Gorbachev in 1987 publicly praised the Cambodia Vietnamese administration for its readiness to promote talks about national reconciliation. As a token of its sincerity he expected Vietnam to quit Phnom Penh. China, now keen to improve relations with the USSR, began to cast adrift the Khmer Rouge. In their view a four-party coalition should take over in the capital.

Would the Khmer Rouge return, overtly or covertly? Sihanouk's government-in-exile included terrorist officers. The maverick leader's insistence in 1989 on including them in any final settlement seemed to be as unwise as his alliance with them when he reeled away from overthrow in 1970. Whatever the inclination of Sihanouk, the White House now wrestled with an embarrassing dilemma. Did inviting the Khmer Rouge to participate in negotiation risk buttressing its position and mortally offending other nations? Or would excluding this faction (along with its unknown rural adherents) bring civil war as a consequence? American and other governments appear to have squared these moral issues by "looking for ways to deal with the realities of the situation", as the White House put it in September 1989. Realism suggested then (as it did to the UN two years later) that giving the Khmer Rouge a role might just prevent it from a return to dominance. That role should only be local, it was widely felt, since many took umbrage that Sihanouk's unacceptable associate sat at the same table in the General Assembly and believed that seat should remain empty pending final settlement. In late 1989 there was fierce accusation that the "comprehensive settlement" publicly desired by the US was a euphemism for anti-Vietnamese manoeuvres where any line-up was permissible. In the face of this the US Permanent Representative told the General Assembly that Washington had to accept that the credentials of Democratic Kampuchea were in order because the UN's Credentials Committee had said so, although this did not imply that his government supported the Khmer Rouge.

Meanwhile, apart from the wrangles in New York the situation on the ground in Cambodia that same year looked inauspicious. An authoritative calculation estimated that there were 50,000 government troops in and around Phnom Penh, some 20,000 Khmer Rouge guerrillas in salients to the north and southwest, an irregular force of 10,000 men in the west claiming to be the Kampuchean People's National Liberation Front (KPNLF), and Prince Sihanouk's 12,000-strong army northwest on the Thai frontier. At the same time, 26,000 Vietnamese, a considerable force, were marking time in the south of the country.

As 1989 drew to a close some light began to dawn. The Vietnamese withdrew from Cambodia. The Security Council was urgently convened and it threw its weight behind a peace process.[1] The Secretary-General appointed a Special Representative with a brief to urge UN members to recognize a coalition government in Cambodia and to co-ordinate a large-scale humanitarian aid programme regardless of political uncertainties. There was already a tangle of 80 NGOs in the field. If major powers such as the United States and China could be persuaded to retire the UN could step in, using perhaps the Genocide Code to expel and possibly arraign the Khmer Rouge. A peace package without strings would ease Vietnam's freedom to withdraw and at the same time clear away the ground for Hanoi's improved relations with the US.

A UN TRANSITION PROGRAMME

Momentum at the UN gathered speed in early 1990. Australia had tabled an initiative at the Security Council calling for the UN to sponsor a period of transition ("expanded peacekeeping") in Cambodia and to interpose a force to do this through a process of enfranchisement, election and rehabilitation.[2] Delegates from the P5 met in Paris and arranged intensive discussion among 17 interested nations and 14 political groups from Cambodia. Questions began to reverberate. What were the precise objectives of a multiphase operation? What would be the role and methods of particular contingents, military and civilian? How best would liaison and the training of UN personnel be effected? Could the agenda be accomplished, say, in two years? What arrangements might be possible for standing down the operation, withdrawing UN elements, without risking the total collapse of a half-built structure? Would the US and Japan help with the cost of the enterprise? In the longer term might it be possible to resurrect the idea of establishing a zone of peace and neutrality in return for mutual force reduction? It must be assumed that Cambodia was to be properly demilitarized through a careful programme of monitored demobilization if the overall scheme was to work.

Outlines were clear and agreed on the drawing board by August 1990. A force to be known as the United Nations Transitional Authority in Cambodia (UNTAC) was to be set up. (Note the difference in terminology between "Transition *Assistance*" in UNTAG (Namibia) and "Transitional *Authority*" in UNTAC (Cambodia). This was to be a significant difference in approach.) The force would go to Cambodia, by invitation, of course, to assist in a process of national rebuilding. Phnom Penh was ready to hand over administrative authority to the UN in five major ministries and UN staff were to carry the portfolios of Foreign Affairs, Defence, Public Security, Finance and Information. In the capital a Supreme National Council, chaired by Sihanouk, would be formed from various groups and it was to govern Cambodia between a cease-fire and the final exit of the UN force.[3] The same body would fill the General Assembly seat rather than leave it vacant. Two months later, the General Assembly endorsed this most ambitious plan, seeing it as a condemnation of the policies and practices of the recent past and as facilitating self-determination. Within 12 months a United Nations Advance Mission (UNAMIC) was to be sent out.

Paris finally set the seal on the initiative on 23 October 1991 when 19 nations approved its treaty plan and authorized a peacekeeping mandate emphasizing that this had to be "realistic, defined clearly, and capable of being readily realized in operational terms". Yasushi Akashi from Japan was appointed Special Representative in Cambodia. The make-up of the UN's biggest ever peacekeeping operation was now clear: 16,000 soldiers, 3,600 police, and 2,400 civilians were to be provided by more than 50 states. Over two years the costs were estimated to be $3,000–5,000 million dollars in a budget of unprecedented size and complexity. The actual mandate as further clarified by the Security Council in February 1992 was to comprise operations in seven fields: survey and report; human rights; military affairs; civil administration; police work; electoral preparation and monitoring; and rehabilitation. UNTAC was distinguished from most other peacekeeping operations in that it would have administrative authority (which had not been the case in Namibia, but was in West Irian), and it would provide the UN with, in the Secretary-General's words, "an historical opportunity to restore peace to Cambodia and to contribute to the advent of a new era in South East Asia and in international relations".

The three areas UNTAC gave priority to during 1991–3 were military disarmament, the structure of civil administration, and arrangements for an election. Disarmament was to be total before any election could be held. Soldiers bearing arms could be mustered and directed to cantonments there to be divested of their weaponry. The Blue Berets who were to carry out this difficult and dangerous task came from such countries as Poland, Ireland, Bangladesh, Indonesia, Peru, the US, the Philippines, the USSR, Bulgaria, France, the Netherlands and Canada. There were frequent misunderstandings and strained incidents when patrols met from nations with diverse languages and military conventions. In two respects the Supreme National Council made disarmament a little easier, first, by agreeing that command and control would not have to await New York's approval but could be placed locally (avoiding a problem that had bogged down aspects of other UN peacekeeping operations), and secondly, that in the absence of any guarantee of total disarmament it would be practicable to aim at a 70% cut in arms followed by regrouping the remainder in the cantonments in the hope that eventually they might be persuaded to disarm.

Despite the care with which all this was handled Cambodia remained armed to the teeth. The white jeeps of UNTAC were regularly shot at. Seventy million or so land mines threaded the roads and verges and maimed at least 80 Cambodians each week. Demining was the number one priority and would take years to complete. UN supplies were stolen, vehicles were hijacked. Certainly, the Khmer Rouge and numerous other groups held arms caches in impenetrable undergrowth. If movement by day was unpredictable and hazardous, any patrolling or convoying during the hours of darkness would bring lethal consequences. In these circumstances, it is debatable whether the mandate neatly parcelled up back in Paris and New York was something of a fantasy in expecting a peaceful scenario in which free and fair, and by implication, lasting developments could be encouraged and structures hoisted into place. Should the mandate have permitted military action using the UN Convention of "appropriate measures" in such chaos? Was the use of force only in self-defence adequate to deal not only with intransigence but with violent confrontation, of which there were many instances?

Civil administration provision had to initiate a detailed range of statutes and general measures to authorize the work in the capital and outlying areas. A new legal system was necessary and that meant UN legal advisors must frame fresh legislative codes and devise appropriate methods for enquiry into violation of human rights. Magistrates had to be sworn in. Premises were found in which courts could function and officials were appointed. There were persistent language difficulties and a corps of translators had to be on hand each day. Vexing problems frequently arose when a UN advisor, perhaps from a sophisticated regime, came up against the fatalistic eccentricities of age-old traditions. Relations between UNTAC's fresh foreign military police and the *gendarmerie* were notoriously troublesome. In some instances UNTAC's recommendations for the arrest of a criminal would raise local objections from a host of kinsfolk, which begged the question of how far UNTAC could enforce its law-making and its peacekeeping.

Cambodian material needs made necessary a task-force approach. Where bankers and accountants put together a currency system and coped with the threat of 100% inflation, out in the field it was teams of military engineers and civilian technicians who set about reconstructing derelict forges and work-shops. Construction units from Eastern Europe, guarded by Bangladeshi infantry, rerouted and remetalled cratered roads, repaired a trailing mass of power lines and useless telecommunications wires, dug wells, connected up a mains system, and tried their best to improve a situation where only 3% of the population had access to drinkable water. UNICEF came in to mount a massive emergency operation, the biggest since the Second World War, to deal with widespread malnutrition, immunization against typhoid, malaria and other diseases, and the plight of at least 20,000 amputees, victims of mines. Agricultural workers, 62% of whom were women, were to receive tools, techniques, seeds and the advice of experts from a host of countries. A target set was that each family might have its own food plot. Schools, libraries and colleges had to be rescued from ashes and a literacy drive was mounted (particularly in anticipation of the election). Replacements for 15,000 teachers who had been lost during the Khmer Rouge regime was a first step in reconstructing the entire educational system. In addition to all this refurbishment of settled communities, there was the agonizing condition of 370,000 refugees flooding south from Thailand, footsore and menaced by bandits, who would demand food, first aid and shelter in a protective Cambodia.

ORGANIZING AN ELECTION

Election preparations were put in hand in good time for the voting on 23–25 May 1993. UNTAC troops were now given fresh orders to move in to protect election workers and premises. People needed to be reassured that in some way UNTAC was their safeguard against ill-treatment, yet it would not be easy to protect them physically. Although experts flown in from New York were experienced in electoral organization in Haiti, Namibia, Angola, Mozambique and 40 other countries, none of them had encountered the nightmare of tension and the latent terror in Cambodia. A democratic election was to take place in a land where a generation had suffered mayhem and where the chief political cliques relied on private armies.

Twenty-one electoral provinces were divided into districts supervised by teams from 47 nations. A flak jacket and helmet were deemed more advisable than a UN armband. The concept of a secret ballot was explained to villagers using a travelling street-theatre. If the village headman were amenable his neighbours crowded round to listen to Radio UNTAC relaying information 15 hours a day. Each Cambodian registered as a voter was issued with a plastic registration card bearing name, age and a photograph. One million people had registered somehow in the first six weeks and in the third week of May the total number of voters was approaching 4.6 million. White helicopters from UNTAC, under vigilant guard, delivered the election leaflets of 20 contending parties, the ballot boxes and bundles of voting slips. Election notices were pasted on billboards while UNTAC's headquarters was refortified.

Two rather ominous events were noted by UNTAC staff at the beginning of May. In New York the Security Council appeared to backtrack on the Paris treaty plan of October 1991 of "free and fair elections in a neutral political environment". It was now hoped, rather ambiguously, that the May election would achieve "a minimum standard of acceptability". Then in Cambodia itself, the Khmer Rouge let it be known that while it boycotted the actual election it reserved the right to "act appropriately", as it now felt threatened by everybody, everywhere. Against a tiger ready to spring UNTAC would be helpless. The stark truth was that if there were no ballot there would be civil war. Moreover, if electoral losers were unable to accept the results of the ballot, then, again, there would be civil war (as was to happen in Angola).

The third week of May, grimly contemplated, was, in fact, an astonishing success. The "stinking theatrical farce" of the election, as the Khmer Rouge termed it, brought 90% of the registered voters, four million of them, to the polls. (Some of them even voted for UNTAC!) A fair majority was won by Funcinpec, a former opposition and royalist group led by Prince Sihanouk's son Prince Ranariddh. Second came the Cambodian People's Party and in third place the Buddhist Liberal Democrats. Khmer Rouge was humiliated and so excluded. No overwhelming win was gained that might have incited a loser to resume hostilities. Narrow margins in voting seemed sufficient inducement for parties to work together in a hung but tense coalition. Sihanouk, the controversial maker and breaker of fences, appeared to be the only acceptable intermediary in the advance of transition. Despite the candour of his own self-advertisement he was grudgingly acknowledged to be the least bad alternative where the best harbinger of progress had not yet emerged.

THE AFTERMATH: DANGERS AND CONFUSION

At the beginning of June 1993 the mercurial Sihanouk almost torpedoed the great UN experiment. Stung by criticism that he had endeavoured to stage a constitutional coup he pulled out of the barely-formed National Government. As so often happens, the political vacuum was soon filled by political power-gaming. All parties were now writhing in anguish at the prospect of not being first. Khmer Rouge followers began openly to canvass support in menacing terms. Previously it had not been impossible to persuade Cambodians to queue up for hours in the hot sun so that their vote might bring peace and a change of power after 25 years of turmoil. If Phnom Penh were to become no-man's-land politically it would wreck the UNTAC scheme at the peak of performance and inevitably plunge the land back into anarchy. Once more the question was asked in the world's press: had the UN taken on more than it could ever manage?

The patchy reconciliation of July 1993 was not altogether satisfactory. The UNTAC mandate was to expire in August 1993. The Australian military commander of UNTAC had held exploratory talks with the remnants of the Khmer Rouge and other groups of similar ilk to see whether they would agree to reliquish their hold over about 20% of Cambodia in return for a guarantee that they would not be annihilated. The justification for these meetings with unsavoury elements was that negotiation was preferred to the use of military force. Nevertheless, the talks resulted in deadlock, even though violence did ebb away for a time. Retrospectively, negotiation seems a very risky thing to have attempted, since it could easily have been the thin edge of a wedge likely to split political consensus irretrievably.

A more positive attempt to bring some order to the confusion in Cambodia was the vote of the multiparty Cambodian Constitutional Assembly in September 1993 to restore the monarchy. Prince Sihanouk, who had abolished the monarchy 40 years previously, was to be reinstated as one who would "reign" but not "rule". Akashi decided that the time had come to pull out the bulk of the UNTAC force by November 1993 at the latest. In view of the uncertainties of Cambodia, as a precaution a sizeable contingent of 3,500 UNTAC police and medical staff would stay on for the time being, together with the mine-clearance squads whose job seemed endless. Should a military presence make itself felt? The Secretary-General decided not to recommend this unless Cambodia itself asked for help – currently it would be better to concentrate on civilian resources. Nevertheless, 20 unarmed military liaison officers (from 14 nations) were sent in for six months with a roving mission to observe matters affecting security. In Phnom Penh an office to co-ordinate civilian activities was established and another, to oversee work for human rights, was set up with an Australian judge as its director. Both of these offices were to service the new civilian infrastructure and put in hand a scheme, using a grant of $20 million, for the reception and rehabilitation of refugees. In such a slim fashion UNTAC's main purpose still was to encourage the people of Cambodia to believe that democracy was worthwhile and that this was their chance, perhaps the last one, to break with the past. More recently, in July 1994, leaders of the Khmer Rouge have been outlawed. Some 9,000 guerrillas have been offered amnesty if they surrender.

Were UNTAC's 26 months of painful effort a success or a failure?[4] The cost in dollars and in the lives of 28 soldiers and civilians was a sobering reflection; another was the sheer impossibility of judging how far and how long the process of reconstruction might be seen to be productive. In common with the earlier and smaller operations in Namibia and West Irian this was an effort by the UN to aid transition from despair to peaceful settlement. In the case of Cambodia the UN was invited into a country where people walked with crutches, figuratively and literally; the UN, in a sense, offered first-aid and prosthetic treatment. When UNTAC folded its tents there was no certainty that Cambodians would have learned to walk unaided. Even so, surely it was worth the attempt?

NOTES

1. Despite meetings in mid 1989 with Cambodian factions in such diverse locations as Tokyo, Hanoi and Paris, the broad strategy then envisioned gained no momentum until the P5 were able to use Australian proposals as a lever. See Note 2 below.
2. Known as the "Red Book" proposals these are described in outline in Gareth Evans, *Cooperating for peace*.
3. Six seats each were to be given the Government and the "resistance". Khmer Rouge would occupy two places.
4. Gareth Evans admits flaws in UNTAC operations, for instance, slow deployment, patchy civil and judicial control, unavailing prosecution of human rights violators. Lessons learned range over needed improvements in staff recruitment, mustering and training, in cost-conscious administrative procedures, and in communication. See *Cooperating for peace* p. 106 ff.

FURTHER READING

Brown, F. Z. *Second chance: The United States and Indochina in the 1990s*. New York: Council on Foreign Relations, 1989.

Duncanson, D. Who will govern Cambodia? *The World Today* 38, pp. 239–45, 1982.

Evans, G. *Cooperating for peace*. Sydney: Allen & Unwin, 1993.

Kroef, van der, J. M. Kampuchea: diplomatic gambits and political realities. *Orbis* 28(1), pp. 145–62, 1984.

Solarz, S. J. Cambodia and the international community. *Foreign Affairs* 69(2), pp. 99–115, 1990.

Thomas, T. Into the unknown: can the United Nations bring peace to Cambodia? *Journal of International Affairs* 44(2), pp. 495–515, 1991.

Wright, M. (ed.) *Cambodia: a matter of survival*. London: Longman, 1989).

The situation in Cambodia after the conclusion of the transition process can be followed in outline in *Keesing's Record of World Events*; see Appendix: Where to find out more about the UN.

Chapter Seventeen

CAMBODIA

1954   Cambodia (Kampuchea, Khmer Republic) independent after being a French colony.

1955   Cambodia joins the UN.

1970   Lon Nol coup ousts King Sihanouk. US bombing raids blast Communist supply lines to Vietnam.

1975   Pol Pot's Khmer Rouge rename land as Democratic Kampuchea and maintain five years of barbarous ruthless repression.

1979   Vietnam "liberates" Cambodia. Danger of external powers exploiting instability.

1981   UN tests the ground for negotiations.

1985   ASEAN's help enlisted towards settlement.

1989   UN sponsors exploratory diplomacy and appoints Special Representative for Cambodia.

1990   Australia's transition plan tabled, discussed in Paris, and UNTAC authorized.

1991   October: design of UNTAC finalized, mandate given. Extensive terms of transition programme.

1993   May: UN supervised elections.

August: UNTAC mandate of finishes and main force is disbanded.

1994   Reconciliation process now slow and in Cambodian hands.

PART SIX

New initiatives

The environment

With the collapse in 1990 of the Cold War superpower confrontation, the world found itself faced with "threats without enemies". The rapidly wasting environment was the threat that eventually caused most public concern. Records of UN debates in previous decades show discussion often centring on such threats to humanity as fall-out from nuclear testing, or debris in outerspace, or gross pollution of seaways and urban areas. The symptoms of mankind's thoughtless use of the world were soil erosion, increasing aridity, and damage to water supplies and settlements; the causes attracted less attention. Although the term "environment" does not occur in the UN Charter, from the very beginning there was a great sense of environmental mission to improve the health, wealth and happiness of people living in habitats that were generally depicted as "undeveloped" or as "inadequately resourced". Years of UN work have addressed economic and social betterment. It is mainly from the late 1960s that the UN articulates and amplifies a note of growing public and expert anxiety about the consequences of heedless exploitation of natural resources, with the inevitable conclusion that we all have a duty to save an endangered biosphere from further despoliation. The UN as a world organization has since attempted to give environmental problems salience by providing a forum, a means of careful observation, and recourse to specific programming. Concern about securing the future not only of an inhabited world but of Planet Earth is grounded in the sober realization that the consequences of our ecological (and economic) fecklessness transgress all human boundaries. Uniting nations in rational and determined action seems the only way forward. Governments that are complacent or tardy about this are being jerked into action above all by young people everywhere: "20% today, 100% tomorrow" expresses the conviction that although young people are not in the majority today, it is particularly their future that is in peril.

This chapter traces UN involvement in environmental issues from the first great international meeting in Stockholm in 1972, convened by the UN, to a commemorative follow-up meeting in Rio de Janeiro 20 years later. The achievements of the Stockholm conference gave impetus to promoting concepts and devising programmes such as the Action Plan and the UN Environment Programme (UNEP). The process of environmental degradation, its diffusion and rate of growth, called for urgent international report and action. A brief survey follows of three seminal reports that highlighted the issues and clarified the options. The new concepts of "sustainable development" and "global commons" are scrutinized. Finally, this chapter examines the discussion and achievements of the Rio conference, *Earth Summit 92*, concluding with some of the questions that international collaboration must raise.

THE STOCKHOLM CONFERENCE, 1972

Official government delegates from 113 states gathered at the UN Conference on the Human Environment (UNCHE) in Stockholm in June 1972. For two weeks they were to consider the protection and improvement of the human habitat; their vision must be global. Three main committees set to work: on human settlement; on natural resources and development; and on pollution. Separately a working group began to frame a Declaration. Fourteen days of intensive discussion resulted in the agreement and publication of an Action Plan and a Declaration on the Human Environment. Fundamental principles for UN action on the environment headed the Action Plan.

(a) Essential objectives must be defined at the outset.
(b) Existing organizations should be used wherever possible to increase efficiency and reduce overlap.
(c) Operating networks would be preferred to another "super-agency".
(d) Action should be evolutionary and flexible despite incomplete knowledge of environmental consequences.
(e) Regional centres for implementation and analysis would be more effective than a long-distance headquarters like New York.
(f) The UN would be the principal centre for co-ordinating international collaboration.
(g) Proposals for change and implementation should take into account the diversity of habitats among countries.

These principles were followed by 109 recommendations for international action. Broadly speaking they relate to three fields of action. First, analysis and monitoring was to be the function of an *Earthwatch* programme, supplied with scientific personnel and information technology. Problems of clear significance, such as climate change and pollution, would be identified, continuously monitored, and remediation proposed. Secondly, there were plans for formulating management strategies to handle specific problems. Thirdly, proposals for supportive measures were outlined to cover the whole range of public information, ongoing scientific and governmental liaison, finance, and training and education. The whole scheme was innovatory in two respects. It spelled out the inescapable duty of governments to collaborate, and it deliberately enrolled the ancillary help of the growing number of NGOs and pressure groups, the so-called "Greens". "Linkage for Action" became a conference slogan.

The Declaration on the Human Environment, although endorsed by everyone in the conference hall, did not escape criticism, especially from those outside. Similar to the 1948 Universal Declaration of Human Rights, it served as an ethical code. There were declarations, general scientific premises, and some international law in its clauses. Those who found it questionable asked: was it merely a worthy statement of ethical principles that would be used as a fire curtain against inflammatory dissent? Could it form a platform for eventual purposive action? Did it have any legal leverage? Most dissatisfaction welled up from Third World delegates asserting that for them the link between environmental considerations and development was crucial and should have topped the agenda. They expressed candidly their concern to reduce poverty first, before pollution. In the fullest sense, they urged, environmental action plans should aim at enhancing the development of less well-off nations; international collaboration by richer nations should aim to raise resources to enable the poorer to meet their environmental responsibilities. This distinction, although energetically voiced, did not result in discord, rather, the sense of it was incorporated into the Preamble to the Declaration.

It is worth noting that already at Stockholm in 1972, certain points of international law, controversial today, were being put into the Declaration. First, there is the prime right of sovereign states "to exploit their own resources pursuant to their own environmental policies". (The possibilities of argument over this seem endless.) This position "as of right" is subject in law to two requirements, namely, that states have a responsibility to ensure that such activities do not cause damage to the environments of other states, and, further, that in the event of such damage being caused, states must co-operate over admission of liability and payment of compensation. Thus, interestingly, the UN was able to persuade a hundred states that the principle of sovereignty, expressed in conventional terms, needed a qualification acknowledging responsibility towards one's neighbours.

Also noteworthy is the number of uninvited who attended. Perhaps 10,000 campaigners from a wide array of grassroots movements converged on the conference hall to buttonhole delegates, to listen attentively to debate, and to hold an alternative fringe forum in the city. They saw themselves as pushing reluctant politicians, it was said, into "greening their sovereignties".[1] Many of the visitors most certainly espoused the theme of the tandem relationship of development and environment issues.

233

THE GENERAL ASSEMBLY AND THE ENVIRONMENT

At its December 1972 meeting the UN General Assembly acclaimed the UNCHE Resolutions. It took up proposals from the conference that the Action Plan should be co-ordinated by the UN and to this end established a UN Environment Programme (UNEP). To be based in Nairobi, in Kenya, this body would not be a fundraising agency but one for research and information banking. *Earthwatch*, as monitoring agent, would pass data to Nairobi who, in close consultation with governments and scientific bodies, would prepare policy documents and initiate programmes of information, training and technical aid. Work went ahead at full speed. Within two years priorities had been set for progress in such areas as ocean dumping, trade in endangered species of fauna and flora, marine-and-shore pollution, population growth and settlement trends, health and water quality, and trans-boundary air pollution.

A number of states began to take topics such as these on board by establishing environment ministries or development departments and by tabling legislation for their parliaments to approve. Global enquiry and application were to be carried out by: the *Earthwatch* system; the Global Environment Monitoring System (GEMS), for monitoring among other things the spread of toxic waste, water quality and indications of climatic change; an International Referral System for Sources of Environmental Information (INFOTERRA), to abstract detailed information on planning, development and technology; and the Global Resource Information Database (GRID), to bank the data. The agenda at Stockholm and the work of UNEP quite quickly inspired clear growth points in government and public consciousness, especially when it was radiated through the press and interest groups. Terms such as "ecology", "ecosystem", "recycling" and "biosphere" became common parlance. The number and variety of "pressure groups" (a significant label) campaigning with an "eco-message" became overwhelming, many of them seeking the UN's formal recognition of their "consultative status".

THE NAIROBI CONFERENCE, JUNE 1982

A constant feature of discussion, whether at conference or in the press, is the growing conviction that finding lasting remedies for many environmental problems depends on building a framework of appropriate international law. Obligations, limitations and sanctions need to be codified. This point was well taken when 105 states reassembled to mark the tenth anniversary of the UNCHE, this time in Nairobi. Which areas of concern, members queried, were still showing slow progress because guidelines and rules lacked stringency? Could there have been faults in the Stockholm design where the UNEP had been envisaged as catalyst and well-meaning co-ordinator of national and regional schemes rather than being given a more positive leadership role? UNEP had inspired and endorsed strategies, conventions, protocols and declarations, but the task of saving certain natural features and resources warranted some degree of prohibition and enforcement. Reaffirming principles agreed at Stockholm, the Nairobi conference went further. It was emphatically agreed that effective management of waning resources required both technical innovation and compulsory measures. Further, the UN should bring into focus development and environmental work undertaken in different sectors by Specialized Agencies.

Another question heard at Nairobi, itself in a developing country, related to the poorer majority of the world. What happens when a struggling nation cannot afford to take on the environmental obligations the richer world thinks it should? Collectively, the Third World, it was pointed out, owed its mainly Western creditors about $1.3 trillion. Should Senegal be blamed for irresponsibility if it has to fell vast forests for timber or mortgage a year's catch of fish to raise foreign exchange to pay off debt? Were Mexico, Brazil and Peru to be condemned for cutting environmental corners to guarantee food and shelter in their teeming slum areas? Representatives of developing lands bitterly criticized the foreign exchange dealing in New York, London and Tokyo, which circulates $95 in every $100 around a rich inner-wheel of advantaged countries and dispenses $5 to a capital-hungry world where environment improvement waits for investment schemes.

Within 15 years of the Stockholm conference the UNEP was able to demonstrate a massive experiment in peaceful political and technical change. The laboratory had been a variety of habitats. Financially, more than $1,000 million had been lodged in UNEP's enabling fund and of this $260 million had been distributed. "The Fund," UNEP boasted, "has catalysed four times the resources for the environment that it has had to spend itself." Even so, the funding base was narrow with six rich states paying in three-quarters of it. Apart from this, governments were spending thousands of millions of dollars on conservation work. Human resources were being marshalled in over 100 countries; UNEP had been devoting one-fifth of its monies to training 27,000 personnel. These people were visibly managing initiatives in three domains: conceptual, technical and legal. An example is the work on clearing up the seas. Conceptually, the focus was on bringing governments together to pool assessment of pollution in mankind's marine rubbish-dump (70% of the earth's surface). Brainstorming the situation were 130 states, 16 UN Specialized Agencies, and 40 NGOs. Technically, the clearance programme was targeted on the very different ecological and human-use characteristics of ten regional seas across the world. Ridding coastal and deep-sea areas of contamination was linked to conservation of fish and mammals. Legally, following agreed concepts, the strictest safeguards and prohibitions had to be rigorously enforced in regard to dumping, coastal engineering and mining, oil spills, and coastal effluence. The cardinal assumption in work of this scale has been that, unless we can estimate with a fair degree of accuracy what is likely to happen, remediation is unlikely to be adequate. UNEP's sophisticated machinery, GRID, was able to make very useful forecasts about marine area deterioration.

THE PROGRESS OF DEGRADATION

Progressive worsening of the environment in the last two decades has been dramatic. In some unhappy circumstances *Earthwatch* has turned into "Doomwatch". The statistics stand like tombstones. WHO estimates that 50–60% of all healthcare costs in developing countries are triggered by water rendered unclean by pollution or interference. Industrial pollution in the developed world has grown 40 times in the last 35 years. Each year 65 million tonnes of waste foul the seas, most often just offshore. Lake and forest are savaged by acid rain and sulphur dioxide; in some places, such as southern California, local humidity turns acid rain into acidic fog with traces of 16 pesticides in it. Mexico City's joggers have been advised to do their circuits indoors where the air is at least breathable. Every 12 months 20 million tonnes of productive topsoil are removed and six million hectares of land become dust. The extinction rate of species of animals, plants and insects, while not easy to confirm, must now run into thousands. Ill-planned rainforest clearance in Amazonia and Indonesia is hacking down timber ten times faster than it can be replanted. Above all, in many lands the prospect of global warming and the erosion of the ozone layer is causing anxiety. The 25km layer of gases in the atmosphere, which has been a beneficial heat shield, is now fast becoming a "greenhouse" heat trap thickened by 24,000 million tonnes of carbon-dioxide, methane, nitrogen and the destructive CFCs. The next generation may well have to cope with warmer temperatures of 1–3°C (enough to cause problems with harvests) and heightened sea levels. Dangers resulting from depleted ozone levels have been predicted by UN sources for some years. The Vienna Convention for the Protection of the Ozone Layer broke new ground in 1985 in anticipating an environmental catastrophe by the end of the century. Increased ultraviolet radiation, skin cancers and eye cataracts had to be prevented by strict prohibition of harmful emissions such as carbon dioxide from fossil fuels. Altogether, world habitats have greatly deteriorated over the past 20 years. Cavalier disregard of the environment has presented the world with brutal options.

INFLUENTIAL REPORTS BRING NEW CONCEPTS

In the 1980s the UN brought together experts from all over the world not merely to restate environmental problems but to work out solutions. Germany's Chancellor Willy Brandt headed in 1980 a commission that discussed the division of rich world North and poor world South, initially in terms of the survival of both and then, two years later, revised its agenda to talk of "a programme for survival and common crisis". The message was that the people who struggled in deprived habitats would best be helped not by further handouts in the begging bowl, but by careful planning that enabled them to go forward with development appropriate to their own circumstances. In 1984 a commission headed by the Swedish Prime Minister Olaf Palme broadened the concept of "security", largely associated with disarmament, to recognize that those denied an equitable share of resources might ultimately resort to force unless more deliberate husbanding and distribution were undertaken.

The prime mover in collective response to environmental problems was to be the Brundtland Commission Report of 1987. Mrs Gro Harlem Brundtland, Norway's Premier, had already had notable success in her own country on conservation matters, when she was invited to chair an independent section of the UN's World Commission on Environment and Development. The report, *Our common future,* concluded that integration of the two concepts of environmental care and development was the only sound and viable way to ensure humanity's future. Richer states would have special responsibilities and poorer ones would have to cope with special handicaps. The 23 Commission members, 11 of them from developing nations, came straight to the point.

> We are not forecasting a future: we are serving a notice, an urgent notice based on the latest and best scientific evidence that the time has come to take the decisions needed to secure the resources to sustain this and coming generations.

They were thus charting a path rather than showing a blueprint. As to the mode of operation, states had to accept that unilateral exercise of sovereignty, when each looked after his own, was no longer possible. "The Earth is one but the world is not" was the judgement. To take unity of action further, the concept of "sustainable development" was introduced. Soon to become a popular phrase, this referred to development that meets the need of the present without compromising the ability of future generations to meet their own needs. This would not be a fixed state of harmony but a process of change. The transition to sustainability in industrial life and in lifestyles was seen by the Brundtland Commissioners as depending on three principles. Primarily, cause and effect must be as accountable in environmental terms as in economic ones. Next, there must be fundamental changes in management behaviour with new objectives and methods to attain them. Finally, incentives to change should be provided instead of relying solely on regulatory measures. What elsewhere became termed an "eco-revolution" would preserve and extend technical benefits, create new opportunities, and add an environmental dimension to development policies and practices.

One other useful concept stated in the Brundtland Report was "global commons" (a term that has become standard in the literature of environmental politics). Those parts of the planet falling outside national jurisdictions, the oceans, outerspace, Antarctica, have special significance in that sustainable development, indeed their very existence as "resource", can be secured only through international co-operation and agreed regimes for surveillance, development and management. The UN Conference on the Law of the Sea in 1982 was an ambitious scheme to meet those desirable ends. Two other "commons" struck the Brundtland Commission as in need of urgent attention. Outerspace is peppered with orbiting satellites and, until recently, the products of weapons testing. A negotiated regime for dealing with traffic and debris was vital. Antarctica had been safeguarded to some degree by the UN's 1959 Antarctica Treaty. Keeping its "silent", unique environment demilitarized and preserved for science would mean strenuous efforts to hold off the exploitative plundering that other continents had suffered.

On the whole, *Our common future* had a good press. Two of its assertions, however, aroused controversy – growth and financial capabilities. One interpretation of sustainable development was that it depended on lowered demands on resource use. Did this mean that growth in quantitative terms would have to be discouraged, that is, where an emerging nation was "going for gold rather than green", exploiting resources regardless of optimal environmental balance? Who would take on the task of admonition? The Brundtland Report had called for a change in the content of growth, "to make it less material-and-energy intensive and more equitable in its impact". Representatives of developing nations were quick to point out that it is generally the advantaged who can afford to make the choice between "quality" and "quantity" of growth. The Report's call for addressing causes rather than symptoms meant squaring up to financiers, investors, profiteers, foreign exchange dealers and creditors who encouraged protectionism and selfish exploitation. Financial capabilities of many countries in the developing world were constrained by their disadvantage in trading and the raising of capital, however much they they wanted to respond to environmental ethics. A good example of the problem is that in Latin America four states, Argentina, Brazil, Mexico and Venezuela, owed roughly 30% of total world debt. To meet this burden they cut timber, mined and over-farmed to produce exports of which 35% went to meet interest on debt payments. In regard to environmental conservation, what was the extent of their "financial capabilities"?

THE RIO CONFERENCE, 1992: EXPECTATIONS

With the dawn of a new decade in 1990, UNEP got down to the work of organizing a mammoth event to mark the twentieth anniversary of UNCHE, held in

Stockholm, 1972. It would be the first "summit meeting" of heads of state on environmental issues. Progress with global clean-up was impressive but rather sporadic. Some governments had keenly embarked on legislation and public relations work to interest industry in filtration, recycling, energy-efficiency experiments and the installation of facilities.[2] Very obviously the packaging and food sectors were ahead with their practice to market "environment-friendly" and "biodegradable" commodities. Controls on nuclear-waste dumping, limiting use of CFCs, proposals for taxation of fuel, were all to be heard from nations in the forefront.

Yet in Eastern Europe, in the Middle East and in most of Africa, there was little evidence of the easy slogan, "think globally, act locally". A meeting of political impulse and expert minds ought to act now and plan for the next century. A Preparatory Committee sought to co-ordinate the planning of UN Specialized Agencies, NGOs and scientific groups with working parties meeting from time to time in such places as Norway, Kenya, Thailand, Mexico, Spain and Egypt. UN member-states were asked to forward to UNEP documents with their experiences, insights and proposals to show what they were doing about sustainability. As a culmination of conference analysis, reporting, proposal framing, and meetings to revise and negotiate, three international Conventions were envisaged, on climate change, on biodiversity and on forestry. A master-plan for specific action enumerated strategies for dealing with 21 separate environmental issues. This would be put to the conference for approval and implementation under the name of Agenda 21, pointing to action in the twenty-first as well as the twentieth centuries.

An elaborate blueprint of 500 closely detailed pages is not easy to summarize. (Indeed, it was to prove rather indigestible for many delegates in Rio de Janeiro.) As a brief for conservation to the Year 2000 and beyond, the structure was factual and statistical covering such topics as the effects of disarmament, trade, population trends, finance and debt. It assumed a hortative note in discussing access to natural resources, human rights, popular participation and forward planning. The text built in analysis and proposals for betterment in those sections concerned with pollution, energy strategies, oceans, and biological, chemical and physical factors of ecological change. Objectives were identified, targets set, completion times and costs provisionally estimated. As its name suggested, this was an agenda for discussion and in no sense a list of enforceable directives.

The size of the conference when it opened in June 1992 was astonishing: 178 UN member-states amassed a delegational cohort of 10,000 officials. There were 120 heads of state. New York and Nairobi headquarters attached 700 staff for administration. Seven thousand journalists constituted an unprecedented Press Corps. The "uninvited" flocked in again, as had happened at Stockholm two decades earlier. Fifteen thousand men, women and children represented everything from alternative eco-religions to mammalian conservation, scientific interest groups and human rights campaigns. During the two weeks of the conference they maintained close contact with official delegates in a huge, vibrant global forum.

THE RIO CONFERENCE: DEBATE AND ACHIEVEMENTS

The achievements of the Rio conference were considerable in the ordering of discussion and the presentation of a great range of suggested measures. More debatable is the extent of political will that UN members are prepared to bring to bear, and particularly the readiness with which they will initiate and follow through some rather radical institutional change. There was some disappointment with the inconsistent visibility of certain Western leaders, among them President George Bush. The readiness with which some observers branded the meeting as a failure may perhaps be traced to understandable exasperation that a volume of words failed to remove "vested interests" from their established points of advantage.

Yet it is interesting in retrospect to look at some of the issues that were raised in the conference hall. For a start, an ethical perspective shone through the declarations of richer countries, who had in mind a triple challenge of environment, development and democracy. Environmental protection and carefully staged development would mean little without liberation of people, justice and open accountability. If all were to work together on sustainability then some developing states would need more transparent and representative government. Poorer nations responded almost predictably. Were rich states trying to slow their development, using UNEP to force financial and other considerations on them? Was this neo-imperialism? Or eco-colonialism? They should not be treated as a botanical garden! Were the wealthier nations prepared to reverse net revenue, which had flowed from South to North over 30 years? Would there be an end to trade barriers so that their own products could compete more equitably in world markets? That way they could also aim at ecologically balancing their agriculture.

There were observers at Rio who were to conclude that what was at stake, and always will be, is money. Quite clearly, it seemed to them, the poorest nations required urgent financial aid to lift them off the bottom of the economic pile. Richer countries such as India, Malaysia and Brazil looked for access to new technology. The richest in the world (the "G7" group) offered an unquantified commitment to "new and additional funding" without disturbing too much the institutional shape of the World Bank, government exchequer structures and the multinational corporations. It was clear, too, that political factors twitched the purse-strings and that, in President Bush's words, "the day of the open cheque book is over". Discussion over what became known, a trifle facetiously, as "Costing the Earth", made much of the rather sad fact that a UNEP appeal for $600,000 million to meet costs for a year's implementation only netted about $8,000 million in pledges from states. Every one, naturally, realized that recession made it difficult for most nations to guarantee appreciable and consistent funding.

A concluding remark by the Conference Secretary-General, Maurice Strong of Canada, puts achievement in perspective. "The road from Rio will be much harder than the road to Rio," he declared. It was a trailblazing exercise. The three Conventions destined for universal endorsement became two. The first, on climate change, aimed at stabilizing concentrations of "greenhouse gases" at levels that would prevent human activities from dangerously interfering with the global climatic system; 153 nations agreed to aim at holding steady 1990 emission levels until the Year 2000. Not all, especially the UK and the US, found it easy to define timetables and targets and the possibility of taxation on fuels.

The other Convention, that on biodiversity, was thrown around a good deal in discussion. The stated aim was effective international action to ensure conservation of genes, species and ecosystems, to promote their sustainable use and ensure equitable sharing of benefits arising from them. This statement of intent was signed by 165 states. Nevertheless, strong words were spoken. The beneficiaries of this collective resolve, it was demanded, should be those local communities and indigenous people who had protected these endangered species for years (the rainforests, for example, were rich in such species). This laudable sentiment was objected to by the US and, less forcibly, by a number of European nations. The Bush Administration refused its signature because it opposed Third World nations' insistence on sharing the wealth created from biotechnology and drugs originating from US territories. The UK and Japan were wary about what they feared might be open-ended commitments, but finally they signed.

The third hoped-for Convention, that on forestry, was never launched from the slipway. The North/South divide blocked agreement. The developed nations set out wanting a binding forest Convention. Developing nations, feeling that more was being demanded of them than of the temperate nations, opposed on the grounds of national sovereignty. They regarded their forests as part of a natural endowment to be used as they themselves thought best. In any case, if a part of those resources was to be set aside at the behest of others, they would expect compensation for the lost revenue. No guarantee of this sort was forthcoming and the Convention was watered down to a nonbinding set of sustainable forestry principles.

The extent of consensus is demonstrated by the measures that were finally approved. These were Agenda 21, a Declaration on Environment and Development, a Statement of Principles on Management, Conservation and Sustainable Development of All Types of Forest, the two Conventions described above, and an agreement to set up working groups and negotiating processes to deal with desertification. Generally, it was obvious that the objectives of the summit had been met to some extent. A set of agreements had signalled a collective firm response to environmental decay. Political commitment to sustainable development had been vouched for at the highest level. New paths and networks for nations in action had been outlined and tentatively secured.[3] Worldwide public awareness had been fostered. The prime objective for many was to make sure that the "bottom-up" approach of a representative global forum would succeed the conventional "top-down" mode of the summit meeting. The essence of sustainable development and global commons was to be put into practice by the work of a new UN Commission on Sustainable Development. Its membership from 53 nations would first investigate the intricacies of finance, monitoring and technological transfer, to be followed by specific programming for developments in health, toxic waste disposal, seas and forests.

ENVIRONMENT: PRESSING QUESTIONS

The road from Stockholm to Rio and beyond is long and tortuous. In 1972 and 1992 a host of issues were raised that still confront us. One of the great questions being asked relates to the "peace dividend" that was expected to follow when nations relaxed their ideological in-fighting with the end of the Cold War. If the fault line is now more North/South than East/West could some of the astronomical military expenditure be diverted into environmental improvement? An unstable world, nurturing fears and some enmities still thinks it necessary to spend $900,000 million a year on arms and to recruit half the world's scientists for defence-related activities. While the bulk of this investment is that of industrial states, the developing nations are spending over $200,000 million on weaponry. Numerous calculations have been made to demonstrate what could be done by diversion of spending. What is spent on arms in 12 hours would help to put tropical rainforests into better shape. Two days' expenditure on defence could be put to curbing spread of dry lands and deserts. A fraction of the world's defence spending diverted into the environment would make a significant contribution towards the preservation of rainforests or curbing the spread of dry lands. Massive provision of funds is crucial. Nothing has yet been done to take up the suggestion in the 1980 Brandt Report that revenue for environmental aid might be gained by tax levied on the use of international commons such as fishing, sea and air transport, and seabed mining. It is not difficult to foresee the political objections to this that some states and their electorate might raise. There have been a number of imaginative schemes for nations to assign a portion of their gross national product (GNP) to environmental resuscitation, although the experience of the UN in persuading nations to put 0.7% of GNP into aid for developing countries is not a happy one.

Two financial problems voiced at Rio are receiving earnest attention in UN circles at the moment. The first is how to work for price stabilization in raw materials so that Third World producers do not have to resort to over-exploitation. Half a dozen multinational corporations and industrial conglomerates have the say-so in respect of 80–90% of such primary commodities as forest products, tea, coffee, copper, oil and bauxite. Producers can do little to prevent external enterprise from denuding their natural resources and they are soon caught in a remorseless cycle of dependence and poverty. Another difficulty, mainly facing nations that industrialized last century, is the fearsome and hugely expensive task (now seen as a duty) of rolling back the toxic remnants of a previous "dash for growth". In Europe, at least, there have been many schemes for rehabilitation. Other regions in the world, victims not of industrial but of early commercial exploitation and urban sprawl, are in desperate need of co-ordinated aid to provide inhabitable locales.

The UN must co-ordinate its cross-sectoral activities if progress is to be effective and steady. Getting the balance right between developmental and environmental priorities will be a most delicate task. Elaborate monitoring schemes, through the medium of technical instruments such as GEMS and GRID, will go on.[4] An expanding UNEP programme will seek to improve legal machinery to codify obligations, limitations and penalties. There will be concern to formulate procedures, analogous to those in the UN Charter, for dealing with disputes and conflicts that have roots in the environment, and for preventing them if possible. If the direction and extent of the wasting of Planet Earth seems now indisputable, the pressure for amelioration must be inexorable. Slowly, and rather erratically, nations are uniting to put fingers in the breached dyke. The words of President J. F. Kennedy are even more relevant today: "Together we shall save our planet or together we shall perish in its flames. Save it we can, and save it we must, and then we shall earn the eternal thanks of mankind".

NOTES

1. Twenty years later, in Europe and North America, new perspectives ("political ecologism"), particularly among younger people, are differentiating Green Politics from the old, conventional Grey Politics. See Dick Richardson & Chris Rootes, *The Green challenge* (London: Routledge, 1995). These approaches are increasingly being urged at UN conferences and in UN published material.
2. In 1995 UNEP is going ahead with programmes exploring links between patterns of industrial production and consumption. The aim is to work out preventive strategies reconciling industrial development and environmental protection.
3. The World Summit for Social Development, meeting in Copenhagen in March 1995, had prominent on its agenda environmental aspects of policies for poverty eradication and re-employment in developing and developed lands. A commission to monitor "eco-friendly" social development programmes has been pro-

posed which will report annually to the UN and prepare an agenda for a follow-up summit in the Year 2000.

4. UNEP is setting up an International Environment Technology Centre in Osaka, Japan, in 1995 to assist developing countries with data analysis where resources and settlements are being managed according to "environmentally sound" criteria.

FURTHER READING

Ahmad, Y. J. *Guidelines to environmental impact assessment in developing countries.* London: Hodder & Stoughton, 1985.

Carson, R. *Silent Spring.* London: Penguin, 1962.

Ekholm, E. P. *Down to earth, environment and human needs.* New York: Norton, 1982.

Falk, R. *This endangered planet.* Toronto: James Lorimer, 1971.

French, H. F. *After the Earth Summit: the future of global environmental governance.* Washington DC: Worldwatch Paper 107, 1992.

Hurrell, A. & B. Kingsbury (eds). *The international politics of the environment.* Oxford: Oxford University Press, 1992.

Imber, M. Too many cooks? The post-Rio reform of the UN. *International Affairs* 69(1), pp. 55–70.

Kimball, L. A. *Forging international agreements. Strengthening inter-governmental institutions for environment and development.* Washington DC: World Research Institute, 1992.

Leontief, W. W. *The future of the world economy: a UN study.* Oxford: Oxford University Press, 1977.

Tessitore, J. & B. Woolfson (eds). *Global agenda. Issues before the General Assembly of the United Nations.* United Nations Association of the USA, 1992.

Thacker, P. S. *Global security and risk management: background to institutional options for management of the global environment and commons.* Geneva: World Federation of United Nations Associations, 1992.

United Nations. *Disarmament, environment and sustainable development.* New York: United Nations Environment Programme, 1988.

—*The United Nations system-wide medium-term environment programme 1990–5.* Nairobi: United Nations Environment Programme, 1991.

—*The global partnership for environment and development: a guide to Agenda 21. Post-Rio edition.* New York: United Nations Public Information Department, 1993.

World Commission on Environment and Development. *Our common future* (Brundtland Report). Oxford: Oxford University Press, 1987.

Chapter Eighteen

THE ENVIRONMENT

Environmental issues, much in public mind, taken up by UN in last 30 years along with general mission to improve human social, economic conditions.

1972 June, Stockholm	the first international conference on environment, UNCHE, launches Declaration on Human Environment, detailed Action Plan for protection, conservation, *Earthwatch* monitoring agency. NGO participation unprecedented.
December	General Assembly establishes UNEP, based in Nairobi. *Earthwatch*, GEMS, INFOTERRA monitor, analyze, bank and disseminate data.
1980	Brandt Commission.
1982 June	Nairobi conference pursues environment: development link more closely. GRID facilitates forecasting. Growing anxiety about ozone layer depletion and global warming.
1984	Palme Commission.
1985	The Vienna Convention for the Protection of the Ozone Layer.
1987	Brundtland Commission Report, *Our common future*. Introduces new concepts of sustainable development and global commons.
1992 June	Rio de Janeiro: conference designs Agenda 21, three Conventions (climate, biodiversity, forestry). Again, great NGO involvement. Dissent in debate evident. Majority endorse Agenda 21, Earth Charter, Climate and Biodiversity Conventions. Forestry Convention replaced with Statement of Principles.

UNEP still needs to address schemes for financial underpinning and institutional change if global attack on environmental degradation is to succeed.

The control of drugs

"The misery caused by drug addiction is immeasurable", reported the Secretary-General to the UN in 1989. His audience would nod assent to his description of the terrifying effects of vast profits on social and economic well-being and the prospect that in some cases "administrative and judicial structures are being undermined to the extent of endangering political stability". Less apparent, however, is what the world is to do about this threat to life, liberty and the pursuit of happiness. If an individual wants to take drugs, it is asked, why should governments interfere? Should we not think out the unthinkable and legalize some drugs thus eliminating the black-marketeers with the consequent price war? Spending so much time on tracking down the producers and tempting them with *ad hoc* agricultural alternatives does not attack the real problem of street demand. What about the UN's laudable efforts to help developing countries stand on their feet and improve living standards, which leads to the temptation to buy and sell narcotics? Why not let each nation take care of its own trafficking problem? Debate resounds and that is good. Even better is that the UN's appeal for "international understanding and co-ordination together with increased resources" is seen as indispensable by members of the UN. The world battle against drug addicts has been joined.

For thousands of years drugs have been employed to relieve pain and aid control of disease, to combat fatigue and hunger, or to alleviate boredom and despair. A great range of products found in nature, herbs, plants and roots, have had supposed curative properties, either in popular practice and superstition or, together with synthetic products, as additives or specially prepared doses administered medically. The relaxing or stimulating side-effects have conferred on a number of these drugs a reputation as providers of serenity, elation and power, an element of magic. The global problems of narcotics are the concern of this chapter. A brief look at the attempts to enforce drug control in the first years of this century is followed by an account of how the UN has been brought in to legislate and set up a system for active control. The comprehensive work of the UN Drug Control Headquarters in Vienna, in association with UN Specialized Agencies, is considered, together with its global strategy for dealing with drug production, trafficking and abuse. Finally, mention is made of some of the possible trends of the problem.

THE EXTENT OF THE DRUG PROBLEM

Drugs or narcotics have become a world problem socially, economically and individually. Socially, most countries have witnessed the emergence of a subculture with distinctive habits and language, the disquieting presence in the streets of "users" and "pushers" and the associated alienation and crime. Curiosity, ignorance and peer pressure compound the problems of drug abuse in societies where jobs and housing are hard to find. Most victims are young and in the US half of those treated in drug clinics are women. Economically, drug-related problems transcend national frontiers and affect all states whatever their stage of development or political structure. In a time of recession when capital and jobs are scarce, drugs trading provides new opportunities for individuals and for syndicates. Trafficking leads to criminal activities such as racketeering, tax evasion, bribery, corruption, conspiracy and violence and terrorism. Powerful networks operate illicit transit and money transfers. In the workplace the effects include incapacity, job failure, accidents and absenteeism.

For the individual, drug abuse lowers bodily defence mechanisms. Confused states such as fantasy, depression, aggression, anxiety and hallucination generally occur. A desire for repeated doses at ever shorter intervals impels those who are dependent into expensive searching for new supplies. Alcohol exacerbates the damage of drug taking. Withdrawal symptoms tear away at the whole psychic health of the individual. In the view of the UN Division of Narcotic Drugs, the tidal increase in drug abuse has become a human tragedy invading home, workplace and school, and affecting persons of all ages and origins. Drugs are enticing, captivating and destructive; they destroy traditional values, lifestyles, families and national economies. Misuse radiates beyond the disadvantaged who find it hard to cope with unemployment, overcrowding and exploitation; it includes those who have yet to leave school, those who are successful and most advantaged and, of course, it impacts on families and the community at large. Understanding and support are needed with intervention and treatment to prevent alienation and a return to deviance. Punishment is no cure; neither ostracism nor over-tolerance are helpful.

EARLY ATTEMPTS TO CONTROL

The expansion of trade and the improvement in communications last century opened up a world market for narcotics. The first initiative to limit supply was the work of the Shanghai International Conference in 1909 when 13 nations instituted an Opium Commission with an International Opium Convention put into force in 1915. After the First World War the League of Nations established in 1920 an Advisory Committee on Traffic in Opium and Other Dangerous Drugs. Three Conventions followed: a 1925 Convention bringing into being a Permanent Central Narcotics Board to regulate lawful international trade in narcotic drugs; a 1931 Convention, again to license and control trading; and a 1936 Convention that recognized that legislation was not controlling shipments adequately and for the first time introduced measures for the severe punishment of illicit traffickers.

In 1946 the UN was able to assume responsibility for drug control from the defunct League. A special committee was made responsible to the UN Economic and Social Council . The availability of synthetic compounds now presented new hazards and a Protocol in 1948 was expressly designed to deal with this supply. It was, of course, very important to distinguish carefully between those substances that could be acquired legitimately for scientific and medical purposes and those that were "diverted" into unauthorized channels. This remains a major problem for drug control since there are possibilities of evasion and disguise. Five years later, the Opium Protocol of 1953 was aimed at clamping down on the growing opium trade. Seven countries only would be allowed to export opium, namely, Bulgaria, Greece, India, Iran, Turkey, the USSR and Yugoslavia.

THE UN AND TIGHTER CONTROL

There were obvious loopholes in much of the early legislation. An ambitious UN scheme in 1961 introduced the Single Convention on Narcotic Drugs, which sought to consolidate all existing legislation and to streamline control machinery. The aim was to limit the quantity of narcotics in use to the amount needed for legitimate purposes. (This proved a difficult exercise.) Moreover, if any country or territory failed to carry out the provisions of the Convention an explanation would be demanded by the UN. Should the explanation be unsatisfactory there might be a penal stoppage of drug imports or exports, or both, to and from the defaulting country. An interesting feature of this Convention was that sanctions could be enforced against states that were not party to the Convention but which could be held to be contravening legitimate standards. UN policy was to keep a tight control on the cultivation of natural materials for drug use, such as opium (yielding heroin), the cannabis plant (supplying cannabis, marijuana and hashish) and the coca-bush (from which cocaine is extracted). Signatories were obliged to limit production of these materials to the quantity necessary for approved medical and scientific purposes. The Convention goes further than its predecessors in prohibiting drug misuse such as eating and smoking opium, chewing coca-leaf and any non-medical use of the cannabis plant. Special controls were levied on very dangerous drugs such as heroin.

All too clearly in the early 1970s the UN realized that tougher measures were needed. Illicit drug handling was becoming an extensive and highly profitable enterprise. Keener detection and more drastic impounding and sentencing were necessary. At the hub of UN enterprise was the International Narcotics Control Board (INCB), which had been set up in the days of the Single Convention. The INCB had a quasi-judicial competence in the hands of 13 experts sitting in their personal capacity. The crux of its work was assembling accurate information from governments to judge the effective performance of UN efforts. What governments were doing to improve their drug control schemes was to be continuously evaluated. Working priority was given to consultation and inspection. Drug control administrators from many nations were to be trained at the INCB headquarters in Vienna. New approaches focused on the need to go beyond the earlier punitive legislation and provide for international standards and techniques of treatment of drug users, for education, for public information campaigns, and for rehabilitation. Also in the 1970s a new area of drug taking was addressed, that of the harmful effects of psychotropic substances. Drugs such as LSD, mescaline, amphetamines, barbiturates, tranquillizers are synthetic products; depending on how often they are taken, they can change mood and behaviour and induce feelings of nagging dependency. The most dangerous, it was thought, should be banned absolutely; the others must be controlled very strictly. Stocks, records and laboratory facilities should have routine inspections. No public advertising of these substances would be permissible. The World Health Organization would be responsible for deciding whether any new substance should be brought under the Convention on Psychotropic Substances, which came into force in 1971. The UN Specialized Agencies could most profitably pool funds, experience and research efforts.

Another decade was to reveal drug abuse and trafficking spreading throughout the five continents. Realism had to succeed the previous optimism; it was now time to review the directions of action so far and to see how best to mount a global battle against drug misuse. Central policy for the UN was in the hands of the Commission on Narcotic Drugs (CND), which had been set up in 1946 as one of the six functional commissions of ECOSOC. Representatives of 40 UN member-states meet to review the overall situation, to make recommendations, and to appraise the progress of the implementation of the UN Conventions. They consult to a great extent with Specialized Agencies and NGOs. The CND is not, however, an executive organ for action in the field. Equally, the INCB pursues information gathering, analysis reporting, inspection and dialogue with governments, but again, these are supplementary functions, not executive ones. What was now needed was a more effective machine for co-ordinating resources and planning a strategy for global action. Some sort of global programme must be mounted. The locus of control was to be in Vienna.

THE VIENNA DRUG HEADQUARTERS AND PROGRAMMES

At present there are three units in Vienna responsible for UN drug abuse control. They are in action continuously and they work closely with WHO in Geneva. The Division of Narcotic Drugs (DND) is a clearing-house for technical and professional advice on dealing with every aspect of the drug problem. It is the nerve centre, serviced by the INCB secretariat; this second unit monitors and evaluates action in 190 territories. Thirdly, the apparatus for the actual execution of programmes is the United Nations Fund for Drug Abuse Control (UNFDAC). Its work is funded by the voluntary contributions of 100 governments. The major fields of its activity are: reducing drug demand; reducing drug supply; and reducing illicit traffic. UNFDAC identifies needs and problems at national, regional and international levels. A network of contacts with a host of different bodies is established and fostered in all countries. Governments that request assistance with plans are given advice from the UNFDAC, which also identifies and provides resources and trains personnel. In its first decade, UNFDAC concentrated on technical aid, and on pilot and experimental projects aimed at spurring governments to mobilize resources. Successful schemes were mounted in Pakistan, Thailand and Turkey where opium was flourishing, and in Colombia and Ecuador where peasant farmers were tied into cultivating the coca-bush. Building on this experience UNFDAC now concentrates its financial resources and expertise on the development and implementation of national and regional programmes known as "master plans". The plan begins with a thorough analysis of the site and its specific problems, assesses the practicability of marshalling particular resources and techniques and then administers the scheme as a partnership between national participants and expatriate experts. Master plans have been devised for more than 50 countries; ongoing schemes are in operation now in Asia, the Middle East, southern Europe, Latin America and in the notorious "Golden Triangle" of Laos, Burma and Thailand.

A global programme can only succeed if there is close liaison between the Specialized Agencies of the UN. The International Maritime Organization (IMO) and the International Civil Aviation Organization (ICAO) are active in matters affecting detection in transit by sea or air, the detention of "mules" (drug carriers), and the seizure and confiscation of goods. UNESCO, particularly, has to tackle misinformation and myth. Complacency and fatalism are to be encountered at every level in the public and governmental sectors. Only weak individuals become addicts, it is said. Why not peripheralize them, imprison them if necessary? The message of UNESCO to users and their associates is that they cannot claim to be victims of society, rather, the community and the family are the victims of the abuser: the consequences of abuse are harmful to others as well as to themselves. Extensive programmes of education are mounted worldwide by UNESCO, in schools, public places and, in Latin America, over a wide radio network. Where possible, public opinion must be encouraged to move beyond disapproval, to keep a government on its toes, and to frame courses of local action that prevent and reduce drug taking and involve professional and lay members of a community in counselling work.

For WHO itself there are three main tasks. Banking information as a prelude to policy decision comes top of the agenda. National programmes can then be designed and put into action. The third onerous necessity is to schedule narcotic substances. Is the drug capable of producing a state of dependence? Could its abuse lead to social and public health problems? Then it warrants control. Dependence, in its fullest sense, can, of course, result from the classic analgesics morphine and codeine, which are normally only obtainable on medical prescription. Guidelines are sent out by WHO to pharmacists, doctors and hospital staff as to the regularized use of therapeutic drugs. The wide range of authorities carrying through a global approach for drug control convinced the General Assembly in 1990 that it should convene a Special Assembly to design and authorize a master plan, the UN Drug Control Programme. Finance would be derived as a charge of 7% of the UN regular budget with the remaining 93% contributed by member-states. Since 1992 the costs of the global programme are around $100 million a year, with 80% or so funding well over 100 projects in 63 countries. At least half of this expense is used for educational purposes, underlining the importance of training professionals to deal with the drugs problem. The programme is decentralized with 16 field headquarters in Asia and Africa, and 11 in Central and Latin America.

THE CULTIVATION OF NARCOTIC CROPS

So far this chapter has discussed what might be termed the consumer's side of the drugs issue. But how does the UN deal with narcotic crop cultivation? In what ways can illicit trafficking be stopped? In the first place, it is clear that in many developing countries narcotic cash-crops find a ready market, which is less vulnerable to falling product prices globally, and this eats away at the notion of all-round development. Such crops can be "harvested" against cash in the hand. A shortage of food crops may be the result. Farmers and drug traffickers become mutually dependent, influenced, perhaps, by extortion and violence: there is a militant constituency for the continuance of the nefarious trade. The global programme approached the limitation of drugs cultivation by way of a scheme for "estimates". How much of the coca-bush derivative, cocaine, is used for medical purposes? Large-scale cultivation must be serving illegal demand to a calculable extent. Horticultural and industrial processes employ cannabis plants for some ingredients. The rest must be supplying marijuana leaves and hashish resin to be hawked in the streets. Opium poppy fields yield extracts for morphine and codeine to a measurable degree; the rest must get into the wrong hands.

It is difficult in poorer countries to divert this reliance – by governments as well as farmers – on income-generating points in agriculture. Might intervention by the UN be deemed interference with economic rights? The nucleus of the drug problem is poverty among peasants and shortage of funds in exchequers. Coca offers a tenfold cash return over any other crop. In Andean countries a farmer with an average 2.5 acre plot turned over to coca earns $5,000 a year. How is he to be persuaded to forgo an income that is ten times the average among his neighbours? Another instance of voluminous profit is the sale of heroin derived from morphine (opium contains 10% morphine). Fairly easy cultivation of a crop worth 15 times more than maize yields heroin, a kilo of which will net $6,000. (Later street value is many, many times more than that and for adulterated samples.) Pressure on governments to deal with their own farmers is the UN's best approach. In Latin America, although eight states have banded together to recruit an elaborately equipped Special Force, which moves with military precision into the haunts of the narcotics producers, there is reluctance to act decisively in some places. Links between government ministers and farmers have been reported. There are cynics at the UN in New York who refer to "narco-democracies". How, they ask, can we tell Colombia and Bolivia that putting an end to narcotics cropping in their fields may lose the government $600 million in revenue? In those countries and elsewhere teams of agricultural advisors from FAO, aided by UNFDAC funds, have put in hand schemes for alternative cropping, and that means providing large-scale resources, from seed-stuffs and tractors to credit and marketing arrangements.

THE UN AND DRUG TRAFFICKING

Illicit trafficking is at the heart of the global drugs problem. At present, sales of cocaine, heroin and cannabis are worth $122,000 million per year in the United States and Europe alone. Britain's share of this is estimated at $12,500 million. The "drug barons" appear to possess a Midas touch. One Neapolitan arrested recently had a supposed annual turnover in the drugs trade of $1,100 million together with an "army" of 4,000 racketeers and assassins. On both sides of the Atlantic a mafia is viciously active. Governments now maintain round-the-clock surveillance and inspection of ports and transit routes.

Guidelines for governments were issued in 1987 when a world conference in Vienna contrived a *Comprehensive multidisciplinary outline of future activities* relevant to drug abuse and handling: 35 objectives were enumerated and specific lines of action proposed. In regard to narcotics trading, stringent penalties would be exacted after detection, confiscation and arrest. Ringleaders tracked down in any country could be extradited. All means of detection and intervention, from electronic sensor equipment, sniffer dogs, armed troop detachments, to tanks and helicopters, are used in what is a dangerous and difficult operation particularly in remote areas. The Caribbean is a notorious transhipment area for large quantities of cannabis and cocaine destined for North American and European city streets. Financial and banking regulations are fragmentary and weak. Transit of drugs among a myriad of islands eludes surveillance patrols. Fifteen African states are not parties to any international drug control treaty and traffickers move easily along open trade routes. Governments in South East Asia are strenuously trying to cope with the problem of backyard laboratories in down-town urban areas and with the buoyant demand for the export of "rogue" narcotics. In Europe major challenges to drug control and law enforcement are presented by the opening of borders between Western and Eastern Europe and by the hostilities raging in former Yugoslavia. The frontline operation is to deal with producers and middlemen in the open, the rearguard task is to investigate the bogus companies that launder the profits from criminal activities.

POSSIBLE TRENDS

Controversy about drug taking was referred to earlier in this chapter. One of the debates is whether "softer" drugs such as cannabis should be legalized. Those in favour argue that eight out of ten drug offences involve cannabis. A free market, in their opinion, would mop up the black-market element by sinking their profits. Making the mere possession of drugs a crime, they say, does not reduce its incidence. Moreover, in many European countries, one in three cases of possession receives just a caution. However, the UN does not agree with the notion of freeing drugs. Vienna holds that any distinction between "soft" and "hard" drugs is not helpful. There would be every likelihood of more people finding it easier to move from one liberated category to another. Legalization would predictably accelerate reliance on commercial narcotic growing. And, of course, there is the evident link between drug use and the human immunodeficiency virus (HIV). One estimate is that 10–20% of AIDS (acquired immunodeficiency syndrome) patients are intravenous users. Many more resort regularly to drugs such as cocaine, marijuana, amphetamines and inhalants. The first two are known to suppress an individual's immune system. UN members are absolutely convinced of one thing – drug abuse is here to stay. Five years ago, Perez de Cuellar, UN Secretary-General, delivered a stern warning: "Drug abuse is a time-bomb ticking away in the heart of our civilization. We must now find measures to deal with it before it explodes and destroys us".

FURTHER READING

See Appendix for UN information services addresses, from which publications on drug control programmes can be obtained.

Chapter Nineteen

THE CONTROL OF DRUGS

Medical and popular use of drugs for pain relief and to aid treatment has escalated this century into a profound problem socially, economically and for the individual. Worldwide spread as result of wider trade, better communications.

Twentieth century attempts to contain opium use and trading generally proscriptive approach in 1909, 1915, 1925, 1931, 1936.

1946 UN improves on ECOSOC's rather loose measures by establishing CND as central policy-making body.

1961 Single Convention on Narcotic Drugs seeks to consolidate legislation, improve detection, control misuse. Governments responsible for street drug abuse.

1970s Tightened control through INCB and discrimination between licit and illicit drugs. New psychotropic menace addressed via 1971 Convention on Psychotropic Substances.

1980s Global strategy formulated by CND.

- INCB from Vienna headquarters has co-ordinated work of drug control units since 1961 – DND, UNFDC, INCB.
- WHO's master plan is global programme, information banking, scheduling, country projects. Specialized Agencies, e.g. FAO, UNICEF, UNESCO collaborate to curb production and trading, disseminate information and advice. IMO, ICAO work on transit problems.
- Crop production of coca, opium lucrative. UN encouragement of crop substitutions.
- Trafficking the cancerous core, with mega-rich profits. 1984 General Assembly condemnation reinforced by 1987 Comprehensive Multidisciplinary Outline of Activities. UN and other authorities use military-style operations, technology. Close liaison with numerous national law-enforcement agencies.

Future trends: states not suffering harmful drug abuse now the exception. International drug cartels still amassing profits, spreading into new markets. Link with AIDS especially worrying. Decriminalization of "soft" drugs a controversial approach in some countries.

The control of AIDS

Many international events with a global significance arouse controversy and even disbelief. The AIDS problem, which is on everybody's lips today, is a pervasive and indisputable threat to mankind. The disease is remarkable in a number of ways. It has spread globally and explosively. The consequences are virulent and almost always fatal; the latent period of physical deterioration can last up to ten years. Science has not yet provided any reliable cure. Essentially, the disease is transmitted sexually, a factor that incites in some victims and amongst the general public psychological responses as diverse as avoidance, concealment and isolation. Above all, AIDS is new, having emerged only in the past two decades.

The sheer scale of the AIDS infection, knowing no human or geographical boundaries, demands a world response. The UN's co-ordinating role in prevention and treatment is now acknowledged and contributed to by 180 nations. This pandemic (worldwide epidemic) is being addressed by a mammoth UN Global Programme against AIDS (GPA) operated through the World Health Authority (WHO), a UN Specialized Agency with 189 member-states. This chapter looks at the spread of the disease and goes on to describe its nature and some possible means of treatment. The economic and social impact are discussed. Finally, the UN's impressive global programme is examined.

It is important to understand that AIDS has a two-stage progression. The first is of infection with the human immunodeficiency virus (HIV). The linked second stage is that of acquired immunodeficiency syndrome (AIDS). Three out of four of those reaching the final stage of AIDS will die because of it.

THE SPREAD OF AIDS

No continent is untouched. It is not easy to get reliable statistics. There is reluctance to declare infection on the part of numerous victims and their associates and families. There is delay in recording and filing data particularly in countries where communication is difficult. Nonetheless, although WHO and other authorities are having to rely on the best estimates they can make from what data is recorded, the general interpretation of those statistics is clear: it is a tremendous world problem. The late-1994 estimate by WHO gives 14 million cases infected with HIV. Of these one million are children under the age of five. Each day brings 5,000 fresh cases. They are being diagnosed at the rate of one million every six months. Something like 50% of these victims are in sub-Saharan Africa, and 25% in Asia. Half of the new adult infections are women. There were more new cases reported in 1993 than in any previous year. Numbers regionally pan out at over 7 million cases in Africa, 2.5 million in the Americas, 1 million in Asia, 500,000 in Europe, 75,000 in North Africa and the Middle East, 30,000 in Australasia, and a swiftly rising 1.5 million in South East Asia and the Pacific. Those figures were for the first stage, HIV infection. The statistics for the terminal phase, AIDS, are even more horrifying. At least 1.75 million cases have been reported by 168 nations. In view of the difficulties in obtaining reliable statistics, this may be a gross underestimate – the real total could be double. Probably eight out of ten of these are in Africa and they are mainly in the 15–24 age group. Globally 500,000 children are thought to have been born with AIDS and most of these die before the age of five.

THE NATURE OF THE DISEASE

The first cases of AIDS were reported from the United States in 1981. Originally the illness was confined chiefly to homosexuals and to drug injectors exchanging needles in some urban areas in industrialized nations. In 15 years it has grown into a pandemic affecting millions of men, women and children in every part of the globe. HIV transmission mainly occurs through unprotected sexual intercourse. It can also be transmitted through infected blood samples or donated organs. A woman may pass on the infection to a foetus or to an infant (perinatal transmission). Parenteral transmission usually involves skin-piercing instruments such as unsterile needles or syringes and only rarely unscreened donated blood. Increasingly, transmission occurs through heterosexual intercourse and perinatally. There is still no evidence that mosquitoes and other biting insects transmit HIV. Nor is the virus spread by ordinary social and casual contact, as it cannot survive easily outside the body. That fact, of course, differentiates this pandemic from various types of plague.

Two characteristics of AIDS are virulence and latency. Infection gradually lowers the resistance of the body so that the patient suffers a series of what are termed "opportunistic infections" such as pneumonia, tuberculosis, severe influenza, or the infection of internal organs. Any of these may bring death within six months in developing countries; elsewhere, where the quality of healthcare is superior, drugs may prolong life by anything up to ten years. During the 1990s HIV-related diseases will be among the chief causes of death in young adults under the age of 40, with, as it were, a latent period during which an infected person will incur appreciable wasting and suffering. In a high-fertility continent such as Africa, where the proportion of young to old is different from that of the industrialized nations, it is estimated that during the present decade some ten million children will be orphaned through the death of one or both parents because of AIDS.

POSSIBLE MEANS OF TREATMENT

Treatment of these infections is at present very uncertain. There is no let-up in the research to find effective antiviral drugs that could be administered as a "cocktail" combining several constituents. A cheaper alternative would be a vaccine. Currently some 15 varieties of vaccine are at the laboratory stage, being developed in the three categories of: (a) preventive, to protect uninfected persons against HIV; (b) therapeutic, to stop or delay the progression of HIV to AIDS; and (c) perinatal, to prevent HIV transmission from pregnant women. However, would such a vaccine be affordable by poorer nations? Would it be possible to carry out trials of the vaccines in the field without encountering resistance from those who fear they are just being used as guinea-pigs? In any case, it seems most unlikely that vaccination can put brakes on the onrush of these infections before the Year 2000.

It is generally agreed that the most effective approach is education about how to prevent transmission through changes in personal behaviour. Two of the UN's Specialized Agencies, WHO and ILO, have worked hard to secure agreements about how those diagnosed as HIV- or AIDS-positive should be regarded in the workplace. Unlike cholera or typhoid victims, HIV carriers do not constitute a threat to others purely by their presence. A worker with HIV who is healthy should be treated without discrimination, either by his colleagues or in the terms of his employment. Abandonment because of a fear of contagion is not to be tolerated – human rights are violated this way and it is counter-productive. Stigmatizing victims may push the problem underground, making prevention and diagnosis difficult, and leading victims and high-risk individuals to behave evasively. WHO continually points out that treatment of HIV and AIDS needs more than medical attention; careful monitoring over the incubation period must be supplemented by accessible, continuous and expensive care. The patient's environment needs to be supportive.

ECONOMIC AND SOCIAL IMPACT

The economic and social impact of HIV and AIDS represents a tremendous challenge in those parts of the world where the infrastructure of healthcare is inadequate and funds are hard to raise. Three out of four hospital beds may have an AIDS-related patient. Families lose breadwinners, children are bereft of parents, the elderly are left to one side without active carers. The infection is also selective, in crippling and killing men and women in what are normally their most productive years. Many sufferers will belong to social, economic and political elites. The loss of their talents and enterprise denudes the workforce severely. Knowledge of their condition places restraints on the patience and tolerance of families, neighbours and colleagues at work.

The pandemic very clearly is not solely a health problem; it is a cancerous threat to socioeconomic development. Nowhere is this more true than in developing countries that have striven to improve the survival and living conditions of infants and young people and are now faced with a calamity that is likely to offset the gains they have made over 30 or so years. The UN, from the onset of the AIDS problem, has been grimly aware of the double burden that women carry. Living not only under their own death sentence they also have to endure a damaged nurturing and child-bearing role. Condemned to a largely subordinate position in traditional societies, their vulnerability may be increased because they lack knowledge of and access to protected sex methods. Women are the main providers of care for families and often for sick or elderly neighbours. They may be ostracized by others, reduced also to widowhood and childlessness. Traditionally in Africa, for instance, a child has belonged to a clan and if parents died would be looked after by next of kin. AIDS and tribal conflicts are currently orphaning African children by the thousand. Villages that offered care to children and the elderly now face the prospect of progressive decimation.

THE UN LAUNCHES A GLOBAL PROGRAMME

Early in 1985 WHO embarked on what was eventually to be known as the Global Programme on AIDS (GPA). The pandemic was escalating at a tenfold rate in all parts of the world. To prevent and control it would need a mammoth plan of action and a co-ordinated network involving all nations. At national level there would have to be close collaboration between government departments and voluntary, charitable and religious organizations. A dramatic need of interdependence would lace all resources together in an agreed strategy with short- and long-term objectives. The fundamentals of the strategy are still valid today but have been appraised in the light of epidemiological developments. The GPA operates a broad front of action. Its priorities, as listed in the

1992 version of the programme, are:

- an increased emphasis on the adequate and equitable provision of healthcare, as the huge numbers of people already infected with the human immunodeficiency virus (HIV) progress from asymptomatic infection to AIDS;
- expanded and more effective treatment for other sexually transmitted diseases which are now known to increase the risk of HIV transmission;
- a reduction of the special vulnerability to HIV infection of women and their offspring through an improvement of women's health, education, legal status and economic prospects;
- the creation of a more supportive social environment for AIDS prevention through the removal of legal and other barriers to frank messages about sexual transmission and to people's ability to act on such information;
- immediate planning in anticipation of the socioeconomic impact of the pandemic;
- a greater focus on communicating effectively the compelling public health rationale for overcoming stigmatization and discrimination.
- The three main objectives of the strategy remain:
  to prevent infection with HIV
  to reduce the personal and social impact of HIV infection
  to mobilize and unify national and international efforts against AIDS.

The motive force in the UN's GPA can be put directly: no country can be safe from AIDS until *every* country is. Global AIDS control, according to the programme, has gone through four phases: silence, discovery, mobilization and consolidation. In the first place, some time in the mid 1970s, HIV spread globally without its significance being remarked. Discovery through diagnosis in 1981 alerted scientists into identifying the virus and determining the means of its transmission. The spread and malignancy of the disease alarmed the medical and scientific world and caused much speculative fear among the public. Several countries have passed laws that make wilful transmission of HIV a criminal offence. Mobilization was set afoot by WHO after a first international conference in 1985. Concerted action was launched with a global strategy.

A new phase, that of consolidation, came about in 1992 working along lines as broad as possible, medically in the treatment area, and socially, especially in developing countries, to improve healthcare and seek the understanding and co-operation of persons in high-risk categories. This phase is "multisectoral", in the words of WHO, including "the health sector, priority product sectors dependent on human resources (industry, agriculture, mining, tourism), other social sectors (planning, finance, education, information, labour, justice, social services), parliaments, the private sector, charitable, religious and other voluntary organizations, and the media".[1] This wide response has to be co-ordinated urgently and on an enormous scale. Who better than the UN to do that?

In every country poverty, low social status and poor education erode the power and freedom of individuals in the run-down zones of big cities. Health and social services are encouraged in the GPA to set up task-forces to undertake urgent rehabilitation. Counselling, contraception and work with drug addicts make for the preventive and supportive social environment that WHO advises. Of very great importance is the prevention of transmission to women of reproductive age. Equally important for the success of GPA is work with young people. One in five AIDS sufferers are in their twenties. Bearing latency in mind, this must point to most becoming infected with HIV as adolescents. Some fruitful work is being done by WHO in cities where fellow sufferers, called "peer educators", may be induced to counsel others in the same position. All too often, however, ignorance and complacency, which in the first place fed the pandemic, put obstacles in the way of prevention and treatment. Obviously the GPA will only succeed if these obstacles are overcome with the need to break through barriers in discussing matters which are considered private, even taboo, in many traditional societies. WHO and UNESCO are working in tandem in places as diverse as Africa, Latin America and Papua devising informational packages that are judged appropriate to the culture.

THE UN AND AIDS: THE THAILAND PROJECT

An example of WHO's wide and culturally appropriate method of addressing the AIDS problem is the campaign being mounted in Thailand. This country has a high incidence of sexually transmitted disease (STD) and HIV notifications have risen from 50,000 cases to 1.5 million in four years. It is not easy to couch the programme appeal in plain terms as there is generally fairly strong resistance to discussing sexually related matters. WHO has secured a strong Thai Government lead to take forward a medium-term plan during 1992–5. Its initial budget of $7 million includes $4.5 million from the GPA reserves and private sources. Management is exercised by 32 GPA staff together with 30 foreign consultants. Thai nationals have been sent abroad on courses for nine months. A task-force of health workers, teachers, members of NGOs, army officers and religious leaders follows the line of carefully encouraging knowledge, attitudes, beliefs and practice. There is a good supply of specially designed health education packs supplemented by the output of television, radio and press. WHO brings in technical support to hospitals and travelling clinics. This source of help and some intensive advocacy and counselling has made fair impact on the extent of HIV. There is much more to do to improve the link between dealing with HIV and the follow-on of AIDS. Thailand aptly illustrates the WHO multisectoral approach. There the Justice Division reviews the legislation on AIDS that has to do with the rights of patients and of family survivors; the Ministry of Labour and Youth brings AIDS education to the workplace and to school leavers; the Ministry of Defence looks after army personnel and their dependants; and the Ministry of the Interior addresses the problem in prisons and among the police. Regionally, and in conjunction with ASEAN, there are careful controls on immigration and emigration.

THE UN AND THE FUTURE OF AIDS

What future developments are likely in the UN work on AIDS? First, there is the hypothetical spread of the problem by, say, the Year 2000. The UN at the start of the GPA in the mid 1980s was using a method known as a "Delphi projection" to forecast future trends. Original figures pointed to a likely total of HIV infections by the Year 2000 of more than 20 million men, women and children. Eventually, this was thought to be a conservative estimate given the substantial increases in Africa and South and South East Asia. That total might

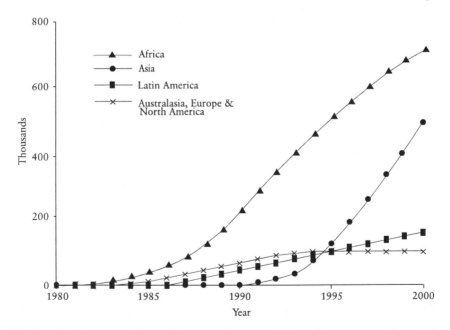

Estimated and projected annual AIDS incidences (number of new cases each year) by "macro" region, 1980–2000. (Source: The HIV/AIDS pandemic: 1993 overview, World Health Organization, 1993.)

well be reached in 1995. The current projection given by WHO planners is between 30 million and 40 million cases of HIV in men, women and children by the start of the next century. Nine out of ten would certainly originate in sub-Saharan Africa. With this total the number of AIDS cases could then reach ten million with again 90% in developing countries. In those countries this would orphan ten million children under the age of ten.

Secondly, there are questions about future costs. The World Bank has already lent the global efforts $500 million. In summer 1994, through an alliance of WHO and the World Bank, the UN renewed an appeal to the 189 members of WHO for a realistic financial response to the consolidation phase of the global programme. Effective control of HIV and AIDS would mean a twenty-fold increase in spending. Would all nations be willing to dig into their pockets to the tune of $2,500 million when there were so many other demands on their resources? There is as yet no sign that another problem will easily be solved, that of asymmetrical spending where only 2% of "aid for AIDS" is spent on Africa where 50% of the patients are to be treated. Are some nations denying the shape and size of AIDS-related problems?

Thirdly, and more hopefully, the UN has managed to co-ordinate an impressive and very costly network of research. A dozen or so UN Specialized Agencies meet regularly as a management committee for the GPA. Experts as varied as epidemiologists, pharmacists, biologists, statisticians, psychologists are working out schemes for laboratory research and field surveys and trials. Three lines of approach are evident. Primarily, there is a linking of short-term preventive measures (for AIDS-related and other associated maladies). Health professions in 180 nations have been brought into this field of action, and wealthier nations are being persuaded that they cannot afford *not* to help with the huge costs of prevention. In the longer term, WHO's policy is to encourage the governments of newer nations to develop their own research sources rather than to rely on handouts from distant sources. Such nations will have to find ways of coping with manpower shortages, lack of funds and poor transport. At the very least, thousands of refrigerators would be needed in which to store the required drugs and vaccines. WHO also believes that families and communities in developing countries need ideally to be educated and empowered to act methodically without waiting to be led by the hand by outside intervention. Finally, the message from Geneva and from New York is that unity-in-action is the overriding requirement.

> For the sake of our common survival we must act with courage and urgency. With every passing day, HIV claims thousands of lives. The only possible answer to the new AIDS challenge lies in global solidarity.[2]

The maxim of the UN's global programme to deal with HIV and AIDS is "AIDS – sharing the challenge".

NOTES

1. World Health Organization (1991) *Global Programme on* AIDS *1991 Progress Report*, (Geneva: WHO), with 1992 update on global AIDS strategy, pp. 97–9.
2. World Health Organization (1992) *Global Programme on* AIDS. *Global strategy for the prevention and control of* AIDS, 1992 update (Geneva: WHO), p. 19.

FURTHER READING

See Appendix for UN information services addresses, from which publications on the UN global programme can be obtained.

Chapter Twenty

THE CONTROL OF AIDS

All continents face a pandemic with HIV developing into AIDS. Estimated 10–20 million cases especially in developing countries. Transmitted mainly through unprotected sex. Main characteristics: immune system progressively destroyed; virulence leading to death; latency to AIDS progression may last up to ten years. Grievous socioeconomic impact.

1970s   Silent spread globally, pandemic-in-being unnoticed.

1981   Discovery of AIDS. Alarmed by nature and spread science identifies virus, determines infection mode, suggests control methods.

1985   WHO launches Global Programme on AIDS (GPA), with a global strategy for the prevention and control of AIDS.

1992   WHO, on reappraisal, initiates further strategy with comprehensive drive for prevention, caring programmes, concentration on highly vulnerable women and children, creation of supportive and non-isolating environments.

1995   Ongoing research into preventive and therapeutic vaccines. GPA co ordinating short term and long term monitored schemes. Some 250 projects costing $200 million a year. Intensive publicity, education, training programmes worldwide. World AIDS Day is 1 December. Possible escalation of HIV to 30 million and AIDS 10 million by Year 2000 with 90% in developing nations has 180 nations conferring. Reliable vaccine and mixed "cocktail" of drugs still awaited.

CHAPTER TWENTY-ONE

Africa's food crisis

In today's world, Africa presents two images, highly visible and much reported. One is of a forest of hands reaching for food from the back of a lorry, labelled with the letters "UN", or of figures scrambling around grain sacks pitched out of low-flying aircraft. Food enables life, sustains hope. The other is of tribal feuding (or its sad consequences), of snaking lines of refugees, or of the violence in brandished rifles and Armoured Personnel Carriers snorting through the dust. Hunger is the common factor. An imperative for nations uniting in some sort of relief action has been the feeding of Africa, and in larger terms, the saving of Africa. Essentially, however, the question is: what does Africa need apart from food?

This chapter discusses the action of the UN to address the food problem in Africa, first by examining some of the causes of recurrent crises. There follows an account of the schemes, launched optimistically by the FAO, for improvement of agriculture, which later were to assume the shape of large programmes for disaster relief of famine victims. The process of rural development and the definition and elaboration of food strategies illustrate how today the UN aims at self-help for developing nations. Finally, some contemporary problems raised by UN work to feed Africa are reviewed.

CAUSES OF CRISIS

Causative factors are broadly physical, economic and sociopolitical. From west to east in Africa there is an area of land, three-quarters the size of the US, which has seen little rain over two years. Twenty-four states, 2.5 million square miles in all, have had no water for the crops. Incomes have plummeted, food prices have risen steeply in the market, and families are forced to join the helpless and hopeless and trek elsewhere in order to survive. The only certainty has been an outbreak of typhoid. What has remained green has generally been savaged by locusts foraging in clouds two miles long. Apart from the physical impact of drought on people normally very much dependent on the land, the interlinked economic and social factors have had a devastating effect. Demand hugely outstrips supply. Africa's population has doubled since 1968 and by the end of this century may have doubled again to reach 1,000 million. WHO has estimated that 40 million of these people are threatened by dire starvation. Those that do find food are hobbled by malnutrition, by Vitamin A and iodine deficiencies, by lack of protein and calories, and thus they are limited as an economic workforce.

Africa's desperation is not so much the aridity that defeats its farmers as the grinding poverty and the lack of infrastructure; what food is provided rarely reaches those without cash or who live in scattered, remote villages. They do not get their fair share in places like Burkino Faso, the Central African Republic, Rwanda, where the incomes of nine out of ten will never keep up with inflation. In Africa as a whole, *per capita* income is a derisory 6% of what it is in Europe. Half of these people are estimated to be living in areas with low agricultural potential subject to environmental deterioration. They can have little resilience when times are bad.

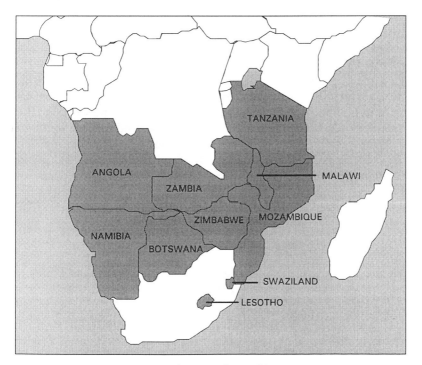

Drought in southern Africa.

Indebtedness cripples most developing countries. Each year the nations of Africa are faced with a demand for repayment of interest on capital loans of some $30,000 million. In practice only one-tenth of this will be repaid leaving the rest to accrue in following years. Zimbabwe, for instance, sold off large maize reserves in 1992 to meet interest payments. Then the country was hit by drought, the worst for a century, and 60% of the grain crop failed. Even if rains materialized in the short term there would be no harvest for a further nine months. Traditionally a maize exporter, Zimbabwe has now had to import $400,000 million worth of foodstuffs to keep the country together. There is no cushion in bankruptcy law for the national debtor as there is for the individual who may be saved from the indebtedness that leads to starvation. If an African country manages to meet repayments and interest charges each year this will certainly gobble up four out of every five dollars earned from exports.

Fluctuations in raw material prices hit the economic prospects of developing countries. Variations in demand, the introduction and use of alternative materials and erratic financial conditions, are all compounded by protectionism in importing countries and the inability of such devices as the General Agreement on Tariffs and Trade (GATT) to bring about stabilization of prices and terms of trade. Retrospectively, the 1960s and 1970s were a time of significant economic progress with Africa as a net food exporter. The 1980s ushered in what has been termed a "lost decade". Commodity prices slumped. Interest rates steepened. Africa's share in global trade greatly declined: debt rose to unprecedented levels. In recent years, 40% of food has had to be imported for a population whose increasing numbers and lengthened life-expectancy make for many more mouths to feed each year.

Mercy feeding in Africa is often pictured as a famished crowd held at arm's length. Helmeted Blue Berets and tanks ring round the food containers, suggesting disaster and endemic strife. Animosities inflame the scene in Liberia, Ethiopia, Rwanda, Sudan, Angola. Until apartheid was dispelled, South Africa harassed the frontline states such as Botswana, Tanzania, Zambia and Zimbabwe with blockade, destruction of food crops and hard political pressure. Mozambique has additional difficulties after 30 years without peace and a third of its people displaced from their homes. The UN's third largest peacekeeping force struggles to keep rival factions from decimating their opponents and their crops. Old tribal animosities surface to banish a tradition of providing a meal and a roof for those needing asylum. In a very grim sense the industrialized nations perceive Africa as a lost continent. The clear despair and dereliction in the media galvanize the public elsewhere into reaching into their pockets, but does nothing to educate them into understanding the economic, social and political factors that have created such an imbalance in global fortunes. It is to the credit of the UN response that there has been a very thorough scrutiny of cause and effect. Yet that response, while not always consistent in its direction, has been dogged by underfunding. The mounting frustration of UN Secretary-Generals is understandable. Boutros Boutros-Ghali in the last two years has been forthright in his observations about Africa's need. Is Africa a special case where economic laws do not apply? Surely not. Are Africans too feckless and too disunited even to feed themselves and revitalize their way of living? That cannot be. These stern remarks are directed at what is currently being termed "the vicious cycle of P–P–E" (population, poverty, environment), which spirals relentlessly ever downward. What *has* the UN done in its scheme to feed the bodies and the hopes of Africans? What must be done in the future?

THE UN BECOMES INVOLVED

The Food and Agriculture Organization (FAO) was founded in 1945 on 16 October, which is now World Food Day. In those heady days of great optimism the aims of this Specialized Agency were twofold: improving agriculture and nutrition in the developing regions of the world, and ultimately promoting self-sufficiency. Better yields of crops and livestock might be attained by applying new technical methods and following the demonstrations and experimental projects of experts. Farm, forest and fishery would profit from more skilled management, the rational use of fertilizers and pesticides, and the control of plant and animal disease. Investment by the state and by the community would bring about self-reliance and in due course a measure of economic independence. Village co-operatives in Africa, particularly, would use an "each one teach one" system to train in resource conservation, production, marketing and distribution. Progress was soon evident. Back in the industrial countries FAO was actively stimulating interest and reciprocal relationships between nations with its World Food Congresses, its liaison with NGOs and its Freedom from Hunger Campaign.

If, in those early days, a rather simple view of "rational participation" had been indispensable to activity it was soon obvious in following decades that in fact progress was not all that even or certain. Africa was not building up the reserves that ultimately would back up independent and self-sustaining provision for meeting the basic demands of an expanding population. In 1962 a reappraisal of FAO programming was given the name of the World Food Programme (WFP). It identified four areas to be given priority. Projects in the field should tie together, as far as possible, social and economic development. Food supplies should not go direct to governments but to specific projects. Work done in the field should, again so far as possible, be administered by those receiving aid. Explicitly, the poor would be helping themselves.

To support these four desirable ways to help communities, the WFP would have a Food Aid Convention that would set out the principles underlying an improved FAO programme, and there would be an International Food Emergency Fund to underpin any relief in what was seen as an emergency. Early optimism was acquiring a more realistic streak. An example of the WFP's reappraised approach is that of Malawi in the late 1960s. Assured food supplies were to be "gift-wrapped" in social and economic terms. No expensive convoy or inaccurate air drop could supply enough food of the right quality to remote villagers. The people were debilitated by malnutrition and malaria; there were 23,000 to every one doctor. Teams from FAO and from WHO went in to help men dig wells, resurface roads, carve out reasonable maize plots from scrubland. They would receive their food if they reported for work and if they turned up to literacy classes. A travelling health unit inoculated children, fed them with booster vitamins and instructed mothers in family planning. The village headman was enrolled as counsellor and as treasurer of a community chest.

REAPPRAISAL AND NEW APPROACHES

Within ten years FAO was forced to look again at the principles and practice of feeding Africa. So great was the need of basic sustenance, and so difficult were the physical problems that make for failed harvest and maldistribution of what was available, that the term "disaster" was now used. In 1972 the UN decided to concentrate its urgent operations in a specially formed UN Disaster Relief Organization (UNDRO). The mission would proceed by despatching observers to a disaster area to calculate what was needed, then muster appropriate resources, deploy them, and follow up the food with programmes for social rehabilitation. Financial pledges were required from UN members. It was not long before there was an obvious shortfall in the number and amount of pledges coming in to New York. For the first time UN officials were heard to speculate about UN members suffering from "donor fatigue". Were there so many calls on the conscience of the industrialized nations that they were losing interest? How could African nations prepare for the future without always having their backs to the wall?

Two years later, in 1974, the General Assembly convened a World Food Conference held in Rome. One result of this was to be a World Food Council, composed of food ministers from 36 UN member-states, which would review problems and co-ordinate policies with the WFP and the FAO. A World Food Bank would assemble buffer stocks of food and fertilizers. Representatives from suffering African countries did not see this proposal as either sufficiently imaginative or immediate. They called for an International Undertaking on Food Security. (This seemed to be taking up the notion, aired, for instance, in the 1984 Palme Report and the 1987 Brundtland Report, that "security" had to do with assurance of basic resources. See Chapter 18.) A system of nationally held reserved food stocks must be co-ordinated internationally and bolstered internationally with commitments to provide finance for food purchase and distribution.

To begin with, a guarantee to fund at least 10 million tonnes of grain for three years would be a reasonable gesture by the UN. There was all-round agreement in Rome that hunger had less to do with scarcity of food than with poverty and the consequent lack of access to sufficient resources. Innovative development projects would do much to attack poverty in particular localities, and to this end the Rome Conference endowed an International Fund for Agricultural Development (IFAD) with $1,000 million. In alliance with the World Bank there would be cash advances on concessional terms to help the poorest rural communities of small farmers, livestock herders, fishermen, and women's groups, to advance their husbandry through self-help schemes. Eventually, IFAD proved an attractive proposition to Africans in 40 countries, although they were wary of the World Bank's stated expectation that "the recipient has financial and political stability and a general commitment to all-round development". Inevitably, there were a number of more radical African governments who suspected the political objectivity of both the World Bank (with so many governing members from capitalist nations) and of the African Development Bank, which never found it easy to dispel ideological differences. (These were, after all, the days of hard East and West polarized positions.)

The basis on which international action could be calculated and planned was a monitoring system set up by the UN in 1975. The Global International Emergency Warning System (GIEWS) was supported by member-states. Data from press, radio and TV, meteorological stations, and satellites, was fed into computers to assess in advance the effects on food supply of adverse weather, changes in planted acreage, price movements, market behaviour, global supply and demand for basic foods, product shortfalls and surpluses. Details of animal and plant diseases, soil conditions, storage and transport data were entered together with satellite monitoring of vegetation patterns. Predictive calculation furnished a series of "risk maps". All this was fine for the participation of industrial countries, but there was an obvious problem for some developing countries, with primitive technology, to access the data quickly and reliably.

THE UN'S FOOD STRATEGIES

The feeding of Africa (and of many other developing countries) took major steps forward in 1979 and 1980. The General Assembly introduced the concept of "food strategies" designed to integrate policies for food production, its distribution and its consumption. In the following year, and not a minute too soon in the eyes of the Third World, a Food Aid Convention, aimed especially at Africa, underwrote the link between food strategies and development strategies. The first-named were to have a bedrock of 7.6 million tonnes of food aid as the absolute minimum level for countries with specific "food deficits". This would operate regardless of the level of world market prices. To enable nations to import food in times of drought or other natural disasters credits would be provided. This facility was vital for any African country having to import five times as much food as before at twice the price and in a state of near-bankruptcy.

Together with the FAO the Convention provided for nations' investment in improved storage and distribution networks and for the strategic prepositioning of essential foodstuffs in vulnerable regions. As for development strategies, it was essential that local communities were directly involved in the improvement of habitats. Another step forward in what was termed "opening doors to growth" was a major innovation in 1986. Again, the UN determined to set in tandem food and development strategies. The UN Programme for African Economic Recovery and Development (UNPAAERD) focused for the first time on getting African nations to prepare or update plans for economic development and policy reform. To ensure a dependable food supply would cost an estimated $120,000 million. Couldn't Africa find two-thirds of this?

Mention was made earlier of the 1980s becoming a "lost decade" as economic vitality worsened. Hard times meant resort to hard enquiry. There was another look at food aid. Does a robust response by the donor nations destroy any incentive in recipients to develop further their own agriculture when the prices for their own raw material commodities are so undependable? Could it be that ready arrivals of foreign foodstuffs dislocate cultural food habits? Are such donations a convenient way of dumping the unwanted food surpluses of Europe? Apart from the obvious necessity of emergency famine relief, doesn't the steady import of foodstuffs tend to lower prices of home-produced commodities and perhaps lead to farm workers deserting their plots for shanties in town? At least one African commentator at the time spoke of food aid shipments as alienating the peasant, placing him in an awkward situation of enforced inferiority. At conferences and seminars and at meetings in the field there was ready acknowledgement that injection of food aid is only a short-term palliative. Better than this, as a major programme to ensure dependable feeding, is a rural development programme to lace together demonstrated small-scale husbandry, herd management (where appropriate) and fishery practice, with primary healthcare, especially for mothers and children, as well as literacy and technical training schemes. The IFAD seemed to be a promising move forward if only it could attract reliable funds from a variety of national, public and private sources. Above all, it was important to dissuade African governments and their farmers from going headlong to produce cash-crops rather than food-crops. Well might the FAO declare in 1987, in a moment of candour, that almost any innovation in development ran the risk of making the rich richer and the poor poorer.

SECURITY AND SUSTAINABILITY

The 1987 Brundtland Commission Report struck a resonance worldwide (see Chapter 18). This report devoted an entire chapter to "Food security". In regard to food production, the phenomenal rise in productivity of Europe and North America had seen the "resource-poor" and technologically poor regions like Africa lag far behind the leaders. The Commission considered that richer states were subverting the poor. Subsidies "featherbedded" food exporters and their short-sighted policies, sometimes in collusion with selfish importers, knocked away security from subsistence smallholders. Women in Africa are responsible for between 60 and 90% of the food production, processing and marketing.[1] The challenge for Africa, it was stated, must be to conserve and enhance the resource base for food production and where it had been diminished or destroyed, to restore it. A detailed plan of action was outlined. It would be in the mutual self-interest of nations to address the interaction between resource depletion and rising, destabilizing poverty.

The waning years of the 1980s saw the UN taking bold decisions about the problems of Africa. The keynote in the new approach was to be sustainable development, which saw development as only admissible and practicable if it went ahead without jeopardizing the needs of future generations (see Chaper 18). The FAO Director-General in 1989 took up the principles of sustainability, namely, that accountability must be environmental as well as economic, that management practices have to be redirected appropriately, and that to provide incentives is more important than to levy penalties. Accordingly, the FAO should put projects into action that were environmentally non-degrading, that were technically suitable, economically viable, and socially acceptable.

In the light of the stated requirements of the FAO, it is interesting to glance briefly at the range of UN programmes initiated in the present decade to revitalize developing economies. More than 1,500 projects are attempting to rehabilitate millions of people in 113 countries. One hundred donor states subscribe to the cost. Food aid, specifically, is of three types.

(a) *Emergency food aid*, 20% of the total, is the one most noticed in press headlines. Whether derived from FAO buffer stocks or donated, say, by the EU, it is injected to relieve a crisis or to match up to recurrent shortfall. Clearly, this form of aid is not a strategy in the usual sense. Its very *ad hoc* nature may, in fact, retard urgent structural improvements in a recipient's economy.

(b) *Project food aid*, 30% of the total, aims to create heightened demand for commodities by supporting and furthering development programmes or nutrition schemes. Generally, it is easier to control organization and distribution at the point of entry rather than at the distant receiving ends.

(c) *Programme food aid*, 50% of the total, is more indirect. Essentially, through import financing and intergovernmental transactions, the objective is to influence ways in which off-loaded food is sold and the proceeds then placed in safeguarded accounts.

There is a long tally of nations in which the last approach has been implemented: Ethiopia, Algeria, Mauritania, Guinea, Côte d'Ivoire, Liberia and Mozambique. Thousands of tonnes of food and many millions of dollars have been disbursed in this way. One look at the names listed perhaps strengthens conjecture about the extent of political as well as economic influence. A more concrete anxiety is the possibility that food released into the market by an external agency is likely to lower farm prices and discourage food cropping.

General Assembly debates of recent years have naturally expressed concern at the frequency with which the African continent encounters crisis. Unlike most of Asia, Africa is fractured by political turbulence. Nevertheless, *A programme of action for Africa 1986–90* was judged to have made some progress with perhaps 40 or so African states putting political and economic reform into practice. United Nations' discussions by way of appraisal produced in 1991 *A new agenda of development of Africa in the 1990s*. This was said to be "the product of consensus between Africa and the donor community with a mutual commitment on a number of priorities". The emphasis would no longer be on big government and central planning, at least not to the same extent as previously. Expert panels in New York or Nairobi could examine key issues but the essence now was to localize the take-up of recommendations. It is particularly significant that a World Food Conference convened by the UN in October 1993 met not in Africa but in Japan. One thousand representatives of 63 nations, of Specialized Agencies, of NGOs, met together as a think-tank in Tokyo to pool Asian and African experience and to shape a progressive multifaceted response to "eco-economic wastage".

STRUCTURAL ADJUSTMENT PROGRAMMES

A point frequently voiced in Tokyo and subsequently by the FAO Committee on World Food Security was that the 30 countries in sub-Saharan Africa most in need of help faced a challenge that they themselves had to meet head on. Expert opinion went straight to the point. Half of the developing countries under survey could produce in total twice as much of the main food crops as they needed. If this, though, was the challenge, how might it best be met? It is worth taking a look at a factor that has caused controversy if not recrimination at many conferences. For some years the World Bank has tried to address the problem of developing countries having a skewed balance of trade where unfavourable world markets penalize their vulnerable exports and tot up indebtedness.

Using the index of GNP as a measure of economic growth, a calculation by the World Bank (and similarly by UN Specialized Agencies) is that Africa as a whole needs an increased growth rate of 4–5% to avert continuous hunger alone. There are nations in Africa, such as Kenya, Nigeria and Botswana, that rate 3%. Much of sub-Saharan Africa does not approach 1% of annual growth. Insensitively, so many African ministers declare, the World Bank has required "structural adjustment programmes" to be contrived by lagging African states where imports are to be held down, and budget deficits contained through financial controls and retrenchment. This often leads to cuts in the social sector. Roads and bridges built with expensive foreign currency can no longer be maintained. Transport is denied diesel oil and spare parts. Schools cannot afford books. Jobs are lost among the poor who then suffer poorer diets and less substantial housing. At all costs the export of cash-crops is to be increased. "Adjustment programmes", it was objected at Tokyo, "are rending the fabric of our African society". This was not the way to encourage self-sufficiency, self-reliance, or indeed, any form of sustainable and equable development. How far was it possible, asked a delegate from UNICEF, to modify the approach of adjustment so that it had "a human face"?

REMAINING QUESTIONS

A last look at the feeding of Africa brings us back to that demanding question: what does Africa need apart from food? The UN has tried a number of approaches, as we have seen, from emergency injections of relief to the less dramatic step-by-step encouragement of self-help development schemes. Certainly there has been duplication of effort by UN Specialized Agencies (sometimes unhappily but pointedly described as "feudal baronies"). Not surprisingly, the first approach by FAO staff in the high-principled and optimistic years of peace just after 1945 was to bring expert and external advice and demonstration to bear on peoples newly liberated from the shackles of colonial power and trade. It was never going to be easy to follow up a part-prescriptive manner with a much more open-ended one when the challenge was passed quite bluntly into African hands.

Down the years there have been countless suggestions about how best to adopt a multisectoral approach to Africa's basic problem where one of the vital sectors is that of African participation. It is clear that much more needs to be done by way of land reform in countries where 15% are landless and 30% virtually so. Land reform cannot be imposed: government and local communities must share a common democratic will. It is not a question of giving everybody a plot, rather, a fairer reordering is needed for more equal responsibility and tangible benefits. Many nations in Africa are slow to move in this direction. Another sensitive issue, barely explored, is that of the rigid and one-sided relationships between multinational corporations (MNCs) of industrialized states and their dependent developing states. What has been done so far has been described as "rearranging the furniture inside the debtors' prison". The belief of the UN Conference on Trade and Development (UNCTAD), a permanent organization in Geneva since 1964, is that effective co-operation is possible with MNCs if equal conditions for all parties are secured, through strict regard for the sovereignty of the host country, and through the sharing of managerial and technological knowledge and skills. If developing countries increase their bargaining power, possibly through regional associations, and if they keep in mind the criteria of sustainable exploitation of natural resources and of balanced social and economic development, the traditional cycle of dominance–dependence could be broken.

If Africa can really produce a good deal of its own food, as seems likely, there is a credible case for sustainability, freedom from constraining financial obligations (such as debt repayment), and reconstructed patterns of production–distribution–consumption. Not long ago, Boutros Boutros-Ghali put stern words to a group of experts in Rome. For 30 years aid and assistance had been poured into Africa with seemingly little effect. Donors had lost optimism because many of the recipients became trapped in "a damaging cycle of dependence". The whole notion of development was wasteful, paternalistic, and lacking in dynamism. More visible results must be achieved rapidly. He concluded: "It is our approach that has failed. Africa has not". Are the member-states of the UN still failing Africa? What *does* Africa need – more than food?

NOTE

1. The Brundtland Commission Report quotes an opinion from a participant in a public hearing in Nairobi, Kenya in 1986 that "No on can really address the food crisis in Africa or many of the other crises that seem to exist here without addressing the question of women, and really seeing that women are participants in decision-making processes at the very basic all the way through to the highest level" (*Our common future* (Brundtland Report), p.124).

FURTHER READING

Brown, M. B. & P. Tiffen. *Short changed: Africa in world trade*. London: Pluto, 1992.
Brundtland Commission (World Commission on Environment and Development). *Our common future*. Oxford: Oxford University Press, 1987.
Green, R. H. Calamities and catastrophes: extending the UN response. *Third World Quarterly* 14(1), pp. 51–6, 1993.
Sottas, E. *The least developed countries UNCTAD*. Geneva: United Nations, 1985.
United Nations. *The state of world rural poverty*. London: Intermediate Technology

Publications (for IFAD), 1992.

United Nations. *Africa Recovery* (bimonthly periodical); *Development Forum* (monthly periodical); *World Development.* New York: UN Department of Public Information (monthly periodical).

Chapter Twenty-one

AFRICA'S FOOD CRISIS

1945   FAO aims improve food production, handling, distribution, nutrition, also organize world publicity campaigns.

1962   WFP and FAO: emergency food relief via International Food Emergency Fund, beginning of food-development linkage. Food Aid Convention. Liaison with World Bank.

1964   UNCTAD: concern with Africa's problems, especially development.

1964   UNDP: funds, programmes with specific object; voluntary contribution of 25% to Africa.

1971   Food Security Assistance Scheme: prepositioned food stocking.

1972   UNDRO: disaster relief missions, reporting, planning.

1974   World Food Conference, Rome. IFAD.

1975   GIEWS to monitor supply, demand, shortages, patterns for risk maps.

1979   General Assembly: promotes concept of food strategies.

1980   Food Aid Convention links relief, food, with development strategies.
International Emergency Food Reserve administered by WFP. Credit schemes, buffer stocks, distribution schemes. (Severe drought year.)

1981   Office of Emergency Operations Africa (OEOA) mobilizes emergency aid.

1986   UNPAAERD encourages African governments' policy reforms; extra funds.

1986   Intergovernment Authority on Drought and Development.
General Assembly: Programme of Action for Africa 1986–90.

1989   Economic Commission for Africa: search for "adjustment with human face" alternatives for socio-economic recovery.

1991   General Assembly: New Agenda of Development of Africa in 1990s (severe drought years.)

1992–3   UN expert panels advise Secretary-General; site visits, seminars, consultations in Europe, New York, Africa.

1993   Structural Adjustment Programme by World Bank to improve developing nations' trade balances, promote economic viability; "austerity regimes".

1992   International Conference on Nutrition, Rome.

1993   UN World Food Conference, Tokyo, October: specific reference Africa.

1994   FAO Committee on World Food Security: report on African food production capabilities.

Appendix

WHERE TO FIND OUT MORE ABOUT THE UN

Books

Barrs, D. (ed.), *The United Nations kit* (Cambridge: Pearson Publishing, 1992).

Boutros-Ghali, B., *An agenda for peace* (New York: UN, 1992).

British Yearbook of International Law (Oxford: Oxford University Press).

Luard, E., *A history of the United Nations volume 1: 1945–55* (London: Macmillan, 1982).

Luard, E., *A history of the United Nations volume 2: 1955–65* (London: Macmillan, 1989).

Osmanczyk, E. J. (ed.), *Encyclopaedia of the United Nations and international relations* (London: Taylor & Francis, 1990).

United Nations, *Basic facts about the United Nations* (New York: UN, 1933, regularly updated).

United Nations, *Everyone's United Nations 1966–78; 1978–85* (New York: UN, regularly updated).

United Nations, *Yearbook of the United Nations* (The Hague: Martinus Nijhoff, annual).

United Nations Association – UK, *Memorandum on an agenda for peace* (for House of Commons Select Committee) (London, 1993).

Other sources

The UN Specialized Agencies provide much material free and for sale.

Journals that carry items of interest are *International Affairs, International Organization, International Relations, International Studies, Journal of Contemporary History, Millennium, Orbis, Review of International Studies, The World Today, Third World Quarterly, World Affairs, World Politics*. Particularly useful newspapers are

Christian Science Monitor, The Economist, The Financial Times, The Guardian, The Independent, The New York Times, The Times, Wall Street Journal, The Washington Post.

Most libraries keep copies of *Keesing's record of world events* (Cambridge: Catermill Publishing). Originating in 1931 and for many years known as *Keesing's contemporary archives*, this is an easy-to-use, invaluable reference source continuously monitoring the world's press and information sources. Supplements update it monthly.

There are various articles in *Encyclopaedia Britannica* (University of Chicago: Encyclopaedia Britannica Inc.), in *Chambers Encyclopaedia* (London: George Newnes) and, from time to time, in *Year Book of World Affairs*. Main articles under the heading United Nations give useful accounts of origins and activities.

Addresses

Full information on all aspects of UN involvement worldwide can be obtained from:

United Nations Department of Public
  Information
Promotion and Public Services Division,
Public Enquiries Unit, UN Plaza, New
York, NY 110017, USA
Tel: 001212-963-9245

United Nations Information Centre
Ship House, 20 Buckingham Gate,
London, SW1E 6LB, UK
Tel: 0171-630-1981

United Nations Information Service
UN Office at Geneva, Palais des Nations,
1211 Geneva 10, Switzerland
Tel: 004122-917-1234

United Nations Sales Section
Room DC2-0853, New York,
NY 10017, USA
Tel: 001212-963-8302

United Nations Association – UK
3 Whitehall Court, London,
SW1A 2EL, UK
Tel: 0171-930-2931

United Nations Association – USA
485 Fifth Avenue, New York,
NY 10017, USA
Tel: 001212-697-3232

Index

Acronyms appearing in this index are listed and explained on pp. ix–xi.
UN peacekeeping operations are listed on pp. 36–7.

Afghanistan 8, 29, 77–87
Africa
  case study 266–78
  economic problems, structural adjustment 274–5, 278
  FAO's early initiatives 269–70, 278
  education 151, 273
  food security and sustainability 273, 278
  human rights 138, 141
  multi-sectoral approach 275–6
  nuclear questions 113, 115, 119
  UN reappraisal, new programs 270–4, 278
  world response to Africa's famine 268
  ANC 164–5, 168, 169, 171
Agenda for Peace ix
Ahtisaari, President Martti 209, 211, 212
AIDS
  case study 256–65
  economic and social impact 259–61
  global incidence 157, 257, 259, 262–3
  likely trends 262–3, 265
  nature of disease 257–8, 265
  possible treatment 258
  research 258, 263
  WHO Global Programme 259–61, 265
  WHO Thailand Project 261–2
Akashi, Yasushi 221, 225
Amin, Hafizullah 78
Amnesty International 138
ANC 164–5, 168, 169, 171
Angola
  front line state 165
  guerillas 207
  MPLA 209–10
  Namibia 209, 210

UNITA 210
Antarctic Treaty 111, 117
Anti-apartheid Movement 167
apartheid ix, 62, 135, 137, 183, 206
  case study 161–73
Arab-Israeli conflict
  see Palestinians, Middle East
Arab League 91
Arafat, Yasser 67, 69, 70, 72, 73, 76, 140
Argentina
  and Brazil 126
  and Falklands Is. 201
arms trading 33, 34, 167, 172, 242
ASEAN 219, 227
Asia 9, 38–9, 107, 113, 119, 140, 142, 151, 215, 257, 262
Atlantic Charter 4
Australia
  aboriginal rights 141
  AIDS 257
  Cambodia 220, 225–6
  Korea 42
  nuclear testing 119, 125
  Palestinians 64
  West Irian 201
Austria 10, 52

bacteriological weapons 95, 121
Baker, James (US Secretary of State) 72
Balfour Declaration 62, 76
Balkans 176, 183
Bandung Conference (1955): Third World 119
Baruch, Senator Bernard 119
Begin, Menachem 70–1

Belgium 31, 42, 164
Bernadotte, Count Folke 65–6
Boesak, Rev. Alan 168
Bosnia
   case study 175–89
   conflict origins 176–8
   Former Yugoslavia 33
   human rights 11n
   peace negotiations 184–6, 187n
   refugees 180–3
   UNPROFOR mission 178–9, 181–2, 184–6, 187n
   see also Former Yugoslavia, Croatia
Botha, President P. W. 169
Boutros Boutros-Ghali
   and Africa 268–9, 276
   and Cyprus 57
   and nuclear testing 126
   and peacekeeping 32–3
   as Secretary General 24
   and UN future ix, 3, 186
Bradley, General Omar 43
Brandt Commission Report 237, 242, 245
Brazil 18, 126
Brezhnev, Leonid 78, 81
Britain
   Afghanistan 78
   apartheid 162, 164, 166, 167, 172, 174
   British Commonwealth 50, 64, 171, 172, 207
   British Empire 38, 50, 60, 78, 135, 162
   Cambodia 218
   Cyprus 50
   drug trafficking 252
   environment 235
   Former Yugoslavia 183–5, 186n
   human rights 152
   Korea 39, 42
   nuclear proliferation 106, 107, 108, 112
   nuclear testing 119, 121, 128n
   Namibia 207–8, 214
   Palestinians 61–4, 76, 89
   refugees 180
   UN Secretariat 19
   UNEF I 30
   UN founder 4–5
   UN reform 22n
   West Irian 194, 201
   women's rights 151–2
   see also P5
Brundtland Commission Report 237–8, 270, 273, 275n
Bunche, Ralph 66

Bunker, Ellsworth 197, 203
Burma 45, 142
Bush, President George 22n, 58n, 89, 92, 93, 210, 240

Cairo Conference (1994): Palestinian problems 73, 76
Cambodia
   Australia's "Red Book" proposals 220, 225, 226n, 227
   case study 215–27
   election organisation 74, 223–4
   General Assembly representation 219–20
   historical origins 216–17
   Khmer Rouge 216, 217–20, 222–5, 227
   refugees 141, 142, 183, 218, 223, 225
   UNTAC transition program 32, 143, 220–6, 227
Camp David accords 70, 76
Canada 64, 139, 207
   nuclear testing 107, 125
   peacekeeping 42, 52, 197
Carrington, Lord 184
Carter, President Jimmy 70, 76, 79, 115, 124, 187n
Central America 8, 142, 156
Charter
   see UN Charter
chemical weapons 95, 98
   see also bacteriological weapons
Chernobyl 110
children's rights 71, 133, 135, 139–40
China
   Beijing Conference (1995): World Conference on Women 157, 158
   Cambodia 218, 219
   Gulf conflict 91, 93
   Hong Kong 201
   human rights 142
   Korea 39, 41–5, 48
   nuclear testing 119, 121, 122, 124
   peacekeeping 28, 56
   UN representation 5, 41
   see also P5
Churchill, Winston S. 4
CIS 125
Claude, Inis 17, 22n
Clerides, President Glafos 57
Clinton, President Bill 22n, 114, 126, 185
Cold War
   confrontation era 10, 28–9, 126, 136, 186, 194
   peacekeeping 27, 30, 46, 81

post-Cold War era 77, 88, 113, 185, 215
collective security ix, 6–8, 11*n*, 21, 27, 99, 270
  see also Security Council
Commonwealth, British
  see Britain
Communism 39, 41, 43, 44, 47, 79, 81, 115, 136, 176, 177, 209, 217
Comprehensive Test-ban Treaty 115, 118, 123, 125–8, 129
Congo crisis 29, 31, 52, 54, 120
Contact Group (UN)
  Bosnia 186, 189
  Namibia 207–8, 214
Cordovez, Diego 80
Croatia
  Croatian Republic 177, 178
  invasion by Serbs 178, 180
  peace negotiations 183–5, 188–9
  refugees 142
  see also Former Yugoslavia
Crocker, Chester A. 210
CSCE (now OSCE) ix, 8, 33, 187*n*
Cuba 93, 210
  missile crisis 121
Cyprus 28, 29
  case study 50–60
  see also Greece, Turkey, TRNC

decolonisation 9, 21, 51, 193, 195–6, 198–9, 200, 203, 204
  see also self-determination
debt crisis
  see Third World, indebtedness
de Cuellar, Javier Perez 24, 32, 58*n*, 79, 91, 93, 212, 219, 254
de Klerk, President F. W. 161, 169, 172*n*, 212
Democratic Turnhalle Alliance 209
Denktash, President Rauf 58*n*
détente 77, 78, 123–4
  see also Cold War
disarmament
  bilateral, multilateral negotiations 10, 106, 107, 111, 124
  UN Conference on Disarmament 123, 129
  UN Disarmament Commission 123, 129
  see also nuclear disarmament, nuclear proliferation, nuclear testing
domestic jurisdiction 7, 8, 13, 34*n*, 135, 140, 141, 144, 145, 190, 206
drug control
  case study 246–55

Commission on Narcotic Drugs 249
Convention on Psychotropic Substances 249
DND CND 249, 255
INCB 249, 255
League of Nations initiatives 248
narcotics cultivation 251–2, 255
possible trends of drugs problem 253–4
UN and drug trafficking 252–3
UN control 247, 248–51, 255
Dumbarton Oaks Conference (1944): UN
  Charter draft 5, 13

economic development
  drug related problems 247, 250, 252–3
  economic aspects of Africa's food crisis 266–9
  economic impact of AIDS 259
  economic redevelopment
    Cambodia 223
    Iraq-Kuwait 96
    Palestinians 73–4
    South Africa 171
  Group of 7 137, 186
  Group of 77 137
  indebtedness 238, 268
  role of Specialized Agencies 20–1, 136
  UN Development Decades 21
  UNDP 58
ECOSOC
  Charter role 13, 14
  drugs control 248, 249
  human rights 138
  NGOs 138, 167
  Specialized Agency coordination 20–1, 136
Egypt 18, 67, 68, 70, 73, 91, 106, 179, 201
Eisenhower, President Dwight D. 107, 120
environment
  Brandt, Palme, Brundtland Commissions and Reports 236–8, 242, 245
  case study 231–45
  economic, financial problems 237–40, 243*n*
  global enquiry, monitoring, research 21, 232, 234, 236, 239, 245
  Nairobi Conference (1982) 234–5, 245
  NGO participation 233, 239
  pollution 21, 231, 232, 233, 235–6
  Rio Conference (1992) 232, 238–42, 245
  Stockholm Conference (1972) 231, 232–3, 235, 239, 242, 245
  sustainable development 237–8, 242

Third World attitudes 233, 235, 240, 241, 243
UNEP 232, 234–5, 240
EOKA 51
Ethiopia 42, 141, 142, 201, 205
Europe 19, 106, 107, 151
 AIDS 257, 262
 Cambodia 215
 Cold War 29
 drugs 250, 252, 253
 environment 232–3, 235, 239, 243n
 EU (EC) 33, 34n, 97, 116n, 151, 171, 172n, 184
 Former Yugoslavia 176, 178, 180, 183, 185
 human rights 138, 141, 151, 175, 180, 186
 nuclear proliferation 106, 107
 refugees 141, 142, 143, 180
 US relations 77, 79

FAO
 Africa 266, 269–70, 271, 272–3, 275
 liaison with other Agencies 21, 107, 136, 211, 255
 narcotics cultivation 251–2
 World Food congresses 269–70
 WFP 269–70
financing, UN
 AIDS program 263
 environmental program 235
 members' contributions 15
 members' arrears 15, 22n
 peacekeeping 27, 33, 34n, 56, 58n, 98
 UNDCP 251
 see also economic development, World Bank
Former Yugoslavia
 case study (Bosnia) 175–89
 conflict origins 176–8
 human rights 11n, 140–1, 156, 183–4
 peace negotiations 184–6, 187n, 188–9
 refugees 180–3
 split into smaller units 22n, 176, 178
 UNPROFOR mission 178, 181–4, 186, 187n, 189
 see also Bosnia, Croatia
France
 apartheid 164, 166
 Cambodia 216, 222, 226, 227
 as colonial power 38, 39, 89, 135, 164, 201, 216, 227
 Contact Group member 186, 207

Former Yugoslavia 183, 186
Gulf conflict 91, 92, 101
human rights 144
MTCR 125
nuclear questions 107, 112, 113–4, 116n, 119, 121, 124, 125
 as P5 member 5, 19, 119, 220
 peacekeeping 56, 183, 220–1, 222
 Suez crisis 30, 76
 US relations 79

G7 137, 186, 240
G77 137
GATT 268
Gaza-Jericho Accord 73
Geneva
 Afghanistan talks 77, 79, 80, 81, 82–3, 87
 Geneva conventions 71
 Gulf conflict: relief aid 96
 human rights 138, 157, 160
 Korea 45
 Middle East conference 69–70, 75n
 NPT conferences 105, 112, 117
 nuclear questions 119–20, 123, 124, 127, 128n, 129
 UNHCR 142
Geneva Accords 77, 82–3, 87
General Assembly
 admission of UN members 22n
 Afghanistan 78, 87
 Africa's food crisis 270, 271, 278
 apartheid 163, 164, 165, 169, 171, 172n, 174
 Cambodia 219–20, 221
 disarmament 15, 119
 environment 234, 245
 functions viii, 13, 14–16, 17, 18, 20, 22n, 24
 Gulf conflict 92
 Korea 40, 42, 43
 human rights 134, 144
 Middle East 61, 63–4, 65, 69, 70, 71, 140
 Namibia 205, 206, 207
 nuclear questions 107, 119, 120, 122–3, 125
 peacekeeping 29, 31, 32
 procedures 9, 11n, 22n
 Secretariat 19
 Secretary General 15, 31
 Security Council 5
 Specialized Agencies 15
 Special Sessions 15, 55
 Uniting for Peace Resolution 43, 48

voting viii, 14, 18
West Irian 196, 197, 199, 200, 201, 203
women's rights 151, 152, 153, 155, 160
Germany
 apartheid 172
 as colonial power 205
 Contact Group member 186, 207
 Former Yugoslavia 178, 186
 Gulf conflict 95, 97
 human rights 141, 144
 Nazi Germany 141, 176, 177, 179
 nuclear questions 122, 125
 refugees 180, 181
 Security Council enlargement 18, 22*n*
 US relations 79
Glaspie, Mrs April 89
Gorbachev, Mikhail
 Afghanistan 81, 82, 87
 Cambodia 219
 collective security 7
 Gulf conflict 92, 95
 nuclear questions 124
Greece 50, 56, 57, 58*n*
Gulf conflict
 case study 88–101
 financial costs 33
 peace enforcement 17, 37
 Saddam Hussein 89–90, 94, 96, 97, 98,
  101
Gyani, Lieut-General P. S. 52

Hammarskjöld, Dag 18, 24, 30–1, 164
human rights
 Africa 138
 case study 133–47
 Charter references 134, 136
 children's rights 133, 135, 137, 139–40
 Commission on Human Rights (UN) 138
 Copenhagen conference (1980) 154
 ECOSOC 138, 152, 160
 education 145*n*
 "ethnic cleansing" 11*n*, 141, 143
 Europe 138, 141
 General Assembly 134, 137, 140, 144
 genocide 141, 147, 216, 218
 Human Rights Committee (UN) 138
 indigenous people 140–1
 International Bill of Human Rights 133–4
 International Covenant on Civil and
  Political Rights 135–6
 International Covenant on Economic,
  Social and Cultural Rights 135–6
 minorities 140–1

 NGOs 138
 Optional Protocol 136
 prospects for human rights 144–5
 racial discrimination 137, 141, 145*n*,
  162–3, 166, 213
 Specialized Agencies 136, 137
 states' inviolability ix
 torture 9, 135, 137
 Universal Declaration of Human Rights
  133–5, 147, 148, 160, 165
 Vienna Conference (1993) 133, 144
 see also refugees
Hurd, Douglas 61
Hussein, Saddam
 invasion of Kuwait 90, 94, 101
 Iraqi–US relations 89–90
 Kurds 96–8
 nuclear questions 101, 111, 114, 116*n*
 political emergence 89
 see also Gulf conflict
Hussein of Jordan, King 70

IAEA
 established 105, 117
 functions 107, 108
 Iraq 95, 98, 101, 116*n*
 North Korea 116*n*
 safeguards 107–111, 112, 115
 verification 111, 114, 116*n*
ICJ
 advisory opinions 20, 56, 127, 201, 214
 apartheid 205, 206, 214
 competence 19–20, 24, 32
 establishment 19
 Decade of International Law 127
 Former Yugoslavia 180
 International Law Commission 20
 jurisdiction 7–8, 20
 limits to use 9, 20
 membership 20
 nuclear questions 127
 UN Charter 7–8, 13
ILO 74, 136, 140, 149, 258
IMO 250, 255
India
 Afghanistan 80, 85
 apartheid 163
 former Indian Empire 38
 Gulf conflict 94
 Korea 45
 nuclear questions 106, 107, 111, 119,
  126
 peacekeeping 29, 52, 197

Security Council 18
Indo-China 38, 217
Indonesia 18, 39, 156, 194–201, 203
  see also West Irian
INSTRAW 154
International Peace Bureau 127
Intifada 71–2, 76
Iran
  Afghanistan 79, 84, 86
  Iran–Iraq War 8, 89, 100n, 101
  Islamic fundamentalism 78, 89
  nuclear questions 100n, 111, 126
Iraq
  former British mandate 89
  human rights 141, 142, 143, 144
  Iran–Iraq War 8, 89, 100n, 101
  nuclear questions 98, 100n, 101, 111,
    114, 116n, 118
  refugees 96–8, 141, 142, 143
  see also Gulf conflict
Islam
  Islamic values 144
  religious persecution 140, 179
  see also Gulf conflict
Israel
  Arab-Jewish hostility 66–7, 71
  Arab-Jewish reconciliation 69, 73–4, 75n
  Camp David meeting 70
  Gaza-Jericho Accord 73–4
  Gulf conflict 92
  Palestinian problem: case study 61–76
  peacekeeping 29
  PLO 67, 69, 71, 72, 73, 74, 76, 80, 91
  refugees 66, 74
  Resolution 242, 67–8, 75n
  see also Palestinians
Italy 94, 125, 181

Japan
  apartheid 172n
  Cambodia 221
  Hiroshima bomb 117, 119
  Korea 39
  nuclear questions 125
  Security Council enlargement 18, 22n
  West Irian 193, 198, 203
  World Food Conference 274
Jordan 67

Kamal, Barbrack 78, 81
Kampuchea
  see Cambodia
Katanga 31

Kennedy, President J. F. 120, 121, 197
Khan, Major-General Said Uddin 197
Khmer Rouge 215, 216, 217–20, 222, 223,
    224, 225, 227
  see also Cambodia
Khruschev, Nikita 120
Kissinger, Henry A. 17, 69, 75n
Korea
  case study 38–49
  Chinese intervention 43, 45
  Democratic Republic of North Korea 30,
    38, 40–42, 44, 45, 47n, 48, 106, 111,
    115, 116n
  nuclear questions 47n, 106, 111, 115,
    116n
  peacekeeping (enforcement) 30, 37, 42,
    43, 46, 54
  South Korea 38, 40–3, 45, 106, 114
  US involvement 39, 41–3, 44, 45, 46n,
    47n
Kim Il-Sung, President 41, 45, 115
Kurds 96–8, 101, 143
Kuwait
  see Gulf conflict

Latin America
  AIDS 261
  defence 10
  drug control 251, 252
  human rights 135
  illiteracy 151
  nuclear questions 106, 111
  Security Council 29
League of Nations
  Covenant 4
  history 3–4, 11n, 28, 61
  mandate: Iraq 89
  mandate: Palestine 61–2, 63, 76, 89
  mandate: South West Africa 204, 214
  narcotics control 248
Lebanon
  Arab-Jewish hostility 67, 76
  former French mandate 89
  human rights 142
  peacekeeping 29, 71, 75n
  peace negotiations 72, 92
  PLO 71
Libya 80, 92, 101, 106
Lie, Trygve 24, 30, 38, 66
literacy 21, 150–1, 155, 159
Luthuli, Chief Albert 164

MacArthur, General Douglas 42–3, 48

Macedonia 178, 187*n*

Macmillan, Harold 167

Madrid Conference (1993): Palestinian problems 73, 76

Malan, President Daniel 163

Makarios, Archbishop (President) 51, 54, 55, 60

Mandela, President Nelson
first black South African President 161, 172
imprisonment 165, 168, 205
Nobel Prize 161, 174
transition negotiations 169–71
see also apartheid

Middle East
AIDS 257
Gulf conflict 88, 89, 93, 99
nuclear questions 95, 98, 114
peacekeeping 29, 46, 52, 83
see also Gulf conflict, Palestinians

Military Staff Committee 6, 32, 93

Milosevic, President Slobodan 177, 179
see also Former Yugoslavia

Mitterand, President François 92

Morgenthau, Henry 10

Mozambique 142, 143, 165, 216, 268

Mujahadeen (*also* Mujahidin) 80, 81, 85, 86

Nairobi
international women's conference 155–6, 160
UNCHE conference 232–3
UNEP headquarters 232, 234

Najibullah, President Mohammed 81, 86

Namibia
case study 204–13
election 74, 208, 209, 211–12, 213*n*, 214
self-determination 199–200, 202, 215–16
South African presence 20, 165, 204–7, 208–9, 211, 212, 213*n*, 214
UNTAG 209, 211–12, 213*n*, 214

Narcotics
see drug control

NATO 8, 32, 51, 52, 106, 122, 182

Nehru, Jawaharlal 119

Netherlands
former Dutch empire 39, 135
Korea 42
South Africa (Boers) 162
West Irian 193–9, 200, 201, 203

NFZ 107, 111–12, 114, 115, 117

NGOs 85, 110, 138, 167, 235, 239

NPT 98, 105, 107, 109–13, 114, 117

NNWS 106, 107, 108–9, 110, 113, 115, 115*n*

Nobel Peace Prize 32, 142, 147, 161

Nol, General Lon 217, 227

Non-aligned movement 56, 108, 113, 119, 120, 129, 207

nuclear disarmament
Antarctic Treaty 111, 117
arms race 106, 112, 121, 124
guarantees 113, 115
Intermediate-range Nuclear Forces (INF) 128*n*
Iraqi capability 98, 100*n*, 101, 111, 114, 118
MTCR 125, 129
NFZ 107, 111–12, 114, 115, 117
non-aligned states 108, 113, 119, 120, 129
outer space 112, 117, 121
Rarotonga Treaty 112, 117
SALT II 124
seabed 112, 117, 121
Strategic Defence Initiative (SDI) 125
Tlatelolco Treaty 111, 117, 121
verification 111–14, 115, 116*n*, 120, 124, 125, 127, 128*n*
see also IAEA, nuclear proliferation, nuclear testing

nuclear energy
"atoms for peace" 107
commercial proliferation 105
peaceful use 107–8, 105, 110, 111, 112, 114, 116, 123–4, 127

nuclear proliferation
Antarctic Treaty 111, 117
case study 105–17
Iraq 98, 100*n*, 101, 111, 114, 116*n*, 118
NPT 98, 105, 108–9, 112–13, 114, 115, 117, 126, 128*n*
review conferences 112–14, 115, 117
see also IAEA, NPT, nuclear disarmament, nuclear testing, NWS, NNWS

nuclear testing
case study 118–29
Cold War impasse 120
Comprehensive Test Ban 115, 123, 125–7, 128*n*, 129
Cuban Missile Crisis 121
MTCR 125, 129
negotiations: bilateral 121, 123–4, 125
negotiations: UN 119–20, 123–4
PNET 123

PTBT   121–3
TTBT   123–4
Nujoma, President Sam   212
NWS   106, 107, 108–9, 110, 113, 115*n*

OAS   ix, 138
OAU   ix, 172, 172*n*, 207
ONUC   29, 31, 36, 54
OPEC   172*n*
opium   248, 249, 255
Oppenheimer, J. Robert   119
Optional Protocol   134, 136–7, 147
OSCE (formerly CSCE)   ix, 187*n*
outer space   112, 117, 121
   Outer Space Treaty   112, 117, 121
Owen, Lord (David)   184, 188
Oxfam   138, 181

P5
   apartheid   163
   arms trading   33
   Cambodia   220
   enlargement of Security Council   17
   Gulf conflict   91
   nuclear testing   125, 127–8, 128*n*, 129
   NWS   10, 106, 107, 110
   peacekeeping   28, 29, 30
   privileged position   17, 38
   sanctions and South Africa   167
   Security Council   17, 113, 127–8
   unanimity   5, 6–7, 17
   veto   5, 17
Pacific Ocean   39, 112, 196
Pakistan
   Afghanistan   77, 78, 79, 80, 83–5, 86, 87
   Former Yugoslavia   179
   Gulf conflict   95
   human rights   139
   Korea   45
   nuclear questions   106, 111
   peacekeeping   29, 197, 199
Palestine
   historical origins   61–3
   mandate era   62–3, 66
   Peel Commission   63
   UN partition scheme   63–5
   White Paper (1939)   63
   see also Israel
Palestinians
   Arab-Jewish hostility   66–8, 71–2
   Arab-Jewish reconciliation   69–71
   case study   61–76
   Gaza-Jericho Accord   73–4, 76

   Geneva conference   69–70
   refugees   66, 68, 74
   Resolution 242   67–8, 75*n*, 76
   see also PLO
Palme Commission Report   237, 245, 270
Papua   156, 193, 197, 198, 200
   see also West Irian
peacebuilding   32–3, 50, 74, 221, 225
peacekeeping
   Agenda for Peace proposals   32–3
   case studies   27–101
   civilian protection   52–3, 96–8, 178–9,
      181–3, 221–2
   Cold War impact   28–9, 30
   collective security   6, 11*n*, 27–8, 99
   conditions required for launching   31–3,
      52, 99
   costs   27, 33, 34*n*, 56, 58*n*
   dispute settlement   viii, 7–8, 17, 28, 38,
      50, 54, 56, 58, 73–4, 77, 88, 184–6,
      200–1, 225
   enforcement   28, 30, 37, 46, 88–9,
      99–100
   General Assembly   31, 43, 65, 78, 92
   intervention as issue   33, 34*n*, 46, 85, 88,
      183–4
   list of peacekeeping operations   36–7
   rapid deployment force   30, 32, 99
   Secretary Generals   30–3
   Security Council   17, 29, 31, 41, 43, 46,
      57, 64, 66, 78, 90, 92, 94, 95, 98, 101,
      175
   tranquillizing as issue   viii, 50, 54, 85
   UN founding principles   5–8, 13, 78, 178
peace settlements   44–5, 82–4, 169–70,
   204, 215, 226
PLO   67, 69, 71, 72, 73, 74, 80, 91, 140
Pol Pot   216, 218, 227
   see also Khmer Rouge, Cambodia
preventive diplomacy   18, 34*n*, 99

Rabin, Yitzhak   73
Ranariddh, Prince   224
Reagan, President Ronald   124, 125, 210
Red Crescent   181
Red Cross   96, 138, 181
refugees
   Afghanistan   82, 83, 84–5, 86
   Africa   266, 268
   asylum   141–3, 180–1
   Cambodia   141, 142, 183, 218, 223, 225
   distribution   141–3
   Former Yugoslavia   180–3

General Assembly 137
incidence 11, 141–3
Iraq (Kurds) 96–8, 141, 142, 143
Namibia 211, 213*n*
Palestinians 66, 68, 71, 74
protection (safe havens) 96–7, 142–3, 178, 182, 187*n*
refoulement 142
resettlement 55, 74, 85, 142–3, 182–3, 215, 221, 223
UNHCR 21, 83, 142, 147, 180
voluntary repatriation 142
Rhee, Syngman 41, 45
Rikye, General Indar 198
Rio de Janeiro Conference (1992): environment 232, 238–42, 245
ROC 51, 54, 55, 56
Roosevelt, Mrs Eleanor 133, 145
Roosevelt, President F. D. 4, 106
Rwanda ix, 141, 142, 267

Sadat, President Anwar 70
sanctions, UN
Afghanistan 79, 87
controversial use 56, 99, 166–7
Cyprus dispute 56
Former Yugoslavia 181, 187*n*
Gulf conflict 90, 91, 95, 100*n*, 101
Security Council 17, 90, 95, 101, 167
South Africa 165, 166–7, 170*n*, 206, 208
Saudi Arabia
Afghanistan 86
Gulf conflict 89, 90, 91
human rights 157
Palestinians 70
seabed
exploitation 21
nuclear free zone 111, 117
nuclear testing 121
UNEP 235, 236, 237, 238, 242
Secretariat, UN 6, 19, 120
Secretary-General
Afghanistan 77, 78, 79, 85
Africa's food crisis 276
apartheid 161, 164, 170
Arab-Jewish negotiations 67*n*
Cambodia 220–1
Cyprus 52, 56, 58*n*
drug control 246, 254
Former Yugoslavia 179, 186
Gulf conflict 93–4, 101
incumbents as Secretary-General 24
Korea 38, 41

Namibia 207, 209, 212
nuclear proliferation 108
nuclear testing 119, 126
Palestine 66
peacekeeping 17, 18, 30–3, 52
Personal Representatives 52, 77, 85
Security Council 78, 93
UNEF 67
war crimes 179–80
West Irian 196–7
Security Council
Afghanistan 78
apartheid 163, 165, 167, 172*n*
Arab-Israeli disputes 63–4, 67–8
Cambodia 17
Charter, UN 5, 220
Cyprus 52
enlargement viii, 17–18, 22*n*
Former Yugoslavia 17, 175, 178–9
Gulf conflict 17, 37, 90, 91, 92–3, 94, 95–6, 98
human rights 97
Korea 17, 41–2
membership viii, 14, 17, 24
Namibia 206, 207, 208, 213*n*
nuclear proliferation 98
nuclear testing 127
peacekeeping 17, 29, 31, 46, 78, 93, 188, 189
powers, procedures 6, 17–18, 24, 43, 78–9
veto 7, 17, 43, 166
voting 17–18, 127–8
West Irian 195
see also P5
self-defence 11*n*, 109, 122–3, 178, 217
self-determination 9, 51, 67, 141, 199–202, 216
Seoul 39, 40
Serbia 176 7, 178, 181, 183 6, 187*n*, 188–9
see also Former Yugoslavia
Sihanouk, King Narodom 217–8, 221
South Africa
apartheid 62, 135, 137, case study 161–73, 183
Boer dominion 162
domestic jurisdiction 145*n*
'front line states' 166, 268
Namibia 20, 165, 204–7, 208–9, 211, 212, 213*n*, 214
nuclear proliferation 114
NWS 106

SADF 205, 208, 209
Sharpeville massacre 164, 168, 174
Soweto massacre 166, 168, 174
see also apartheid
sovereignty, national ix, 22n, 56, 69, 74n, 82, 109, 196, 199–200, 237
Specialized Agencies
  Africa's food crisis 269–75
  AIDS 256, 258, 260–1, 263
  Cambodia 223
  children's rights 140
  drug problem 247, 249, 250–1, 255
  ECOSOC 20, 24
  functions 14, 15, 16, 21, 136, 140
  membership 10
  Palestinians 74
  refugees 142
  relief programs 7, 20, 85
  technical assistance 21, 107
  women's rights 139, 154, 156
  see also individual Agency acronyms
Stalin, Joseph 41
Stockholm Conference (1972): environment 231, 232–3, 235, 239, 242, 245
Stoltenberg, Torsten 185, 188
Strong, Maurice 241
Sukarno, President Achmed 194, 197
Syria 67, 72, 80, 89, 90, 91

Thailand 42, 220, 223, 261–2
Thant, U. 24, 31, 52, 121, 197
Third World
  Afghanistan 80
  AIDS 257, 258, 261
  apartheid 163
  civil strife 10
  environment 233, 235, 237, 238, 240, 241
  Group of 77 137
  human rights 137, 138, 139, 140, 141, 142–3, 145
  indebtedness 238, 268, 276
  literacy 21, 150–1, 155, 159
  maternal mortality 158, 159n
  MNC exploitation 243, 275–6
  nuclear testing 119
  poverty 235, 237
  refugees 82, 83, 84–5, 86, 96–8, 142–3, 183, 211, 218, 223, 225, 266, 268
  uncommitted states 56, 108, 113, 119, 120, 129, 207
  West Irian, case study 191–201
  women's rights 151–2, 155, 156, 157–8,

159n
  see also individual states, Africa, Non-aligned movement
Tito, Marshall Josip 176, 177
Tlatelolco Treaty 111, 115, 117
torture 9, 135, 137
TRNC 55, 56, 58n
  see also Cyprus, Turkey
Truman, President Harry, 41–2, 43, 79, 119
Trusteeship Council 9, 39, 196
Turkey
  Cyprus 50–4, 55, 56, 57, 58n
  Gulf conflict 96, 182
  Korea 42
  refugees 142
  TRNC 55, 56, 58n
  see also Cyprus

UN
  collective security ix, 6–8, 11n, 21, 27, 99, 270
  decision making 6, 11n
  financing 15, 22n, 27, 33, 34n, 56, 58n, 98, 235, 251, 263
  founding principles 3–11, 13, 166, 167, 168, 201, 206
  idealism 4–5, 28
  major organs 5–6, 14–21, 22n, 24
  membership viii, 5, 9, 10, 22n, 24, 220
  NGO role 19
  realism 4, 6, 7, 17, 29, 220
  reform viii, 11n, 17–18, 22n
  regionalism 7–8
  Special Sessions 15, 55
  trusteeship system 8, 9, 13, 39, 76, 196, 206
  voting viii, 14, 17–18, 127–8
  see also ECOSOC, General Assembly, Human Rights, Peacekeeping, Secretariat, Secretary General, Security Council, Specialized Agencies, UN Charter
UNAMIC 37, 221
UN Center against apartheid 166
UN Charter
  amendment viii, ix
  collective security (Chapter VII) 6–8
  dispute settlement (Chapter VI) 7–8
  drafting 5, 13
  ICJ 6
  peacekeeping 27
  principles 3–4, 166, 170, 201, 206
  regional arrangements 7, 8
UNCHE 231, 232–3, 235, 239, 242, 245

UN Commission on Human Rights   138
UN Committee on South West Africa   205
UN Council for Namibia   206, 214
UNCRO   37, 187n
UNCTAD   276, 278
UN Division of Narcotic Drugs   247
UNDOF   29, 36, 72
UNDP   86, 152, 156
UNDRO   270
UN Drug Control Program   251
UNEF I   30, 36, 67
UNEP   232, 234–6, 238–9, 240, 243n
UNESCO   21, 107, 136, 156, 207, 250–1,
   261
UNFDAC   250, 255
UNFICYP   36, 52–4, 56, 57, 58n
UNGOMAP   36, 77, 83, 84–5, 87
UNHCR   58, 83, 142, 156, 181
UN Human Rights Committee   135, 137
UNICEF   159, 181, 211, 223
UNIFIL   29, 36, 72
UNIKOM   37, 96
UN Institute for Namibia   207
UNITA   210
United States
   Afghanistan   78, 81, 85
   AIDS   257, 262
   apartheid   166, 172n
   Cambodia   217, 218, 219, 220, 222
   domestic jurisdiction   8
   drugs   252, 253
   environment   235, 236, 240, 243n
   Former Yugoslavia   179, 183, 184, 185
   Gulf conflict   89–94, 96, 97, 100, 101
   'hot-line' link   121
   human rights   133, 138, 139, 141
   Korea   39–43, 44, 45, 46n, 47, 48–9
   Namibia   207, 208, 210
   nuclear proliferation   106, 107, 108, 111,
      112, 113, 114, 115, 116n, 117
   nuclear testing   119, 120, 121, 122, 123,
      124, 125, 126, 128n
   P5   5, 17, 22n, 28, 29, 38
   Palestinian problem   63, 66, 69, 70, 73,
      75n, 76
   peacekeeping   69–70, 71, 72, 73, 76, 220
   UN Secretariat   19
   West Irian   197, 201, 203
UNOMSA   170
UNPAAERD   272, 278
UNPREDEP   37, 187n
UNPROFOR   37, 178, 182, 183–4, 185, 186,
   187n

UNRWA   66, 72, 74, 76
UNSCOP   64, 76
UNSF   197
UN Special Committee on Apartheid   168
UNTAC   37, 221–6, 227
UNTAG   36, 209. 211–12, 213n
UNTEA   197–9, 203
UN Temporary Commission   41
USSR
   Afghanistan   77–82, 83, 84, 86, 87
   Cambodia   218, 219, 222
   Cyprus   56
   domestic jurisdiction   8
   drugs   248
   Former Yugoslavia   185
   Gulf conflict   90–1, 92, 95, 101
   human rights   135
   Korea   39–40, 41, 42, 45, 47n
   Namibia   210
   nuclear proliferation   107, 108–9, 111,
      115
   nuclear testing   119, 120–1, 122, 124,
      125, 126, 128n
   Russia (successor state)   56, 86, 87, 115
   see also Cold War, Gorbachev, P5

Vance, Cyrus   184, 188
Versailles Conference   5
Verwoerd, President Hendrik   163, 174
veto   7, 18, 166, 208
   see also Security Council, P5
Vietnam   79, 142, 182, 216, 217, 218, 220,
   227

Waldheim, Kurt   24, 31, 69, 79, 148, 207
war crimes   179–80
Warsaw Pact (Treaty)   8, 32, 125
West Irian (West New Guinea)
   case study   193–203
   see also Indonesia, Netherlands
WHO
   AIDS   256, 257, 258, 259–61, 262–3, 265
   drug control   249, 251, 255
   human rights   136, 156
   Geneva   21
   Namibia   211
   nuclear proliferation   107
women
   AIDS   257, 259, 261, 262–3, 265
   drug control   157, 247
   literacy   150–1, 155, 159, 159n
   maternal mortality   158
   refugees   157, 183

women and children 133, 135, 139–40, 159, 159*n,* 160, 259, 265, 270, 271, 272

women's rights 137, 139, case study 148–60

World Bank 240
  Afghan economy 81
  AIDS program 263
  G7 240
  loans to Africa 271
  loans to Palestinians 74
  P5 members 10
  peacekeeping 34*n*
  South African economy 171

structural adjustment programs 274–5
World Council of Churches 75*n,* 138
WFP 269–70, 278
World Summit for Children 139–40, 147

Yalta Conference 4, 13, 39
Yemen 29, 91, 93
Yom Kippur War 68–9, 76
Yugoslavia Peace Conference (1992) 184

Zambia 166
Zimbabwe 268
Zionism 62, 70, 71, 75*n,* 76